NEW INTERNATIONAL BIBLICAL COMMENTARY

Old Testament Editors,
Robert L. Hubbard Jr.
Robert K. Johnston

JOSHUA, JUDGES, RUTH

Old Testament Series

NEW INTERNATIONAL BIBLICAL COMMENTARY

JOSHUA, JUDGES, RUTH

J. GORDON HARRIS
CHERYL A. BROWN
MICHAEL S. MOORE

Based on the New International Version

© 2000 by Hendrickson Publishers, Inc.
P. O. Box 3473
Peabody, Massachusetts 01961–3473

First published jointly, 2000, in the United States by Hendrickson
Publishers and in the United Kingdom by the Paternoster Press,
P. O. Box 300, Carlisle, Cumbria CA3 0QS.

Printed in the United States of America

First printing — November 2000

Library of Congress Cataloging-in-Publication Data

Harris, J. Gordon.
    Joshua, Judges, Ruth / J. Gordon Harris, Cheryl A. Brown,
Michael S. Moore.
       p. cm. — (New International biblical commentary. Old
Testament series; 5)
    Includes bibliographical references and indexes.
    ISBN 1–56563–214–1 (pbk.)
    1. Bible. O.T. Joshua—Commentaries. 2. Bible. O.T. Judges—
Commentaries. 3. Bible. O.T. Ruth—Commentaries. 4. Bible. O.T.
Joshua—Canonical criticism. 5. Bible. O.T. Judges—Canonical
criticism. 6. Bible. O.T. Ruth—Canonical criticism. I. Brown, Cheryl
Anne, 1949– II. Moore, Michael S. III. Title. IV. Series.

BS1295.3 .H36 2000
222'.2077–dc21

                                       00-063352

ISBN 1–56563–214–1 (U.S. softcover)
ISBN 1–56563–590–6 (U.S. hardcover)

British Library Cataloguing in Publication Data
A catalogue record for this book is available
from the British Library.

ISBN 0–85364–726–7 (U.K. softcover)

Table of Contents

Judges—Cheryl A. Brown

Foreword
New International Biblical Commentary

As an ancient document, the Old Testament often seems something quite foreign to modern men and women. Opening its pages may feel, to the modern reader, like traversing a kind of literary time warp into a whole other world. In that world sisters and brothers marry, long hair mysteriously makes men superhuman, and temple altars daily smell of savory burning flesh and sweet incense. There, desert bushes burn but leave no ashes, water gushes from rocks, and cities fall because people march around them. A different world, indeed!

Even God, the Old Testament's main character, seems a stranger compared to his more familiar New Testament counterpart. Sometimes the divine is portrayed as a loving father and faithful friend, someone who rescues people from their greatest dangers or generously rewards them for heroic deeds. At other times, however, God resembles more a cruel despot, one furious at human failures, raving against enemies, and bloodthirsty for revenge. Thus, skittish about the Old Testament's diverse portrayal of God, some readers carefully select which portions of the text to study, or they avoid the Old Testament altogether.

The purpose of this commentary series is to help readers navigate this strange and sometimes forbidding literary and spiritual terrain. Its goal is to break down the barriers between the ancient and modern worlds so that the power and meaning of these biblical texts become transparent to contemporary readers. How is this to be done? And what sets this series apart from others currently on the market?

This commentary series will bypass several popular approaches to biblical interpretation. It will not follow a *precritical* approach that interprets the text without reference to recent scholarly conversations. Such a commentary contents itself with offering little more than a paraphrase of the text with occasional supplements from archaeology, word studies, and classical theology. It mistakenly believes that there have been few insights into the Bible since Calvin or Luther. Nor will this series pursue an *anticritical* approach whose preoccupation is to defend the Bible against its detractors, especially scholarly ones. Such a commentary has little space left to move beyond showing why the Bible's critics are wrong to explaining what the biblical text means. The result is a paucity of vibrant biblical theology. Again, this series finds inadequate a *critical* approach that seeks to understand the text apart from belief in the meaning it conveys. Though modern readers have been taught to be discerning, they do not want to live in the "desert of criticism" either.

Instead, as its editors, we have sought to align this series with what has been labeled *believing criticism*. This approach marries probing, reflective interpretation of the text to loyal biblical devotion and warm Christian affection. Our contributors tackle the task of interpretation using the full range of critical methodologies and practices. Yet they do so as people of faith who hold the text in the highest regard. The commentators in this series use criticism to bring the message of the biblical texts vividly to life so the minds of modern readers may be illumined and their faith deepened.

The authors in this series combine a firm commitment to modern scholarship with a similar commitment to the Bible's full authority for Christians. They bring to the task the highest technical skills, warm theological commitment, and rich insight from their various communities. In so doing, they hope to enrich the life of the academy as well as the life of the church.

Part of the richness of this commentary series derives from its authors' breadth of experience and ecclesial background. As editors, we have consciously brought together a diverse group of scholars in terms of age, gender, denominational affiliation, and race. We make no claim that they represent the full expression of the people of God, but they do bring fresh, broad perspectives to the interpretive task. But though this series has sought out diversity among its contributors, they also reflect a commitment to a common center. These commentators write as "believing critics"—scholars who desire to speak for church and academy, for academy and church. As editors, we offer this series in devotion to God and for the enrichment of God's people.

ROBERT L. HUBBARD JR.
ROBERT K. JOHNSTON
Editors

Abbreviations

4QMMT	A priestly document from Cave 4 at Qumran, "Some of the Works of the Law"; E. Qimron and J. Strugnell, eds., "Qumran Cave 4.V, *Miqsat Ma'ase HaTorah,*" *Discoveries in the Judean Desert*, vol. X (Oxford: Oxford University Press, 1994).
4QRuth^a	Hebrew text of Ruth found in Cave 4 at Qumran; R. H. Eisenman and J. M. Robinson, *A Facsimile Edition of the Dead Sea Scrolls* (Washington, D.C.: Biblical Archaeology Society, 1991) PAM # 42.287 & 43.090 (Palestine Archaeology Museum #).
AB	Anchor Bible
ABD	*Anchor Bible Dictionary* (ed. D. N. Freedman; Garden City, N.Y.: Doubleday, 1992).
AJSL	*American Journal of Semitic Languages*
ANET	*Ancient Near Eastern Texts Relating to the Old Testament* (ed. J. Pritchard; Princeton: Princeton University, 1969).
ASOR	*American Schools of Oriental Research*
ASV	American Standard Version
b.	Babylonian Talmud (London: Soncino, 1933–).
B. Bat.	*Baba Batra* ("Last Gate")
BA	*Biblical Archaeologist*
BAR	*Biblical Archaeology Review*
BASOR	*Bulletin of the American Schools of Oriental Research*
BDB	*Hebrew and English Lexicon of the Old Testament* (eds. F. Brown, S. R. Driver, & C. Briggs; Oxford: Clarendon, 1907).
B. Qam.	*Baba Qamma* ("First Gate")
Bib	*Biblica*

BibInt	*Biblical Interpretation*
Ber.	*Berakot* ("Blessings")
BLS	Bible and Literature Series
BR	*Bible Review*
BSac	*Bibliotheca Sacra*
CAD	*Chicago Assyrian Dictionary* (Chicago: University of Chicago Oriental Institute, 1964–)
CB	*Century Bible*
CBC	*Cambridge Bible Commentary*
CBI	Currents in Biblical Interpretation
CBQ	*Catholic Biblical Quarterly*
CBW	Cities of the Biblical World
DAT	The Deir 'Alla plaster texts; translation in J. Hackett, *The Balaam Text from Deir 'Alla* (Chico, Calif.: Scholars, 1984).
DNWSI	*Dictionary of North-West Semitic Inscriptions* (eds. J. Hoftijzer & K. Jongeling; Leiden: Brill, 1995).
EA	*Die El-Amarna Tafeln* (ed. J. A. Knudtzon; Aalen: Zeller, 1964; reprint of 1915 ed.).
EQ	*Evangelical Quarterly*
GHB	P. Joüon, *Grammaire de l'Hébreu Biblique* (Rome: Institute Biblique Pontifical, 1982; originally published in 1923).
Git.	*Gittin* ("Bills of Divorce")
Gk.	Greek
GKC	W. Gesenius, E. Kautzsch, & A. E. Cowley, *Gesenius' Hebrew Grammar* (Oxford: Clarendon, 1910).
Hb.	Hebrew
HUCA	*Hebrew Union College Annual*
IBT	Interpreting Biblical Texts
ICC	*International Critical Commentary*
i.e.	"that is"
IES	Israel Exploration Society
JAOS	*Journal of the American Oriental Society*
JBL	*Journal of Biblical Literature*
JJS	*Journal of Jewish Studies*
JSOT	*Journal for the Study of the Old Testament*
JSOTSup	Journal for the Study of the Old Testament Supplement

KAI	*Kanaanäische und aramäische Inschriften* (ed. H. Donner & W. Röllig; Wiesbaden: Harrassowitz, 1962–64).
KB	L. Koehler and W. Baumgartner, *Hebräisches und Aramäisches Lexicon zum Alten Testament* (Leiden: Brill, 1967–96).
Ketib	"that which is written" (the reading preserved in the received text)
Ketub.	*Ketuboth* ("Marriage Deeds")
KJV	King James Version
LXX	Septuagint translation (Greek) in A. Rahlfs, *Septuaginta*, 9th ed. (Stuttgart: Wurttembergische Bibelanstalt, 1935).
m.	Mishnah
MT	Masoretic Text of the Hebrew Bible, *Biblia Hebraica Stuttgartensia* (K. Elliger and W. Rudolph, eds.; Stuttgart: Deutsche Bibelgesellschaft, 1983).
NASV	New American Standard Version
Nazir	*Nazir* ("Nazirite Vow")
NEB	New English Bible
NICOT	*New International Commentary on the Old Testament*
NIV	New International Version
NJPS	New Jewish Publication Society version
NRSV	New Revised Standard Version
NT	New Testament
OG	Old Greek
OSA	Old South Arabic
OT	Old Testament
OTL	*Old Testament Library*
PSSD	*A Compendious Syriac Dictionary* founded upon the *Thesaurus Syriacus* of R. Payne Smith (ed. J. Payne Smith; Oxford: Clarendon, 1903).
Qere	"that which is read" (the reading preferred by the Masoretes)
Qidd.	*Qiddushin* ("Holy Things")
Rab.	*Midrash Rabbah* (London: Soncino, 1983).
Rashi	*The Megilloth and Rashi's Commentary* (ed. A. & Y. Schwartz; New York: Feldheim, 1983).

RB	*Revue Biblique*
RQ	*Restoration Quarterly*
RSV	Revised Standard Version
RTR	*Reformed Theological Review*
Sanh.	*Sanhedrin* ("Assembly")
Shabb.	*Shabbat* ("Sabbath")
SJOT	*Scandinavian Journal of Theology*
SJT	*Scottish Journal of Theology*
SOTBT	Studies in Old Testament Biblical Theology
Sot.	Sotah ("Suspected Adulteress")
s.v.	*sub verbo* ("under the word")
Syr	Syriac translation in *The Syriac Bible* (Stuttgart: United Bible Societies, 1979).
TBS	The Biblical Seminar
TDOT	*Theological Dictionary of the Old Testament* (eds. G. J. Botterweck & H. Ringgren; Grand Rapids: Eerdmans, 1974–).
Tg	Targum (Aramaic translation & commentary) in A. Sperber, ed. *The Bible in Aramaic: Vol. IV A, Ruth* (Leiden: Brill, 1968).
TOTC	*Tyndale Old Testament Commentaries*
TynBul	*Tyndale Bulletin*
Ug	Ugaritic
Vg	Vulgate translation (Latin) in *Biblia Sacra Vulgata* (Stuttgart: Deutsche Bibelgesellschaft, 1983).
VT	*Vetus Testamentum*
VTSup	Supplements to Vetus Testamentum
WBC	*Word Biblical Commentary*
Yeb.	*Yebamot* ("Sisters-in-Law")
ZAW	*Zeitschrift fur die alttestamentliche Wissenschaft*

General Introduction

Welcome to a commentary on three books of the Bible that include everything: love and violence, faith and greediness, respect and harassment, sex and war, riddle and fable, powerful feats and ritual warfare, geography and idolatry, conquering and revenge. Joshua, Judges, and Ruth create controversy and inspire courage. Here women are treated as objects *and* as partners in mission. Foreigners are killed without mercy and also accepted into the people of God, even into the lineage of David.

The authors of these three commentaries take a canonical-historical approach to the books, viewing the books as a whole and relating them to other books in the canon. For instance, Joshua, Judges, Samuel, and Kings comprise the Former Prophets in the Hebrew canon. These reflect themes from Deuteronomy and so are called books of the Deuteronomic History by M. Noth. He proposed that Deuteronomy originally introduced the Former Prophets.

The relationship of Joshua and Judges with Deuteronomy appears when they critique events of their period. Joshua especially reflects themes of Deuteronomy in chapters 1 and 23–24. The influence of Deuteronomy continues within the framework of Judges 2:11–16:31. Judges 17–21 explains how a lack of kingship leads to chaos, violence, and idolatrous behavior. Gordon Harris and Cheryl Brown discuss these canonical relationships in their commentaries on Joshua and Judges.

Ruth is not included in the books in the Former Prophets, but is in the third division of the Hebrew canon, Writings, between Song of Songs and Lamentations. The Septuagint, however, places Ruth after Judges and before Samuel in its canon, because Ruth has its setting in the period of the Judges. Michael Moore points out that although stories in Judges and Ruth tell of events prior to kingship, the ways they do so are in stark contrast. Judges 17–21 pictures the period as a time when Israel was without faithfulness, bent on self-destruction, and without controls. Ruth, by contrast, shows that through faithfulness courageous women can rise above loss and pessimism to experience protection and happiness with a faithful kinsman-redeemer. Ruth ends with a final genealogy that prepares the way for the finest moment of kingship, the house of David.

Joshua, Judges, and Ruth also stand together as narratives. The books respond well to literary methods that critically open the story as a whole. Joshua and Judges tell complex stories in various forms and styles; irony provides interesting twists and interpretations in the narratives. In these books burials provide endings to sections (Deut 34:5–8; Josh. 8:29; 24:29–33; Judg. 2:7–10; 16:31). Ruth tells the saga of two women. Fate provides both tragedy and a happy climax to the story. The narrator sensitively describes the bitter losses of Naomi and Ruth and how they move from emptiness to fullness. Its form is unique among the three books; nonetheless, a literary analysis of the story remains the key to understanding the three books.

Theology is an integral part of these three books. Joshua, Judges, and Ruth explore the dynamics of God's relationship with those called to be God's people. War and love are secondary to the power and work of God, who gives land to and provides deliverers for the people. The people's responsibility in this relationship is made clear in covenant renewal ceremonies (Josh. 8:30–35; 24) that call the people to fear and serve the Lord in light of God's goodness. The book of Joshua teaches that faithfulness to God leads to a homeland. Judges 2:11–16:31 shows how unfaithfulness brings oppression and hardship in the land, and repentance brings deliverance. Ruth explores how faithfulness to one another brings deliverance from God.

The three books are tied together also by a common historical context. Joshua, Judges, and Ruth all reflect the setting of the tribal settlement of Canaan. Consequently, the commentaries on Joshua and Judges deal with the date of the exodus and the nature and date of the settlement, issues on which archaeological findings continue to fuel debate. A history of the literature focuses on the setting of the audience of the book's final form and dismisses chronological issues of the settlement. Commentaries on Joshua and Judges in this volume will discuss options of understanding the historical setting of the books.

I am pleased to have the opportunity to introduce this volume. The authors want to thank colleagues and friends for their support during the writing of the commentaries. Our families played a major role in enabling us to write our respective sections. The editors have encouraged and directed us professionally through the writing and production. May God speak clearly to you, the reader, through this volume.

J. Gordon Harris
North American Baptist Seminary
Sioux Falls, South Dakota

Joshua

J. Gordon Harris

Introduction: Joshua

The book of Joshua captures the imagination of readers as do few other books, for it challenges and builds their faith. However, the message of Joshua remains a difficult one to interpret and apply. On the positive side, the book calls for a high level of courage and commitment to God and teaches that following the orders of God leads to success. By contrast, people who disobey God fail. Courageous and committed leaders win battles. The book says believers receive rest from enemies and security when they fight for God and God's chosen leader. However, these teachings can be misused in churches today.

There certain aspects of the theology of Joshua that Christians cannot easily accept. Readers often struggle with God's sanctions and commands of violence and the way in which God gives territory to a favored nation that exterminates the inhabitants of its land. God's brutality upsets readers who expect the God of the OT to love enemies as Jesus commanded. Readers also feel uncomfortable with Joshua's promises of material success; Christians who read their NT identify success with meekness and spiritual maturity. Another difficulty is that readers may question Joshua's nationalistic overtones. Exhortations about total devotion to a nation increase their concern about the book. These challenges the commentary seeks to answer.

This commentary is limited in size and addresses a general readership. It must focus on the theology of Joshua and how those teachings can be applied in the modern Christian context. It lacks the space to address in detail controversial critical issues discussed in larger, technical commentaries. This volume provides a theological bridge to transport readers from a book about tribal events to current Christian teachings. The commentary points out common human and religious situations in the book and asks what God is saying through each one. Scriptures then are interpreted in light of the NT. This approach produces a commentary focusing on life situations and biblical theology.

Title of the Book

The book is named after its chief character, Joshua, who dominates the warfare and allotment of land to tribes later known as Israel. The name Joshua means "The Lord is salvation," and it is formed by adding a shortened Hebrew form of the covenant name for Israel's God *(yhwh)* to the word "salvation." (The Greek form of the Hebrew name Joshua is Jesus.) Moses changes Joshua's earlier name, *Hoshea* ("he saves"), into Joshua (Num. 13:16). The book pictures God as the Savior who gives Canaan to the tribes and portrays Joshua as God's agent who leads the tribes to victory.

Joshua is the first of four books that the Hebrew canon calls the Former Prophets (Joshua, Judges, Samuel, and Kings). Deuteronomy introduces the Former Prophets and provides ideals for judging the actions of subsequent generations. Events in the book of Joshua provide the bridge from Moses' death in the wilderness to the taking of land west of the Jordan River, where the tribes subsequently become the nation Israel.[1] Joshua is a prophet like the one Moses foretold would arise (Deut.18:15–19). As the successor of Moses, he models a royal figure.[2] He exemplifies a successful leader who faithfully follows the instructions of Moses and God.

Structure of the Book

The book divides naturally into three parts: battles for the land (1–12), allotments of the land (13–21), and commitment for remaining in the land (22–24). These larger portions can be broken into smaller sections:

Introduction to the challenge of taking the land, 1:1–18

Preparation for and crossing the Jordan, 2–4

Preparation for holy war, the battles of Jericho and Ai, and covenant renewal, 5–8

Gibeonite deception, southern and northern campaigns, and a summary of victories and remaining threats, 9–12

Tribal land allotments, towns of refuge, towns for Levites, 13–21

Covenant for eastern tribes and their threat to tribal unity, 22

Joshua's farewell address, 23

A covenant for the future, 24

Historical Questions about the Events of Joshua

For a century, debate raged about chronology issues of the premonarchical period of ancient Israel as exponents of source-critical theory increasingly questioned the historicity of the biblical sources. In the 1950s and 1960s new discoveries fueled optimism that biblical archaeology could solve chronological questions about the exodus and settlement. However, evidence found by archaeologists has led scholars to propose a number of competing reconstructions of the period. Study of the history of biblical literature has reinforced further pessimism about the historical reliability of the biblical accounts.

Archaeological Evidence about the Exodus and Settlement in Canaan

Determining the date of the exodus could provide a starting point for the chronology of the settlement, but the date of the exodus remains one of the unsolved mysteries of premonarchical chronology. Those scholars who dismiss the historicity of the Bible also reject the biblical account of the exodus. Scholars who accept the basic historicity of the exodus remain divided on its date. One group proposes a mid-fifteenth-century date (ca. 1446 B.C.E.), and others point to a thirteenth-century date (ca. 1290 B.C.E.).[3] The balance of archaeological evidence in my opinion points toward the thirteenth-century date rather than the earlier one. However, conclusions should be considered tentative in light of the scarcity of clear evidence.

Archaeologists are just as divided on the chronology and nature of the settlement of the tribes in Canaan. They propose three constructs of the way Israel entered and settled the land. First, W. F. Albright and others cite archaeological evidence pointing toward a unified, military conquest.[4] Alt and his followers, however, suggest that Israel entered Canaan as desert nomads by peaceful infiltration, subsequently joining together in a tribal confederation.[5] Taking a different view, G. E. Mendenhall and then N. Gottwald propose a revolt theory. In their reconstruction the settlement originated in the cataclysmic sociopolitical changes of a "peasant revolution" against oppressive overlords in urban Canaan, perhaps precipitated by a small group of former slaves. Refugees from low, exploited classes of urban Canaanite society[6] ultimately settled the highlands and were bound together by an ideology (i.e., the worship of Yahweh). As with the date of the exodus, archaeological evidence both supports and denies aspects of each construction.

Investigations in the hill country, Galilee, and the Jezreel Valley indicate a very complex picture of the settlement. For example, archaeological findings support the military conquest construction in the thirteenth century only at Hazor. Instead of building a consensus, archaeologists continue to propose other settlement constructs.[7]

I. Finkelstein suggests that archaeological evidence points only to a general deurbanization of Canaan at the end of the Late Bronze Age and during the beginning of Iron I.[8] The settlement period in his reconstruction encompasses Joshua, Judges, and 1 Samuel. Evidence from the hill country points to an influx of settlers overrunning the region and a number of communities appearing in the central hills of Israel, traveling from east to west. In this view, archaeologists suggest that the settlement era lasted from 1200 to 900 B.C.E. or until David conquered the urban centers of Jerusalem and Megiddo. During this period, pastoral groups make the transition to a sedentary existence. Movement west increases conflict between tribes and inhabitants of the urban Canaan. This view of the settlement resembles features of the book of Joshua, but the conclusion places the events as happening over a longer period of time.

The various reconstructions of the settlement point to the limits of archaeology. Readers should not reject the historical quality of Joshua's narrative because archaeology does not directly support the book.[9] Apparent conflicts in chronology and interpretation can be attributed to the difficulty of using limited evidence for reconstructing biblical events. In this commentary, interpreting the book of Joshua does not depend on archaeological evidence. Instead I will use archaeological evidence primarily for clarifying biblical settings.

Literary study of Deuteronomy, Deuteronomistic History, and Joshua

M. Noth, who pointed out the relationship of the book of Joshua to Deuteronomy (e.g., Josh. 1; 23–24), shifts discussion from the historicity of the events of Joshua to the history of traditions forming its literature. He proposed that Deuteronomy was not originally linked to Genesis–Numbers but only later was separated and linked to the Torah as the Pentateuch. He suggested that Deuteronomy introduced Joshua–Kings (Deuteronomistic History) because of the history's Deuteronomic theology and literary forms.[10] History of tradition studies developed a theory tracing the book of Joshua from its origin during the reign of Josiah through two or maybe three levels of Deuteronomic editing.[11] In this scheme, the early form of Joshua addressed Israel of the seventh century; the final form, Israel in exile in Babylon.[12] The theory assumed the final editing connected Deuteronomy to Joshua–2 Kings.

J. G. McConville points out some weaknesses in assumptions and methods used by tradition history in its study of Joshua. First, though teachings from the book can apply to a nation in exile, the book does not address specifically concerns of the exile. Second, the history of traditions approach has trouble determining the history of some passages in the book (e.g., Josh. 24). Third, circular thinking remains suspect. Circular thinking accepts a theory and then interprets the Bible by it.[13] In general, the atomizing and theoretical approach of tradition history does not do justice to the book of Joshua.

Narrative Analysis and Joshua

Narrative analysis is a more appropriate method for studying Joshua because it focuses on a close reading of a text and interprets the book as a whole. Narrative methods challenge the assumption that a variety of viewpoints indicates different authors, sources, or editors. Narrative analysis also recognizes dynamics such as conflict and plot[14] and multileveled mediation of events.[15] Such studies follow R. Polzin,[16] who identifies the unity of Joshua within its internal tensions and conflicting themes. A careful reading of the text promises a more fruitful approach for interpreting its meaning than does a history of its literature.

One hopes that commentaries will utilize the methods of narrative studies even more. In his commentary M. H. Woudstra[17] moves in that direction, reading the book as a whole while not neglecting a variety of viewpoints and themes. Woudstra charts multileveled mediation of events and does not identify them as coming from different sources or editors. He also refers to archaeological evidence but refrains from stating dogmatic conclusions about it. Woudstra approaches Joshua as a message about God's gift, calling readers to live responsibly.

Worship in the Book of Joshua

The book of Joshua frequently describes worship experiences. Tribal representatives renew covenants, prepare for holy war, and build altars as memorials to their God. Worship ceremonies are celebrated at the sites of Gilgal, Shiloh, and Shechem.

Gilgal

A number of Gilgals are mentioned in the Bible, the one in Joshua being located somewhere near Jericho and the Jordan River. The Israelites camped there upon crossing the Jordan and remained in their camp during the conquest of the central hills. Joshua ordered the tribes to set up a memorial of standing stones at Gilgal to commemorate the crossing (Josh. 4:19ff.). Gilgal also was the place where a generation of men was circumcised.

Shiloh

Shiloh was an ancient center where during the time of Eli the tribes built a tabernacle to house the Ark (1 Sam 1–4). It was located in the central hills just 10 miles north of Bethel, halfway between Bethel and Shechem. The Tent of Meeting was set up there after the tribes entered Canaan (Josh. 18:1). Here too Joshua apportioned land to the tribes (Josh. 20–21). Eleazer was priest (Josh. 21:1–2). The eastern tribes built an alternative altar near the Jordan River at Geliloth and nearly caused a civil war as the western tribes rushed to defend Shiloh, their worship center. Only the mediation of Phinehas and quick thinking by leaders of the eastern tribes averted a conflict (Josh. 22:9–34).

Shechem

Shechem was located in the pass between Mount Gerizim and Mount Ebal, north of Shiloh. Shechem is mentioned first as an altar of uncut stones on Mount Ebal, where the tribes offered sacrifices and renewed the covenant in the pass (Josh. 8:30–35). Shechem entered the tribal entity by treaty (Josh. 8; 24). No destruction layer remains in Shechem from the end of the Bronze Age to the beginning of Iron I (ca. 1200 B.C.E.).[18]

Standing Stone Sites and Worship

Standing stones *(masseboth)* represented the deity in desert shrines. Memorials of standing stones like those placed at Gilgal and heaps of stones that mark graves also may have hosted worship celebrations (e.g., Josh. 10:27). These worship centers included a flat slab of stones for offering sacrifices and had a circle of stones placed in front of the standing stones to enclose the worship.[19] Joshua placed a standing stone at Shechem as a witness to the covenant between God and the people (Josh. 24:26).

Worship during the settlement utilized symbols and worship places in Canaan to give birth to new faith in the Lord of the heavens and the earth.

Worship Ceremonies

Prebattle ceremonies abounded in Joshua, because purity in the camp prior to battle determined success in warfare as much as did fighting. Consulting God about the battle set the stage for divine support of the conflict. God gave instructions about what part of the booty belonged to God or what was *herem*. What belonged to God was devoted to God, and warriors were banned from keeping the booty themselves. Circumcision also purified the warriors for warfare (Josh. 5:2–9). After the warriors were healed, the tribes celebrated the Passover (Josh. 5:10–12).

Battlefield ceremonies included lifting up the ark of the covenant, a wooden box on which the LORD was enthroned, and carrying it in front of the troops. It indicated that the LORD was leading the troops into battle. Marching around a city like Jericho also was performed in a ritualistic order. The blowing of trumpets and the war cry demoralized the enemy and as the voice of God knocked down the fortress walls (Josh. 1–20). These ritualistic acts on the battlefield ensured success and gave the leaders an opportunity to repeat prebattle instructions to the soldiers. Sacrifices and covenant renewal celebrated victory in battle (Josh. 8:30–35).

The Text of Joshua

The text of Joshua shows substantial differences between the Old Greek (OG) and the Hebrew (Masoretic Text, MT). The Greek text is about 5 percent shorter than the Hebrew. In some places, however, both expand the text or show evidence of omissions and additions. Recent studies indicate that the OG is a reliable translation of a Hebrew text that equals the value of the MT.[20] Two town lists illustrate the value of the OG: eleven names in the

Judah list (15:59) and Levitical cities in Reuben (21:36–37). The OG is the earliest recoverable form of what is known as the Septuagint (LXX).

The OG and MT are so different in Joshua 5, 6, 20, and 24 that R. D. Nelson concludes that one text (either OG or MT) has been revised or modified in those chapters.[21] The MT has been revised in Joshua 5:2–9, 6:1–15, and 20:1–9. In Joshua 24 the OG is the revised text (see discussions on Josh. 24 in commentary).

Two Dead Sea Scroll fragments of Joshua from cave 4 at Qumran have been found. The fragment 4Qjosh(a) positions the reading of the law at Shechem (8:30–35) before 5:2–7 and after the crossing of the Jordan. This change puts the book in agreement with the command in Deuteronomy 27:2 (see discussion in commentary note under 8:30–35).

Interpreters of the passages need to study both the OG and MT before deciding how to understand the text. Both texts deserve equal consideration using standard textual-criticism principles. Readers can isolate an earlier text by comparing the two texts and then eliminating expansions appearing in either the OG or MT.

Theological Themes of Joshua

Readers need to interpret the theological themes by asking what the theme teaches about God. For example, the leadership theme points out how God encourages righteousness and strength in leaders. God's gift of the land shows that God, the divine warrior, freely provides victory and gives rest in the land. God's grace also promises divine faithfulness for the obedient. Finally, the book's concern for unity teaches that God promotes unity, not discord and defeat. Readers need to consider the theological dimension of a passage because God dominates the book.

Leadership

The book presents a number of insights into the nature of leadership. Joshua 1 begins with the death of the great leader, Moses. Moses, the servant of the Lord, dominates the exodus experience and events of the wilderness. He is the great lawgiver, the intermediary between God and the people. Joshua, the assistant of Moses, no doubt faces a crisis of confidence upon succeeding the great Moses. Chapter by chapter, the book describes how Joshua emerges as a leader like Moses until he too is called the "servant of the Lord" (24:29) after his death. Joshua tells how God develops leadership and defines its characteristics. Key words challenge Joshua to lead the people successfully. He is to be strong, courageous, obedient, not afraid, not confused, a follower of God's ways, and successful (1:1–9). Joshua's leadership shows that leaders can act decisively, prepare well, be unprepared, make mistakes, be manipulated, and compromise outside of God's will. As a leader Joshua does not model the ideals of leadership throughout the book. He combines success with disappointment. Though Joshua leads with mixed results, he remains faithful to God and serves his people. Consequently, the success of Joshua teaches that leaders ultimately can succeed with guidance from God and loyalty and respect from their subordinates.

Land as Gift

God's gift of the land of Canaan to the tribes dominates the book. Military might, however, does not enable the tribes to defeat the Canaanites. Though passages often celebrate victory in battle and defeat of enemies using traditional battle account forms, they do so to praise the divine warrior who made victory possible at Jericho, Ai, Gibeon, and Hazor. The book contains little information about fighting. Battles for Canaan would humble professional soldiers, and these encounters are decided by ritual, deceit, a night march, extended daylight, and thunderstorms. Victory comes when the people follow God's guidelines for war (see commentary on Jericho and Ai).

The distribution of allotments by the casting of lots emphasizes that the land is a gift from God (13–21).[22] Eleazar the priest helps Joshua determine the will of God for the allotments. Frequently Joshua also directly addresses the tribes to remind them that the Lord is giving them their inheritance (23:3–5). God's allotment of cities of refuge and towns for Levites reminds the tribes that the Lord owns the land and controls its use. The gift of the land obligates tribes to respect and serve the Lord wholeheartedly and unswervingly (24:13–15).

Obedience and God's Grace

In an act of grace, God freely promises and gives land to the tribes. God's grace in return demands obedience to the commands of Moses and to the instructions of the Lord. Those instructions vary from prebattle calls for utter destruction of life and

booty *(herem)* at Jericho to the later call to collect booty and preserve cities as a reward to troops. The annihilation of Achan and
his family in the valley of Achor because of violations of *herem* at
Jericho (7:2–13) underlines the importance of obeying these instructions. What remains consistent in God's instructions through
Joshua is the call to do as God commands (11:15). Faithfulness becomes synonymous with obedience to divine instructions.

Unity

Joshua begins and ends with concerns about the unity of
the tribes. The book expresses a special concern about tribes east
of the Jordan River cooperating with those west of the river
(1:10–18; 22:7–34). A geographical barrier such as a river often
promotes jealousy, regionalism, and civil war; regional customs
potentially can distort the worship of the Lord. Success in the
battle for Canaan depends on fielding forces from both the east
and the west. That unity depends on loyalty first to Moses and
now to Joshua.

Judges chronicles the breakdown of tribal unity. The out-
rage at Gibeah and the civil war against Benjamin (Judg. 19–21)
demonstrate why Joshua was concerned about unity. Joshua's
farewell address (23:6–16) and the covenant renewal ceremony
(24:15–24) emphasize the importance of religious unity in the future. Both ceremonies address representatives of all the tribes and
reflect concerns about idolatry expressed in Deuteronomy. The
passages warn the people against marrying people in the land
and worshiping other gods. Worship of the Lord who rescued
the people from slavery in Egypt must be the glue that binds
the tribes.

Ultimately, unity springs out of faithfulness to God, not loyalty to a leader. Joshua warns the tribes against attitudes and actions that can harm their unity. Worship of the God of Moses and
faithfulness to the commandments hold the people together in
the land. Idolatry and unfaithfulness to the covenant drive the
people apart and out of the land. Judges–Kings chronicle the loss
of unity as faith drifts away.

Challenges and Questions

The book of Joshua begins and ends with challenges and
questions. A change of leadership creates anxious moments for a

new leader and the people. Joshua faces the especially daunting task of succeeding Moses and leading a collection of tribes to possess a land full of hostile enemies. The passing of Moses signals the end of an old era. In his place Joshua assumes the responsibility for leading the people through a transition to a new era. Joshua knows he will succeed when the tribes succeed. These are the best of times and yet the most stressful. God wants to give the land and charges Joshua with the responsibility of leading the people to receive the gift.

The book maintains suspense as it seeks answers to a series of questions: Will the tribes receive and obey a new leader? Will the new leader follow the law of Moses? Will the tribes obey the instructions (law) of God to possess the land and their promised rest? Will the people compromise their covenant with the Lord? Will the Jordan River and division of the land bring about disunity and conflict? Will the tribes eliminate idolatrous residents from the land? Will Israel develop the devotion necessary to retain the land? Does God possess enough power as a warrior to give the tribes promised rest? Unresolved tension continues throughout the book, as from the first chapter to the final verses the questions are answered yes or no or sometimes. The death of Joshua raises a new question: Can the people conquer the remaining areas without Joshua and his generation of leaders? Doubt returns and continues through the time of Judges.

Notes

---

1. For a summary of recent evidence on the early history of the settlement see R. S. Hess, "Early Israel in Canaan: a summary of recent evidence and interpretations," *PEQ* (1993), pp. 125–42.

2. J. R. Porter, "The Succession of Joshua," *Proclamation and Presence* (ed. J. I. Durham and J. R. Porter; Richmond, Va.: John Knox, 1970), pp. 102–32.

3. Supporters of the mid-fifteenth-century date locate the exodus during the Amarna period (1 Kgs. 6:1; 1 Chron.; Judg. 11:26). Those who accept the thirteenth-century date emphasize the four hundred years the tribes were in Egypt (Gen. 15:13 and the building of Pithom and Ramses by Ramses II, who ascended to the throne ca. 1300 B.C.E. [Exod. 1:11]).

4. See W. F. Albright, "The Israelite Conquest of Canaan in the Light of Archaeology," *BASOR* 74 (1939), pp. 11–23 and J. Bright, *History*

of Israel (1st ed. [Philadelphia: Westminster, 1959], pp. 117–20, as compared with the 3d ed. [Philadelphia: Westminster, 1981], pp. 129–33) and G. E. Wright, *Biblical Archaeology* (rev. ed.; Philadelphia: Westminster, 1962), pp. 69–84.

5. A. Alt, "Josua," *BZAW* 66 (1936), pp. 13–19, and *Essays on Old Testament History and Religion* (trans. R. A. Wilson; Garden City, N.Y.: Doubleday, 1967), pp. 174–221.

6. G. E. Mendenhall explores this option in "The Hebrew conquest of Palestine," *BA* 25 (1962), pp. 66–77, along with N. Gottwald, *The Tribes of Yahweh* (Maryknoll, N.Y.: Orbis, 1979).

7. Reconstructions of the settlement can be found in F. M. Cross, ed., *Symposia Celebrating the Seventy-fifth Anniversary of the Founding of the ASOR (1900–1975)* (Cambridge, Mass.: ASOR, 1979), pp. 1–84; B. Halpern, *The Emergence of Israel in Canaan* (SBL Monograph 29; Chico, Calif.: Scholars, 1983), pp. 47–106; R. B. Coote, *Early Israel: A New Horizon* (Minneapolis: Fortress, 1990), pp. 59–93.

8. For a discussion of Israelite settlement in light of earlier models and additional evidence see I. Finkelstein, *The Archaeology of the Israelite Settlement* (Jerusalem: IES, 1988) and V. Fritz, *An Introduction to Biblical Archaeology* (JSOTSup 172; Sheffield: JSOT Press, 1994), pp. 137–42.

9. The authenticity of the narrative of Joshua is dismissed by M. D. Coogan, "Archaeology and Biblical Studies: The Book of Joshua," in *The Hebrew Bible and Its Interpreters* (ed. W. H. Propp; Winona Lake, Ind.: Eisenbrauns, 1990), pp. 19–31, and N. P. Lemche, *Ancient Israel: A New History of Israelite Society* (TBS; Sheffield: JSOT Press, 1988), pp. 88–114. R. S. Hess expresses a more positive view in *Joshua: An Introduction and Commentary* (TOTC; Downers Grove, Ill.: InterVarsity, 1996).

10. The traditional historical-critical approach to the book emphasizes the role of a series of Deuteronomistic and priestly redactors in composing the book. F. Volkmar, *Das Buch Josua* (HZAT I: 7; Tübingen: J. C. B. Mohr, 1994). R. Polzin (*Moses and the Deuteronomist: Deuteronomy, Joshua, Judges* [New York: Seabury, 1980], pp. 74–80) takes a narrative approach but assumes a relationship between the book and the Deuteronomist.

11. For additional information on this approach see M. Noth, *The Deuteronomic History* (JSOTSup 15; Sheffield: JSOT Press, 1943, 1981), A. D. H. Mayes, *The Story of Israel Between Settlement and Exile: A Redactional Study of the Deuteronomistic History* (London: SCM, 1983), and R. D. Nelson, *The Double Redaction of the Deuteronomistic History* (JSOTSup 18; Sheffield: JSOT Press, 1981).

12. T. E. Fretheim, *Deuteronomic History* (IBT; Nashville: Abingdon, 1983).

13. J. G. McConville, *Grace in the End: A Study in Deuteronomic Theology* (SOTBT; Grand Rapids: Zondervan, 1993).

14. L. D. Hawk, *Every Promise Fulfilled: Contesting Plots in Joshua* (CBI; Louisville, Ky.: Westminster John Knox, 1991).

15. L. Eslinger takes a creative narrative approach in *Into the Hands of the Living God* (BLS 24; JSOTSup 84; Sheffield: Almond, 1989).

16. Polzin traces the voices of *authoritarian dogmatism* in conflict with *critical traditionalism* and changes in viewpoints throughout the sustained meditation on interpreting the Word of God (*Moses and the Deuteronomist*, pp. 84–145).

17. M. H. Woudstra, *The Book of Joshua* (NICOT; Grand Rapids: Eerdmans, 1981).

18. Information on the cities appears in *Mercer Bible Dictionary*, pp. 332, 816–17, 820; their locations can be found on Bible maps.

19. See discussions on standing stones and worship centers at Tel Dan in A. Biran, "Sacred Spaces," *BAR* 24 (1998), pp. 38–45, 70, and in the desert (Uzi Avner) in V. Horowitz, "Picturing Imageless Deities: Iconography in the Ancient Near East," *BAR* 23 (1997), pp. 46–51, 68–69.

20. Read more about the texts of Joshua in A. G. Auld, "Joshua: The Hebrew and Greek Texts," *Studies in the Historical Books of the Old Testament* (ed. J. A. Emerton; VTSup 30 [Leiden: Brill, 1979]), pp. 1–14, and "Textual and Literary Studies in the Book of Joshua," *ZAW* 90 (1978), pp. 412–17.

21. The best discussion of the textual issue in a commentary is the one by R. D. Nelson, *Joshua* (OTL; Louisville, Ky.: Westminster John Knox, 1997), pp. 22–24.

22. The best discussion of the allotments of Joshua is found in Hess, *Joshua*, pp. 53–62. The commentary discusses the geographical issues under 13–21, §19–32.

§1 Joshua: A New Leader Takes Over (Josh. 1:1–9)

1:1 / The narrator sets the context of the events in the first verse. Joshua 1:1 states that a new era is beginning **after the death of Moses.** The narrator connects the book of Joshua with the final chapters of Deuteronomy (Deut. 32:48–52; 34:1–12) describing the death of Moses in Moab. Moses, a victim of his anger, will not lead the people into the promised land (Num. 20:6–12; Deut. 1:37; 3:26). Instead Joshua, Moses' assistant (lit. "minister," lieutenant, aide), faces the assignment of following the premier **servant of the LORD.** The rest of the book answers the question of whether Joshua will lead the tribes to their promised rest.

1:2–9 / God's point of view dominates these verses, in which the Lord, speaking directly to Joshua rather than through Moses' report (Deut. 31:7–8), addresses him about matters summarized in Deuteronomy 31:23. As if grieving the loss, the Lord states the obvious: **Moses my servant is dead.** Despite the grief, God moves on to discuss the future. God tells Joshua and the tribes to move to the challenge ahead: **Get ready to cross the Jordan River** (lit. "Now arise, pass over this Jordan!"). The period of grieving (Deut. 34:8) is over; the tribes must go forward. People find the past more comfortable, but God provides new leadership and pushes them toward the future. Moving the tribes toward the future in no way diminishes the memory of the earlier leader or the severity of the loss. Rather, God compliments Moses by directing the new leader and followers toward his goal of entering **the land.**

The land of opportunity will come as a gift from God's grace as **promised** to **Moses,** and that gift unifies fighting in Canaan (1–12) with dividing allotments (13–21) among tribes and clans. God promises a land stretching from the desert (wilderness) in the south to Lebanon in the north, from the Euphrates in the east to the Mediterranean (Great) Sea on the west (vv. 3–4). These limits do not mark the actual borders of the emerging nation. Rather, God points Joshua and the tribes toward the potential gift, the Fertile Crescent, the part of the Middle East that reaches across the northern Syrian Desert and extends from the Nile Valley to the Tigris and Euphrates rivers. The tribes will need to wait until the reign of David to achieve anything near to those borders. God's promise of land becomes the challenge for subsequent generations.

This gift will be won on the field of conflict, for God directs Joshua to attack enemy forces and to expect victory through God's support. God promises: **No one will be able to stand up against you all the days of your life** (lit. stand before you). The divine warrior removes barriers to winning the prize. Victory will come because God promises to be present personally and powerfully. **I will be with you; I will never leave you nor forsake you.** That promise echoes the one given to Moses at his call (Exod. 3:12). As in the past, the divine warrior promises gifts by offering a personal and powerful relationship.

The promise of the divine warrior's presence encourages an insecure Joshua. **Be strong and courageous,** the Lord tells him (1:6). Strength and courage will enable the people to **inherit** the land that God promised through an oath to Israel's ancestors. The inheritance of the tribes becomes a key theme when the land is distributed. Claiming the promises of God and their inheritance demands strength and courage when the gift includes hostile opponents. The gift will be received when it is seized.

God challenges Joshua also to be strong and very courageous in keeping the law (torah). The teachings of Moses will show the tribes how to take the land. The law, or instruction, was what **Moses gave** to Joshua. The **Book of the Law** ensures success (1:8) when Joshua follows it, keeps it in his mouth for speaking, thinks about it day and night, and obeys it carefully. If Joshua obeys the law in this way, God promises him, **Then you will be prosperous and successful.** Joshua will achieve prosperity and success (regular victories against the enemies) by following the instructions of the divine warrior. The passage should not be interpreted as promising financial security. Instead, God connects obedience to Moses' gift, the law, to successfully receiving God's gift, the land. Faithfulness to both gifts demands courage and strength.

The final challenge to the new leader repeats God's encouragement. Joshua needs to remember earlier instructions: **Have I**

not commanded you? Be strong and courageous (1:9). Joshua need not be frozen with terror or disabled by discouragement, because **the LORD your God will be with you wherever you go.** The Hebrew reverses the word order to emphasize that God is near: "Because with you is the Lord your God." God's presence as the divine warrior ensures perseverance and ultimate victory under difficult circumstances. The presence of God is the greatest weapon of a chosen servant. God the warrior transforms an unknown wilderness into familiar territory. God's presence is the ultimate contingency plan for believers. It is the final solution for fear and pressures. It ensures the success of God's mission and servant.

Additional Note §1

1:1 / The term **servant of the LORD** is missing in the Gk. version in vv. 1 and 15. However, that term is used as a title frequently in Deut. It appears in God's reported speech in vv. 2 and 13. It not only refers to slaves but also describes a person in a subordinate position. That person can be a strong leader such as Abraham, Moses, or David. Subjects to a king refer to themselves as servants of the king (the word "servant" often refers to an official; see Gen. 14:14; Exod. 32:13; Lev. 25:55; 1 Sam. 3:9; Ezra 9:11). The most significant leaders would be called "servant of the LORD." Joshua is called "servant of the Lord" only twice (Josh. 24:29; Judg. 2:8).

"LORD" *(Adonai)* refers to how readers should pronounce the covenant name of the God *(Yhwh)* of Israel. During and after the exile in Babylon, the Israelites determined that they would not violate the holiness of God by saying the holy name of God. Rabbis substituted the vowels of *Adonai* (lit. LORD) to suggest that the divine name *(Yhwh)* be read as LORD. The personal name of God remains a mystery, which God revealed to Moses with the simple explanation: "I am who I am" (other translations can be "I create" or "I will be present"; Exod. 4:14). See the discussion in R. G. Boling and G. E. Wright, *Joshua* (AB 6; Garden City, N.Y.: Doubleday, 1982), pp. 118–20. The meaning of the name, however, remains unknown. See the discussion of the self-introduction formula in Exod. 6 and Ezek. 20 (W. Zimmerli, *I Am Yahweh* [ed. W. Brueggemann; trans. D. W. Stott; Atlanta: John Knox, 1982], pp. 1–16).

§2 Excursus: Joshua in the Canon

Joshua, Moses' "servant" or "minister" (Hb. *mesaret*; Exod. 24:13; Josh. 1:1), is called Hoshea in Numbers 13:16. In that passage, Moses renames him "Joshua" (Hb. *yehosua*), or "Yahweh is salvation." The Bible identifies Joshua as one who served Moses in the wilderness, led the tribes into the land of Canaan, and apportioned land to the tribes. Joshua's inheritance in the tribe of Ephraim (Josh. 19:49–50), his burial site (Josh. 24:30), and a genealogical note (1 Chron. 7:27) indicate that he belonged to the tribe of Ephraim.

Some scholars try to reconstruct the history of the Joshua traditions and question the historical reliability of stories about Joshua. G. W. Ramsey discusses this viewpoint ("Joshua," *ABD* 3:999), and R. D. Nelson also questions whether the materials confirm the historicity of Joshua by pointing out royal elements in the stories (Num. 27:15–23), especially parallels between Joshua and Josiah (Nelson, *The Double Redaction*, p. 125). However, a close reading of the canonical materials produces a clear picture of Moses' successor.

Numerous passages point out the close relationship between Joshua and Moses. Joshua first appears as a warrior who fights the Amalekites under Moses' command (Exod. 17:9–13). As an apprentice he accompanies Moses to Mount Sinai (Exod. 24:13; 32:15–18) to receive the law. He serves in the tent of meeting (Exod. 33:11; cf. Acts 7:44–45). He evaluates the land of Canaan as a spy and joins with Caleb to affirm that with God's help Israel can take the land (Num. 13–14). As Moses faces his death, he designates Joshua to be his successor (Num. 27:12–23; Deut. 3:23–28). Joshua helps the people to possess the land by following the commands of Moses.

Joshua begins to lead the people under the most difficult of circumstances. In chapter 1 God repeatedly encourages Joshua. Joshua grieves the loss of his friend, Moses, and then faces the difficult task of succeeding this great leader. He must lead a people to take a land they refused to take under Moses. Joshua experiences achievements and disappointments but always rises to the occasion. At the end of his career, Joshua gathers tribal leaders to renew the covenant with the Lord (lit. *Yhwh;* Josh. 24). The narrator gives Joshua the title "servant of the LORD" upon his death, the label by which Moses is best known.

Though Joshua demonstrates courageous leadership, the Bible as a whole rates the leadership of Moses over that of Joshua (Num. 11:26–29; 27:20–21). Moses accomplishes more, especially signs and wonders (Exod. 7–11; 14:21–31; 15:22–25; 17:1–7; Num. 20:2–13). Moses intercedes regularly for the people (Exod. 32:11–14; Num. 11:2; 12:13; 14:13–19; 21:7) and speaks for God more often than does Joshua (Deut.). Even the book of Joshua makes it clear that Joshua and the people succeed when they follow the teachings of Moses (Josh. 1:7–8, 13; 4:10; 8:30–35; 11:12–15; 22:2; 23:6). As well, the NT mentions Moses more frequently than Joshua (eighty times compared with three).

The supremacy of Moses, however, diminishes in no way the accomplishments of Joshua. The book of Joshua pictures him as a prophet, speaking for God (Josh. 1:1; 3:7; 4:1, 15; 8:18; 20:1). Though he needs the mediation of a priest to do some tasks (Num. 27:15–23; Josh. 14:1; 19:51), he speaks for God using the formula "thus says the Lord" (Josh. 7:13; 24:2). Kings treats Joshua as a prophet in telling about a fulfillment of his words coming "in accordance with the word of the LORD spoken by Joshua son of Nun" (1 Kgs. 16:34). Joshua intercedes for the people as did Moses (Josh. 7:6–9). God calls him in language reminiscent of the call of Moses (Josh. 5:13–15), and Joshua leads the people to cross the Jordan as Moses led the people to cross the Reed Sea. Joshua also is filled with the "spirit of wisdom because Moses had laid his hands on him" (Deut. 34:9; see G. Mitchell, *Together in the Land: A Reading of the Book of Joshua* [JSOTSup 134; Sheffield: JSOT Press, 1993], pp. 33–34). In these ways Joshua exemplifies the standards of a prophet like Moses whom God would send (Deut. 18:15–19).

The book of Joshua also describes other ways in which Joshua is a leader like Moses. As the Lord had been with Moses, so God will be with Joshua (1:5, 17; 3:7). As the people experienced awe for Moses, they will feel the same way about Joshua (4:14). The eastern tribes promise to obey Joshua as they followed Moses (1:16–18; 22:2). Joshua assigns property to nine and a half tribes in Canaan as Moses did to two and a half tribes settling east of the Jordan River (22:7). Finally, after renewing the covenant, he "drew up for them decrees and laws. And Joshua recorded these things in the Book of the Law of God" (24:25–26) as did Moses (Deut. 31:9, 24–26).

Joshua, the trained warrior, is the strongest candidate to lead the march into Canaan. By his death, Moses turns over the tribal leadership to one skilled in military campaigns. The book of Joshua shows that God places the right person in leadership for the challenges in Canaan.

§3 Preparation to Cross the River and a Threat to Joshua's Leadership (Josh. 1:10–18)

Crossing the Jordan River presents a number of challenges. To cross the river is to claim the territory on the other side, but the river also threatens to split the forces of Joshua between the east and the west. Thus the Jordan River could become a divisive boundary and a threat to the unity of the emerging people. Moses sought to resolve that issue by requiring the tribes of Reuben and Gad, and the half-tribe of Manasseh, to fight with the western tribes to liberate Canaan as a condition for receiving their land east of the Jordan (Num. 21:21–35; 32:1–27).

The moment of truth has arrived. Will the two and a half tribes carry out their promise to Moses and cross the river to help the other tribes take the land of Canaan? Will they obey Joshua as they had promised Moses? Violation of that promise and resulting disunity could threaten the crossing of the river. Maintaining tribal unity would affirm the authority of the new leader.

1:10–11 / In these verses the narrator shifts the speech from God to Joshua. As a faithful subordinate, Joshua repeats the order of his commander in chief (God, 1:2). Joshua commands his subordinates (lit. officers; LXX, recorders) to have the people prepare to move the camp. Although no location for the camp is mentioned in this chapter, Shittim (2:1) is assumed, and that location is probably the same as the Shittim in Numbers (Num. 25:1). The staging area for crossing the Jordan had previously been the site of sexual immorality and worshiping the gods of the land (Num. 25:2–3).

Joshua orders the **officers of the people** to go through the camp and tell the people to **get** their **supplies ready**. With this order Joshua changed the wilderness habits of the tribes. While they were in the wilderness the tribes had depended on manna from heaven for their supplies. A successful military campaign at the river Jordan and in Canaan, however, would depend on supplies and provisions of the people. This operations order heralded a new period in the life of the people.

An operations order like the one given by Joshua states the army's mission, lists tasks it must do, and gives a time period in which it must complete the assignments. Joshua gives the tribes **three days** to prepare to leave the camp. The reported mission is to **cross the Jordan** River and to **take possession of the land** God is giving the people (lit. you; 1:11). Joshua repeats the order directly in the second person reminding the people that the Lord is **your God,** the divine helper of the entire body. Though the mission seems impossible, the covenant God of Moses (and the true commander) assures tribal leaders the mission is attainable. The tribes have three days to complete preparations, to break camp, and to begin the mission.

1:12–18 / The audience changes from the officers to representatives of the eastern tribes, the **Reubenites,** the **Gadites and the half-tribe of Manasseh.** Joshua evokes the name and position of Moses to impress on the tribes that they must carry out their agreement with Moses to secure God's gift of **rest** (secure borders, land to possess, and a relatively peaceful life). Moses had conquered and distributed land to the eastern (transjordan) tribes, and Joshua reminds them, God **has granted you this land** (east of the Jordan; Num. 21). The eastern tribes owe a debt of gratitude to God for their land (Num. 32:6–32). Joshua tells them that their families can remain east of the Jordan, but the warriors must fight for the west bank until all the tribes have **rest.**

In his speech, Joshua echoes Moses' concern for unity (Num. 32). Human nature tends to look after itself and forget about community responsibilities, an attitude that is summarized in the contemporary saying "Not in My Back Yard" (NIMBY). The point of this saying is that citizens favor what they can gain from but oppose what does not benefit them directly. That attitude leads citizens to oppose building a public service building near or behind their houses because it lowers property values on the houses. If the eastern tribes follow human nature, they will not support fighting for land of their fellow tribes. The back yard of the eastern tribes is secure; why should they fight west of the Jordan? Joshua settles that issue by calling members of fellow tribes **brothers** (1:14). Community is built on helping **your brothers until the LORD gives them** rest (1:14–15). Assuming community responsibility and providing assistance remains a vital task for people of God.

Leaders of the eastern tribes respond to Joshua with the same faithfulness they showed to Moses. They pledge, **Whatever you have commanded us we will do, and wherever you send us we will go.** At the end of this pledge they utter a blessing for Joshua, **the LORD your God be with you as he was with Moses.** Then they threaten those who do not follow Joshua with a curse, **whoever rebels . . . and does not obey your words . . . will be put to death.** Encouraging Joshua, they seal this vow by saying, **Be strong and courageous!** (1:16–18).

Statements of loyalty to the new leader from leaders of the eastern tribes come as a surprise. Those loyal to Moses also accept the new leader, a circumstance that rarely happens in religious organizations. A pledge of faithfulness to the new leader out of obedience to the commands of Moses indicates that the eastern tribes are ready to help the western tribes possess the land. It is crucial that Joshua lead a united front as he prepares to possess the land of Canaan.

This passage shows us four things about God. God encourages leaders when they feel insecure and weak. God performs miracles by uniting divided forces for the task at hand; God is a force for unity and encouragement. When leaders faithfully prepare to do God's will, they discover that God has prepared the way for success. Courage and unity also are divine gifts for believers.

Additional Note §3

1:10 / **Joshua ordered the officers of the people . . . camp:** The tribes set up camp in the plains of Moab at Shittim, northeast of the Dead Sea, as they prepared to cross the Jordan River to enter Canaan. At Shittim, the location of the idolatrous and immoral worship of Baal-Peor, twenty-four thousand Israelites died because they took Moabite and Midianite wives and participated in the cult of Baal-Peor. There the tribes took a census of men twenty years and up to fill their military ranks and to determine the allotment of land to tribes (Num. 26). Also, Joshua was announced here as the successor to Moses (Num. 27:12–23). Third, Moses gave the eastern tribes their allotments of land (Num. 32) and delivered his farewell speech (Deut. 31). Fourth, the tribes defeated the Midianites from the camp at Shittim.

Shittim is probably the same as Abel-Shittim (Num. 33:49), even though there remains some confusion over the location of Abel-Shittim because the biblical name no longer remains in the area. What can be said with certainty is that Shittim was located in the once-forested hills of Moab (see J. C. Slayton, "Shittim," *ABD* 5:1222–23.

The forces of the camp were organized by officers (the Hb. word for officers in Josh. 1:10, *sotere*, is translated in Gk. [OG, LXX] as *grammateusin*, or recorders). These officers act as military leaders responsible for calling out the people or mustering the troops for movement or battle. As faithful subordinates they pass on their commander's orders. In the narrative, they are the lower level of command through which Joshua tells the people the commands of God.

§4 *Spies and Rahab the Prostitute (Josh. 2:1–24)*

Military history illustrates the importance of spies for gathering intelligence prior to battles, and army doctrine states that victory requires thorough reconnaissance. In the United States, General George Armstrong Custer shunned reconnaissance and lost his life and the lives of many troops at the battle of Little Big Horn.

The Bible gives a mixed picture of the importance of spies for warfare. In the wilderness of Sinai, Moses sent spies to gather intelligence on Canaan, but fearfulness spread when the majority brought back a negative recommendation (Num. 21:32, Jazer; Num. 13; Deut. 1:22–23). At other times skillful reconnaissance provided opportunities for surprise in warfare and ensured victory (Judg. 7:10–11; 1 Sam. 26:6–7). Faulty reconnaissance (Josh. 7:3; 8:1) cost Joshua and the people the element of surprise, and disobedience cost them a victory at Ai (Josh. 7:1, 2–5, 10–12). Ultimately the support of the Lord, not clever reconnaissance, enabled the people to possess the land of Canaan. In the book of Joshua, intelligence gathering was a dangerous enterprise that produced mixed results.

2:1–7 / Joshua's first act after securing his authority is to send out **secretly** two spies with instructions: **Go, look over the land, . . . especially Jericho** (lit. view the land and Jericho). From this time on the two spies are simply called the two men. Note how the narrator reports that God ordered Joshua to arise and cross the Jordan, but instead Joshua orders spies to go to Jericho and Canaan. By sending the spies, Joshua risked the success of the mission. To save their lives, the spies spared Rahab, a Canaanite in Jericho, and accepted a Canaanite into what was to be limited to the people of God (see Eslinger, *Into the Hands of the Living God*, pp. 34–38).

Ironically, the spies see only Jericho and go no farther than the house of Rahab the harlot. The narrator tantalizes readers by using words that have double meanings and sexual connotations. The two men enter (lit. go into) the house of Rahab and lie down there. The narrator continues the humor by mentioning that Rahab and the king of Jericho speak of the two men who came into (lit. entered into) the house of the prostitute. To their credit, the soldiers go to the best place to get information on the physical and psychological state of Jericho, because a house of prostitution preserves anonymity and can be used as a refuge or an inn for strangers. Likewise, the narrative does not mention immoral acts that the spies might have done in Rahab's house.

The spies accomplish only part of their mission at Rahab's house. Even though they enter the city under the cover of darkness to **spy out the land,** citizens of Jericho quickly discover them, and they are in danger. The unnamed king of Jericho sends a message to Rahab asking her to **Bring out the men who came to** [lit. entered into] **you and entered your house.** The spies no longer have the element of surprise. Their mission and their lives seem lost. Success depends on the support of a prostitute. If she does not help, the spies will die and damage the opportunity to take the land.

Rahab's words dominate the rest of the chapter. The narrator explains how Rahab protects the spies, hiding them under flax on the roof and then helping them escape. In her own words, Rahab tells the men of the king a lie that sends them to look for spies on the road to the fords of the Jordan River. Some readers are shocked that she would lie and yet have the respect she achieved in the book of Joshua and in the NT. Deception in Rahab's case expresses her loyalty to the strangers who were her guests. Without the power to fight, Rahab lives by her wits. Rahab's deception is the way God rescues the blundering spies and ensures that the tribes will possess Canaan. Deception remains the weapon of the marginal and helpless.

2:8–14 / The spies learn about Jericho because Rahab comes to the roof where they are hiding and tells them about her city. Her speech expresses her faith. It begins with Israel's common statement of faith, **I know.** Personally she knows that the Lord has given the land to the people of the spies, confirmed by earlier victories and panic in Jericho. She also realizes that the God of the tribes is **God in heaven above and on the earth below.** The speech echoes the teachings of Deuteronomy. Rahab offers her allegiance to the God who possesses all power, so it is easy for the spies to **show kindness** (lit. show faithfulness) to Rahab and to spare her and the lives of her family when Jericho falls. Not realizing the implication of sparing inhabitants of Jericho, the spies sincerely swear, **Our lives for your lives!** They promise to give their lives to preserve her life and the lives of her family. If she does not inform on them, Rahab and her family will survive **when the LORD gives us the land.** On the one hand, the spies violate the requirements of total destruction of Jericho by pledging to spare Rahab. Sparing Rahab increases tension in the plot of the battle of Jericho and raises questions about the entire campaign. On the other hand, this incident tells readers that God accepts all types into the people of God. God can make even a prostitute from Jericho an example of faith for the rest of the people, including Christians (Heb. 11:31; Jas. 2:25).

2:15–24 / This account about the escape of the spies offers some information about the city wall structure. Rahab helps the men escape from the city by a rope that let down the men through her window. Her house is **part of the city wall** (lit. in the wall; perhaps a casemate wall [see Additional Notes]). As Rahab lowers the men over the wall, she instructs them to hide for three days. The spies then tell her how to save her life and the lives of her family. She must tie a **scarlet cord in the window** and bring her family members into her house when the tribes attack. The verse is ambiguous about whether "this cord" was the one she used to lower the spies or not. In any case, a scarlet cord hanging out a window in a house on the wall would mark visibly where Rahab lived (2:18, 21).

A scarlet cord would get the attention of the troops and save Rahab and her family. Details about the rope strengthen the art of the narrative and should not be considered theological points. Early church fathers used typology to associate the red cord with the red blood of Jesus. They taught that as the cord saved the lives of Rahab and her family, so does the blood of Christ. However, the original passage in Joshua did not place any particular prominence on the color of the cord. Red would be visible at a great distance. Even NT allusions to Rahab did not associate the color of the cord with the color of Jesus' blood. Despite the similarity of the two types, modern interpreters need to use typology sparingly and carefully. It is enough to realize that God saved the lives of Rahab and her family through the red cord tied to the window.

Three days later, coinciding with the three days necessary for the tribes to collect supplies and to prepare for leaving, the spies return to the camp and tell Joshua about the events, their oath, and the conclusion. Unlike the ten spies who gave an unfavorable report in the wilderness, they affirm that **the LORD has surely given the whole land into our hands; all the people are melting in fear because of us.** The spies through Rahab strengthen the resolve of the people and reinforce the theological truth that the land is a gift from the Lord, ready to be possessed.

Additional Notes §4

2:2–3 / Jericho: OT Jericho, at 670 feet below sea level, is located at Tell es-Sultan, next to a spring on the western side of the Jordan River. A Neolithic settlement on the site dates to 8000 B.C.E.. The tell has been the center of archaeological controversy since the work of K. Kenyon in the 1950s (see K. M. Kenyon, *Digging up Jericho* [London: Ernest Benn, 1957] and Kenyon and T. A. Holland, *Excavations at Jericho V: The Pottery Phases of the Tell and Other Finds* [Jerusalem: British School of Archaeology, 1983]). Kenyon dated the destruction of the Middle Bronze Age city during the sixteenth century. A Late Bronze Age section of a house and tombs, she dated around the late fourteenth century B.C.E. Kenyon concluded that the tell generally remained vacant until the eleventh century. At best she found no evidence of a fortress conquered by Joshua during the thirteenth century. B. G. Wood, however, studied the common pottery found by Kenyon at Jericho and on this evidence proposed that Joshua destroyed the city in the Late Bronze Age, not the thirteenth century (B. G. Wood, "Did the Israelites Conquer Jericho? A New Look at the Archaeological Evidence," *BAR* 16 [1990], pp. 44–59, and "Dating Jericho's Destruction: Bienkowski Is Wrong on All Counts," *BAR* 16 [1990], pp. 45–69). On the contrary, Bienkowski considered Kenyon's evidence and supported Kenyon's conclusion by reinforcing that Jericho was destroyed in the Middle Bronze Age, not the Late Bronze Age or 1300 B.C.E. (see P. Bienkowski, "Jericho Was Destroyed in the Middle Bronze Age, Not the Late Bronze Age," *BAR* 16 [1990], pp. 45–69).

Jericho was an impressive fortress in the Middle Bronze and perhaps in the Late Bronze Age. Truly it was a gateway to southern Canaan. Limited evidence, however, makes it hard to reconstruct the history or life in Jericho during the sixteenth to the thirteenth centuries B.C.E. Egyptian records ignore Jericho, and the Amarna letters do not mention it (J. R. Bartlett, *Jericho* [CBW; Grand Rapids: Eerdmans, 1982], p. 98). Consequently, Bible students can suspend judgment about the time, nature, and location of the Jericho of Joshua and still learn the lessons of Jericho in Joshua's excellent narrative.

2:1, 4–7 / Rahab the prostitute: Rahab remains a controversial character in the Bible. A resident of Jericho, she is called a harlot (Hb. *zona*; Josh. 2:1). Her name comes from a root word meaning "to be broad" or "wide." Her occupation has sparked disagreement over whether she was a secular or sacred prostitute, or even an innkeeper as suggested in Josephus and the Targums. The word used for "harlot" is the one for a secular harlot, not a sacred one. M. Noth refutes the view that she was a sacred prostitute or priestess as held by H. Gressman (1914), G. Holscher, S. O. P. Mowinckel, and J. Heller (see discussion in J. A. Soggin, *Joshua* [trans. R. A. Wilson; OTL; Philadelphia: Westminster, 1972], p. 39). Her house also may have functioned as an inn for travelers (Hess, *Joshua,* pp. 83–84 and D. M. Howard Jr., *Joshua* [NAC; Nashville: Broadman & Holman, 1998], pp. 98–99). Still, Rahab the harlot represents a profession with marginal social status. The story points out that marginal, non-Israelite outsiders entered the people of God by demonstrating faithfulness (Hb. *hesed*) in helping the tribes conquer Canaan. In R. Polzin's work he presents another way to interpret the incident: the sparing of Rahab illustrates the wickedness and faithfulness of Israel (Polzin, *Moses and the Deuteronomist,* pp. 888–91). He points out that the narrative reflects the point of view of dispossessed nations and people instead of that of the Deuteronomist. In this view, Rahab is a typological representative of people spared from destruction, and the spy mission represents a human attempt to conquer the land.

2:15 / Rahab is said to have lived in a house on the wall itself (2:15). Archaeological excavations indicate casemate walls of ancient fortresses commonly contained rooms inside them. Casemate walls are built with space in the middle, which builders frequently filled with earth for reinforcement. Houses also could be built on top of the wall and within the wall. Middle Bronze fortifications at Jericho had considerable space between the stone revetment wall (used to support an embankment), a mud brick parapet wall (a low, protective wall on a roof or balcony), and the upper wall. Evidence from the excavation of Jericho shows poorer houses built in that space. See the description of fortifications in the Levant (the area bordering the eastern Mediterranean) and at Jericho in Wood, "Did the Israelites Conquer Jericho?" p. 56, and Z. Herzog, "Fortifications, " *ABD* 2:844–52.

§5 Crossing Over the Jordan (Josh. 3:1–17)

The action of the story slows down in the crossing narrative (Josh. 3–4). Commands are repeated and events are described in laborious detail to indicate the importance of crossing the Jordan for the faith of Israel. The narrator also describes a liturgical drama that would be used for instruction of the young. The fords of the Jordan River and then Gilgal, the camp after Israel crossed the river, become the central locations for the narrative and the events to follow. The Israelite narrator's point of view dominates the two chapters. Officers, Joshua, the Lord, and finally Joshua again give commands. Then the tribes cross the Jordan as a result of their obedience and God's miracle.

3:1–4 / Crossing the Jordan is tied to the preparation period by chronological references. Joshua arose early in the morning and moved the camp from Shittim to the river. After three days, Joshua's officers walk through the camp giving final instructions on the order for crossing the Jordan. The operation plans order the people to wait for the signal to move. When priests pick up the ark of the covenant, the symbol of the presence of God, and begin the march, the people then follow at least two thousand cubits behind the ark. (A cubit is about eighteen inches or half a meter.) The ark will guide the march through the river for possessing the land.

Marching behind the ark reinforces the theological belief that God as supreme commander leads Israel. Only the Lord knows the future and can guide the people to victory in the land of Canaan. The people remain a half-mile behind the ark in respect of the power of God, because the Lord is holy, and that holiness is dangerous. At every point the people depend on God, for they do not know the way to victory. The journey to Canaan depends on God's showing them the way.

3:5–13 / The central section of this narrative contains a three-part speech, in which Joshua speaks first to the people and then to the priests. Next the Lord gives advice and instructions to Joshua, and then Joshua motivates the people and delivers final instructions. Another chronological note ties the first part of the speech to the events of preparation. **Consecrate yourselves** (lit. make yourselves holy), **for tomorrow the LORD will do amazing things** (lit. wonders, miracles) **among you.** Holiness is the basis on which God does miracles, and the holy God demands a holy people. In turn, worship and holy warfare demand ritual and personal holiness. There is no time to waste, because only hours remain to worship and prepare spiritually. The next day can be a day of wonders for a prepared people.

Verses 6–13 assume that the morning has arrived for God's wonders. Acting on Joshua's orders, the priests pick up the ark and move to the front of the people. God in turn encourages Joshua by telling him, **Today I will begin to exalt you in the eyes of all Israel, so they may know that I am with you as I was with Moses** (cf. Exod. 14:31). God equates crossing the Jordan with crossing the Reed Sea under Moses. The miracle elevates Joshua's leadership to the level of that of Moses and will confirm God's presence with Joshua.

Crossing a body of water teaches much about God. The crossing melts the hearts of the enemy in Canaan but also makes sure the tribes **know** (3:7, 10) the power of their divine commander and the importance of God's leader. When the priests carrying the ark enter the edge of the waters, they are to **go and stand in the river** (3:8). They are not to hesitate when they reach the river but are to lead the way into the water. Then they will experience the miracle of God's power.

The rest of God's message is told through a motivational speech from Joshua. In this speech Joshua first calls the people to gather and **listen to the words of the LORD your God** (3:9). He then directs the people to expect victory. **You will know that the living God is among you and that he will certainly drive out before you** inhabitants of Canaan (3:10). The list of inhabitants reminds the Israelites that the task of possessing the land is formidable and can be carried out only by the **Lord of all the earth.** The God of Israel is a "living God," unlike the "dead" idols of the inhabitants of Canaan. Victory over the inhabitants of the land will confirm who is living and who is dead.

In the final part of the speech, Joshua relays God's instructions to choose twelve men to represent the tribes for some future task and to expect the waters of the Jordan to **stand up in a heap** when the leaders set foot in the Jordan. Joshua's exhortations prepare the tribes to expect victory. Just as a winning football, baseball, or basketball team expects to win every game, so successful believers also expect God's victories and attempt great tasks. God delivers wonders to those who expect them.

3:14–17 / In these verses a narrator summarizes clearly and succinctly the wonders of crossing the Jordan. This summary gives a weather report and picture of the events that change the direction of the tribes that would become Israel. The weather report describes why what was normally an easy river crossing was a miracle. During March and April, the Jordan overflowed its inner banks when melting snow swelled its normally shallow fords. The river forecast also indicates that the event occurred during the barley (LXX, wheat) harvest, or at the end of the rainy season.

This account gives geographical notes that indicate generally where the event took place: Adam (Adamah), Zarethan, Sea of the Arabah (Salt), and near Jericho. These places are in the geological fault known as the southern extension of the Great Rift. The river Jordan flows down the rift on a curving route into the Salt Sea, later referred to as the Dead Sea. Places mentioned along the river are Adam and Zarethan. R. G. Boling interprets the references to **Adam,** 16 miles north of Jericho, to **Zarethan,** approximately 12 miles north of Adam, as the extent that water backed up the river from the temporary damming of the Jordan. Scholars who favor a northern crossing point interpret mention of Adam and Zarethan as a reference to a natural route for entering the land through the north-central hill country. The most plausible suggestion is that of Boling, who thinks that the ford al-Mates, about 8 miles southeast of Jericho, is the ford for the crossing (Boling and Wright, *Joshua,* p. 170).

Other information, however, is more important for interpreting the passage. The symbol of the presence of the Lord leads the tribes to the Jordan. The priests carrying the ark enter the river, and the water from upstream stops flowing (3:16). Water flowing down to the Sea of the Arabah is cut off. As the priests carrying the ark of the covenant stand on dry ground in the middle of the Jordan, the people complete the crossing. The passage outlines how generations celebrate this story as God's miraculous accomplishment.

Additional Notes §5

3:3, 6, 13, 17 / Ark of the covenant: The ark is a box or chest, a container for keeping the law tablets of the covenant (Exod. 25:21; 40:20; Deut. 10:5). It is mentioned as the ark of the covenant forty times in Deuteronomist materials (Noth, *The Deuteronomistic History,* pp. 91–93). Priestly narratives call it the ark of the testimony, a synonym for covenant (Josh. 4:16). From the time of Shiloh it seems to be associated with the cherubim throne of God (R. E. Clements, *God and Temple* [Philadelphia: Fortress, 1965], pp. 28–35). The ark assures the people that the Lord is present (Num. 10:33, 35) and so leads the people into battle as a war palladium (Num. 14:44; 1 Sam. 4:2–9). The Ark Narrative (1 Sam. 4–6) recounts the capture of the ark by the Philistines and the power of Israel's God found in the ark. Surrounded by figures of the cherubim, it is placed in the Holy of Holies in Solomon's time. The ark is never mentioned after the temple was demolished by the Babylonians (C. L. Seow, "Ark of the Covenant," *ABD* 1:386–93).

3:10 / The OT contains twenty-one similar lists of nations, varying in names and order. The most common number of the list of nations is seven: **Canaanites, Hittites, Hivites, Perizzites, Girgashites, Amorites and Jebusites.** The Canaanites gave their name to the land, but the country was open to a migration of several peoples from the north during the Late Bronze Age. The political fragmentation of that era is reflected in letters found at Amarna, written before the existence of the seven nations in Josh. 3. The Greeks called Canaanites living in Lebanon Phoenicians.

Scriptures mention Hittites at Hebron (Gen. 23), Beersheba (Gen. 26:34), Bethel (Judg. 1:22–26), Jerusalem (Ezek. 16:3, 45), and elsewhere (Num. 13:29; 1 Sam. 26:6; see A. Kempinsky, "Hittites in the Bible," *BAR* 5 [1979], pp. 21–45). Little wonder that Josh. 1:4 refers to the promised land as the land of the Hittites (omitted from the LXX).

Hivites are mentioned in eighteen of the twenty-one lists of nations. The Amarna letters mention their living near Shechem, and Gen. 34 refers to Shechem as the town led by Hamor the Hivite (G. E. Mendenhall, *The Tenth Generation* [Baltimore: Johns Hopkins University Press, 1973], p. 156). Anatolian archaeological evidence at Shechem indicates the presence of Hivites. Hivites are also located at Gibeon (Josh. 9:7; 2 Sam. 21:2; lit. Amorites or westerners) and at the foot of Mount Hermon, in the land of Mizpah (Josh. 11:3). Fourteen of the lists place Jebusites after the Hivites.

The ethnic identity of Perizzites and Girgashites is more obscure. The Girgashites are mentioned in Ugaritic and Egyptian sources of the Late Bronze Age, but little else is known about them. Perizzites remain unattested by extrabiblical material, even though Josh. 11:3 locates them in the hill country of Canaan (also Gen. 15:19–21; Josh. 17:15). The land of the Perizzites was promised to Abraham and his descendents (Gen.

15:20). Israelites married them (Judg. 3:5), and the people remained among them (Ezra 9:1; see S. A. Reed, "Perizzite," *ABD* 5:231, and Mendenhall, *The Tenth Generation*, p. 145).

Amorites refers to remnants of western immigrants (Josh. 7:10; Gen. 15:19–21) in Canaan. The term *amurru* first occurs in Old Akkadian as "the West." As an ethnic designation, the term identifies a foreign population from northeast Syria. During the Late Bronze Age the Amorites dispersed into Canaan and set up a kingdom in the Orantes Valley of Syria. The Amorites were among the early enemies of the tribes. Their kings were Sihon and Og of Bashan in the Transjordan region (Num. 21). Eventually the Amorites ceased to exist as a separate cultural group (G. E. Mendenhall, "Amorites," *ABD* 1:199–202).

Jebusites lived in Jerusalem as descendents of the clan of Jebus (Josh. 15:8; 18:28; Judg. 19:10–11). Amarna letters and documents from Ebla in the mid-third millennium attest that the earlier name for Jerusalem was Urusalim. Few remains of the Jebusite city have been discovered (see the discussion in Boling and Wright, *Joshua*, pp. 165–67).

§6 Memorials for the Crossing of the Jordan (Josh. 4:1–24)

4:1–24 / The story of chapter 3 picks up again in Joshua 4:14. The first thirteen verses explain why the tribes chose twelve representatives (3:12). These representatives were to pick up rocks that would be fitting memorials to the crossing of the Jordan. The importance of this endeavor is underlined by the repetition of the commands as coming from God and Joshua and the note that the **stones are to be a memorial to the people** (lit. sons or descendants) **of Israel forever** (4:7). Children would ask about the stones, and adults could tell them the story of the victorious crossing (4:6).

Twelve stones were placed in two places: in the middle of the Jordan (4:9) where the priests and the ark stood on dry ground and at the place where the people would lodge after crossing the river (4:3). Soggin concludes that the first set of stones may have been picked up on the east bank of the river to indicate the joining of the east and west bank tribes. The story waits to give the location of the second set, with the narrator finally telling readers that the second set was picked up from the middle of the river (4:3, 8) and placed at the camp of Gilgal. Large rocks were commonly set up at sacred centers in Canaan, so these rocks may have become a circular (Gilgal means "circular") worship center for ceremonies reenacting the crossing and covenant renewal. In any case, the rocks at Gilgal stood as a reminder of the crossing of the Jordan (4:20–23).

Out of the wonders of the crossing came two results. That day the Lord exalted (lit. made great) Joshua in the sight of all Israel, and they revered him all the days of his life, just as they had revered Moses (4:14). Joshua's leadership was viewed as nearly identical to that of the greatest leader. God's power and might also became well known to everyone. He effected the crossing so that all the peoples of the earth might know that the hand of the Lord is powerful and so that they might always fear the Lord (4:24).

Through this event all the nations (lit. peoples) of the earth would know what the God of the freed slaves can do (lit. mighty hand of the Lord). The subsequent part of this recognition calls upon the people of God to respect and worship their God. Both Joshua and God gain obedience and status from the wonders by the Jordan.

Additional Notes §6

4:6 / What do these stones mean? Creating a story to match standing stones or some other natural phenomenon is called etiology (aetiology), and Noth influenced the study of Joshua most by noting its use of that literary form. He concluded that an early account of Joshua existed prior to the Deuteronomist. This account consisted of "a series of aetiological stories relevant to the Israelite incursion"; it was combined into a series of heroic legends that "dtr" took over. To this was added an introduction, an epilogue, and supplementary material (Noth, *The Deuteronomistic History*, pp. 36–41, and Soggin, *Joshua*, pp. 10–12).

Etiology is not unique to Israel or the book of Joshua. Comparative literature shows that ancient people often explained a geographical phenomenon or a liturgical ceremony by telling stories about it. For example, Joshua's information about Gilgal and the twelve stones explains why the round hill (Gilgal) remains for later generations a Benjamite sanctuary, a place for celebrating crossing the Jordan River and covenant renewal. Recent discussions of the use of etiology in Joshua do not dismiss etiological explanations included in narratives but rather point out that etiological elements are not primary in the narratives as suggested by Noth.

4:19 / Camped at Gilgal on the eastern border of Jericho: In the OT Gilgal is a common place name that refers to a circle such as a circle of rocks or a round hill. At least three and perhaps five locations for Gilgal are mentioned in the Bible. A Gilgal near Jericho is the memorial for the crossing of the Jordan and a site of a circumcision and Passover in Joshua (5:2–11). Gilgal is the location of the tribal camp to which the Gibeonites came to deceive the invaders and the base from which the tribes marched to attack the anti-Gibeon coalition (9:6; 10:6–15).

During the time of Samuel, Gilgal seems to be an important cultic center (1 Sam. 7–11). It is mentioned as the location where David greets the men of Judah as he returns victorious after the death of Absalom (2 Sam. 19:15). After these incidents, Gilgal is not mentioned until the eighth century B.C.E. in the book of the twelve prophets, where it appears as a center where Israel committed apostasy in the name of worship (Amos 4:4; 5:5; Hos. 4:15; 9:15; 12:11; Mic. 6:5). Scholars speculate that Joshua 3–6 reflects an annual cultic festival celebrating the crossing of the Jordan (see Soggin, *Joshua*, pp. 51–54). However, the silence of Scripture about this celebration makes it unlikely that an annual covenant renewal festival was celebrated at Gilgal, near Jericho.

The Bible also mentions a Gilgal in the Central Highlands south of Samaria (2 Kgs. 2:1–2; perhaps 4:38–41). E. Sellin (1917) associated the Gilgal in Joshua with Deut. 11:30, an area near Shechem. Changing the location of Gilgal from the vicinity of Jericho to the Central Highlands also changes the tribal penetration of the land of Canaan from the south to the north (A. Zertal, "Israel Enters Canaan—Following the Pottery Trail," *BAR* 17 [1991], pp. 38–47). Few scholars, however, accept the northern hypothesis for the location of Gilgal in the book of Joshua (W. R. Kotter, "Gilgal," *ABD* 2:1024). Still, archaeological remains that have been recovered do not verify decisively the location of Gilgal in the book of Joshua.

§7 Religious Preparation for War (Josh. 5:1–15)

5:1 / The wonders of crossing the Jordan demoralize the enemy for the tribal attacks. Enemy kings find their **hearts melted and they no longer had the courage to face the Israelites** (lit. there was no spirit in them). Rahab's analysis proves true as residents of Canaan experience the "melting of hearts" and "loss of spirit" when they hear of God's victories east of the Jordan (2:11). Jericho and the cities become vulnerable when the God of the tribes conquers the Jordan.

Joshua 5 names not nations in the land but rather enemy kings of the western bank who fall into two categories, Amorites and Canaanites (Phoenicians in the LXX). Amorites inhabit the highlands west of the Jordan, and Canaanites live in cities of the coastal plains. The demoralizing of the enemy provides another sign that God has given the land to Joshua and the people. Still, God's support and victory in battle demand that the tribes prepare liturgically and religiously for battle.

5:2–9 / Circumcision, the primary sign of the people of God and prerequisite for participating in the Passover (Exod. 12:44–49), is the first ritual for battle preparation. This ritual is tied to the shock of the enemy kings by the temporal clause **at that time** (5:2). Without wasting any time, God commands Joshua, **Make flint knives and circumcise the Israelites again** (lit. a second time). Circumcision makes troops vulnerable to attack, so Joshua must act quickly while the enemy has lost its spirit.

The command assumes that Joshua is repeating an earlier event, but a better interpretation of the word "again" is to recognize that Joshua circumcised this second generation as those leaving Egypt had been circumcised. Verses 4–7 explain that families had neglected to circumcise young men during the wilderness travels, and the earlier generation had perished. So God commanded that Joshua use the traditional flint knives to circumcise the uncircumcised men. After the circumcision, the men remained in the camp until they were healed and ready for battle.

Circumcision in the OT represents the outward sign of an inward condition. Circumcision marks every male as a descendant of Abraham (Gen. 17:10–11). The NT is concerned that believers be sons and daughters of Abraham by faith, not by physical circumcision. Therefore, Paul talks about the circumcision of the heart as the sign of the believer, not physical circumcision. This change of attitude and thought patterns produces faith that will be victorious over evil. In this spiritual sense, the change of heart is as crucial to victories in the Christian life as circumcision was to prepare the tribes to possess the land and to defeat the kings of the Amorites and Canaanites.

An etiology about Gilgal completes the narrative. The circumcision at Gilgal brings a declaration from God: **Today I have rolled away the reproach of Egypt from you** (5:9). The Hebrew word for "roll" comes from a root (*galal*) that is similar to Gilgal (circle or wheel). How the circular area relates to the place known as the "hill of foreskins," or Gibeah Haaraloth (5:3), remains unknown. Nevertheless, Gilgal appears to be the most significant place associated with the circumcision ceremony. The play on words declares that God has rolled away Israel's embarrassment over slavery in Egypt by circumcision at Gilgal. At this point enemies will regard the Israelites as better than "just slaves." The community has fully identified with the divine warrior who will give them the land and victory.

Christians can celebrate their own Gilgals. For many it will be baptism. Others will remember a special experience in which Jesus confronts a sinful past and transforms it with hope and confidence. This transformation can be celebrated as the event when the embarrassment of slavery to sin and weakness will be rolled away. Most believers would like to forget their shameful past. A new start in faith buries that period of life under the forgiveness of God. The experiences of Gilgal prepare all for victories. At a modern Gilgal, God calls believers, sons and daughters, identified with Christ, no longer slaves to sin.

5:10–12 / Circumcision qualified the community to celebrate the Passover and eat the *seder* meal. The celebration follows those days on which the people celebrated the Passover in Egypt. **On the evening of the fourteenth day of the month, while camped at Gilgal on the plains of Jericho, the Israelites celebrated the**

Passover (5:10; Exod. 12:3, 6, 18). The narrative does not mention either Egypt or the lamb in this account, nor does it describe in detail the Passover liturgy or meal. Instead, it focuses on eating the feast and then eating bread made from produce in the land.

The Passover inaugurates a new era in which the tribes received no more manna from God. **The manna stopped the day after they ate this food from the land; there was no longer any manna for the Israelites, but that year they ate of the produce of Canaan** (5:12). From this point God provides only indirectly by assisting them in battle and giving them the land. Conflicts and poverty in the wilderness and shame from slavery now lie behind the people. Ahead stands the challenge of possessing the land and overcoming its hostile kings. The tribes now must secure their food through conquest or treaty.

Christianity benefits greatly from building its communion service on the Passover. As the Passover celebrates an immanent era of freedom and independence, so the final supper of Jesus before his crucifixion celebrates a new period in the lives of the disciples. Jesus would no longer be present physically to help them. Now the Spirit of Christ will assist them by giving gifts and encouragement. The past was filled with lessons of God's grace, but new challenges will build the kingdom of God beyond what was possible while Jesus was physically present. That was true in ancient Israel and remains true today. God is in the process of building effective disciples, not in feeding dependent believers.

The first Passover in the promised land can continue to teach its lessons through Christian communion, which celebrates regularly the cost of new opportunities made possible through the blood and body of Jesus. Communion does not feed the congregation as a meal but rather empowers through prayer and faith efforts to conquer evil. Christians are not dependent on communion but are challenged by its example to extra efforts and victories through its evidence of God's love.

5:13–15 / Once the people are prepared to do battle in the name of the Lord, Joshua meets a mysterious visitor near Jericho (lit. in Jericho). The stranger is **a man standing in front of him with a drawn sword in his hand** (5:13). Joshua reacts like an alert sentry. He calls the man to identify himself: **Are you for us or for our enemies?** That request is especially relevant for a warrior standing with a drawn sword.

The reply of the stranger puzzles interpreters. The NIV translates it, **Neither, . . . but as commander of the army of the LORD I have now come** (5:14). The answer could be literally, "No!" or the Hebrew could be understood as an emphatic "Indeed!" (Soggin, *Joshua*, p. 77). The question calls for a positive answer, but the negative one can also make sense in the context. The negative answer has the sense that as commander of the army of the Lord, the visitor does not need to take sides. The Lord remains independent and will judge what side to support by how the people obey or do not obey their orders from God. In either case, the answer identifies the stranger as the commander of the heavenly hosts and does not commit God to support one side or the other. The surprising answer is comforting in the sense that the heavenly commander is present, but it is disturbing to know that commander reserves the right to change sides in any conflict. Either answer undermines the doctrine of holy war, with its view that God fights for a chosen nation. The Lord remains independent from any ritual or magical incantation, and divine support can never be assumed.

Joshua prostrates himself before the messenger and asks for any message that one might bring. **What message does my Lord have for his servant?** The messenger, however, makes no announcement about the battle or God's support of Joshua. Interpreters suggest that the report of the incident is broken and the message has been cut off. By doing this they do not recognize the importance of what the commander does say: **Take off your sandals, for the place where you are standing is holy** (5:15). The command parallels that at the burning bush where the Lord calls Moses to liberate the people and gives him the divine name (Exod. 3:5). Both speeches tell these men to take off the symbols of power and strength, the sandals, and to consider the place holy. Joshua 5 ends as the commander of the heavenly hosts tells Joshua that Jericho and subsequently the land of Canaan belong to God. The Lord has made it holy by divine decree and can give that city to the people. Joshua follows orders and thereby recognizes the holiness of God and the land of Canaan. No other message is needed to encourage Joshua and the people. They can only obey their commander in chief.

Additional Notes §7

5:1 / For comments on **Amorite kings . . . and . . . Canaanite kings,** see the notes on nations from ch. 3 [§5].

5:2 / **Make flint knives and circumcise:** Circumcision is the removal of the foreskin. The law (Lev. 12:3) requires the ceremony on the eighth day after birth (Gen. 21:4). Flint knives used for the ceremony indicate that the rite (Exod. 4:25; Josh. 2–3) existed before metal knives (R. de Vaux, *Ancient Israel: Social Institutions* [New York: McGraw-Hill, 1961], 1:46–48). The origin of the custom is obscure and unclear. Priests in Egypt were circumcised, but the extent of circumcision in Egypt is unknown. Israel used circumcision as a sign of the covenant with its God and the necessary preparation for observing the Passover (Exod. 12:43, 49). In the setting of Josh. 5, circumcision incorporates the men into the community and prepares them for war.

The name "hill of foreskins" may indicate that the tribes took over a place of circumcision used previously by residents of the land (Boling and Wright, *Joshua*, p. 189). No clues in the text indicate the location of this hill. In any case, the fighting men who had not been circumcised in the wilderness were circumcised and properly related to their God for battle.

§8 Excursus: Holy War in Israel

Behind the concept of holy war is the tradition of the sovereign Lord fighting for a chosen people as a divine warrior (F. M. Cross, "The Divine Warrior in Israel's Early Cult," in *Biblical Motifs: Origins and Transformations, Studies and Texts* 3 [Cambridge: Harvard University Press, 1966], pp. 11–30). The events from the exodus, through the wilderness, and into Canaan are framed as the triumphant battle of the divine commander in chief leading a combination of earthly and heavenly forces to victory (Boling and Wright, *Joshua*, p. 27). The ark of the covenant represents the presence of the Lord, leading the people into battle. In holy war, the victory belongs to the deity. Participants had to be sanctified by sacred rituals to fight alongside of God.

The term "holy war" is not appropriate as a category for describing the early warfare of Israel. Ancient people approached all of life without distinguishing between sacred and secular. A more appropriate term would be to call the battles to possess the land the wars of the Lord (lit. *Yhwh*). These unique battles of weak, former slaves through whom the power of the Lord is revealed should not be generalized into a doctrine for warfare among nations or religions.

Rules for sacred battles are listed in Deuteronomy 20. These instructions describe what is called a ban or devoted plunder (Hb. *herem;* Deut. 7:1–2). Booty—objects or people who would pollute the faith or camp of Israel—is accursed and must be destroyed. Such objects are banned from ordinary use and therefore dedicated to destruction (E. J. Hamlin, *Joshua* [ITC; Grand Rapids: Eerdmans, 1983], pp. 52–53). According to Deuteronomy, plunder or war booty is devoted to the divine warrior and must be destroyed as a sacrifice to the deity. Earthly warriors will not profit from a victory secured by God. Extermination of the enemy removes the temptation to serve the gods of the defeated people.

From the reign of David to the end of the first temple, Israel adapted its warfare rules for plunder to assist a standing army. Some divine warrior rituals and ideologies influenced Israel's literature and worship throughout its history, but rules of booty distribution changed considerably. Divine warrior motifs in the NT primarily describe spiritual warfare (T. Longman and D. G. Reid, *God Is a Warrior* [SOTBT; Grand Rapids: Zondervan, 1995], pp. 91–135).

Considerable flexibility appears in the booty or ban rules in narratives about battles in Joshua. What plunder must be devoted does not always follow the rules of Deuteronomy 7 or 20. Instructions are given before each battle, and the soldiers are accountable to follow only those. Obedience is not always gauged by the rules of Deuteronomy. In some ways, Joshua modifies the rules and stands in tension with the ideals of Deuteronomy. As the narrative describes the battles, notice the variation in application of the devoted rules to the victories of the tribes.

Additional Notes §8

5:1–6:27 / **Kings along the coast heard:** The account of Joshua's conquest has striking similarities to Assyrian royal inscriptions (J. van Seters, "Joshua's Campaign of Canaan and Near Eastern Historiography," *JSOT* [1990], pp. 1–12). Many inscriptions, especially from Esarhaddon and Ashurbanipal, mention an oracle of encouragement for the king before a battle. The march is described in detail with talk of physical difficulties such as a river at flood stage. A few battles are described in detail, while others are summarized. Special attention is given to the capture of kings and the fame and terror of the Assyrians spread throughout the land. Assyrians fight against coalitions, and other populations repopulate the decimated areas. Inscriptions regularly conclude with summaries of the conquests and booty taken. In Assyrian texts the land of Canaan is known as the land of the Hittites. Assyrian kings also use omens to win battles. Elements of the Assyrian inscriptions also appear in the Joshua accounts of conquests in Canaan. Van Seters concludes that the forms utilized by the Deuteronomic Historian to tell of Joshua's campaign depend on Assyrian royal inscriptions and the invasion was an invention of that historian, six hundred to seven hundred years later.

A close study of Joshua 9–12 reveals a structure to the conquest accounts reflecting a common structure and ideology found in other ancient conquest accounts (K. L. Younger, *Ancient Conquest Accounts* [JSOTSup 98; Sheffield: JSOT Press, 1990], pp. 98, 197–331). There are some differences between ancient Near Eastern inscriptions and conquest narratives in Joshua, but many similarities also exist (e.g., Josh. 9, Gibeonite vassalage; Josh. 10–11, conquest accounts of the north and south; and Josh. 12, summaries and lists). There are enough similarities to suggest that Joshua 9–12 reflects a transmission code similar to that in ancient royal inscriptions.

§9 Possessing Jericho and Rescuing Rahab (Josh. 6:1–27)

Many readers reject the book of Joshua because they think it describes only warfare. In reality, the narratives concentrate on God's role in giving the land and summarize the warfare. Joshua 6:20–25 covers the fighting in summary fashion. That section points out the results of what could have been an intense battle. It describes the falling of the wall, the killing of the population, the burning of the city, and the rescue of Rahab and her family. Most of the chapter details marching instructions to Joshua and subsequently to the people and the liturgical march around the city. This format emphasizes not the violence of the warfare but rather the sounding of the trumpets and the war whoop of the ritual. The chapter makes the point that Jericho falls because of the power of God and the faithfulness of the people instead of battlefield strategy or skills.

6:1–11 / Narration about the situation in Jericho interrupts the story and sets the stage for the battle. The first verse tells readers that the gates of Jericho are closed due to a siege and fear of the imminent battle. As in earlier chapters, God gives instructions to Joshua in verses 2–5. These contain announcements and instructions by the Lord that one would have expected to come from the commander of the heavenly army (5:13–15). The narration, however, separates the battle narrative from the appearance narrative in Joshua 5 and shifts the attention of the reader from the appearance of the commander of the heavenly army to the imminent siege of Jericho.

The Lord's motivational speech begins with a typical promise of victory over Jericho. **See, I have delivered Jericho into your hands, along with its king and its fighting men** (6:2). This announcement predicts victory with the confidence of Babe Ruth pointing toward the right field fence to predict a home run. There is no question about the outcome of the battle and the one responsible for the victory. God's instructions detail the liturgical march through which God will deliver Jericho into Joshua's hands (6:3–5). Joshua, the earthly commander, repeats the operations plans to the priests who carry the ark. Then he orders the forces to march behind the ark. The narrator reveals details of the liturgical march and additional instructions as the story progresses. As a result, the narrative quickly and efficiently tells the story.

God's instructions on the liturgical march are clear. The troops march around the city once for six days. The army marches accompanied by seven priests carrying and blowing seven ram's horn trumpets *(shophar)*, the common instruments for celebrating atonement and the New Year festivals. During temple worship, priests blow them to indicate the voice of God in the liturgy. On the seventh day, the army and priests are to march around the city seven times. A long blast from the ram's horn will signal for the people to shout loudly, and the wall of the city will fall down in its place (6:3–5). Marching seven days around a city would devastate its morale, and a breached wall would provide easy access to the heart of Jericho. The victory is summarized: **the people will go up, every man straight in** (6:5).

As noted in earlier chapters, Joshua transforms the original operations plans into his orders. The ark of the covenant becomes the focus of his orders. An honor guard **(the armed guard)** leads the processional. Next come priests blowing the *shophar* and then the ark. Priests sound the horns continually. The ark of the covenant follows the priests in front of the army, picturing the Lord leading the troops into battle. Changes in details through the various instructions and orders cause some scholars to look for various documents or sources to explain the variations, but commentators need not propose such elaborate hypotheses to explain the differences. Commanders historically adapt a plan to a battle as long as they do not violate the spirit and directions of the operations plans. The narrator also increases the suspense of the narrative by changing the commands.

Joshua directly warns the people against a mistake that would undermine the operations: **Do not give a war cry, do not raise your voices, do not say a word until the day I tell you to shout. Then shout!** (6:10). Silence increases the power of the war cry and heightens the shock factor of the march. The narrator does not picture Joshua as an unthinking functionary who can not evaluate and adapt the plans of God. Finally, the narrator completes the picture by describing the first day of marching around the city and notes that the forces return to the camp and spend the night there (6:11). The suspense builds with every pause as the battle for the minds of Jericho begins.

6:12–19 / Joshua gives additional instructions during days two through seven. The day begins at dawn. Days two through six are summarized in three verses (6:12–14). Narration describes the seventh day and brings readers up to the lengthy blast of the shophar and the order to shout (6:16), only to prolong the suspense by repeating instructions about devoting those living in the city except Rahab and her family. The *herem* instructions play two roles in the narrative. First, the instructions make clear what booty the tribes must devote to destruction to preserve the support of their God. This will be very important when Achan is confronted later. Second, the sparing of Rahab is an exception to the rules of *herem* written in Deuteronomy, and the rationale for that exception needs to be clear. The troops must spare Rahab and her household because she hid the spies and the spies gave their word to save her.

Joshua's booty instructions end with a warning: **Keep away from the devoted things, so that you will not bring about your own destruction by taking any of them. Otherwise you will make the camp of Israel liable to destruction and bring trouble on it** (6:18). Taking booty is a common motivation for going to war and often is the pay of soldiers. Joshua makes clear the rules of this battle and warns soldiers of the consequences for violations of *herem*. Individuals and the community will suffer trouble if one violates the instructions. The second concern is spelled out clearly in the final instruction. **All the silver and gold and the articles of bronze and iron are sacred to the LORD and must go into his treasury** (6:19). Items that would be useful to worship of the Lord go directly into the Lord's treasury. Valuable items are to be stored for the future worship center. This guideline also will be important for understanding the enormity of Achan's violation.

6:20–25 / Jericho is ripe for taking. The tribal forces know what to do and how to do it. The narrative resumes where it left off with the sound of the *shophar* and the war whoop. Will God provide the victory? Will Rahab be rescued? Will the troops follow the rules of encounter required by God and communicated by Joshua? At last the reader will find out. The waiting is over.

All seems to be answered with a resounding yes. At the shout of the people, the wall collapses and the troops enter the city. The troops begin to destroy all life with their swords. Joshua steps into the situation and orders the two former spies to rescue Rahab and her family because they know her house and are the logical ones to rescue them. The entire family is kept in a safe place outside the camp (6:21–23).

Despite the importance of the battle, the narrative focuses on the rescue of Rahab, a prostitute and a citizen of the enemies of the tribes. The rules of *herem* require that she and her family be exterminated. Yet the summary of the battle mentions her rescue twice, and Joshua directly intervenes to send two soldiers to help her. The two descriptions of the rescue add different insights into the event. After the rescue, the troops settle her and her family outside the camp, which must remain dedicated to the Lord. To bring in strangers would violate its sacred role in holy war. In the second account, however, the passage mentions that **she lives among the Israelites to this day** (6:25). The rescue explains why a family tracing itself to a resident of Jericho, Rahab the prostitute, remains a part of Israel up until the time of the writing of this story. The presence of this family points out the mixing of the tribes with the people of the land from the beginning, a situation unchanged with the passing of time. The tribes already are violating their calling by including people in the land in their alliance.

6:26–27 / The passage gives no indication of why Jericho receives a severe penalty. No order comes from the Lord to place a curse on the one who would rebuild Jericho. Instead Joshua pronounces his oath as a part of his command privilege and as an extension of *herem* on the city. In ancient warfare a curse on a defeated city is not unusual (S. Gevertz, "Jericho and Shechem: A Religio-Literary Aspect of City Destruction," *VT* 13 [1963], pp. 52–62), but this curse extends the devastation or ban forever. The ancient curse formula is mentioned in 1 Kings 16:34, when during the reign of Ahab, Hiel of Bethel rebuilds Jericho. Hiel's youngest son dies when the builder sets up the gates and is seen as a fulfillment of the curse formula.

The curse formula does not warn against resettling the area (Josh. 18:21; Judg. 3:13; 2 Sam. 10:5). Instead the formula calls for the deaths of children when one rebuilds the walls of Jericho. The curse states that the builder who sets the foundations of the walls will do so at the **cost of his firstborn son**. A builder who sets up the gates of Jericho will do so **at the cost of his youngest** (6:26).

The Bible describes child sacrifice as an abomination to the Lord in Israel (2 Kgs. 21:2–6). De Vaux takes the view that Joshua

6:26 refers to child sacrifice as a part of foundation ceremonies current with Canaanites (de Vaux, *Ancient Israel: Social Institutions,* 2:442). E. V. Hulse suggests that the curse of Joshua 6 refers to the unhealthy aspect of living in Jericho with its high rate of infant mortality (E. V. Hulse, "Joshua's Curse and the abandonment of Ancient Jericho: Schistosomiasis as a Possible Medical Explanation," *Medical History* 15 [1971], pp. 376–86). In this view, children die in the family that rebuilds the city because of disease (Boling and Wright, *Joshua,* p. 214). The intent of the passage is not clear; the sequel in Kings says only that during the reign of Ahab, Hiel the builder from Bethel lost his firstborn son Abiram when he laid a new foundation and his youngest son Segub when he set up the gates of Jericho (1 Kgs. 16:34, NIV). This fulfillment reinforces the power of Joshua's curse but does not mention any other implication of the passage.

The victory and subsequent burning and devastation of Jericho demonstrate that the Lord is with Joshua. Joshua's reputation, along with that of the Lord, spreads throughout the land. The narrator summarizes well the impact of Jericho. Ironically, all seems well and ends happily. Neither Joshua nor the people anticipate that the seeds of disaster are being planted at that moment. Joshua 7 begins an unhappy appendix to this event anticipated only by the narrator.

§10 Spies, Achan, and Failure at Ai (Josh. 7:1–26)

Victory is often a prelude to disaster in the Bible. The joy of the song of Moses after the exodus has hardly died down before the people complain (Exod. 15:24). Moses faces a golden calf upon coming down the mountain after receiving the commandments of the covenant (Exod. 32). Likewise sin rears its ugly side at Jericho. Power gives birth to selfishness and miscalculation of the strength of the enemy. Joshua's campaign to take Canaan also is a series of successes and failures.

7:1–9 / The narrator sets the stage for failure at Ai (Hb. ruin; LXX, city). From an omniscient view, the narrator warns readers that all is not well in the camp after victory at Jericho. The people have **acted unfaithfully in regard to the devoted things** because Achan of the tribe of Judah has taken some of the forbidden booty for himself. The impact of this violation of *herem* means that **the LORD's anger burned against Israel** (7:1). The point of view of the narrator focuses the story on the ban violation and its implications for the entire people. These responses explain why the army of the tribes was defeated, suffered casualties, and felt embarrassed when God did not fight for the people.

Verses 2–9 tell readers the military side of the story. Spies again bring disaster. In Joshua 2, spies not authorized by God blunder into the house of a prostitute, Rahab, receive protection from her, and bring a Canaanite family into the people of the Lord (see discussions in Polzin, *Moses and the Deuteronomist*, pp. 85–91, and Hawk, *Every Promise Fulfilled*, pp. 61–70). At Ai Joshua's spies underestimate the strength of the enemy (7:3) and suggest two or three thousand soldiers easily could take Ai. They say casually, **Do not weary all the people, for only a few men are there.** They reverse the mistaken survey of twelve spies who surveyed the land of Canaan and overestimated the enemy to Moses and the people (Num. 13:16–14:4). Again they demonstrate that poor reconnaissance is worse than no reconnaissance. The people rely on spies, do not plan carefully the battle, and do not seek the support of the Lord. Their blunder costs at least thirty-six soldiers their lives and nearly wrecks the reputations of Joshua and the Lord. One defeat threatens the fame of Joshua and the Lord (7:9).

Defeat at Ai melted the hearts of the people into water (7:5) and sent Joshua and the leaders into mourning. He tore his clothes and fell facedown to the ground before the ark of the Lord, remaining there until evening. The elders of Israel did the same and sprinkled dust on their heads (7:6). The leaders felt deeply the sting of the defeat. In a lament, Joshua cries out in concern to God:

> **Ah [lit. *ahah*], Sovereign Lord, why did you ever bring this people across the Jordan to deliver us into the hands of the Amorites to destroy us? If only we had been content to stay on the other side of the Jordan! O Lord, what can I say, now that Israel has been routed by its enemies? The Canaanites and the other people of the country will hear about this and they will surround us and wipe out our name from the earth. What then will you do for your own great name?** (7:7–9)

Joshua's lament seems shocking to a westerner. He does not confess any wrongdoing but seems to blame God and crossing of the Jordan for defeat. What had been the blessing and victory building up God's reputation becomes the curse. The defeat now makes the future so vulnerable that Joshua fears elimination of God's people. In the final entreaty, he calls God to reestablish the reputation that had been tarnished by the defeat.

The lament form follows that commonly found in Psalms. The worshiper protests before God that a disaster threatens the existence of the people of God. He calls on God to deliver the people of the Lord for the sake of the divine reputation (lit. name). God will be blamed if the tribes fail to possess the land. Western religion looks for someone to blame or seeks some reason to explain a loss. Eastern laments describe the loss and its consequences as God's problem and hope that God will be moved to resolve the situation. With this lament, Joshua imitates the intercessory role of Moses (Num. 14:13–14). However, the lament itself sounds more like the grumbling of Israel in the wilderness than the intercessory prayer of Moses (Num. 14:11–12, 20–25; Hawk, *Every Promise Fulfilled*, pp. 76–77). God virtually ignores the lament when answering the plea of Joshua.

7:10–26 / Instead of telling Joshua how the Lord will rescue the tribes, God names their sin and explains to Joshua how to discover the sinner. God says the loss happened because members of the army violated *herem* booty rules. The Lord expresses more anger over this than bungling spies or the casual approach of commanders to the battle. The Lord says: **He who is caught with the devoted things shall be destroyed by fire, along with all that belongs to him. He has violated the covenant of the LORD and has done a disgraceful thing in Israel** (7:15). Violation of the rules of booty is a direct affront to *herem* instructions of God. The wrongdoer violates the agreement by which the Lord joins with Israel. Disobedience is a disgraceful act threatening the covenant relationship of God with the people.

God reverses Joshua's entreaty in the lament: "What will you [God] do for your great name?" (7:9). The Lord tells Joshua what to do. **Go, consecrate the people. Tell them, "Consecrate yourselves in preparation for tomorrow; for this is what the LORD, the God of Israel, says: That which is devoted is among you, O Israel. You cannot stand against your enemies until you remove it"** (7:13). The holy nature of God requires that justice also issue forth from a holy people. Holiness is God's requirement for support and a relationship (cf. 3:5). Spoils of war obtained in violation of God's instructions must be removed from the people before Israel can defeat enemies in the land and possess its inheritance.

The chronological notes of "tomorrow," **in the morning,** and **early the next morning** move the story into its trial account. Tribe by tribe, clan by clan (lit. family, which refers to the extended family or kin), and households (lit. houses or units such as the "father's house") file by to be judged. Guiltiness may have been determined by casting lots or some test. In any case, Achan, son of Carmi, son of Zabdi (see marginal notes), of the tribe of Judah, was found guilty. Achan, silent until discovered, confesses. Joshua orders him to tell what he has done. Achan does not hide anything when he replies: **It is true! I have sinned against the LORD, the God of Israel. This is what I have done: When I saw in the plunder a beautiful robe from Babylonia, two hundred shekels of silver and a wedge of gold weighing fifty shekels, I coveted them and took them. They are hidden in the ground inside my tent, with the silver underneath** (7:20–21).

Sin began with seeing and coveting. The Ten Commandments and Jesus warned against wanting what is valuable and does not belong to us. Discovered, Achan told that he buried the plunder—an imported robe, silver, and gold—under the floor of his tent. Achan buried silver beneath the rest, for it was the most valuable metal. Precious metals belonged in the treasury of the Lord. He buried what was devoted to destruction and stole goods set aside to finance the worship center of God. Little wonder Achan recognized that his coveting and disobedience were sins against the Lord.

Readers often react against the punishment of Achan and his household in the valley of Achor (lit. trouble). Stoning and burning him and his household and possessions seem harsh (7:25). Yet Joshua sums it up well when he asks: **Why have you brought this trouble on us? The LORD will bring trouble on you today.** Sin like Achan's sin affects the entire body. Corporate guilt requires that the household share in Achan's guilt and hence in his punishment. Executing the source of Israel's sin disciplined and purged the people and enabled them to possess the land. A cancer is removed to preserve the body. Rocks remain piled over the bodies as a reminder "to this day" that coveting and disobedience have consequences (7:26). The name for the place of execution and rock pile, the valley of Achor (trouble), also reminds those who pass by that sin brings trouble but hope can come out of trouble (see Hos. 2:15).

Ironically, the fate of Achan was written in contrast with that of Rahab. Rahab's family shared in her deliverance as Achan's family shared in his disgrace and execution. Achan represented an enemy from within, Rahab one from without. Historically, the family of Rahab lived as a part of the later nation of Israel as a monument of faith; Achan and his family lived only by reputation through a pile of rocks, a reminder of greed and its consequences. The tribes went to battle and discovered that defeat begins from within the community. Churches need to examine their ranks also as they do battle with evil.

Additional Note §10

7:2 / **Ai, which is near Beth Aven to the east of Bethel:** Ai ("the ruin") is mentioned as a place of Abram's early migration into the land of Canaan (Gen. 12–13) and as the location of Joshua's second conquest (Josh. 7–8). A number of archaeologists identify the site with et-Tell, east of Bethel (J. A. Callaway, "Ai," *ABD* 1:125–30). A problem remains at the site of et-Tell. Archaeological excavations find no evidence of occupation of the site during 1400 to 1200 B.C.E., the proposed dates of the conquest. The absence of occupation evidence points to three options: identifying another site as the biblical Ai; finding a date for the conquest when the site was occupied; or dismissing the story. Since archaeologists identify sites only tentatively, the search needs to continue for the Ai of Joshua's time.

§11 Ambush and Victory at Ai (Josh. 8:1–29)

8:1–2 / Now that the people were consecrated and Israel's primary sin eliminated, God gave Joshua marching orders to take Ai (lit. ruin). The Lord said to Joshua, **Do not be afraid; do not be discouraged** [lit. dismayed]. **Take the whole army** [lit. people of war] **with you, and go up and attack Ai. For I have delivered into your hands the king of Ai, his people, his city and his land** (8:1). The Lord instructed Joshua about rules of plunder for Ai. The king of Ai and its residents would be killed, but the army could keep the spoils and domestic animals seized there. Ironically, if Achan had waited, he could have taken booty from Ai. Jericho was to be a whole burnt offering to God as a response of gratitude for God's victory, but Ai was fought by different rules of plunder. These rules recognized that forces live off the land to fight and survive.

The Lord again predicted victory for Israel but took no risk. Rather than allow the commanders to develop a plan of attack, the Lord told Joshua to plan an ambush **behind the city** (8:2). In this way, God noted that Joshua must not fight according to the recommendations of bungling scouts or casual commanders. An ambush using the "entire army" would correct the mistakes of the earlier fiasco.

8:3–17 / The Lord made the point that success requires careful planning. God demanded holiness but also took seriously the threat and planned the operation to accomplish the mission. Five thousand of the thirty thousand men hid in ambush between Bethel and Ai on the west side of Ai. In this encounter, unlike the first one, the enemy underestimated the tribal forces. As the frontal force attacked, the forces of Ai hurried to meet the attack and pursue the soldiers they easily had beaten earlier.

8:18–29 / Once the enemy left their protection and chased the troops a sufficient distance, Joshua signaled the ambush to begin as God directed him: **Hold out toward Ai the**

javelin that is in your hand, for into your hand I will deliver the city (8:18). The ambush succeeded.

The narration underlines the importance of decisive leadership in the victory by noting that **Joshua did not draw back the hand that held out his javelin until he had destroyed all who lived in Ai.** As Moses won the battle against the Amalekites by holding up his arms (Exod. 17), so Joshua secured victory at the "ruin" by holding out his javelin. The fire set in Ai by the ambush forces surprised and demoralized the enemy. Tribal forces being chased swung around to fight a battle in which twelve thousand soldiers and the inhabitants of Ai died. This time the tribal forces followed the plunder instructions of God and Joshua. Joshua ordered his troops to remove the body of the king from a tree at sunset (Deut. 21:22–23). Decisive leadership contributed much to the victory and kept the forces obedient to the Lord.

Heaps of stones close the narrative about Achan and the account of victory at Ai (8:28–29). Mounds of rocks indicate what happens to enemies of the Lord, both from within the community and from outside. In Joshua 7 Achan's heap reminds all the Israelites of the consequences of sin and an embarrassing defeat "to this day." The pile of rocks in Joshua 8 memorializes a most significant victory **to this day** (8:29). By the power of God a ruin (Ai) becomes a **heap** and defeat becomes victory. The heap at Ai celebrates the victory of the Lord and the folly of opposing God.

The Bible describes the comparatively insignificant battle at Ai in more detail that the one at Jericho. This is because the lessons learned at the ruin named Ai are more important than the collapse of the walls at Jericho. Defeat at Ai teaches the perils of coveting and disobeying the commands of God. One should never underestimate the enemy, and ever-present danger demands a total dedication of resources, careful planning, and decisive action by the leader. The heaps of stones can teach every generation that the Lord ultimately provides victory when they eliminate sin and work with God against evil. Together, God and obedient followers can conquer any enemy.

§12 Worship at Mount Ebal (Josh. 8:30–35)

8:30–35 / Immediately the scene changes. The action shifts suddenly to the northern highlands, from battle to liturgy, and from death to covenant renewal. Soggin interprets the ceremony at Mount Ebal as a doublet of the renewal ceremony at Shechem (Josh. 24; Soggin, *Joshua,* pp. 222ff.; LXX inserts this section after 9:2). However, considering the unique roles of both passages in the book, I do not view the ceremonies as doublets. Joshua followed the teachings of Moses by building an altar at Mount Ebal and renewing the covenant early in the campaign (Deut. 27:4). The ceremony at the altar on Mount Ebal celebrated victories at Jericho and Ai and repaired damage to the covenant caused by Achan's violations of *herem* (cf. violations anticipated in Deut. 31:23–29).

Mount Ebal and Mount Gerizim, mountains surrounding Shechem, became important worship sites in the time of Abraham (Gen. 12:6–7). The most important aspect of building an altar and the renewal ceremony in Joshua 8 is that the people fulfilled the commands of Moses. Joshua follows Moses' instructions by building **an altar of uncut stones, on which no iron tool had been used** (Josh. 8:31; Deut. 27). Copying the law on stone makes everyone reponsible for covenant requirements (Deut. 27–31).

The community assembles on both sides of the ark; half of the people stand in front of Mount Gerizim and the other half in front of Mount Ebal. Assuming the role of covenant mediator as the new Moses, Joshua reads **all the words of the law—the blessings and the curses.** He then informs the **whole assembly of Israel, including the women and children, and the aliens who lived among them** (8:34–35) about the covenant responsibilities. Joshua does not omit any of the requirements of the covenant from his reading. Members of the tribes (Israel) hear what will happen (blessings and curses) if they violate the covenant relationship (cf. Deut. 27–30). Violations in the future cannot be attributed to ignorance of the provisions of the law. Everyone, including women, children, and strangers (outsiders), knows what is required for a covenant with the Lord.

Covenant renewal completes the narrative on crossing the Jordan and initial victories. At Mount Ebal, the community reflects on and reaffirms its covenant relationship with the Lord and prepares for possessing the remaining land. The ceremony at Mount Ebal reminds tribal members of covenant requirements for the people of God. How long this agreement will survive depends on the people's faithfulness. In this sense, the ceremony at Mount Ebal closes the early campaign and parallels in function Joshua 24.

Additonal Note §12

8:30 / Then Joshua built on Mount Ebal an altar to the Lord: A. Zertal discovered a worship site on the lowest peak of Mount Ebal dating to the thirteenth and twelfth centuries B.C.E. The site is on a stony hilltop crossed by a stone wall. The earlier, thirteenth-century level includes a round installation with ashes and animal bones. Around 1200, a larger structure was built. The second level lasted fifty years and was then abandoned. Pottery found there could have been used for votive offerings. Zertal also identifies a ramp on the north side and a veranda on the top of the altar. This evidence points to cultic use of the site and according to Zertal seems to be an early Israelite altar (see Zertal, "Israel Enters Canaan," *BAR* 17, no. 5 [1991], pp. 44–47; "Has Joshua's Altar Been Found on Mt Ebal?" *BAR* 11, no. 1 [1985], pp. 26–43; A. Kempinski, "Joshua's Altar—An Iron Age Watchtower," *BAR* 12, no. 1 [1986], pp. 42, 44–46, 48–49; and H. Shanks, "Two Early Israelite Cult Sites Now Questioned," *BAR* 14, no. 1 [1988], pp. 48–52).

§13 The Gibeonite Treaty of Deception (Josh. 9:1–27)

9:1–2 / A new phase of possessing the land begins here, and conquering the hill country is the next challenge for possessing the land. The narrator tells of independent ethnic enclaves who plot war against the tribal threat (9:1). These ethnic groups live in the hill country, in the western foothills (Shephelah), and along the coast of the Mediterranean, or Great Sea, as far north as Lebanon. The narrator tells readers that the nations in Canaan **came together to make war against Joshua and Israel** (9:2).

9:3–11 / The narrator also tells of Hivites in Gibeon who decide to take advantage of the migration. News of Joshua's victories at Jericho and Ai (9:3) inspires the Gibeonites to plan a ruse to convince Joshua and the tribal leaders that they live in a far country and are no threat to the tribes. The Gibeonites arrive with donkeys carrying worn-out sacks and wineskins, cracked and repaired. The men wear old clothes and worn sandals. Their bread is dry and moldy, as if they have come from a distant country. The ruse mirrors the statement in Deuteronomy (20:15), which allows the tribes to make treaties with distant cities and exempts them from the obligations of *herem*. The Gibeonites arrive asking for clemency: **We are your servants** (9:8).

In their proposal the Gibeonites flatter Joshua and **the fame of the LORD your God** by recounting reports of God's mighty deeds (9:9–13). What the Gibeonites say and do not say is instructive. First, the Hivites have heard of what God did in Egypt (cf. Deut. 11:3–4), so the narrative includes the exodus in the list of mighty deeds. Second, the list of battles recounts only victories of Moses prior to the crossing of the Jordan (cf. Deut. 2:24–3:11; 29:2–8). Omitting mention of recent victories is a part of the ruse to make it appear that these visitors have come from afar and possess only old news. Finally, the representatives from Gibeon repeat instructions from their leaders. They commit the city to a

covenant by saying, **We are your servants; make a treaty with us**
(lit. cut a covenant for us; 9:11).

9:12–27 / The narrator provides an important clue for
interpreting this passage. Gibeonites were accepted into the
people of God because **the men of Israel sampled their provisions but did not inquire of the LORD** (9:14). That is, the tribal
leaders test the Gibeonites' story by sampling their moldy, dry
bread, but they leave out the most important test. As happened
with the spies at Ai and with Rahab at Jericho, the leaders of Israel
now do not seek a message from the Lord. Again, depending on
frail human wisdom, the leaders violate their rules of possessing
the land. Phase two starts out as phase one did, with a covenant
and an oath with the enemy who would tempt the assembly to
worship their gods (Deut. 7:25–26; 11:16–17). **Then Joshua made a
treaty of peace with them to let them live, and the leaders of the
assembly ratified it by oath** (9:15). This agreement is worse than
the one with Rahab, for the Gibeonites give no statement of faith,
as Rahab did, prior to receiving their covenant.

Three days later, the truth becomes known. Gibeon lies
near Gilgal, hardly three days' journey. It is also a part of a league
with three other cities: Kephirah, Beeroth, and Kiriath Jearim.
Nevertheless, despite the deception, the tribal forces did not fight
the cities because of the oath. As would be expected, the people
grumbled against their leaders. Leaders always get blamed for
mistakes of the assembly. The leaders defend themselves because
they have given an oath, but they find a compromise that allows
the treaty to stand and *herem* to be served. Aliens living in the land
will be the "choppers of wood and carriers of water" (Deut. 29:11),
and so will be the Gibeonites (9:23). The leaders accept the teachings of Deuteronomy as the appropriate compromise and allow
the Gibeonites to live. **They continued, "Let them live, but let
them be woodcutters and water carriers for the entire community." So the leaders' promise to them was kept. Then Joshua
summoned the Gibeonites and said, "Why did you deceive us
by saying, 'We live a long way from you,' while actually you
live near us? You are now under a curse: You will never cease to
serve as woodcutters and water carriers for the house of my
God"** (9:21–23).

Burning of sacrifices and purification rites require wood
and water at a house of worship. Thus the Israelites will remember that the Gibeonites joined the people of God through de-

ception when they see them serving the congregation (the LXX expands the verse to include "congregation of the Lord to this day"; 9:21). The curse makes the point that deception is no way to enter the people of God. Since Israel, from the time of Jacob, has been famous for its deceptive ways, the message speaks to both strangers and community members. There is no room for deception in the relationship between God and human beings. That message speaks to readers everywhere more than does the servant status of Gibeonites in the tribal federation.

The Gibeonites humbly accept the compromise: **We are now in your hands. Do to us whatever seems good and right to you** (9:25). Then the narrator reminds readers that the compromise is a generous act of saving the Gibeonites from extermination. So the narrative summarizes the message that Gibeonites serve as **woodcutters and water carriers for the community and for the altar of the LORD at the place the LORD would choose. And that is what they are to this day** (9:27). The location of "the altar . . . the Lord will choose" remains ambiguous. Later readers will assume that the place is the temple in Jerusalem, but that point is not stated here. God still has the freedom to appear wherever appropriate. No one location can claim to possess God. In any case, the Gibeonites continue to serve God and the people as woodcutters and water carriers to the time when the story is retold and becomes Scripture. The humility of the Gibeonites points out that they have learned their lesson and now deserve a place in the people of God.

§14 Five Kings Attack Gibeon and Joshua Counterattacks (Josh. 10:1–28)

10:1–5 / Adoni-Zedek, king of Jebusite Jerusalem, gathers other kings to make war on Joshua and Israel (9:1–2). The king of Jerusalem is upset over Joshua's treaty with Gibeon and the treatment of kings in Ai and Jericho. He perceives Gibeon to be more of a threat than Ai because it is a more significant town (lit. great), a city with a king (lit. royal), and has a skilled army (lit. all her men are warriors; 10:2). The king forms a coalition with **Hoham king of Hebron, Piram king of Jarmuth, Japhia king of Lachish and Debir king of Eglon.** Adoni-Zedek sends out a call to punish Gibeon for its treaty with the intruders: **Come up and help me attack Gibeon . . . because it has made peace with Joshua and the Israelites** (10:4). Then the five kings move their troops into positions to attack Gibeon. The ill-advised treaty with residents in the land already is bringing Israel into war.

10:6–11 / Gibeon responds quickly to the threat by calling to Joshua for protection. Joshua is in Gilgal when he receives the call for help: **Do not abandon your servants. Come up to us quickly and save us! Help us, because all the Amorite kings from the hill country have joined forces against us** (10:6). As the king in Jerusalem overstates the threat of Gibeon by calling it "great" and a "royal" city, so Gibeon overstates the threat of the Amorite kings. Only five kings in the hill country are attacking Gibeon. However, the message, stated in the common rhetoric of calls for help, gets Joshua's response. The narrator describes how **Joshua marched up from Gilgal with his entire army, including all the best fighting men** (10:7). Lessons of the past improve Joshua's leadership. This time he consults the Lord and receives assurance: **Do not be afraid of them; I have given them into your hand. Not one of them will be able to withstand you** (10:8). Joshua will learn later how important it was to consult the Lord and to receive this promise.

Joshua's counterattack on the five kings demonstrates he had learned two lessons from previous battles. He fights a wise, well-planned operation, and yet victory depends largely on support from God, the divine warrior. Joshua launches a forced march, a 32-kilometer journey that is a demanding, twisting, steep climb from Gilgal. A night march ensured the victory by the element of surprise (10:9–10), as the coalition's troops are thrown into confusion. The other side of the victory is that the Lord hurls large hail (lit. great stones) upon the fleeing troops at the descent of Beth Horon. More soldiers died in the hail than in battle (10:11). God's hail emphasizes the dependence tribal forces have on support from the divine warrior.

10:12–28 / A poem from the Book of Jashar celebrates the Lord's support of the troops. In the poem's introduction, Joshua calls out to the Lord, the ruler of the heavens, in front of Israel. He mentions the **sun** standing **still over Gibeon** and the **moon, over the Valley of Aijalon.** The poem states that **the sun stood still, and the moon stopped,** until the tribes **avenged** themselves against the enemy (10:12–13).

The narrator summarizes in prose the events of the day. He mentions that the valley of Aijalon (Beth Horon Pass) and Gibeon are so oriented that early in the morning a person could see the sun rising in the east over Gibeon and the moon setting in the west over the valley. The Lord's control over the moon and sun gave the people an extended day that would allow them enough time to complete their victory. The narrator explains the extraordinary day as **a day when the LORD listened to a man** and as affirmation that **the LORD was fighting for Israel** (10:14).

The account of the battle ends by stating that **Joshua returned with all Israel to the camp at Gilgal** (10:15). The return to Gilgal also is mentioned after the pursuit of forces from Makkedah to Debir and the summary of victories in the south (10:43). However, verses 15 and 43 are missing from the best manuscripts of the Greek translation (LXX) and do not seem to have been a part of the narrative. The narrative reads smoothly without the account of a return to Gilgal.

The slaughter of the fleeing kings has its own account and setting. This story takes place at a cave at Makkedah. Large rocks at the entrance of the cave remain **to this day** (10:27). The narrator divides the event into three parts (10:16–27). First the tribes roll rocks to block the mouth of the cave to contain the enemy kings while the troops pursue and inflict casualties on the fleeing enemy. Second, the tribes make the conquered kings indicate the superiority of the tribal forces through a ritual. Third, the tribal forces feel encouraged by the victory, including the execution of kings and exposure of their bodies, as instructed by Deuteronomy (Deut. 21:22).

At Makkedah Joshua follows *herem* guidelines carefully in eliminating hostile forces (10:28). He leaves no survivors and executes the king of Jerusalem as was required for the king of Jericho. As at Jericho, the spoils are devoted completely to God and the forces leave no survivors. Everything belongs to the divine warrior who gave the victory at Makkedah.

Additional Notes §14

10:5 / **Then the five kings of the Amorites:** The coalition is made up of Adoni-Zedeq (my lord is righteous; LXX, Adonibezeq, lord of Bezeq, as in Judg. 1:5–7), king of Jerusalem; Hoham (Ailam in LXX), king of Hebron; Piram (Pheidon, LXX), king of Jarmuth; Japhia (Iephtha in LXX), king of Lachish; and Debir (Dabein in LXX, a city?), king of Eglon (LXX; Odollam, here and in v. 23). Hebron (Qiryat-Arba, 14:13–15) is located high in the central highlands south of Jerusalem. Jarmuth (Khirbet Yarmuk) is located forty km west of Jerusalem in the Shephelah, the foothills between the coastal plain and central highlands. Lachish (Tell ed-Duweir) is about forty km southwest of Jerusalem. Debir appears as a place name (15:7; 21:15), and Eglon is located at Tell 'Aiton (disputed location) on the route from Lachish to Hebron. An earlier name for the non-Semitic coalition would have been the "five kings of the Amorites." The king of Jerusalem chose neighbors to the west and south who would protect approaches to the central highlands.

10:13 / **as it is written in the Book of Jashar:** The Book is probably a book of poems celebrating Israel's victories in wars (see also "The Book of the Wars of Yahweh," Num. 21:14; the poem on Deborah, Judg. 5:1–31). It is mentioned as a source book of early Israelite poetry here and in 2 Sam. 1:19–27 (perhaps also 1 Kgs. 8:12–13). Jashar means "upright" or "straight," and the book may have been a collection of national songs about Israel's heroic past. Little remains of its content and structure.

10:28 / **That day Joshua took Makkedah:** The city is described as an Amorite royal city in the Shephelah, located in the center of the battle area. The five Amorite kings who escaped from the battle for Gibeon were trapped in a cave there. Joshua executed the kings and then attacked and defeated Makkedah. No site has been located for Makkedah except for the foothills.

§15 Report on Southern Victories (Josh. 10:29–43)

10:29–43 / Reports of victories in the southern part of the land follow a form common in the ancient Near East. As in the book of Joshua, those reports vary in size and style. Reports on crucial victories or important conquests are long and involved, whereas routine raids are described in stereotyped summaries etched on a stele or standing stone. Southern campaign summaries begin with Makkedah and move city to city until Debir (10:29–39). Then the narrative summarizes Joshua's subjugation of the region from Kadesh Barnea to Gaza and from Goshen to Gibeon (10:40–42).

Three major themes appear in the reports. First, the Lord gives each city and king to the tribal confederation. Second, Joshua and the people carefully carry out the demands of *herem* and execute the king, the army, and the population of each city (**no survivors were left;** lit. no remnant). Third, Joshua captures the region in one campaign because the Lord, the God of Israel, fights for Israel. Notice that the summaries do not mention the destruction of either Jerusalem or Gezer. Both fortresses remain in place. The region has come under the general control of the tribal forces by these raids.

§16 Report on Northern Victories (Josh. 11:1–15)

11:1–5 / Joshua 11 begins as Joshua 10 did (10:1). **When Jabin king of Hazor** hears of the destruction of Jericho, Ai, and the coalition of the five kings, he sends word to other kings (cf. 10:3–4) in the region to make war on Joshua and Israel. As the king of Jerusalem rallied the kings of the south, so Jabin calls out the northern coalition forces. They respond with their might: **They come out with all their troops and a large number of horses and chariots— a huge army, as numerous as the sand on the seashore** (11:4). The added dimension in the north is horses and chariots, which strike fear in the tribal forces from the highlands. Chariots were the ultimate fighting machines of that era, and only wealthy and powerful kings possessed them. These weapons reminded the tribes of their weaknesses.

11:6–15 / As in Joshua 10:8, the Lord encourages Joshua and the people: **Do not be afraid of them, because by this time tomorrow I will hand all of them over to Israel, slain. You are to hamstring their horses and burn their chariots** (11:6). The Lord gives the tribal forces words of encouragement along with *herem* instructions. The tribal forces not only will win but also will cripple the horses that pull the chariots and burn the chariots, symbols of urban warfare. Truly the God of Israel will triumph over the most advanced weapon of warfare in giving the people the land.

The battle has three facets. One is that Joshua surprises the forces of Hazor at the Waters of Merom, an ideal place to corner an army and to make chariots ineffective. Joshua then pursues the forces until no remnant is left. Finally, the Israelite forces cripple the horses and burn the chariots. Again, decisive leadership, effective pursuit, and faithfulness to *herem* instructions allow the people to triumph.

Joshua next attacks the fortresses themselves. The narrator reports that **Joshua took all these royal cities and their kings and**

put them to the sword (11:12). He burns only Hazor as he razed Jericho and Ai. The Israelites carry off plunder for themselves but put the people to the sword, **not sparing anyone that breathed** (11:14). Again Joshua is faithful to the commands of Moses (11:12; that is, the book of Deuteronomy). **As the LORD commanded his servant Moses, so Moses commanded Joshua, and Joshua did it; he left nothing undone of all that the LORD commanded Moses** (11:15). The narrator points out that Joshua obeys the teachings of Deuteronomy by exterminating the population of fortresses and burning one city. As Polzin suggests, there may be some humor intended in the phrase "he left nothing undone of all that the LORD commanded Moses." Joshua does as instructed, but he does not fulfill the *herem* requirements of total destruction (Deut. 7:2).

The narrator paints a picture of a successful conquest while admitting its limited nature. The *herem* standards for the northern raids require only that the enemy be annihilated, so the tribal forces burn only Hazor, and raiders keep the booty. Because aliens in the land could threaten Israel's religious purity in the future, Joshua obediently destroys them. Otherwise, the statement that "he left nothing undone" (11:15) has an ironic twist to it.

Verse 15 states that Joshua obeyed the Lord's instructions given in verse 6 and that Joshua added the burning of Hazor to the requirements. In this way, the book of Joshua modifies the teachings of Deuteronomy as it adjusts *herem* requirements for each situation. The summary suggests that Joshua's modifications can be cataloged as faithfulness even if they do not meet the standards of *herem* in Deuteronomy.

Additional Notes §16

11:5, 7 / **At the Waters of Merom:** The waters of Merom have been identified with the village of Meirom on the eastern slopes of Jebel Jarmaz in upper Galilee. Several seasons of excavation have prompted Meyers to suggest that they are separate locations. Historical and geographic evidence supports Aharoni's and A. Rainey's identification of the Waters of Merom with Tell el-Khureibeh, which is just over three km south of Marun er-Ras. Meron is mentioned in the campaign annals of Thutmose III (1504–1450 B.C.E.) and Rameses II. Tiglath Pileser III (733/32) of Assyria also claims to have taken Merom, indicating the strategic nature of the place (D. C. Liid, "Merom, Waters of," *ABD* 4:705).

11:11 / **And he burned up Hazor itself:** The site of the fortified town is located in northern Galilee at the southwest corner of the Huleh plain, north of the Sea of Galilee. It stands at what were the crossroads of strategic routes from Megiddo to Damascus and Beth-shan to Sidon. Hazor also is mentioned in Judg. 4 as the fortress of Jabin, king of Canaan, who sends forces led by Sisera. Deborah and Barak defeat the Canaanites with the help of Jael. One of the problems in the accounts is that Jabin is mentioned in both of them.

Excavations at the ruins of Tell el-Qedah indicate that the Canaanite city was destroyed in 1300 B.C.E. and never reoccupied. The destruction of Hazor fits the date, which has been recognized by archaeologists as the time of the conquest (J. M. Hamilton, "Hazor," *ABD* 3:87–88). A. Ben-Tor of Hebrew University continues to excavate the site made famous by Y. Yadin, and additional discoveries about the fortress will be forthcoming.

§17 Summaries of Victories in the Land (Josh. 11:16–23)

11:16–23 / A summary report on the campaign for possessing the land begins with the statement that **Joshua took this entire land** (11:16) and ends with the result: **Then the land had rest from war** (11:23). As is the case with Joshua 9–11, the point of view remains that of the narrator. The point of the report is that the tribal forces have possessed the land as the Lord had instructed Moses. God has given the land as an inheritance, and as a result the land could enjoy a period of time without warfare.

The narrator notes why some kings and groups responded as they did when they heard of Joshua's victories. The Lord directly hardened the hearts of the kings so that they waged **war against Israel, so that he might destroy them totally, exterminating them without mercy, as the Lord had commanded Moses** (11:20). Their behavior explains the warfare and its *herem*, although some readers have great difficulty with this picture of God. We should remember, however, that hardening of enemy hearts is another way of saying that when an enemy opposes the tribes—the people to whom God promised the land—that enemy must be destroyed. Those who asked for sanctuary, as Rahab and the people of Gibeon, received it. Also, in the OT, belief in the sovereignty of God attributes all events to God. The Lord initiates everything. God uses the resistance of groups in the land to underline the importance of removing from the land aliens who resist the directives of Israel's God.

Additional study in the hardening of the hearts of enemy can be found in narratives about signs and wonders in Egypt (Exod. 7–8). These verses say that God hardens Pharaoh's heart (7:3), Pharaoh has a hard (lit. stubborn) heart (7:14), and Pharaoh's heart is hardened (7:13, 22; 8:15, 19). The passages describe how Pharaoh's heart (mind or will) hardens through resistance to God's will, increasing his innate stubbornness. The passages describe a leader resisting the power of the Lord and so causing hardship for himself and his people.

In Joshua (9:1; 10:1; 11:1) leaders in the land harden their resistance when they hear about victories of the invaders. They gather coalitions from their region to wage war against the tribes and their allies. Ultimately, the narrator tells us, the enemy's resistance is increased by the acts of a sovereign God who fights for Israel. Their hardness of heart provides another way through which the Lord gives the tribes their inheritance.

Three interesting anecdotes appear in the report. In one the narrator mentions that raids under Joshua took a "long time" (11:18). The campaign was not a quick strike or an instant success as one might think by reading the campaign reports. The report also mentions that Joshua did not destroy the Gibeonites because of the treaty with the Hivites. No other groups had **made a treaty of peace with the Israelites;** therefore people who oppose the tribal forces and their God are exterminated. Finally, the summary mentions that Anakites, the proverbial giants in the land (Num. 13:32), were left in Gaza, Gath, and Ashdod (Aseldo, LXX) within the territory of Israel (11:22). The report does not explain this omission and does not mention that Philistines lived there.

The last point reminds readers that Israel is not totally faithful to the commands of God because they allow aliens and their allies to remain in the land. The tragic results of this mistake will become clearer in future narratives. Otherwise, the report that **Joshua took the entire land, just as the LORD had directed Moses, and he gave it as an inheritance to Israel according to their tribal divisions** (11:23) generally stands up. Joshua "took" the land through raids and broke the initial resistance of people of the land. Subsequent reports on continuing fighting, however, clarify what the word "took" means in this summary. At least Joshua's control gave the land rest from war.

By taking the land, Joshua is able to move on to the second task, dividing the land among the tribes according to lots and their inheritance. The primary point made here by the narrator is that Joshua took control in the land of Canaan to a sufficient degree as the Lord directed Moses. In this achievement, Joshua is faithful and God gives him the land.

Additional Notes §17

11:16 / **So Joshua took this entire land:** The area defined in Josh. 11 is a geography lesson on ancient Canaan. It includes several places that readers may not recognize. For instance, **Arabah** refers to the Great Rift Valley, primarily the section south of the Dead Sea. Arabah can refer to the Jordan River valley and hence to the Arabah south of the Kinnereth Sea (Sea of Galilee; 11:2). **Mount Halak** also is a desert peak east of Kadesh Barnea representing Israel's southern boundary. **Baal Gad** is a Canaanite city in the northern region of Laish (later, Caesarea Philippi) in Lebanon below Mount Hermon. It is a northern border of Joshua's territory. **Anab** is a city in the southern Judean hills, three miles west of Debir. It was one of the cities inhabited by the Anakites.

11:21 / **Joshua went and destroyed the Anakites:** The Anakim are descendents of Anak, who occupied Canaan before the arrival of Israel. Anak was the son of Arba (Josh. 15:11; 21:11), the founder of Kiriath-arba (Hebron). The name refers to neck or necklace, perhaps "long-necked" or giant. Josh. 11:21 indicates the people occupied a larger territory than Hebron. After the defeat remnants of the Anakim lived in Philistine cities and left descendents such as Goliath of Gath (G. L. Mattingly, "Anak," *ABD* 1:222).

12:1 / An introduction to the list of kings connects this chapter with reports of conquests in the land. The list names kings from east to west of the Jordan and ends with a total of thirty-one (twenty-nine in LXX) defeated kings ruling west of the Jordan (12:24). The different forms and content of the list indicate that the narrative combines two independent lists in the report. The list of eastern kings includes border descriptions (12:2–6), while the list of defeated kings west of the Jordan mentions kings by city (12:9–24).

12:2–6 / Narratives on Sihon and Og outline the borders of the two eastern kingdoms and mention again that Moses (second "servant of the Lord" is omitted in LXX) conquered the area and gave the land to the Reubenites, the Gadites, and the half-tribe of Manasseh (see also 1:12–13).

12:7–24 / An introduction describes the conquered area west of the Jordan before listing defeated kings (12:7–8). Thirty-one kings (12:24) conquered west of the Jordan are listed by the name of their city, not by a personal name. A list of six (not seven) ethnic groups on the western side of the Jordan appears in verse 8 (see the list also in 9:1). The narrative here does not divide the area into ethnic enclaves. The passage contrasts the work of Joshua as conqueror of the western area and thirty-one kings with that of Moses, the conqueror of two. The impressive list elevates Joshua's role in defeating enemy rulers. Both passages state that Moses (12:6) and Joshua (12:7) gave Israel the land as a possession or inheritance. Surprisingly, the introduction to each section stresses that the tribes conquered the enemy kings and omits any reference to the Lord's part in the victories (12:1, 7). The entire passage points out the importance of leadership and praises the fighting of the people as keys to defeating enemy leaders.

Readers should not minimize human aspects of the campaign by stressing the divine warrior role of God. At the same time, celebrating victories that come to a believer remains a won-

derful way to praise God. Christians will increase in their appreciation of God by listing blessings they have received in the way
Joshua lists victories in chapter 12.

Additional Note §18

12:7 / **These are the kings of the land that Joshua and Israel
conquered on the west side of the Jordan:** Summarizing statements
and lists of defeated lands are very common in Assyrian royal inscriptions about military campaigns (see Younger, *Ancient Conquest Accounts,*
pp. 230–37). Lists of cities are selective and partial in the inscriptions.
Josh. 12 naturally fits the narrative, as do lists and summaries in Near
Eastern conquest accounts. The order in which towns are listed generally
fits the events described in Josh. 6–11. Hormah and Arad appear in the
list of cities in the south from Num. (21:3). Geder, a city south of Gaza in
Philistine territory, is mentioned only here. Even though there is no record of their conquest, Bethel and four neighboring cities are mentioned.
Bethel is mentioned twice, once as the neighbor of Ai and then as a city
that was conquered. Gezer is on the list but was not conquered until later
(16:10). Shechem and Dothan are not listed in Josh. 12, indicating they
were friendly to the invaders. The ten sites of the northern campaign include a number of sites not mentioned in campaign documents. The
lists indicate that the narrative of Josh. 6–11 is partial and selective in
its report of the campaign. The omission of some areas of Canaan prepares the narrative for mentioning land not conquered (see Hess, *Joshua,*
pp. 226–29).

§19 Instructions about Land Remaining to Be Conquered (Josh. 13:1–6)

13:1 / Joshua's age, estimated as ninety to one hundred, provides the chronological setting for two sections of the book (13:1; 23:1–2). The issues of age and of unconquered land are introduced when the LORD said to him, "You are very old, and there are still very large areas of land to be taken over" (lit. very much land remains to be possessed). God delivers first-person instructions to Joshua, a direct oracle, reminding him that possessing the land has not ended. In his old age Joshua must depend on others to complete the conquest.

13:2–6 / Areas dominated by the Philistines (five southern coastal cities), the Canaanites (coastal areas south of Lebanon), an unknown group (Amorites?) east of the Jordan (area of Og and Sihon), and the Gebalites (Byblus or Lebanon) remain outside of tribal control. In the instructions, God promises again to drive out the inhabitants, even the Sidonians, but Joshua needs to allocate unconquered areas to tribes who would feel obligated to take land now dominated by neighbors.

The divine instructions include several features. God refers to Israel as the inhabitants of the mountain regions from Lebanon to Misrephoth Maim (13:6). Describing tribal holdings as the mountain regions reflects the scope of the earliest settlement as determined by archaeology. Misrephoth Maim was a city on the coast, a few miles south of Tyre. In addition, the omission of the northeast group and the description of the land of the Canaanites as land east of the Jordan indicate that a group living in the northeast area of the land has been deleted from the passage. The land of the Canaanites normally is west of the Jordan. Next, God emphatically states that the Lord will personally drive out the inhabitants of Lebanon, even Sidon. Sidon receives special contempt and treatment in these instructions. It was a particularly difficult fortress to conquer and remained a Phonecian stronghold for generations. The report also mentions a coalition of five Philistine cities and the *Avvim* who lived near Gaza prior to the invasion of the Philistines. Philistines entered the coastal area from Anatolia and are called Sea Peoples. In the warfare passages Joshua nowhere encounters the Philistines. The passage refers to Philistine rulers using an Aegean term meaning "tyrants" (13:3).

This introduction tells readers that the tribes can no longer expect Joshua to lead them into warfare. Instead, completion of the struggle now depends on the tribes. The followers must become courageous leaders. This is God's bad news that goes with the good news of giving an inheritance. An inheritance brings with it a set of challenges. As it was in the time of Joshua, today some people inherit resources but are overwhelmed by challenges accompanying them. Others alertly confront the challenges and enjoy the blessings of God's inheritance by overcoming temptations that come with the inheritance. This is the challenge that comes with the blessings of God's promises.

Verses 1–6 open the section of Joshua 13–22 in which Joshua distributes land to tribes. Interesting narratives are interspersed within reports about the distribution of land. The narratives tell how tribes do or do not confront enemies who control the land they receive. At times the tribes clash with each other instead of the enemy. From this time on, however, responsibility for possessing the land shifts from Moses and Joshua to individual tribes and their leaders.

§20 Division of Land East of the Jordan
(Josh. 13:7–33)

13:7–33 / The narrative shifts from describing land not yet conquered to dividing land among the tribes. Verse 7 begins with a summary statement about land west and east of the Jordan. The Greek version (LXX) of the passage includes a section of the verse left out of the Hebrew (MT) and not in the NIV. Verse 7 begins (NIV) with the following: **and divide it** (the west) **as an inheritance among the nine tribes and half of the tribe of Manasseh.** The Greek adds, from the Jordan to the Great Sea westward you shall give them: the Great Sea shall be the boundary (13:7). The NIV picks up the reference to the half tribe of Manasseh: **The other half of Manasseh** (lit, with him), **the Reubenites and the Gadites had received the inheritance that Moses had given them east of the Jordan, as he, the servant of the LORD, had assigned it to them** (13:8). References to the eastern and western halves of the tribe of Manasseh hold together dividing of land in the east and west. Following the chronology of the conquest, Joshua divides first the land east of the Jordan.

§21 Excursus: Gad, Reuben, and the Half Tribe of Manasseh

In the books of Joshua and Deuteronomy, Reuben is mentioned before Gad, whereas in Numbers 32 the versions vary as to which precedes the other (MT, LXX, and Samaritan). Gad precedes Reuben in the list of cities in Numbers 32:34–38. In other verses, Gad precedes Reuben in the Hebrew text (MT) except for verse 1. Numbers probably preserves the older order of the tribes. Gad lay north of Reuben and the half tribe of Manasseh north of Gad.

Some scholars recognize the mention of the half tribe of Manasseh in Joshua 13 to be a later addition (S. E. Loewenstamm, "The Settlement of Gad and Reuben as Related in Num. 32:1–38—Background and Composition, in *From Babylon to Canaan* [Jerusalem: Magnes, 1992], pp. 112–30). Granted that Numbers 32:1–32 omits the half tribe of Manasseh, it is still hard to argue that the inclusion of the half tribe of Manasseh indicates that Joshua 13 is a late layer of the book, an addition by a later hand. The half tribe of Manasseh does appear in Numbers 32:33, 39–42, in the discussions of allotments and battles of the eastern tribes.

Joshua returns to Moses' instructions for dividing the eastern land (Num. 21:23–33; 32:1–42). Land east of the Jordan includes areas such as the Arnon Gorge, the plateau of Medeba, towns of Sihon, Gilead, Mount Hermon, and Bashan. Ammon is the eastern border. An interesting note here is that the tribal forces "did not drive out the people of Geshur and Maacah, so they continue to live among the Israelites to this day" (13:13).

A footnote about the tribe of Levi interrupts the narrative about dividing the eastern territory. Moses did not parcel out land to the Levites, for they received "offerings made by fire to the LORD, . . . as he promised them" (13:14). Priests must work as impartial worship leaders, and they can carry out this function better without territory to defend or land to tie them to one region of the nation. Levites do not depend on land for making a living; they receive their livelihood from worshipers who support them with sacrifices and offerings.

Joshua then turns to the inheritance of the tribe of Reuben. The area designated by Moses for the clans of Reuben details the geography of the region and then mentions towns on the plateau and the entire realm of Sihon king of the Amorites (13:16–21). The narrative tells how Moses defeated Sihon and his allies. A refrain closes the description of the land of Reuben. "These towns and their villages were the inheritance of the Reubenites, clan by clan" (13:23).

The narrative mentions Balaam in this section on the land of Reuben (13:22). Balaam, son of Beor, is the prophet summoned by Balak, king of Moab, to place a curse on Israel (Num. 22). Elders tempt Balaam with a fee of divination (Num. 22:7); Balak also promises to reward Balaam handsomely if he puts a curse on the invaders (Num. 22:17). Joshua 13:22 explains, "The Israelites had put to the sword Balaam son of Beor, who practiced divination." Balaam's death becomes a warning against practicing divination in Israel.

Many readers may remember Balaam primarily because of his donkey—the animal sees the angel of the Lord and refuses to move toward the angel despite three beatings (Num. 22:33). The donkey tires of getting beaten and explains to Balaam why he refuses to move. Ultimately Balaam does not curse the people of God but only blesses them (Num. 23–24).

Descriptions of the inheritance of Gad and of the half-tribe of Manasseh follow similar formats. An introduction states that Moses gave the land to the tribe, clan by clan (13:24, 29). A conclusion claims that the area is the tribal inheritance given by Moses to descendants, clan by clan (13:28, 31). The division of the land also is the same: a geographical description followed by a list of towns and villages.

In a second note about the tribe of Levi, the narrator explains, "Moses had given no inheritance [to the tribe of Levi]; the LORD, the God of Israel, is their inheritance, as he promised them" (13:33). Unlike the earlier explanation (see 13:14), this conclusion states that the tribe of Levi needs no physical inheritance. This passage does not teach that religious leaders should take a vow of poverty or own no property. Rather, it says the presence of the Lord equals any physical inheritance. That remains a wonderful promise for today's spiritual leaders. It parallels Jesus' promise of sending the Holy Spirit, the Counselor (John 14:26), who quiets the fears of believers and guarantees Jesus' presence with followers (Matt. 28:19–20). The presence of God provides a blessing equal to possessing land. That presence remains the cherished inheritance of Christians.

§22 *Inheritance of Tribes West of the Jordan (Josh. 14:1–5)*

14:1–5 / Joshua 14 introduces the dividing of land west of the Jordan with a summary statement on areas inherited in the **land of Canaan** (14:1). The phrase "land of Canaan" refers to land west of the Jordan, where the Canaanites live. The narrator repeats the instructions in a concluding summary (19:51). **Eleazar, the priest,** Joshua, son of Nun, and clan heads (lit. heads of father's houses) will determine the allotments by casting lots. As the Lord commanded through Moses (14:2, 5), they distribute a tribe's inheritance by lot, taking into account the names of the ancestors and size of tribe (Num. 26:52–56). The narrator's introduction stresses that the priest, military leader, and local heads follow instructions from the Lord that came through Moses. The role of heads of clans indicates that tribal inheritances reflect a democratic, representative process. Clans represent the basic social organization of the tribes, the strong and the weak together. Later, a closing summary of the west-bank division of land adds that the ceremony took place in Shiloh at the entrance to the Tent of Meeting (19:51).

For the third time a narrative introduction discusses how the tribe of Levi will be treated in the allotment of land. The continuing importance of Levites in the narrative indicates a particular interest in the tribe and that descendants of Levi in some way preserved or recorded the account.

A summary finally tells what the tribe will receive: **The Levites received no share of the land but only towns to live in, with pasturelands for their flocks and herds** (14:4). Because of its sacred role, the tribe forfeits territorial rights but does inherit cities in which to live and land for flocks and herds to provide food and clothing. The narrative gives readers information about a place for the tribe of Levi in increments. Suspense continues because readers still do not know the names and locations of the towns.

Readers must wait until after land is apportioned to the other tribes (ch. 21). The Lord ensures a future for the spiritual leaders, however, through promises.

So the Israelites divided the land, just as the LORD had commanded Moses (14:5). The next five chapters fill in the details as to how tribal leaders faithfully accomplish this. The chapters affirm that the leaders followed divine instructions from Moses and discovered the will of God through casting sacred rocks (bones).

Additional Note §22

14:1 / **Eleazar the priest:** Eleazar appears here for the first time in the book of Joshua. He is a son and successor of Aaron and a leader of the Levites. Moses commissions Joshua before Eleazer while Eleazer guides Joshua by casting the Urim (lots, Num. 27:19–22). Moses commands Eleazer and Joshua to divide the land for the tribes (Num. 34:17), assisted by a representative from each tribe. Eleazer casts the sacred lots as a priest emphasizing that the land was a gift from the Lord.

§23 Excursus: Boundary Lists

Boling points out that Joshua 13–21:42 shows evidence of having a form and history separate from that of Joshua 1–12, 21:43–22:34, and 23. The variety of form and content in the boundary lists also indicates a complicated history behind its final form. Joshua 24:1–33 represents a different tradition, the history of which cannot be recovered (Boling and Wright, *Joshua*, pp. 66–72). Although a time when the various parts formed a cohesive whole cannot be determined, a number of scholars place that time during or after the exile.

A careful reading of the boundary and city lists shows how complicated the allotment lists are. Scholars propose several options for determining the historical setting of the boundary lists. Readers may consider the lists as material existing before the monarchy (Alt, except for Judah, and Aharoni), administrative lists created during the monarchy (Noth, Kallai, Na'aman, Svensson, and others), or parts of treaty forms from the time of the settlement to protect tribes from boundary conflict (R. S. Hess, "Asking Historical Questions of Joshua 13–19: Recent Discussions Concerning the Date of the Boundary Lists," in *Faith, Tradition, and History: Old Testament Historiography in its Near Eastern Context* [ed. A. R. Millard, J. K. Hoffmeier, and D. W. Baker; Winona Lake, Ind.: Eisenbrauns, 1994], pp. 191–205). Treaty boundary lists have a rich history, for they appear in treaty documents from 2000 B.C.E. of the Hittites and Syrian city-states of Ugarit and Charcemish (R. S. Hess, "Late Bronze Age and Biblical Boundary Descriptions of the West Semitic World," in *Ugarit and the Bible* [ed. G. J. Brooke, A. H. W. Curtis, and J. G. Healey; Munster: Ugarit-Verlag, 1994], pp. 123–38).

Several points can be made about the boundary and city lists of Joshua 14–21. First, the lists represent ideal allotments for the tribes. One does not need to place the lists into a context in which Israel controlled the land of Canaan. Next, the tribal allotments receive divine support by the casting of lots (Hb. *goral*). The painted rocks or bones declare to the people the will of God and thus give divine approval to each inheritance. In addition, nearly three hundred toponyms enumerated in Joshua 14–21 cannot be identified with any certainty. Archaeologists have identified many more sites than those listed in Joshua, so the lists are selective and ideological in their final form (J. Svensson, *Towns and Toponyms in the Old Testament with Special Emphasis on Joshua 14–21* [Stockholm: Almqvist & Wiksell, 1994], pp. 97–98, who associates the list with the Davidic kingdom). Finally, allotments of land stress that Israel's God owns the land and gives it to tribes to use as long as the treaty relationship continues. Interest in boundaries can be found also in Ezekiel 47–48, where God after the exile gives land again to those in a covenant relationship.

There is a lesson for Christians in these lists. Boundary lists remind Christians that their possessions come from the One who owns everything. Consequently, they need to be good stewards of their possessions and give generously to the causes of Christ. All possessions are loaned from God to believers for carrying out the business of God.

§24 Inheritance for the Calebites (Josh. 14:6–15)

14:6–15 / Surprisingly, allotment of land in Canaan begins with confirming the inheritance of an outsider. Caleb, son of Jephunneh the Kenizzite, represents a number of peoples who intermingle with the descendants of Jacob to form the nation of Israel. Caleb, like Rahab, becomes a model of faith for those who inherit the land as legitimate heirs of Jacob. To emphasize the importance of the Kenizzite leader, the narrator places Mosaic promises for Caleb ahead of those given to the tribes of Jacob and Joseph. Moses gives land to Caleb in the wilderness forty-five years before the current allotment (14:10). The priority given to Caleb in Joshua 14 and 15 confirms the importance of Caleb. In these narratives also, Caleb models the bravery that other clans and tribes need to fight for their inheritance.

The allotment of land takes place at Gilgal, the circle (14:6). Caleb comes with the men of Judah, but only Caleb speaks. He reminds Joshua of their journey to spy out the land when he was forty years old (Num. 13:30; Deut. 1:34–36). Though the majority of the spies and people rejected their report, Caleb reminds Joshua, **I, however, followed the LORD my God wholeheartedly** (14:8). This faithfulness is the motivation for Moses' promise of an inheritance in Canaan (14:9). At age eighty-five, Caleb claims land for himself and his descendants. He is ready and able to assume responsibility for receiving land filled with hostile enemy.

Caleb indicates that willingness by saying, **I am still as strong today as the day Moses sent me out; I'm just as vigorous to go out to battle now as I was then.** He builds on his positive self-image by asking permission to conquer the difficult hill country. **Now give me this hill country . . . the Anakites were there and their cities were large and fortified.** He recognizes that he will have **the LORD helping,** so he has confidence that he **will drive them out** as he had been promised (14:11–12).

A summary ends this narrative (but see also 15:13–19 for more about Caleb's allotment). Joshua blesses Caleb and gives him Hebron as his inheritance. So Hebron has belonged to the tribe of Caleb **ever since, because he followed the LORD, the God of Israel, wholeheartedly** (14:14). The narrator does not mention any fighting to take the land. Joshua blesses Caleb with the land his descendants retain until the day of the narrator and the writing of the account.

A footnote to the summary adds historical information about ancient Hebron. Before it became known as Hebron (lit. union), it was called **Keriath Arba** (lit. town of four) in honor of Arba, the greatest Anakite. The anecdote adds to the prestige of Caleb, for he took the city of the greatest giant of the land. The summary adds the refrain **then the land had rest from war** (14:15). The conquests of Caleb, like those of Joshua, brought a temporary period without war.

15:1–12 / Allotment of the land of Judah includes a detailed description of its boundaries. The boundary list begins in the south and then moves to the east, north, and west. On the east the boundary is the Salt, or Dead Sea to the mouth of the Jordan, and on the west it is the coastline of the Great Sea, or Mediterranean. Descriptions of the southern and northern boundaries indicate a thorough knowledge of ancient geography. The area is small in comparison with ancient empires, but it is a precious heritage for people who have been landless to this point in their history.

15:13–17 / A second narrative ties the inheritance of Caleb to the allotment of Judah. After the territory of Judah is described in great detail, the narrative returns to discuss Caleb's inheritance, **a portion in Judah** (15:13). In the narration of the introduction, Arba is said to be the **forefather** (omitted in the LXX) of Anak. Caleb drives out three descendants of Anak from Hebron.

Next the narrative mentions Caleb's battle for Debir (**formerly called Kiriath Sepher,** town of the book; 15:15). This narrative gives some insight into how a person at age eighty-five takes mountain fortresses. Caleb does not lead the battle but promises to give his daughter Acsah in marriage to the man who attacks and conquers Debir. Othniel, son of Caleb's brother (younger brother, Judg. 3:9), conquers Debir, marries Acsah, and hence assumes a leadership position in the clan.

The positive attitude of Caleb shows how an older person may feel good about his or her health. At the same time, older people need to be realistic about the changes time brings to the body. An older leader does not need to step aside from leadership and to turn over challenges to younger people. Rather, an older person has the ability to challenge and motivate a younger generation to accomplish outstanding feats. Leadership demands participation of all generations. The generation of Joshua and Caleb may be called Israel's greatest generation, and its importance as a model will be clear in the final verses of Joshua 24.

15:18–19 / A story subdividing the inheritance completes the Calebite narrative. Acsah urges Othniel to ask Caleb for a field. The story seems broken, but Caleb gives them a field located in the semi-arid Negev. Because water is limited in this area, Acsah asks her father, Caleb, for a special favor, springs of water. Caleb gives her upper and lower springs (15:18–19). Fathers always have difficulty saying no to daughters.

The story becomes a bridge to Judges, where Othniel, son of Kenaz, Caleb's younger brother, saves the people (Judg. 3:9). Caleb and his descendants receive their inheritance in land given to Judah and apparently become part of that tribe. Caleb first and then Othniel inspire courage and faithfulness in the early days of the settlement in Canaan.

15:20–62 / A list of towns follows the boundary list in verses 1–12. The format of boundary descriptions and list of towns follows the outline for allotment of land east of the Jordan. The towns and villages are listed from the south; to the western foothills, in the hill country, and in the desert. There are twenty-nine towns and villages listed in the south, in the western foothills, thirty-nine towns and villages as well as Philistine towns and surrounding communities; thirty-eight towns and villages in the hill country; and six towns and villages in the desert. As northern settlement lists also indicate, the town list shows that the tribe settled primarily in the hill country of the land.

The inclusion of Philistine towns in the list may indicate that the list originated at a later time, when the cities were a part of Judah. It may be a district list from the time of Josiah, or the list may be an ideal gift that includes area and cities that remain to be conquered. Both the boundary and city lists begin with brief introductions pointing out that the inheritance of the tribe of Judah extends clan by clan (lit. family; 15:1, 20).

15:63 / The allotment concludes with a statement pointing out land not conquered. Judah could not dislodge the Jebusites, who were living in Jerusalem; to this day the Jebusites live there with the people of Judah (15:63). The mention of "to this day" underlines that Judah was unsuccessful in conquering the Jebusite fortress until the time of the narrator (i.e., the time of David). Benjamin also could not conquer this city that lies on its border. That contrasts with the conquests by Caleb and his forces, outsiders who were incorporated into the tribe of Judah. The enemies of the tribes remain in the land, living side by side with followers of the Lord. Periods of apostasy during the time of the judges will not be far away. The people of God are failing to fulfill their duties of possessing the land as spelled out in Deuteronomy.

Additional Notes §25

15:12 / **These are the boundaries around the people of Judah by their clans:** The territory of Judah is divided into four districts: Negev (south), Shephelah (lowlands, foothills), mountain (central highlands), and wilderness (around the Dead Sea). A local, administrative division can be recognized in the lists of towns. Judah includes Simeon but not Benjamin. The southern boundaries of Judah and Benjamin are given in detail. Both of the tribes have boundary and city lists, whereas Simeon and Dan have only town lists. Ephraim has detailed boundary descriptions with Benjamin and Manasseh; Manasseh's northern boundary is general. The area of Samaria lacks city lists. The boundary of Zebulun is clear-cut, but the rest of the boundaries and city lists in Galilee are mixed between boundaries and city lists, especially in the case of Asher. Only four clear boundaries appear in the lists: Judah south (15:2–4), between Judah and Benjamin (15:5–11), between Benjamin and Ephraim (16:1–6), and between Benjamin and Cis-Manasseh. Generally the boundaries for the final three are considered earlier than the first. Hess divides the allotment lists by the method they use to combine cities within boundary lists. For example, Type A includes only tribal boundary descriptions: Reuben, Gad, Judah, Manasseh, Benjamin, Zebulun, Asher, and Naphtali; Type B integrates town lists into tribal boundary descriptions: Reuben, Gad, Zebulun, and Asher; and Type C gives town lists distinct from tribal boundary descriptions: Benjamin, Dan, Judah, Simeon, Issachar, Naphtali, Manasseh, towns of asylum, and towns of the Levites (R. S. Hess, "A Typology of West Semitic Place Name Lists with Special Reference to Joshua 13–21," *BA* 59 [September 1996], pp. 160–70).

15:21 / **Southernmost towns of the tribe of Judah:** Scholars date allotment lists by the administrative nature of a list and by archaeological excavations of the earliest strata on an occupied site. Those criteria remain tentative factors for dating. The lists as they appear may have changed during the monarchy as lists shifted from allotment lists to administrative ones. The administrative use of city lists, however, does not determine the date of origin for texts. Lists for guiding the process of settlement would be adjusted when they were used for administrative purposes. As well, some cities listed in the allotment may have been founded later and may represent a stage in the process of occupation of the land (Hess, *Joshua*, p. 249). In any case, the city lists provide minimal help when determining the origin of allotment materials in Joshua (see maps

31–32, B. J. Beitzel, *The Moody Atlas of Bible Lands* [Chicago: Moody, 1985], pp. 100–101).

15:63 / Judah could not dislodge the Jebusites, who were living in Jerusalem: Minimal evidence remains in Jerusalem supporting the Jebusite occupation. Excavations in the City of David (Hill Ophel) reveal stone terraces erected on the steep eastern slope above the Gihon Spring as foundations for buildings of the Jebusite city but no significant data about Jebusite culture or history (A. Mazor, *Archaeology of the Land of the Bible, 10,000–586 BCE* [Garden City, N.Y.: Doubleday, 1990], p. 333). However, the term "Jebusite" is included in twenty-two of twenty-seven lists of pre-Israelite neighbors. The Jebusites appear in Gen. 10:16 as descendents of Canaan and are one of the last groups to be conquered in Canaan. Jebusites probably were non-Semitic people. Judah's conquest of Jerusalem in Judg. 1:8 has been understood as a partial or temporary victory over the Jebusites. The Bible mentions also that Jebusites remained in Jerusalem until David conquered them (S. A. Reed, "Jebus," *ABD* 3:652–53; for finding boundaries and city lists on maps, readers can consult Beitzel, *The Moody Atlas of Bible Lands,* pp. 96–103).

§26 Inheritance of Ephraim and Manasseh (Josh. 16:1–17:18)

16:1–17:18 / After Judah receives its inheritance, the tribes of Joseph receive theirs. Now that the territory of the north has been separated from Judah, the allotment describes the boundaries of Ephraim and the half-tribe of Manasseh. Ephraim receives its territory first in compliance with the wishes of Jacob, who blessed Ephraim over Manasseh (Gen. 48:14, 19). Ephraim and the half-tribe of Manasseh receive land west of the Jordan. The description of the southern border of Ephraim indicates the boundary list begins by separating the northern territory from Dan and Benjamin. That southern border of Ephraim moves east to west from Jericho to Bethel in the highlands and down to Gezer and the Mediterranean Sea (16:1–4).

An anti-Ephraim viewpoint appears in the allotment list of the northern tribes. The Ephraimite boundary narrative does not include details such as those in the narrative about Judah, and it omits a list of cities. The summary includes fragments regarding the northern boundary of Ephraim, which runs from the Jordan to the highlands near Shiloh, south of Shechem, and then follows the Wadi Kanah down to the Mediterranean (16:5–9). The boundary list mentions lines that run westward (lit. seaward). Only a description of the eastern and northeastern perimeters meeting in Jericho remains intact (16:6b–7). Though the tribe of Ephraim later becomes synonymous with the powerful northern kingdom, this narrative places its towns and villages within the area of Manasseh and does not name them. These comments diminish the reputation of Ephraim. Rivalry with Ephraim continues to appear in the book of Judges within stories about Gideon (Judg. 8:1–3) and Jephthah (Judg. 12:1–7).

As in the Judahite allotment, the tribe cannot completely possess the land (16:10). Gezer, a Canaanite city, remains in the hands of the Canaanites until the time of Solomon. After this time, Canaanites live as forced labor among the people of Ephraim to the time of the narrator. Still, the passage notes that Ephraim, like Judah, does not drive out the enemy from its territory.

The next allotment document discusses the inheritance of Manasseh. Narration points out that Manasseh is **Joseph's firstborn** (17:1). This reminder about the priority of Manasseh again diminishes the importance of Ephraim. The document traces the genealogy of the eastern half of Manasseh through Makir and his clans (lit. families). The rest of the tribe is listed under six clan heads. The narrative mentions five daughters of Zelophehad and Manasseh's inheritance request to Eleazar the priest, Joshua, and the princes. The importance of Manasseh's request is underlined by its grounding in promises from Moses. Clans west of the Jordan receive ten plots of land in addition to Gilead and Bashan, which were given to clans in the east (17:5–6).

The narrative also explains why six clans receive ten tracts. The five daughters of the son of Hepher will divide Zelophehad's portion. Since Zelophehad, only son of Hepher, has no sons, his daughters inherit and divide five ways his one-sixth inheritance. The division of the inheritance recalls an ancient practice through which women without a brother inherit the allotment of their father (Num. 27:8–11). The allotment document provides little information about the ten clans' plots of ground or their boundaries and points out the inclusive nature of their inheritance.

The allotment document then outlines the borders of Manasseh's territory: from Asher to Michmethath, opposite Shechem, southward, turning back toward En-tappuah (spring), down to Kanah Ravine, and along the north side of the ravine to the sea. Asher is on the north and Issachar on the east. The Manasseh border descriptions are general and incomplete as were those of Ephraim.

Several border conflicts appear in explanatory notes (**Manasseh had the land of Tappuah, but Tappuah itself, on the boundary of Manasseh, belonged to the Ephraimites,** 17:8). Notes also point out that Manasseh claims the northern side of the Kanah Ravine (Wadi) and Ephraim, the southern side. Towns belonging to Ephraim also mingle with those in Manasseh. This information could be used as a legal document to settle disputes over cities and land ownership (R. S. Hess, "Asking Historical Questions of Joshua 13–19," in A. R. Millard, J. K. Hoffmeier, and D. W. Baker, *Faith, Tradition and History* [Winona Lake, Ind.: Eisenbrauns, 1994], p. 203).

The Manassite heritage document ends with a city list. Unlike previous city lists, the account mentions cities that the tribe did not control. Cities and their surrounding territory in the list remain dominated by the Canaanites: Beth Shan, Ibleam, Dor, Endor, Taanach, and Megiddo. The narrative explains the problem by saying **the Manassites were not able to occupy these towns** with the excuse that **the Canaanites were determined to live in that region** (17:12). This city list is an embarrassment to Manasseh. The tribe can take little consolation that when it became stronger it forced the Canaanites to labor for them. The fact remains that Manasseh did not drive out the peoples and thereby disobeyed instructions from Moses and Joshua (17:13). As a consequence, the Manassites also contribute to the chaos of the period of the judges.

Only in complaining do the tribes of Joseph find unity. The allotment narrative for these tribes ends in an unflattering story. Tribal leaders come to Joshua and complain about the insufficient size of their territory. They feel that **one allotment and one portion** is not enough for **an inheritance** for **a numerous people** whom the LORD **has blessed . . . abundantly** (17:14). The irony is not hard to miss. Joshua has given each tribe a sufficient portion and for Manasseh a portion on each side of the Jordan. Manasseh's portion is second only to Judah, and much of Judah's land is wilderness (17:15).

Joshua shows no sympathy for their whining but replies with strong irony. He suggests that if they are so many, they should use their strength and numbers to prepare land for cities and agriculture by clearing their heavily forested areas. They also could overcome the Perizzites and Raphaites who live in the forests (17:15). Unfortunately, the people have learned little from their failure to enter the land forty years earlier. They continue to want a convenient allotment that is easy to settle. Driving out enemies and clearing forests do not fit their plans or gifts.

Numerous parallels between the tribal complaining and behavior in Christian congregations come to mind. Christian congregations follow the tribes' example and complain about shortages but want convenient and easy solutions. The passage also says much about God. God has little sympathy with whining. God calls disciples to hard work and courage, not narcissism. Christians want God's blessings but will not sacrifice to achieve them.

Not satisfied, the tribes of Joseph complain again. Canaanite military forces block access to the plains. Again they say, **The hill country is not enough for us,** but this time they give the excuse that **the Canaanites who live in the plain have iron chariots.** So they are limited to the hill country because Canaanites **in Beth**

Shan and its settlements and those in the **Valley of Jezreel** have superior weapons (17:16).

Joshua responds that Canaanite technology is also not enough to warrant an additional allotment. Instead, he challenges them to overcome their technological disadvantage and to drive out the Canaanites with the iron chariots. Joshua believes these numerous and powerful tribes are capable of conquering the cities of Beth Shan at the eastern entrance to the Jezreel Valley as well as the rest of the cities of that plain. That would solve their shortages (17:17–18). As Joshua had defeated the forces of Hazor, burned the chariots, and hamstrung its horses, the large tribes were to possess the territory themselves. Unfortunately, the tribes do not believe themselves capable of defeating the chariots and so decide to wait until David and Solomon solve the problem of chariots with iron parts.

Additional Notes §26

16:10 / **They did not dislodge the Canaanites living in Gezer:** Ancient Gezer is located at Tell Jezer, a thirty-three-acre mound five miles south-southeast of Ramleh. It is 750 feet above sea level, on the final hill of the foothills of the central highlands. It rests at the important crossroads where the roads leading to Jerusalem and sites in the hills branch off from the Way of the Sea to approach the Valley of Aijalon. The town is mentioned in the Bible and in Egyptian and Assyrian texts.

The book of Joshua mentions that the king of Gezer joined in the southern coalition to fight the tribes. Joshua kills the king, but the tribal forces could not conquer the city (Josh. 10:33; 12:12; 16:10; Judg. 1:29). Canaanites controlled the city until Philistines occupied the site (2 Sam. 5:25). Finally, the Egyptian pharaoh captured it and gave it to Solomon at Solomon's marriage to his daughter (1 Kgs. 9:16). Solomon fortified the city along with other projects in Jerusalem, Hazor, and Megiddo (1 Kgs. 9:15–17).

Gezer reached its highest point during Middle Bronze Age II-III (ca. 1800–1500 B.C.E.). The three-way gate, large walls, and high place of ten large stones, some more than ten feet high, are evidences of the strength of the early city. Post-Philistine Gezer began a time of decline. Under Solomon, the post became only an unimportant administrative city. The site declined in importance after Shishak's raid in 924 B.C.E. (1 Kgs. 14:25; see W. Dever, "Gezer," *ABD* 2:998–1003).

17:3 / **Now Zelophehad ... had no sons but only daughters:** Makir, the firstborn son of Manasseh, receives the allotment for the tribe of Manasseh as represented by clan (lit. family) heads. A legal issue halts for a moment the distribution of land to the tribe of Manasseh. Zelophehad, a descendent of Manasseh, has no male heirs. Would the family, namely, his daughters, Mahlah, Noah, Hoglah, Milcah, and Tirzah (Num. 26:33), receive their father's inheritance?

To resolve the inheritance issue, the young women go to the tribal leaders, Eleazar the priest, and Joshua: **The LORD commanded Moses to give us an inheritance among our brothers** (Josh. 17:3–4). They quote a decision given to Moses by the Lord in Num. 27:1–11. The case sets a precedent that grants daughters the inheritance of a father who dies without a son. Two requirements qualify daughters for inheriting their father's land: the father must not disqualify his claim by joining in a rebellion, and the daughters must marry inside their father's tribe (Num. 36:1–11).

These daughters meet both conditions. They argue that their father had not committed treason with the sons of Korah. As well, Zelophehad's daughters married cousins on their father's side (Num. 36:11). The inheritance, therefore, went to the daughters and so remained in their father's clan/tribe to sustain the name of their father.

Two interesting comments can be made. The leaders had to be reminded that the daughters could inherit the claim of their father as had been the law since Moses. Unfortunately, men do not automatically support the rights of women when land is being divided—even legal precedents do not make men that sensitive. In addition, the women assert their own case. There is nothing wrong with women asking for what rightfully belongs to them; in fact, the Bible commends them. Neither should men deride such women by calling them "forward" or "aggressive." Instead, their persistence ensures that the memory and inheritance of their father would remain alive into the next generation. I would like to think that Christians today willingly would advocate for the rights of women more than men did in the time of Joshua.

17:12 / **Canaanites were determined to live in that region:** Significant cities remained in the hands of the Canaanites in the Jezreel Valley: Megiddo, Taanach, Ibleam, Endor, and Beth Shan. The fortresses dominated passes that served as entrances to this fertile plain. These cities made it impossible for the tribes to unify their territory (see map 33, Beitzel, *The Moody Atlas of Bible Lands*, p. 103).

18:1–10 / A narrative summary shifts the scene from Gilgal (Josh. 14:6) to a tribal **assembly** at Shiloh (Josh. 18:1), ten miles northeast of Bethel. The narrative mentions that the assembly set up the Tent of Meeting at that place. The Tent of Meeting at this time is more important than a permanent structure, for it is the symbol of the presence of God. Only later did the tribes house the ark of the covenant in a more permanent structure at Shiloh (1 Sam. 1–4). The Bible reports that Eli and his sons later ministered in a permanent shrine until the Philistines conquered Shiloh and captured the ark (1 Sam. 4:1–22).

By stating that the tribes assembled at Shiloh, the narrator ties the passage to Deuteronomy. The word **gathered** ("assembled," Hb. *kahal*) first appears here (Josh. 18:1) in the book. The assembly frequently is mentioned in Deuteronomy (Deut. 5:19; 9:10; 10:4; 18:16; 23:2, 3, 4, 9). The narrator gives no number of the representatives attending the assembly but rather says representatives of all the tribes attended. Again, the summary repeats the claim that the conquest is complete: **The country** (lit. land) **was brought under their control** (lit. subdued; 18:1). The narrative then focuses on allotments to the remaining seven tribes.

Despite the confident statement that Israel already controls the land, Joshua chides the people for waiting so long to possess the land God has given them (18:3). Control over an area is not the same as settlement. Therefore, he instructs three representatives from the seven tribes to survey the remaining territory. Representatives were to walk through the land, describe it, and divide it into seven portions. Joshua then would cast lots (lot of inheritance, 14:2) for the tribes and thereby assign each a surveyed territory. Joshua states that he will **cast lots . . . in the presence of** (lit. before) **the LORD our God** (18:6). The Tent of Meeting symbolizes God's presence, and the casting of lots reveals the will of the people's personal, covenanted God.

The narrative repeats information about the inheritances of Judah, the tribes of Joseph, the tribe of Levi, and the east bank tribes of Gad, Reuben, and the half-tribe of Manasseh. The Levites do not receive an allotment **because the priestly service of the LORD is their inheritance** (18:7). Priestly service is inheritance enough for a tribe of priests.

Next Joshua repeats his instructions to the tribal representatives. Then the men leave to survey the land and to prepare boundary descriptions. Finally, Joshua casts lots for them in Shiloh at the door of the Tent of Meeting and thereby allots land according to tribal divisions (18:8–10). This brief narrative sets the stage for describing the territorial boundaries of the seven tribes in Joshua 18–19.

Additional Note §27

18:1 / **The whole assembly of the Israelites gathered at Shiloh:** Shiloh was one of three key worship centers in premonarchic Israel. (The other two were Shechem and Gilgal.) The site was located between Bethel and Shechem in the Ephraimite hills. The book of Joshua makes Shiloh the first permanent home of the ark of the covenant. Little can be said about the worship center at Shiloh (cf. Judg. 21:18–23), but excavations indicate that Shiloh's cult had extensive architectural features (I. Finkelstein, "Excavations at Shiloh 1981–1984," *Tel Aviv* 12 [1985], pp. 169–70). Shiloh was destroyed in the mid-eleventh century B.C.E., presumably by the Philistines. However, the site seems to have been occupied throughout the Iron Age and into the exile. It remained an important religious center. Ahijah, a Shilonite prophet from the late tenth century, encourages Jeroboam's rebellion against the house of Solomon (1 Kgs. 11:26–40; 14).

§28 Territory of Benjamin, Simeon, Zebulon, Issachar, Asher, Naphtali, and Dan (Josh. 18:11–19:48)

18:11–28 / The territory of Benjamin is described as a boundary list and a list of cities. (For more information see map 31, Beitzel, *The Moody Bible Atlas of Bible Lands*, p. 100.) Its northern boundary coincides with that of Ephraim and its southern one with that of Judah. On the east is the Jordan River, and on the west its boundary stops in the hills overlooking the Aijalon Valley. Boundary lists of northern tribes follow the style of abbreviated summaries, not repeating boundaries that are held in common with another tribe (Y. Aharoni, *The Land of the Bible: A Historical Geography* [rev. ed.; trans. A. F. Rainey; Philadelphia: Westminster, 1967], p. 250). With the exception of the detailed Benjamin-Judah border around Jerusalem, they offer little detail about the tribal territory. Surprisingly, the Benjamin boundary description makes the point that Jerusalem fits within Benjamin, not Judah.

19:1–9 / The tribe of Simeon received an allotment within the territory of Judah. Of the seventeen cities assigned to Simeon, fifteen are also mentioned as cities in Judah. Simeon is located primarily in southwest Judah, the western Negev, between Beersheba and the Mediterranean Sea. Simeon remained a district or tribal entity in Judah until the time of King Hezekiah (728–696 B.C.E.; 1 Chron. 4:41–42).

19:10–16 / Zebulun borders other tribes in Galilee; Issachar, Naphtali, and Asher border it on the southeast, northeast, and northwest. On the south its border runs from Sarid westward to Babbesheth and then eastward from Sarid to Baberath, Japhia, and Gath Helpher. The northern border touches Rimmon, passing through the modern Bet Netofa Valley to Hannathon. The western border runs southwest and south through the Valley of Iphta El (Wadi el-Mahik) to Kishon (C. G. Rasmussen, *Zondervan*

NIV Atlas of the Bible [Grand Rapids: Zondervan, 1989], pp. 98–99). Fourteen cities are listed in Zebulun. The tribal allotment is located near several major trade routes that ran through the Jezreel Valley.

19:17–23 / The towns given to Issachar are located in the valleys and basalt heights of eastern Lower Galilee. They are located near major international highways that run close to southern and western tribal borders. Major cities such as Beth Shan and Anaharath remain under control of non-Israelites until the period of David and Solomon.

19:24–31 / The tribe of Asher land is located in the northwestern corner of Israel. South and east of the tribe are Manasseh, Zebulun, and Naphtali, and on the north is Phoenicia. Its abbreviated boundary list is combined with a city list. Its territory stretches from Mount Carmel in the south to the Litani River on the north, including the coastal plain and western hills of Upper and Lower Galilee.

19:32–39 / The borders of Naphtali meet Issachar in the south and in the west Zebulun and Asher. There is no northern border mentioned, but probably it goes as far north as Israelites settled. Its eastern borders go to the Jordan River and the Sea of Galilee. The mention of Judah (Josh. 19:34) is problematic. The boundary list description includes a city list.

19:40–48 / Dan at first inherits western territory later incorporated into the tribal inheritance of Benjamin, Judah, and Ephraim. Eventually the tribe of Dan moves north to the upper Jordan valley under pressure from the Philistines (Judg. 18). They conquered the city of Leshem (Laish; Josh. 19:47; Judg. 18:2–10, 27–29), renamed it Dan, and settled it as their new inheritance.

Territorial descriptions in these chapters present tribal inheritances as recorded by at least the time of the book of Judges, which lists foreign populations living in tribal territories whom tribes must subjugate or in whose midst tribes must live. Judges 1:27–36 mentions unconquered populations in Canaan. By contrast, Joshua presents an ideal picture of tribal inheritances, including land not yet conquered. The lists in Joshua divide the land of Canaan and eliminate its gaps. Boundaries of the tribes coincide with those of Canaan.

The lists in Joshua do not include topographical notes about springs, hills, and streams, as earlier or local lists might have done.

Instead they give generalized descriptions of boundaries and settlements. For example, lists do not tell where a boundary passes in the vicinity of a city. As well, Joshua describes the allotments of Issachar, Dan, and Simeon only by city lists. These northern tribal borders may never have been established clearly. At best, Joshua defines their boundaries by those of neighboring tribes.

Primarily the lists tell readers God has assigned territory to the tribes. The Lord and Joshua have done their work. Now the responsibility for possessing the land rests on individual tribes. Judah, Manasseh, and Ephraim cannot possess the entire land of Canaan.

§29 *Territory for the House of Joshua (Josh. 19:49–51)*

19:49–51 / After Joshua and Eleazer the priest finish dividing the land among the people, the tribes grant Joshua an inheritance in the hill country of Ephraim, the center of the country. The divine designation of this land for Joshua also comes by casting lots, the Urim and Thummim. Joshua claims the land and builds up the city of Timnath Serah, the place of his burial (24:30).

Verse 51 summarizes the completion of the division of the tribal lands. The land belongs to the tribes and families that will become the nation of Israel, not to feudal lords. God's gift of the land is thorough, and the passage makes it clear that God owns the land. God freely offers it to the faithful and can take it away from those who abuse its privileges. As Christians know, the meek do inherit the earth (Matt. 5:5).

§30 *Cities of Refuge (Josh. 20:1–9)*

20:1–9 / God reminds Joshua of some unfinished business in the division of the land. God commands in Numbers that cities be set aside to protect those who face the threat of blood revenge (Num. 35:8–34), and Moses repeats that command in Deuteronomy (Deut. 19:1–13). Joshua 20 states that cities need to be set aside as places of "refuge," "admittance," or "inclusion" (the term does not appear in Deut. 19). The passage in Joshua lists three cities west of the Jordan from north to south (v. 7) and three cities east of the Jordan south to north (v. 8). The verses designate the cities as geographical regional centers of asylum. The lists also mention cities east of the Jordan by tribe. The cities of refuge are Kedesh, Shechem, and Hebron in Canaan, and Bezer, Ramoth-Gilead, and Golan in Transjordan. These are designated as Levitical or priestly cities in Joshua 21. As religious centers they may provide asylum for those running for their lives.

The six cities offer asylum to those who cause the death of another without intending to, killings that today would be called "manslaughter" as contrasted to homicide, or deliberate, premeditated killing. Those who murder deliberately and defiantly (with a high hand) cannot find protection here (Num. 35:16–21; Deut. 19:11–13). Persons who kill someone are to come to the gate of a city of refuge and wait there until the elders determine their status and either accept or reject the killer. The elders would offer asylum to persons who unintentionally cause the death of another until that person could be judged properly with a trial. In modern terminology, the cities of refuge prevent the lynching of one deserving legal protection.

Setting aside cities of refuge teaches an important lesson about God. The God of Israel believes in the right of all to a fair trial and has created places of asylum to protect the accused from rash anger or revenge. God believes in due process and protects even potential criminals from retribution. God's protection stretches to all but the most flagrant, violent criminals. Vigilante revenge is no substitute for justice by due process.

Additional Note §30

20:3 /   Old Greek and Hebrew manuscript variants in this passage point out some interesting differences between two ancient texts. For example, the word "inadvertently" (v. 3) does not appear in the Old Greek (OG) version. The authorized Hebrew text (MT), more than the OG version, elaborates on who is eligible for protection in a city of refuge. The shorter OG version does not contain vv. 4, 5, and 6(bc). The OG combines fragments from two verses as a sentence: "and the killer shall not be put to death (not in the MT) until he can stand before the community for judgment" (Josh. 20:3c, 6a; Nelson, *Joshua,* pp. 227–30). In this case, the shorter OG version represents an unrevised text rather than the Hebrew one. Vv. 7 and 8 in the OG attribute the selection of the cities to Joshua alone as outlined in Num. 35:13–14. The OG sentences use the third-person masculine singular pronoun. The revised verses (MT) remind the reader that Moses also established the cities by using the masculine plural pronoun (Deut. 4:41–43; 19:1–7).

§31 Levitical Cities (Josh. 21:1–40)

21:1–40 / Finally, the tribes assume responsibility for supporting the religious leaders of Israel. At Shiloh the heads of the families of Levites request cities to live in and land for their cattle. The Levites possess no land of their own (13:14 [33 MT]; 18:7; Deut. 10:8–9). The descendents of Aaaron receive nine cities in Judah/Simeon (vv. 13–16) and four from Benjamin (vv. 17–18). Korathite descendents get four cities from both Ephraim and Dan and two from the half-tribe of Manasseh (vv. 20–26). Descendents of Gershon are given two cities from the half-tribe of Manasseh, four from both Issachar and Asher, and three from Naphtali, for a total of thirteen cities (vv. 27–33). Descendents of Merari receive four cities from each of the tribes of Zebulun, Reuben, and Gad (vv. 34–40). Together the tribes provide forty-eight cities with pasturelands for the clans of Levi.

The passage asserts the priority of the Aaronic priesthood and reports the completion of orders given in Numbers 35:2–8. The tribes are listed geographically from the south to the central tribes to the north and then to the east. The list appears also in 1 Chronicles 6. The lesson of the granting of Levitical cities points out that God provides for religious leaders and does so through the generosity of the people of God.

§32 Summary: Rest in the Land (Josh. 21:41–45)

21:41–45 / Distribution of the land thereby completes God's gift of the land to the tribes. A summary reports that God has fulfilled all the divine promises to Israel's ancestors. The people now possess the land and live in it. Rest and victory over their enemies are realities of God's gift. With the **rest,** war would be a thing of the past. Now the people can focus on making a living and putting down roots. God makes good on promises sworn to obedient people. The statement closing this part of the book seems idealistic when it is compared to statements that land remains unconquered. Yet God's rest comes by facing challenges. Christians as well overcome obstacles to enjoy God's rest. Faithful believers can rely on the promises and power of God, for in those promises believers find rest.

§33 An Altar Crisis on the Eastern Side of the Jordan River (Josh. 22:1–34)

Joshua closes with three chapters that form an addendum pointing out challenges for the next generation. These chapters include speeches that address concerns of Deuteronomy and use Deuteronomic language. Crises in these passages point toward the book of Judges and the rest of the so-called Deuteronomic History (Samuel and Kings). The closing chapters of Joshua parallel the final chapters of Deuteronomy with its farewell speech of Moses and story of his burial.

The final chapters address questions mentioned earlier in the book and also ask the questions for consideration of future generations. God has given land to tribes through battle and inheritance; can the tribes keep the land? Will future generations sustain their unity and faithfulness to God? Will the tribes divided by a river lose their unity of worship and fracture in suspicion and mistrust? Will people sharing a land with worshipers of idols slide into idolatry? Will strong leaders replace the obedient and courageous leadership of Joshua and his generation? Will the tribes continue their covenant relationship with their God? The chapters address the questions as ever-present challenges to worship and faith. Modern believers also will face the issues of Joshua 22–24. Disunity and unfaithfulness to God remain constant threats to the people of God.

22:1–8 / Joshua 22 reports Joshua's speech at Shiloh. He commends the east bank tribes for their support of the battles to take over the land of Canaan. In helping the western tribes receive their inheritance, they have been faithful to promises made to Moses and their leader, Joshua (22:2, 3, as in 1:13, 15, 18). Now the western tribes have **rest** from extensive warfare. Joshua then gives permission to the eastern tribes to return with booty to their inherited land and to share the spoils of battle with their families (22:4, 8).

The chapter reports the event from the geographical view-point of the western tribes. The narrator talks about the west bank as the land of Canaan (22:9–11), the area belonging to the children of Israel. Joshua sends the eastern tribes to **the other side of the Jordan** (20:4, 7; Transjordan) for their inheritance. Joshua reminds the eastern tribes, especially Reubenites and Gadites, that their support for the western tribes has earned them a position in the people of God. Joshua also gives them permission to keep their booty. This shift away from Deuteronomy (22:8) points out that the rules for holy warfare remain flexible and dependent on cir-cumstances. The faithfulness of the eastern tribes to the earlier commands of Moses and Joshua becomes the setting for dealing with future deviations from covenant requirements.

Verses 1–5 report Joshua's speech to the eastern tribes. This passage parallels covenant requirements given to the western tribes in Joshua 23 and 24. Joshua's warning reflects the language of Deuteronomy 30:20. He observes that the tribes have done everything that **Moses the servant of the LORD commanded** (also 1:13) and **have obeyed me in everything I commanded** (22:2; 1:18). Verse 5 reports Joshua's challenge to the Gadite and Reu-benite tribes and the message of Deuteronomy 22:5 and 6:5. The key phrases remind the people to **be very careful to keep the com-mandment and the law** given by **Moses the servant of the LORD.** They are **to love the LORD** their **God, to walk in all his ways, to obey his commands, to hold fast to him and to serve him with all** their **heart and . . . soul.**

Every generation of believers needs to hear the message of the covenant with the eastern tribes (v. 5). The essence of follow-ing God is summed up in keeping completely covenant responsi-bilities. That consists of loving the Lord God, living as God would live, obediently following his standards, cementing oneself to him, and serving him with single-minded devotion. Christians need to follow Jesus with the same dedication.

Verses 4, 6, and 7 contain some duplication. Joshua sends the eastern tribes to their tents three times and blesses them twice. The repetition strengthens Joshua's statement that the eastern tribes have earned the right to leave Shiloh and go home. Joshua gave to the half-tribe of Manasseh land in Canaan to sweeten its homecoming. Verse 8 reminds the tribes they also can take spoils of war and divide their booty with other members in the east. Finally the eastern tribes leave for home. But before they cross the

river, they leave on the western side of the Jordan a large altar.
That altar sparks anger, misunderstanding, and threats of war.

22:9–21 / Once again the eastern tribes threaten the unity
of the tribes. Oblivious to the implications such an altar would
present to the western tribes, they naïvely build a large, striking
altar on the Canaan side of the Jordan. The western tribes interpret that altar as one providing eastern competition for Shiloh
and gather for war. In their minds the altar violates the command
for one center for worship (Deut. 12:5).

The ten tribes send Phinehas, son of Eleazer the priest, with
ten chiefs of the western tribes, to negotiate a peaceful settlement
to what borders on a religious war. Numbers pictures Phinehas as
one who deals well with deviance in worship when he stops Israel's acts at Baal Peor in Transjordan (Num. 25:6–18). This time
the eastern tribes will test the priest. His negotiating skills provide
readers valuable lessons.

The western delegation confronts the eastern leaders with a
list of charges. They angrily attack the integrity of the eastern
tribes. They accuse them: **How could you break faith** [lit. What
unfaithfulness have you done against the God of Israel?] **with the
God of Israel like this? How could you turn away from the LORD
and build yourselves an altar in rebellion against him now?**
(22:16). They equate the building of the altar with the people's immorality and idolatry at Peor and Achan's violation of the ban at
Jericho. They are afraid that this altar will anger God, who will
then punish everyone. They seem concerned for their own preservation as much as that the altar violates the command that Israel
worship only in one place. Western leaders blame and shame the
eastern tribes.

22:22–25 / Eastern leaders respond graciously and in humility: **The Mighty One, God, the LORD! He knows! And let Israel
know! If this has been in rebellion or disobedience to the LORD,
do not spare us this day. If we have built our own altar to turn
away from the LORD and to offer burnt offerings and grain offerings, or to sacrifice fellowship offerings on it, may the LORD
himself call us to account** (22:22–23). The eastern leaders seem
shocked, sputtering out one divine name after the other. They willingly offer to take whatever punishment they deserve from God.
They deny, however, that they intended to rebel against God. Instead, they say that they feared future western tribes might say to
eastern descendants: **"The LORD has made the Jordan a boundary**

between us and you—you Reubenites and Gadites! You have no
share in the LORD." So your descendants might cause ours to
stop fearing the LORD (22:24–25).

22:26–31 / In this way the eastern tribes defend themselves against charges of building an alternative altar for sacrifices.
They deny building the altar in rebellion against God: **That is why
we said, "Let us get ready and build an altar—but not for burnt offerings or sacrifices." On the contrary, it is to be a witness between
us and you and the generations that follow, that we will worship
the LORD at his sanctuary with our burnt offerings, sacrifices and
fellowship offerings** (22:26–27). Some key words underline their
purpose and mission for building the altar: "No share in the LORD,"
"replica," and "witness." First, the eastern tribes say they fear the
tribes of Canaan will one day shut them out of the worship center in
the west and a share in the Lord. Second, the eastern tribes think that
building a replica of the western altar will keep their descendants
true to the God of Israel as they have a replica visible to the east.
Third, a replica will remind the western tribes that those east of the
Jordan also desire a share in God. The altar will witness to the unity
of the tribes at their east-west border. In the Bible altars are common
witnesses. A memorial is erected to keep two enemies apart in the
Jacob narratives (Gen. 31:48–52). In their defense, the eastern tribes
clarify what may have been conflicting motives and turn the building of an altar from an act of rebellion into a witness of religious unity
and a source of revival.

Although the eastern tribes are naïve to believe that the western tribes will not see the altar as a violation of the command to worship in one center, Phinehas shows great wisdom in listening to the
explanation of the eastern tribes. He does not argue the legitimacy of
their viewpoint. Instead he affirms the sincerity of the eastern tribes
and says, **Today we know that the LORD is with us, because you
have not acted unfaithfully toward the LORD in this matter. Now
you have rescued the Israelites from the LORD's hand** (22:31). His
gracious statement confirms that the eastern tribes do indeed have a
share in the Lord. He praises them for their attitude of contrition
rather than rebellion. Calling the eastern tribes to accountability no
doubt helps them focus better on their motives for building the altar.

22:32–34 / So the delegation takes home a positive report that praises God and silences talk of war. Cooler heads avert
war by listening to and affirming the other's good intentions.
Phinehas remains an example of skillful mediation and the impor-

tance of listening. Tempers can cause irreparable damage unless someone is willing to listen and affirm good intentions where they exist. The Gadites and Reubenites then name the altar **A Witness Between Us that the LORD is God** (22:34). What nearly brought about war becomes a statement of faith for eastern and western tribes: "The LORD is God"!

23:1–5 / Saying goodbye is difficult for everyone, leaders and followers. In Joshua 22 the time arrives for final farewells. The narrator does not tell readers when Joshua gave his farewell, but a long time had passed. Readers can know only that Israel had rest from their enemies and Joshua was **well advanced in years** (lit. days). Joshua summons the local leadership of the tribes—elders, leaders, judges, and officials—to hear his final words. He begins by calling them to reflect on what they had seen the Lord God do for them.

Joshua delivers this speech in first-person autobiographical style. He speaks of his audience of western tribal leaders as **you** (second person plural). The speech points out the value of life review for both elders and the generation left behind.

Joshua gently reminds his listeners that **it was the LORD your God who fought for you. Remember how I have allotted as an inheritance for your tribes all the land of the nations that remain—the nations I conquered—between the Jordan and the Great Sea in the west.** They do not need to fear challenges of the future, for **the LORD your God himself will drive them out of your way. He will push them out before you, and you will take possession their land, as the LORD your God promised you** (23:3–5). God and Joshua earlier helped the tribes through battles and the dividing of the land. Therefore they owe an enormous debt of gratitude to God and Joshua. God's support will continue long after Joshua has died.

23:6–11 / God's gracious deeds build the confidence of the people for their future challenges. Joshua returns to the words of Joshua 1, spoken before the tribes began to take the west bank of the Jordan. He commands them to **be very strong; be careful to obey all that is written in the Book of the Law of Moses, without turning aside to the right or to the left.** He tells them to **not associate with these nations that remain among you;** and to **not invoke the**

names of their gods or swear by them, not to **serve them or bow down to them** (23:6–7). The essence of Joshua's advice to the next generation needs to be heeded by every generation. He stresses that they are to "be very strong," obey without turning aside, not worship other gods, and **hold fast** [cement] **to the LORD your God.** Believers will turn away from competitors of their God and at the same time bind themselves completely to their God. True strength includes obedience to God without wavering before temptations. Separation from temptation is the first step toward faithfulness.

Joshua's speech challenges the people to live up to the teachings of Deuteronomy. He addresses them saying, **Because the LORD ... God fights for you** to make you a productive warrior, you need to make every effort (lit. watch exceedingly) **to love the LORD your God** (23:9–11). An interesting phrase that appears in this verse is the phrase "until this day." This refers to how during the conflict the tribes cemented themselves to God and how no enemy was able to stand against the tribal warriors because God was fighting for the people. In this context, the phrase reflects the time from when the tribes entered the land up to when Joshua gave his farewell address. The phrase in this setting does not refer to a later time when the material was edited or written, as other uses of the phrase might suggest. The reported speech suggests that the tribes should love God in response to God's saving power during the battles and continue a close relationship with God that began under the pressure of taking the land. It addresses human nature, which tends to lose its need to depend on God when a crisis subsides. The people should put extra effort into loving God to counter apathy that sets in when an emergency ends.

23:12–16 / The reported speech of Joshua also warns the tribes about intermingling with and marrying the people in the land. They will become **snares ... traps ... whips on your backs and thorns in your eyes, until you perish from this good land, which the LORD your God has given you** (23:12–13). Joshua underlines the threat of breaking the covenant and serving other gods in his final words. Concern about worshiping alien gods and mixing with people in the land reflects warnings from Deuteronomy. Violation of these two commands will bring about loss of the land God has given the tribes and nullify the work of Joshua.

Joshua concludes the message by reminding the people he is **about to go the way of all the earth.** He warns that God will punish unfaithfulness with as much thoroughness as God has kept all the promises he gave to the tribes. God's nature is to keep promises completely for the obedient and to eliminate the promised good land from those who are disobedient. With this warning clearly stated by Joshua, the tribal representatives are ready to determine their future by choosing whom they will serve (Josh. 24). Joshua, the competent leader, fulfills his responsibility of warning and directing his people before his death. The subsequent chapter places responsibility for the future on the next generation. No leader can carry a people indefinitely. The way of the earth ends the earthly ministry.

§35 Covenant Renewal Ceremony at Shechem (Josh. 24:1–28)

24:1–13 / Joshua assembles representatives of the western tribes at Shechem. The chapter parallels the farewell address in Joshua 23. The farewell address anticipates Joshua's death, and Joshua 24 describes it. This chapter gives no indication of its compositional history, and scholars disagree on its origin or use in the worship of Israel. The ceremony may reflect an early covenant renewal liturgy at Shechem (see Deut. 11:29–32; 27:1–26; reported in Josh. 8:30–35). Joshua's reported message in Joshua 22:1–6 summarizes a similar covenant ceremony for the eastern tribes, perhaps at Shiloh.

Joshua 24 includes a report of a covenant renewal ceremony that is introduced by a narrative call to assemble (24:1) and concludes with a narrative about witnesses to the agreement (24:25–28). Finally, the chapter (book) ends with three grave narratives (24:29–33). The introduction contains no indication of the time of the ceremony and states only that Joshua gathered all the tribes to Shechem: elders, tribal heads, judges, and officers. They gather to present themselves before God as one would come before a king. All of those present hear Joshua review God's mighty deeds for the tribes, challenge them to put away alien gods, and urge them to serve the Lord their God without reservation. Joshua places the alternatives plainly before them and calls them to choose where they will place their loyalty. Joshua 24 challenges them to serve the Lord (Yahweh) exclusively.

Joshua reviews the history of God's mighty acts as a messenger reporting the words of God in the first person (24:2–13). A prophetic messenger formula, **This is what the LORD, the God of Israel, says,** puts this history into God's words about the past. The review places the early ancestors of Israel in a setting of idolatry. From this God brings them to the land of Canaan until they migrate to Egypt. The Lord overpowers the forces of Egypt and brings out the people to the land of the Amorites. Here Balak and

Balaam also are no match for the power of the God of the tribes. From the land of the Amorites, God gives the people of Canaan into the hands of the tribes. A summary of the battles to take the land mentions crossing the Jordan and coming to Jericho. **The citizens of Jericho fought against you, as did also the Amorites, Perizzites, Canaanites, Hittites, Girgashites, Hivites and Jebusites** (24:11). This review of the history of the tribes and their ancestors reminds the tribes that God has given them their success and possessions. They need to be grateful for such grace.

24:14–24 / The reported speech switches from the first-person message of God to an indirect warning from Joshua (24:14–15). The challenge begins with a call to **fear** and **serve** the Lord **with all faithfulness.** Both "fear" and "serve" describe faithful worship. Joshua continues to call the people to put aside the gods of their ancestors to serve the Lord. The idolatry of the past continues into the present. Canaan once again places before the tribes the temptations of the past. Now is the time to choose personally, **this day,** the God of the present. Each generation must make this choice. Commitment to the living God is always one generation away from dying out.

In response to this warning, the people begin to dialogue with Joshua. Key verses of commitment appear at the end of each speech. Joshua says, **As for me and my household, we will serve the LORD** (24:15). The people respond to Joshua out of gratitude for God's blessings: **We too will serve the LORD, because he is our God** (24:18). Joshua warns them: **You are not able to serve the LORD** (24:19). God has high standards of faithfulness because the Lord is a **holy God, jealous** [uncompromising], **will not forgive** [repeatedly] **your rebellion and your sins.** Joshua also reminds the people that God punishes with the same intensity that God does good. Serving God is dangerous unless the people are determined to do good as God does. The people remain determined and reply, **No! We will serve the LORD** (24:21). The dialogue effectively brings the level of commitment needed to establish a relationship with God.

Finally Joshua says that the people are witnesses to this commitment by what they have said. The people gladly accept that they are witnesses of their oath of service. Joshua then challenges them to demonstrate that they mean what they say by throwing away their idols and yielding their **hearts** [wills] **to the LORD.** Their testimony demands negative and positive acts of devotion to the God of Israel. So the people say again to Joshua, **We**

will serve the LORD our God and obey him (24:24). Challenging the ability of the people to do what they say they will do is a marvelous method of getting true commitment from them. In the end, the people commit themselves to worship and obey their God. That is the ultimate witness to a vow.

24:25–28 / A epilogue concludes the covenant making. A narrative reports that Joshua cut a covenant with the people, writing down their responsibilities to God in decrees and laws. He did three things to formalize the agreement. He wrote the covenant in the Book of the Law of God and set up a large stone under a sacred oak tree, near the holy place of the Lord. Then he turned to the people and declared, **See! . . . This stone will be a witness against us. It has heard all the words the LORD has said to us. It will be a witness against you if you are untrue to your God** (24:27). An impartial witness now stands to remind all of their agreement with God. A book containing the responsibilities of the covenant can be read at any time to testify against violations of this agreement. People may rationalize their behavior, but these witnesses cannot be changed. They will verify whether the people live up to their commitments or not and thereby dispense either blessings or curses, rewards or punishment.

§36 Burial in the Promised Land
(Josh. 24:29–33)

24:29–33 / The book of Joshua ends with three grave traditions that set the context for the book of Judges. Joshua and Eleazer die. The religious leaders of the tribes will govern no more. A new generation must arise to challenge the people to commitment. The bones of Joseph are buried in Shechem in the burial cave of Jacob, as Joseph had requested (Gen. 50:24). Truly the land belongs to the tribes. Their ancestors now rest in Canaan.

The narrator pays a high tribute to Joshua. For the first time, Joshua is called **the servant of the LORD** (24:29). That is more important than his age, 110 years. Joshua 1:1 refers to Joshua as Moses' aide (assistant), but now he is a servant of the Lord in his own right. The death narrative recognizes that Joshua lived and died as a servant of the Lord after the model of Moses.

Verse 31 points toward Judges 2:6. The narrator mentions that the tribes served the Lord during the lifetime of Joshua and the lifespan of the elderly who had experienced the mighty acts of God for Israel. Unfortunately, the narrator in Judges 2:10–23 tells the rest of the story. The next generation did evil, not good; disobeyed rather than obeyed the covenant. Judges tells of the cycles of God's anger, punishment, and temporary salvation for the next generation. It records violations of the covenant and disasters that follow.

§37 Excursus: Divergences between the Old Greek Text and the Masoretic Text (Josh. 24:29–33)

24:29–33 / Three significant differences exist between the Old Greek text and the MT in verses 29–33. The OG is the longer text and is closely associated with Judges 2:6–10, 13; 3:7, 12, 14. The issues for distinguishing the documents are that OG reverses the order of verses 29–31 in agreement with Judges 2:6–10; Joshua is buried with flint circumcism knives in the OG (see Josh. 5:2–3 for reference to flint knives); and Eleazar is introduced by the phrase **after these things**, repeated from Joshua 24:29. The mention of Phinehas, son of Eleazar, allows the OG to insert events about Phinehas and the ark from Judges 20:27–28. Finally, Eglon appears in the LXX text as in Judges 3:12, 14.

Clearly the MT is the earlier form of the text. The OG connects Joshua even more closely to Judges by including readings out of Judges. However, the entire text indicates that MT and OG have incorporated a number of changes from the earliest recoverable text (for additional reading on differences between OG and MT, see Nelson, *Joshua,* pp. 22–24, 280–83).

Judges

Cheryl A. Brown

Introduction: Judges

The book of Judges is not about judges, at least not in the way we commonly understand the English term.[1] Only one figure, Deborah (4:4–5), serves in a legal capacity as judge. The Hebrew word *spt* has a broader semantic range than does the English term "judge." The Hebrew can also mean "leader" or "deliverer," for it appears together with such verbs as "saved" or delivered (2:16, 18; 3:9–10). The type of leadership that judges provided was unique in the ancient Near East.[2] They were charismatic figures, divinely raised up in times of crisis from outside the traditional power circles to meet a specific threat, namely, enemy oppression. They worked alone, in the sense that they alone were gifted by God (3:10; 6:34; 11:29; 14:6) to bring deliverance. They did not transfer leadership to their children; it was a nondynastic leadership. The only exception to this is Abimelech (chs. 9–10), but his example is the exception that proves the rule, because his leadership role was illegitimate in every way.

Judges as an Old Testament Book

Before we turn to details about the book itself, we must first briefly address a fundamental issue for Christians who read Judges or any book of the OT—sometimes called the Hebrew Bible, the First Testament, or the Jewish Scriptures. Our struggle to know what to call it reflects a basic ambivalence about these texts. These are Christian Scriptures, and at the same time they are not; for they chronologically and theologically preceded the fuller and final, as Christians view it, revelation in the NT. Added to this basic theological dilemma is the fact that the OT, especially books such as Judges, contains material that flies in the face of everything we identify as biblical morality. We do not know what to do with the rape, murder, genocide, sexual immorality, child sacrifice, lying, idolatry, and stealing. While "all Scripture is God-breathed [inspired] and is useful for teaching, rebuking, correcting and training in righteousness" (2 Tim. 3:16), some parts of Judges do not

readily appear "useful." A significant body of Christian interpreters have solved the problem by allegorizing it, reading a message
into the text rather than out of it, in essence, making it say whatever they wanted, often with the help of ingenious hermeneutical
gymnastics. Others have ignored the problematic or embarrassing passages.[3] But these are no solutions for those who take the
whole of Scripture seriously.[4]

A useful paradigm suggested by G. E. Ladd[5] takes into account the unique character of the Bible, which is both revelatory
and historical. The Scriptures are revelatory in that they are God-
breathed, and from this perspective the message they communicate is timeless and supracultural. But God spoke through and to
human beings within history (i.e., within a particular chronological, linguistic, sociological, and religious context), so the Scriptures are likewise encased within a specific time and culture.
Hence, in interpreting Scripture we must take both aspects into
account. We cannot ignore the historical context and focus entirely on the revelatory (theological), for Scripture is firmly rooted
in time and place. At the same time we cannot ignore the revelatory aspect and focus entirely on the historical. Much of what is
called biblical interpretation comes down almost exclusively on
either side and fails to integrate the two.

How does this paradigm help us interpret Judges? It has
two important implications. First, we must use every means possible to understand the book's original context, for as we discover
what the text meant to its first readers or hearers, we are better
able to understand its meaning for us. Granted, it is often a challenge to successfully discern what a text originally meant, especially since most of these texts had a long, complicated history of
formation. But many tools are now available, and we are learning
increasingly more as new data come to light. Second, having considered the historical aspects of the text, we must look beyond the
original context to the underlying theological, anthropological,
and/or ethical principles communicated by the text (i.e., that
which has been and remains true at all times and in all places).
These fundamental principles are authoritative for Christians reading Scripture any place in the world, at any time.

Judges and Canon

The book of Judges does not stand alone but is a part of a
greater whole. Canonically it is part of a collection of books com-

monly known as the Deuteronomic History,[6] which encompasses Joshua–2 Kings minus Ruth. In most Christian Bibles, this collection is found together with Ruth in a section designated as Historical Books, which reflects the traditional Christian understanding that the texts are essentially historical in genre. Jewish tradition, however, calls the same grouping the Former Prophets and links them with the Latter Prophets, Isaiah–Malachi (minus Daniel) into one canonical unit called the Prophets. Hence, Jewish tradition has understood these books to be essentially prophetic in character and purpose, while not denying their essential historicity. As prophetic history their intended purpose was to interpret events in light of God's revelation, particularly embodied in the Torah (Pentateuch), to exhort God's people to keep their covenant commitments to God, to chastise them when they failed, and to encourage them when they needed a word of hope. In other words, it was preached history!

The model for this genre was the book of Deuteronomy, which stands at the end of the first Jewish canonical unit, the Torah.[7] Its name means "second law" (Deut. 17:18), and according to the text it was essentially Moses' final three addresses to the Israelites before his death. Its character is homiletical, accenting ethical behavior, calling Israel to love (obey) the Lord in very specific ways, as well as spelling out consequences for those who refuse. It, more than any other book, emphasizes covenant theology, such as Israel's election, God's gracious commitment to Israel, purity of worship, torah obedience/blessing and disobedience/cursing, and the promise of the land. The vocabulary of Deuteronomy is covenant vocabulary: torah, love, forsaking, chosen, land, remember, forget, faithfulness, unfaithfulness, obedience, witness, to name a few.[8]

Before leaving the subject of canon, we must look at one other aspect of the Torah that brings to bear on interpretation of the Deuteronomic History, including Judges. The Deuteronomic History tells a story that began not at the beginning of Joshua but at the beginning of all things. To find that story we must trace through the Torah, all the way back to Genesis, where Scripture first reveals the bigger picture of God's plan for creation and humankind's role within creation.

According to Genesis 1:26–27, God created humankind in his image. What does it mean to be in God's image? M. Guinan offers an insightful interpretation of this pregnant phrase:[9]

To be an image is to reflect another who comes first, another with whom we are tightly bound in relationship. This means we are not number one, but number two. This involves on our part a humble recognition of creaturehood and of limitation; a recognition that we and all the relations to others and to the material world which make up our lives exist only as a gift. (pp. 24–25)

The two commands given to humankind as God's image were to "be fruitful and increase in number" [NIV] and to "have dominion over the . . . earth" [RSV] (Gen. 1:28), both of which mirror God's activity. Guinan elucidates what it means to have dominion:

In creation, we [see] God subduing the dark, watery chaos, bringing an ordered habitable universe out of the formlessness and void. In this way God exercises dominion. . . . To have dominion is a royal activity, which involves maintaining an orderly realm in which peoples and nature can live in harmony and right relationships (26), summarized in the twin concepts of *shalom* (peace) and *sedaqa* (justice), which point to integrity, wholeness and harmony and are the opposite of chaos. . . . To share dominion, then, implies . . . working to build and maintain a universe marked by right relations and peaceful order. (p. 26)

Humankind has failed miserably to live out its imagehood but repeatedly and willfully has chosen to usurp God's authority, resulting in a breakdown of *shalom* and a return to chaos. But God has continually sought to find a way to restore *shalom* and *sedaqa* to the world. He first worked through various people, then through a man and woman, Abraham and Sarah (Gen. 12:2–3). These became the progenitors of a people, Israel, through whom God committed to work to bring *shalom* and *sedaqa* to the creation. He rescued them from slavery and made a covenant with them at Mount Sinai, laying down the ground rules by which they could be in relationship with him and serve as his instruments to restore order and harmony—in a word, *shalom*.

That was the plan. But Israel often failed in living out its imagehood, preferring to be god rather than to reflect God. At other times they submitted to God, and *shalom* followed. This dynamic was perhaps most obvious in the period of the judges, which was characterized by alternating *shalom* and chaos, with decreasing *shalom* and increasing chaos as the story moved from beginning to end. The path of our own journey through Judges will be much more clearly marked if we keep in mind this bigger picture of what God was doing in Israel, through Israel, and at times in spite of Israel.[10]

The Composition of Judges

There is wide agreement that Judges is a composite work that arrived at its present form through a lengthy, complex process. Likewise there is general consensus about the process by which the book took shape. According to this view, the individual judges' stories were originally oral and circulated orally for some time before being transferred to written form.[11] They continued to circulate as independent units for quite some time, most likely within the tribal groups that were featured in the stories. Next these were joined together into larger units, such as the Samson stories (the Samson cycle) and the Jephthah stories (the Jephthah cycle). Possibly they were all loosely drawn together, excluding the minor judges' stories (3:31; 10:1–5; 12:8–15). At some point, the Deuteronomic editor integrated them into his interpretive survey of Israel's history between Moses and the exile, placing them within a framework and prefacing the whole document with an introduction (2:6–3:6) that explicitly set forth the lessons he believed the stories illustrated and the message he wished to communicate to his own compatriots. Thus, all six major judges' stories follow a similar pattern:

Israel did evil in the eyes of the Lord.

God punished Israel by allowing an enemy to oppress them for x years.

Israel cried out to the Lord.

The Lord raised up a judge, who delivered them.

The land had peace for x years.

Finally, whether in one, two, or several stages, the second introduction (1:1–2:5) was added, along with the epilogue (chs. 17–21).

There are differing views regarding the dating of the final form of Judges. The question is closely related to other, overarching issues of chronology and historicity that are discussed greater detail below (pp. 134–35, n. 18), though we can draw some general conclusions from a few clues within the text itself. Note, for example, the following:

Judges 11:26, in which Jephthah maintains that Israel has occupied the territory in question for three hundred years (i.e., implying that the conquest was three hundred years earlier).

Judges 18:30–31, where it describes the illegitimate priests as serving "until the captivity of the land" and Micah's idols as being used "as long as the ark was in Shiloh."

Judges 17–18 reveals a very negative polemic against Israelite worship at Dan and Bethel (implied), the two central cultic centers of the northern kingdom.

Judges 19–20 features stories that present tribes of the northern kingdom in a negative light and Judah in a positive light.

Judges 17–20, where appears the recurring refrain "In those days there was no king in Israel . . ."

From these data we can reasonably draw only limited conclusions. There is no compelling reason to interpret the fifth point as literal and thus to assume that the book was composed before the monarchy began, for the refrain is clearly part of an editorial framework imposed onto older narrative units. It seems likely that Judges took final form after the division between the northern and southern kingdoms and Jeroboam's establishing of the (illegitimate from the Deuteronomic perspective) cultic centers at Bethel and Dan (1 Kgs. 12:25–33). Thus, Jeroboam's reign (930–909 B.C.E.) establishes the outer parameters for redaction of the book of Judges. It would seem that the second point would narrow the field considerably. But the "captivity of the land" is ambiguous. It could refer to several events, the two most likely being the fall of the northern kingdom (722 B.C.E.)[12] or the fall of the southern kingdom (587 B.C.E.). The reference to the "ark at Shiloh" is difficult, and as of yet there is no scholarly consensus regarding its interpretation. If it refers to the destruction of Shiloh (Jer. 7:12, 14; 26:6), the date would be quite early, though we do not know exactly when it was destroyed. Both chronological references in Judges 18 appear to be editorial comments and could well be intentionally ambiguous, pointing to the destruction of both the northern and southern kingdoms. Finally, the reference in Judges 11:26 is very difficult and must be treated within the context of the larger issue of chronology of the exodus and conquest and settlement (see pp. 129–30). All in all, the internal evidence is of only limited value in helping us determine the dating.

A number of theories have been suggested, in some cases based on external data such as historical material, explicit or implicit, from elsewhere in the OT, especially from Deuteronomy and the Former and Latter Prophets. Many scholars more or less follow the classic theory significantly developed by M. Noth that, along with Joshua and Samuel–2 Kings and an older form of Deuteronomy, Judges forms the Deuteronomic History, edited during the time of the exile as an apology for the destruction of Judah and subsequent exile of its people.[13] F. M. Cross offered a modified version, positing two redactions—a Dtr_1 from the time of Josiah and a Dtr_2 from the time of the exile, which he distinguished according to different perspectives on the monarchy. Where it is positive, it reflects Josiah's reign; where it is negative, the exile.[14] A similar theory also posits two principal redactions. The first was during the period of chaos, rebellion, and injustice that followed upon the premature death of Josiah (609 B.C.E.) and under the very bad leadership of Jehoiakim (2 Kgs. 23:36–24:7; 2 Chr. 36:4–8). This was the time of Jeremiah's ministry, which repeatedly sounds a refrain calling for repentance from idolatry, immorality, and abuse of power (Jer. 7:5–11; 22:13–17; 23:9–14), all essential concerns of the author of Judges. Then, sometime during the exile, there was a second redaction when the book was placed in the wider context of the overall Deuteronomic History relating the story of God's covenant people from their entrance to the land until their eventual exile because of failure to live up to their covenant obligations to the Lord.[15]

In light of both internal (content in Judges itself) and external (other prophetic texts) evidence, the construct that presents two redactions, one during the period of apostasy following Josiah's death and a second during the exile, best accounts for the book of Judges as we know it. It is possible that the editorial notice "at that time there was no king in Israel" does not anticipate a first united monarchy under David and Solomon but comments about past failures of Israel's and Judah's kings and at the same time anticipates a future Davidic king who will lead a repentant, restored nation according to God's Torah, inaugurating an era of *shalom* and *sedaqah*, thus fulfilling God's purpose for his people and, ultimately, the world.

In spite of this lengthy process and all these layers of tradition, the original material in the individual stories, which by and large has been preserved intact, is quite old, perhaps even dating to the early monarchy (tenth century B.C.E.).[16] For the sake of simplicity, in this commentary I will refer to "the author," recognizing that there was probably no single author or editor, but numerous authors along the way.

Judges as Biblical Literature

Related to the question of composition is how we understand and approach the text. Even if the text were formed in stages, the completed book is still the final composition of a single inspired author. I use the word "author" very intentionally, for the person who gave us the book of Judges as we read it today was a gifted literary artist, a point that has not always been recognized by interpreters who have focused solely on identifying layers of tradition and have often missed the forest for the trees. The scholarly pendulum has now swung toward the side of an approach that takes seriously the text as a whole and seeks to discern meaning through interpretive principles that apply to literature in general. At the same time, dialogue between Jewish and Christian scholars has opened up the world of Hebrew narrative in a new way, adding valuable tools to the exegete seeking to understand the text.

This literary approach is truer to the nature of the Scriptures themselves. Rather than imposing contemporary western categories on the text, we must read it on its own terms, within the construct of its own world. The following are some of the characteristics of Hebrew narrative style that have informed my own exegesis of the text and to which I will refer in subsequent discussions of individual passages:[17]

> *Repetition* of a statement, a word, or a theme. Often a single variation within a repeated element indicates a special point of meaning.

> *Wordplay,* whether upon a word or a root. The structure of the Hebrew language lends itself especially to this literary technique, and the text is full of them.

> *Excessive detail.* Hebrew is a language that does not waste a word. Most of the time, understatement is the keynote; hence, when the author pauses to focus upon some element in detail, it clearly reveals an important feature.

Dialogue. In Hebrew narrative, important points are communicated through direct speech. But at the same time, silence is also significant.

Juxtaposition. Joining two elements renders one a commentary on the other, even if it is not explicitly stated.

Type-scenes. The audience is so familiar with a stereotypic situation that it anticipates beforehand what will happen, and variations on the expected particularly emphasize important points.

A final aspect of Hebrew narrative is that it rarely explicitly comments or tells the reader how to respond but tells the story and moves on, leaving the reader to draw the appropriate conclusion(s). The few times the narrator interrupts with an explicit comment or to give additional information to help the audience interpret the story (narrative intrusion) are especially noteworthy indicators of meaning.

Critical Issues in Interpreting Judges

A variety of interpretive issues, some of which are more controversial than others, continue to attract scholarly attention. Here I will mention only the most important in a general way, as many of these are discussed more comprehensively in the literature listed in the For Further Reading section. Most debate clusters around questions of chronology and history, one of which we have already touched upon in discussion about the composition of Judges. But broader issues remain. For example, how does the book of Judges fit into an overall chronology of the premonarchical period? How do we understand the biblical sources as history and yet theologically interpreted history? These questions lead us directly into the hornet's nest of issues surrounding the exodus and conquest and settlement. On this subject scholarship has been and remains divided into two basic camps: those who accept the essential historicity of the biblical accounts (though surely recognizing the difficulties in interpreting specific passages) and those who do not, with moderates to extremists on both sides. Regarding the dating of the exodus, accepted as historical by those in the first group, interpreters hold to an early date (ca. 1446 B.C.E.), a late date (ca. 1290 B.C.E.), or some combination of both dates (i.e., two waves of exit from Egypt and entrance into the land). Each bases his or her position on clear evidence, whether biblical or archaeological, but in reality, neither can claim definitive proof.[18]

It seems that the view that best accounts for the whole evidence is a thirteenth-century exodus. This is only a tentative conclusion based upon the evidence now available; none of the theories is without difficulty.

Another related issue concerns the chronology of the period of the judges itself. All the judges' terms of office plus the periods of apostasy total a period of approximately 410 years, a length of time that is historically problematic. For this reason, it is widely held that the terms of the judges do not follow chronologically one upon the other but overlap. Many of the judges appear to have had only local influence, involving one tribe or a few that were geographically contiguous, and the material seems to have been arranged so as to communicate a particular message, much like the author of Mark's Gospel arranged his material.[19] For example, it is likely that the story of the Levite and his concubine and the civil war that ensued (Judg. 19–21) dates from an earlier time, perhaps even the beginning of the period of the judges.

Finally, there is the question of the relationship between Judges and Joshua. For the most part Joshua presents a very different view of Israel's early experience in the land (i.e., a total conquest, summarized essentially in Josh. 10:28–43), while Judges begins with its own version of the events, which was anything but a complete conquest. It is likely that Judges portrays the more real picture and Joshua the more ideal.[20] But even in Joshua's ideal presentation we find references that correspond to Judges' version (Josh. 11:18, 22; 13:2–6; 15:63; 16:10; 17:12–13). The relationship between the two accounts must be understood in terms of the theological tendencies of each book and the overall presentation of the Deuteronomic History.

Major Themes of Judges

Although it is best to establish these through an inductive approach, here the major themes are briefly noted so as to be aware of them as we work through the text. The theme of *covenant* underlies the entire story, in keeping with its Deuteronomic character. More specifically, Judges is about God's covenant people, Israel, about their faithfulness and unfaithfulness to covenant commitments made first at Mount Sinai and later renewed, especially at Shechem under Joshua's leadership (Josh. 24). This includes subthemes of *obedience* and *blessing,* on one hand and *sin* (Israel's failure to live up to covenant commitments) and *punishment* on the other. As story moves into story, we will see that each time, Israel's sin worsens in degree and scope, and likewise in the punishment. Related to the theme of covenant also is *unity,* and its corollary, *disunity.* Israel's covenant with the Lord also was a covenant with each other; thus they were to be committed to unity in attitude, purpose, and action. They did not consistently fulfill their obligations either to the Lord or to their fellow covenant community, and their rebellion against the Lord, their rejection of imagehood, precipitated an increasingly serious breakdown of *shalom* in every area of life, individually and corporately. By the end of the story, *shalom* has all but disintegrated and chaos has set in.

The theme of *leadership* also stands out in Judges, as to be expected in a book named after its leaders. In keeping with the thrust of the Deuteronomic History, we will see that good leaders influenced Israel to fulfill covenant obligations and bad leaders influenced them to go astray from God's covenant, God's way of life and liberty. It is no wonder that without good leadership, Israel found itself in bondage from which it could not extricate itself apart from God's miraculous intervention, likewise in the form of a leader. And this brings us to another important theme of Judges, one that many Christian readers in particular might miss: *God's grace.* God's amazing grace is demonstrated as time and again he forgives and helps and restores the nation. The depth and breadth of his grace are revealed in the fact that there even is an Israel by the end of the book. The theme of God's grace points to the final theme, *God's sovereignty,* which undergirds and pervades the book. Even in and through Israel's rebellion, God was faithfully working out his purposes on their behalf.

Notes

1. The meaning of the Hebrew root *spt* is clarified by usage in extrabiblical contexts, such as Ugaritic, where it appears in parallelism with *mlk* ("rule, reign"). The early Romans used similar terms (*sufes* or *sufetes*) in reference to civil leaders.

2. This is pointed out by A. Malamat in his insightful article, "Charismatic Leadership in the Book of Judges," in *Magnalia Dei: The Mighty Acts of God: Essays on the Bible and Archaeology in Memory of G. Ernest Wright* (ed. F. M. Cross, W. E. Lemke, and P. D. Miller Jr.; Garden City, N.Y.: Doubleday, 1976), p. 152.

3. Marcion (ca. 140 C.E.) suggested a third alternative: to excise the entire OT and even parts of the NT that were deemed too Jewish. Although no evangelical Christian today would recommend such a radical solution, many are guilty of the same by treating the texts as if they do not exist.

4. D. R. Davis summarizes the attitudes in *Such a Great Salvation: Expositions of the Book of Judges* (Grand Rapids: Baker, 1990), p. 7: "The church (in general) has a problem with the Book of Judges. It is so earthy, so puzzling, so primitive, so violent—in a word, so strange, that the church can scarcely stomach it. As with many Old Testament books, the sentiment seems to be, 'If we just study the epistles long enough, maybe it will go away.' The church has her way of dealing with embarrassing Scripture: ignore it."

5. G. E. Ladd, *The New Testament and Criticism* (Grand Rapids: Eerdmans, 1989).

6. A similar term is Deuteronomistic History, which some scholars use to designate a different redaction of the Deuteronomic History, while others use it to refer to the Deuteronomic History. The fact that the terms are not used consistently makes for great confusion. In this study, at the risk of obfuscating the distinction (which is not universally acknowledged), I use the term "Deuteronomic History" to refer to the final redaction.

7. The meaning of the Hebrew word "Torah" has unfortunately been influenced by its Greek term used in translation of the Septuagint and in the NT. *nomos,* which means "law." While Torah sometimes has a legal character, its primary meaning is more accurately rendered by the word "guidance," "direction," or even "revelation." It comes from the Hebrew root *yrh,* meaning to "point" (i.e., the way to God, or the way to life).

8. It has been widely recognized that the form and vocabulary of Deuteronomy correspond remarkably to those of ancient Near Eastern treaties. A succinct, useful summary of the parallels is found in W. S. LaSor, D. A. Hubbard, and F. W. Bush, *Old Testament Survey: The Message, Form, and Background of the Old Testament* (Grand Rapids: Eerdmans, 1982), pp. 144–45. See also J. G. McConville, *Grace in the End: A Study in Deuteronomic Theology* (Grand Rapids: Zondervan, 1993), pp. 57–64, and R. B. Dillard and T. Longman III, *An Introduction to the Old Testament* (Leicester, England: Apollos, 1995), pp. 97–99.

9. For much of this discussion on imagehood, I am indebted to M. Guinan, *The Pentateuch, Message of Biblical Spirituality 1* (Collegeville, Minn.: Liturgical, 1990), pp. 21–31.

10. I want to make it clear that when I refer to Israel throughout, especially in contexts in which I point out Israel's weaknesses and failings, I do not have in view present-day Jews. Of course, they are Israel, but in light of the horrendous history of anti-Semitism, in most cases perpetrated by those who have identified themselves as Christians, I want to avoid any semblance of adding to the sin of my Christian ancestors. Moreover, I do not point the finger at "them" without at the same time pointing it at myself and the church today. Israel is not alone in failing to live out its imagehood. So whenever I refer to the failures of Israel, I infer also, *more so*, that the text speaks about the church as well.

11. LaSor, Hubbard, and Bush (*Old Testament Survey*, p. 221) comment about the different styles that are discernible in the book, which, they conclude, "would support the theory that the stories were composed by different authors and transmitted in different forms."

12. The area of the tribe of Dan, being situated in the far north of the country, was one of the first to fall to Assyria (ca. 732 B.C.E.; 1 Kgs. 15:29–30). Some scholars have suggested that this is what is referred to in Judg. 18:30, but it is more likely that a wider captivity is in view here.

13. The work was first published as *Überlieferungsgeschichtliche Studien* 1 (Tübingen: Max Neimeyer Verlag, 1943). The English translation is *The Deuteronomistic History* (JSOTSup 15; Sheffield: JSOT Press, 1981).

14. Cross's hypothesis is discussed at length in *Canaanite Myth and Hebrew Epic: Essays in the History of the Religion of Israel* (Cambridge: Harvard University Press, 1973), pp. 274–89. The issue of seemingly conflicting tendencies, essentially promonarchical and antimonarchical, continues to be investigated and debated. Many scholars posit that the original version was antimonarchical, especially reflected in Jotham's parable (9:7–15), and then a promonarchical epilogue (chs. 17–21) was added. A question that remains, however, is whether or not Jotham's parable is antimonarchical. It could equally be understood as referring to leadership in general, that people deserve the leaders they get and the leaders deserve the people they get, that good people choose good leaders and bad people choose bad leaders.

15. Noth's proposal that Deuteronomy was not originally linked canonically with Genesis–Numbers but was joined to Joshua–2 Kings to form the Deuteronomic History and only later separated and linked with the first four books, does not commend itself, despite the close relationship between Deuteronomy and the Deuteronomic History. The Pentateuch *(torah)* must remain a distinct canonical unit.

16. It has been suggested that these were committed to writing during the united monarchy, the golden age of the nation, when order and stability provided the environment for a flowering of scribal activity (2 Sam. 8:17; 20:25; 1 Kgs. 4:3). See A. E. Cundall and L. Morris, *Judges and Ruth: An Introduction and Commentary* (TOTC; ed. D. J. Wiseman; Downers Grove, Ill.: InterVarsity Press, 1968), p. 26.

17. These guidelines are taken largely though not exclusively from R. Alter, *The Art of Biblical Narrative* (New York: Basic Books, 1981).

18. The following is a brief summary of the fundamental arguments of each position. Those who hold to an early date base it upon a literal reading of biblical chronology coupled with archaeological evidence. For example, 1 Kgs. 6:1 states that Solomon began to build the temple (probably ca. 967 B.C.E.) 480 years after the exodus, which would mean sometime around 1446 B.C.E. Another text, 1 Chron. 6:33–37, indicates that there were eighteen generations between Korah and Heman, a musician during David's reign (ca. 1010–970 B.C.E.); 18 times 25 (the approximate length of a generation) yields a date quite close to 480 years. Likewise Judg. 11:26 supports the early view, for 300 years from the time of the conquest until the time of Jephthah (ca. 1100 B.C.E.) would have been mid-fifteenth century B.C.E. Some supporters of an early date locate the exodus during the Amarna period (fifteenth century B.C.E.), a time of social chaos in Palestine, when local city-states were in decline, leaving a power vacuum that was then filled by the invading Hebrew people. Some even identify the Israelites with the *'apiru* of the Amarna letters; which closely resembles *'ibri* (Hb. for "Hebrew") and who invaded Palestine during that time. But this view is not without problems. For one, it is now known that the *'apiru* were not necessarily an invading people, neither confined to the area of biblical Palestine, neither to the time of the Amarna letters. At the same time, it is highly debatable that the word even corresponds to the Hb. term. Also, the biblical references could be interpreted differently, for 1 Kgs. 6:1 suggests a symbolic number, because it equals 12 times 40, both highly symbolic numbers in biblical literature. Moreover, the Hb. term *dor* ("generation") does not necessarily connote a generation but can refer to a period of time [LaSor, Hubbard, Bush, *Old Testament Survey*, p. 127]. Even if it does refer to what we understand as a generation in 1 Chron., there is no agreement as to how many years it included; anything from 25 to 40 years has been suggested. It is interesting that many who insist on a literal interpretation of the numbers in these texts do not hesitate to squeeze them into the mold of an early date. One difficult text that remains is Judg. 11:26, but 300 is divisible by 3 and 10, which are both equally symbolic numbers.

The later date (thirteenth century B.C.E.) has much to commend itself, with evidence both historical and archaeological. Historical references in Egyptian sources indicate that they used foreign slaves (called the Egyptian equivalent of *'apiru*) in their building projects, even specifically Pithom and Ramses (cf. Exod. 1:11), and that Pithom and Ramses were likely built by Ramses II, who ascended to the throne ca. 1300 B.C.E. In the same way, the Hyksos period in Egypt (seventeenth century B.C.E.) could well be the most likely time for Joseph to have risen to power, corroborating the number of years the Israelites were in Egypt before the exodus, more or less according to Gen. 15:13 (400 years) and Exod. 12:40 (430). Moreover, the Mernephtah stele (see *The Ancient Near East: An Anthology of Texts and Pictures* [ed. J. B. Pritchard; 5th ed.; Princeton, N.J.: Princeton University Press, 1971], p. 231) implies that Israel was present in the land of Israel in 1220 B.C.E.. Additionally, Num. 20:14–21 states that Israel was not able to pass through Moab and Edom, which did not emerge as nation-states until about the thirteenth century B.C.E. Archaeology too points to a thirteenth-century date, for there is a widespread destruction layer in "Israelite" cities during this period. As with the early date, none of this evidence is conclusive. Objections have been raised to interpretations of all these data, mostly based on a different reading of the evidence. Because neither the early date nor the late date is clearly indicated, some interpreters (though few) hold to a view that combines both—that there were two exoduses, one in the fifteenth century and a later one in the thirteenth century.

Two other perspectives are similar in that neither posits a historical exodus and conquest of any kind but rather a protracted process of settlement or a revolt of those already living in the land. The settlement view was first proposed by A. Alt, who suggested that the Israelites were a loosely connected group of desert nomadic peoples who gradually settled in the land, by and large peacefully, and only subsequently joined together into a tribal federation, particularly in groups related to their common matriarchal ancestor, whether Rachel, Leah, Bilhah, or Zilpah (see A. Alt, *Essays on Old Testament History and Religion* [trans. R. A. Wilson; Sheffield: JSOT Press, 1989], pp. 135–69). This view received more widespread exposure through the work of M. Noth (*The History of Israel* [trans. P. Ackroyd; 2d ed.; Philadelphia: Westminster, 1986]).

The revolt theory, first suggested by G. E. Mendenhall and developed more thoroughly by N. Gottwald (*Tribes of Yahweh* [Maryknoll: N.Y.: Orbis, 1979]), posits that the cataclysmic sociopolitical changes that took place in Palestine during the thirteenth century were due to a "peasant revolt" against oppressive Canaanite overlords, perhaps precipitated by the incursion of a small group of Israelite (former) slaves. This group obtained cohesion not through common ancestry but through common ideology (i.e., Yahweh worship). For further discussion, see R. B. Dillard and T. Longman III, *An Introduction to the Old Testament*, pp. 111–12. This view, with some variation, is embraced by R. B. Coote and K. W. Whitelam (*The Emergence of Early Israel in Historical Perspective* [The Social World in Biblical Antiquity Series 5; ed. J. W. Flanagan; Sheffield: Almond, 1987]) and H. H. Rowley (*From Joseph to Joshua: Biblical Traditions in the Light of Archaeology* [London: Oxford University Press, 1950]).

19. See the statement of Papias the Elder (ca. 130–140 C.E.): "The elder said this also: Mark, who has been Peter's interpreter, wrote down carefully . . . , recording both sayings and doings of Christ, not however

in order." Quoted in R. P. Martin, *New Testament Foundations: A Guide for Christian Students*, vol. 1, *The Four Gospels* (Grand Rapids: Eerdmans, 1975), p. 211.

20. Archaeologist W. Dever ("Archaeology and the 'Conquest,' " *ABD* 3:555) comments that "[w]hile modern archaeology may call into question the historicity of Joshua, it provides rather dramatic corroboration of the account in Judges, even in obscure details." Joshua's presentation is quite similar to other ancient Near Eastern conquest accounts, which are characteristically hyperbolic (see Dillard and Longman, *An Introduction to the Old Testament*, p. 112).

§1 Southern Tribes' Settlement (Judg. 1:1–21)

Judges 1:1–21 sets the stage for the book. It focuses upon the primacy of Judah, which will appear again at the close of the book, as a lead into the story of the united monarchy. Judah, in response to divine guidance, takes the lead in obeying God's command to possess the land and is for the most part successful. The themes of leadership, unity, and land are especially highlighted, along with an introduction of the theme of disobedience (sin), which will develop into a dominant theme in the rest of the book. Only at the end of the section is there any hint that Judah did not fully enter into their inheritance promised by the Lord. Since failure to do so represents disobedience, this opening section sets the tone for the entire story.

1:1–3 / The book of Judges looks backward as well as forward. Its canonical link with what goes before it is immediately evident from the first words of the book: **After the death of Joshua.** This important notice both demonstrates continuity with Israel's history and signals a new epoch in that history. The story of Joshua's death (Josh. 24:29–30) follows upon a great covenant renewal ceremony at Shechem (Josh. 24:1–27), in which he and all the people made a solemn commitment to "serve the LORD . . . and obey him" (v. 24). Joshua had fulfilled his mission on earth: Israel was one united people, completely settled in the promised land with "rest" from enemies "on every side," in short, having realized "all of the LORD's good promises to the house of Israel" (Josh. 21:44–45).

Given all that background, we look expectantly for great things from Israel in its land; the words "after the death of Joshua" signal a significant transition in Israel's history, pregnant with possibility of their fulfilling the blessing of the patriarchs and matriarchs: "all peoples on earth will be blessed through you" (Gen. 12:3).

From this inspiring beginning, however, we read on: **the Israelites asked the LORD, "Who will be the first to go up and**

fight for us against the Canaanites?" and a question immediately arises. Why are the Israelites deliberating about who will go up first and fight against the Canaanites if they have already been wiped out and their territory taken? As the story continues, it appears as if the nation is back to where they were at the beginning of the book of Joshua (Josh. 1:15), merely anticipating entering the land and realizing God's promises. How do we understand the whole of Judges 1 in the light of the book of Joshua (see p. 130)?

The differing accounts are juxtaposed without explicit comment. Implicitly communicated, however, is the author's emphasis upon the fact of Israel's apostasy after the death of Joshua and consequent punishment by captivity to the enemies around them. It continues to press home the message that Israel has been unfaithful to the Lord even from the time they entered the land. We will see that the degree of unfaithfulness increased in scope and intensity throughout the period of the judges.

But first, the Israelites faithfully sought to obey God's command to possess the land and faithfully sought the Lord's guidance as to how to proceed after Joshua was no longer on the scene (v. 1b); they united in submission to the Lord's will. How they asked the Lord is not clear. The Hebrew term denotes a kind of divination, which, although practiced widely in the ancient Near East, was limited to three types in Israel: Urim and Thummim (Exod. 28:30; Num. 27:21), the ephod (1 Sam. 14:18, 41), and prophetic utterance.

The question reflects Israel's quest for guidance concerning leadership after Joshua's death, which was the first time in their brief history that such a question had been asked. It was not raised at the transition after Moses' death, for Joshua was clearly named by the Lord as Moses' successor (Deut. 31:1–3, 7–8, 14; 34:9). Now, however, no one leader had been named; rather, the tribe of Judah, named by divine speech, took precedence over the others. Judah's primacy accords with the Deuteronomic author's agenda, foreshadowing Judah's primacy at the time of the united monarchy. The book of Judges begins and ends with a similar motif, almost exact in wording: In times of crisis the Lord chose Judah to lead the nation in battle (1:2; 20:18). Both references form an *inclusio* that frames the book, highlighting the central theme of leadership and the move toward a dynastic monarchy.

The Lord further indicates that Judah inherited the mantle of Moses and Joshua by including a promise that recalls a similar promise to Joshua (Josh. 1:2–5): **I have given the land into their hands.** Judah then solicits the help of the **Simeonites their brothers,** pledging that they **in turn** will help the Simeonites fight for their inheritance. This close relationship between Judah and Simeon, sons of the same mother (Gen. 29:33, 35), is highlighted already in the book of Joshua (Josh. 19:1–9, esp. v. 9; cf. Josh. 15:26–32, 42; 1 Chron. 4:28–33). The appositional phrase, "their brothers," especially points to the unity enjoyed at this time in Israel's history, yet so close to the time of Joshua's leadership. But that unity did not last long.

1:4–8 / As Judah and Simeon attempted their first foray into their inheritance, God faithfully fulfilled his promise of success (v. 4). The omission of reference to Simeon reveals the author's interest in the leadership of Judah exclusively. The terms **Canaanites and Perizzites** appear together in a generic sense of inhabitants of the land. The precise distinction between the two is unknown; R. G. Boling (*Judges: A New Translation with Introduction and Commentary* [AB 6A; Garden City, N.Y.: Doubleday, 1975], p. 54) suggests that the pair may pejoratively refer to city dwellers and rural residents, respectively: "city slickers and country bumpkins."

With the next phrase we are confronted with one of the more difficult interpretive issues in biblical literature. The text reports that **they struck down ten thousand men.** How are we to understand the number here translated as "thousand"? The Hebrew word *'elep* is a term whose semantic range extends beyond the English word "thousand," often connoting a military contingent of uncertain number, as few as five to fourteen men and later many more, though not literally a thousand.

The most difficult interpretive issue in these verses centers on the names **Bezek** and **Adoni-Bezek.** The location of Bezek is problematic because as it has presently been identified, it lies far to the north or to the west of Judah's allotted territory, in the area allotted to the tribe of Manasseh or Ephraim rather than Judah. Judges 1:1–36 implies that each tribe was responsible for conquering its own territory, so what was Judah doing so far away from its inheritance? Related to this is the question of identifying Adoni-Bezek. A similar name, Adoni-Zedek (Josh. 10:1, 3), appears in some Greek manuscripts of Joshua as *Adonibezek,* with a clear reference to the king of Jerusalem, thus leading some commentators to posit that a better reading of the text in Judges is *adoni-sedeq* (i.e., that the king in question is the king of *sedeq* or Jerusalem; cf. Gen.

14:18–20). This reading would also fit the context better, as Jerusalem is geographically within the sphere of Judah's inheritance (Josh. 15:8).

The Judahites defeated the Canaanites and Perizzites and took Adoni-Bezek captive; they also **cut off his thumbs and big toes** (v. 6) Although this sounds extremely harsh, it was commonly practiced in antiquity because it guaranteed that the prisoner would never again take up arms, in addition to serving as an example to others who might attempt to rebel against the victorious adversary. Adoni-Bezek himself acknowledged the justice in his fate, having inflicted the same punishment on his own subjugated enemies (v. 7a). This vignette also points to the fate of Sisera, who likewise will flee his enemy but who will lose more than just his thumbs and big toes (Judg. 4:21; 5:26–27).

There follow two puzzling notices about Jerusalem. In the first case, we are told that the Judahites **brought** Adoni-Bezek **to Jerusalem, and he died there** (v. 7b). In the second, they **attacked Jerusalem also and took it. They put the city to the sword and set it on fire** (v. 8). These notices are puzzling for several reasons, the main one being that the book of Judges indicates that Jerusalem had not been taken and moreover attributes the latter attempt to the Benjamites rather than the Judahites (v. 21). Also, the reference in Judges 19:10–12 to Jerusalem as Jebus, "a city of foreigners," on the surface would seem to mean that Jerusalem later reverted to Canaanite hegemony. But, as noted in the introduction, the setting of the story was much earlier, and the story was placed at the end of the book for theological reasons, to highlight the degree of Israel's sinfulness at the end of the period. Some commentators have sought to harmonize the various accounts by suggesting that Jerusalem changed hands several times. In all likelihood the historical reality was that Israel did not fully control the city until the time of David and that the author of Judges placed this story at the beginning to highlight the association between Judah and Jerusalem and to proleptically anticipate the time when Jerusalem will become the capital of the united monarchy under David and Solomon and then the capital of the southern kingdom of Judah. It is no accident that the author begins with both Judah and Jerusalem.

1:9–15 / The author summarizes in a general way Judah's next activity as they moved southward, attacking **the Canaanites living in the hill country, the Negev and the western**

foothills (v. 9). Then, in typical Hebrew narrative style, he goes back to detail a single episode in the campaign, the taking of **Hebron** (cf. Gen. 23:2; 35:27; Josh. 15:54; 20:7), the most prominent city in the southern hill country and later David's first capital before he moved to Jerusalem (2 Sam. 5:1–4). This story has a parallel in Joshua, though with a significant variation (Josh. 15:13–14): Joshua attributes the victory to Caleb, while Judges attributes it to Judah. Most likely, Joshua's version represents the earlier tradition, which has been modified by the author of Judges in accordance with his special interest in Judah and also foreshadowing David's making Hebron his first capital.

The next episode almost exactly parallels Joshua 15:15–19. Both state that the Judahites next attacked **Debir** (formerly called **Kiriath Sepher**), a strategically important town south of Hebron. **Othniel son of Kenaz, Caleb's younger brother,** led the attack and was rewarded well by Caleb: He was given Caleb's **daughter Acsah,** who was offered as a bride **to the man who attacks and captures** the city. Later (3:7–11) Othniel will be presented as the paradigmatic judge, which is perhaps why his story is repeated. Here he is introduced, appropriately, as a courageous and competent warrior. Moreover, he married a woman of his own clan, an important value in a book whose author viewed exogamy and idolatry as going hand in hand. This is a concern of the Deuteronomic History, the story of Ahab and Jezebel perhaps being the most vivid example of this form of sin against the Lord (1 Kgs. 16:31–33). Finally, the theme of marriage appears again in Judges 21, thus forming an *inclusio* framing the book and underscoring the message of covenant fidelity and infidelity.

1:16 / In the middle of the narration about Judah's exploits, the author injects a flashback-style reference to the movement of the Kenites. Possibly this is suggested by alliteration with Kenaz (v. 13)—a common Hebrew literary technique—or by the fact that it foreshadows the story of Jael the Kenite, or both. The Kenites were essentially a nomadic people who allied themselves with Judah and others (4:11, 17). The text indicates that they camped with Judah on the plain of Jericho (the City of Palms; Deut. 34:3; 2 Chron. 28:15) and then participated in Judah's conquest of desert towns in the Negev.

1:17–20 / Here are further references to Judah's activity in conquering the promised land, along with the **Simeonites their brothers.** Again the theme of communal unity is emphasized by the appositional phrase, "their brothers"; two tribes worked together, and God blessed their joint effort. The conquered city's name changed from **Zephath** to **Hormah,** because it was destroyed (see Num. 21:3). The Hebrew word *horma* is linguistically related to the word *herem*, which means "completely devoted to the deity," completely prohibited from nonsacral use, and hence destroyed. Though it is admittedly foreign to present-day western understanding, *herem* was widely practiced in the ancient Semitic world. According to Deuteronomy 7:2–6 and 20:16–18, Israel was to practice *herem* in every case as they conquered and settled the promised land. Failure to do so was a grave offense against the Lord, for which they would be severely punished.

Then Judah **took Gaza, Ashkelon and Ekron** (v. 18), three of the five Philistine capital cities. The text is admittedly difficult, for the next verse (v. 19) reports that Judah was **unable to drive the people from the plains.** These statements seem irreconcilable. Perhaps the author has juxtaposed the second account with that of verse 18 in order to introduce both the theme of (even) Judah's sinfulness and the Philistines' opposition to the Israelites, serving as God's instrument to punish Israel for their rebellion.

Surely this paradoxical perspective is indicated by the fact that the summary statement of Judah's exploits relates both successes and failures. The text affirms that **the LORD was with the men of Judah;** thus, **they took possession of** their inheritance in **the hill country.** We will again encounter the motif of the Lord's presence as early as the story of Gideon (6:12); it is implied as well in references to the Spirit of the Lord coming upon a judge. The statement that "the LORD was with the men of Judah" again highlights the special place and important role of Judah. These same words had been used to describe Moses and Joshua, and now the mantle has fallen, as it were, upon Judah.

But despite this favored status, Judah was not strong enough to drive the people from the plains, **because they had iron chariots.** The Philistines' ability to work in iron, which they learned from the Hittites, gave them a strategic advantage over other peoples of the region who had not yet developed this technology and thus had to rely on inferior weapons. This, the first directly negative statement in the book, previews the major theme of Judges. We know from later accounts in Judges that even iron chariots should be no challenge for those whom the Lord helps (4:14–15). So why was Judah unable to drive out the people from the plains? Not because the Philistines had iron chariots, but because of spiritual factors that will be explained later (Judg. 2:1–3, 10–15).

There follows a second brief reference to Caleb, whose inheritance fell within the territory of Judah (Josh. 15:13, 54). **As Moses had promised, Hebron was given to** him. Caleb was a Kenazite (Gen. 36:11, 15, 42), an Edomite (from Esau) who joined with the people of God and received an inheritance along with them. This is a beautiful picture of the Lord's grace and inclusiveness, even pointing to the very partial fulfillment of the God's promise to Abraham: In you all the nations of the earth will be blessed. Again, in keeping with the author's perspective, note that Caleb received an inheritance within the tribe of Judah.

1:21 / Finally, the author summarizes Benjamin's activity—or lack of it. It is a brief account in comparison with the others, and it focuses exclusively upon Jerusalem. Although Jerusalem bordered on Judah's territory, the actual allotment fell to Benjamin (Josh. 18:27). As with Judah, the statement that Benjamin **failed to dislodge the Jebusites** is essentially negative. The author's use of the later Israelite name for the city, Jerusalem, gives the impression that he believed the original name of the city was Jerusalem and that it was later renamed when taken over by the Jebusites; in other words, that the city never belonged to the Jebusites.

Additional Notes §1

1:1 / **After the death of Joshua:** M. Noth was the first to interpret this portrayal of Israel as one united worshiping community as modeled after Greek amphictyonies, loose associations of tribal groups whose social cohesion lay in their common worship at a central shrine (e.g.,. at Delphi); a regular and important component of this cultic activity was a yearly renewal their covenant commitment to the god and to each other for harmonious relationships and mutual defense. Noth pointed out that in biblical tribal lists the number twelve remained constant, though the individual components may have varied. He believed that biblical Israel came to exist in the context of this amphictyony, as in this worship context they created a common religious history as the primary force for social cohesion (see M. Noth, *The History of Israel*, pp. 85–109). In recent years, scholarship has rejected this paradigm because the differences between Israel's experience and Greek amphictyonies are more numerous than their similarities and also because there is no textual evidence that such existed in early Israel (see A. D. H. Mayes, *Israel in the Period of the Judges* [SBT 29; Naperville, Ill.: Allenson, 1974]).

1:6 / Cut off his thumbs and big toes: The principle of *talion*, or reciprocal punishment, appears frequently in early Jewish and Christian literature. Adoni-Bezek did not have any kind of faith in the God of Israel, though the author placed within his mouth the statement of this principle in order to highlight its veracity by the king's graphic example. It is also possible that this verse served as an apologetic for Judah's and Israel's conquest of the land of Canaan. Israel did not do anything to the people of the land that they had not already done to others; hence their fate was just. E. J. Hamlin (*At Risk in the Promised Land: A Commentary on the Book of Judges* [Grand Rapids: Eerdmans, 1990], p. 27) makes the intriguing suggestion that cutting off thumbs and big toes desacralized a Canaanite king, who also served as a priest, and that this action signaled "the end of the Canaanite order of sacred kings."

1:8 / The men of Judah attacked Jerusalem also and took it: The absence of clear distinction between Judah and Benjamin is understandable because although Jerusalem fell within the tribal allotment of Benjamin, it bordered on Judah (Josh. 15:8). Later, in the time of the monarchy, it came to be exclusively associated with Judah, the larger, more prominent tribe.

1:9–10 / The men of Judah ... advanced against ... Hebron: Caleb was not an Israelite but came to worship the God of Israel and was eventually integrated into Judah. He is listed as a Judahite in Num. 13:6. Josh. 15:13 states that the Lord commanded Joshua that Caleb be given a "portion (inheritance) in Judah."

1:12 / I will give my daughter: There is a foreshadowing of another father's story, a father who promised his daughter to the one who conquered his enemy (Judg. 11:31) and who gave his daughter to that One (v. 39), to the Lord, who is judge (11:27).

1:19 / They were unable to drive the people from the plains: The LXX appears to harmonize: "Judah ... did not take possession of Gaza, nor ... Ascalon, nor ... of Akkaron ...": the MT represents the more difficult reading.

1:21 / To this day: What the author means by "to this day" is not clear, and commentators interpret the date differently. The parallel passage in Joshua reads that Judah continued to live with the Jebusites in Jerusalem "to this day" (15:63). Again, the relationship between Judah and Benjamin was rather fluid. Other sources within the Deuteronomic History indicate that although Jerusalem was later conquered by David, who moved his capital there (2 Sam. 5:9–10, 13–14), some Jebusites continued to live in the city (2 Sam. 24:16).

§2 Northern Tribes' Settlement (Judg. 1:22–36)

The account proceeds to the northern tribes' settlement of the land. Things start out well enough, with the house of Joseph moving to take its inheritance in the central hill country. We expect success because "the LORD was with them" (v. 22). But instead the situation almost immediately begins to deteriorate, in keeping with the major theme of Judges. What was begun even with Judah, the most prominent tribe, now moves into full swing with the northern tribes. One by one, each tribe disobeys the Lord's explicit command by failing to drive out the Canaanites from its respective allotted territory. Each account is quite brief in comparison with Judah's, which further confirms the author's greater interest in Judah.

1:22–26 / The first campaign in the central hill country was against **Bethel.** The author begins with a general summary of the account and then specifies the details (vv. 23–26). He does not need to tell us explicitly that the house of Joseph was successful, because the theologically weighted statement **the LORD was with them** implicitly communicates the same. Bethel played an important role in Israel's history, being associated with significant encounters between the Lord and ancestors in the faith, Abraham and Jacob (Gen. 12:8; 13:3–4; 28:19–22; esp. 35:1–15), as well as serving as a major cultic center before the united monarchy (Judg. 2:1–5; 20:18; 26; 21:2) and in the northern kingdom (e.g., 1 Kgs. 12:28–33; 2 Kgs. 10:29; 17:28).

Why did the author choose to tell the story of Joseph's taking Bethel first in the area of the central hill country, in comparison with Joshua's account, which begins with Jericho and Ai and does not mention Bethel? The version in Judges points to the author's interest in cultic centers, particularly Jerusalem, Bethel, and Dan. Bethel and Dan were the two major cultic centers of the northern kingdom; surely it is intentional that the author's account of the northern tribes' activity begins with Bethel and ends with Dan. Thus these references are not solely geographical or historical but theological as well.

In their way of taking Bethel the tribes of Joseph first disobeyed God's command to destroy the Canaanites, and thus the downward spiral toward chaos began. The tribe of Joseph was successful, but the displaced people would later come back to trouble them. Significantly, after this point in the narrative appear essentially only negative assessments of the tribes' success in conquering their enemies.

1:27–29 / This division treats together the twin tribes of Ephraim and Manasseh, as they naturally belong (Gen. 48). We are told only what these tribes did not do; they did not **drive out** the indigenous peoples. The Hebrew of verse 28 *(wehores lo' horiso)* emphasizes the negation of the verb "to drive out"; the nuance is that they were not willing to do it and did not make a serious attempt to obey God's command. Indeed, the Canaanites appear to have had more willpower than did the Israelites (v. 27b), for the Hebrew *(wayyoel)*, translated "were determined," means to make up one's mind or to resolve. The Israelites, by contrast, compromised their calling and merely **pressed the Canaanites into forced labor** when the opportunity arose (cf. Josh. 17:12). The word for "forced labor" *(mas)* is the same as the word used for what Pharaoh did to the Israelites in Egypt. There is great irony here: The Israelites treated the Canaanites as they had been treated, and although they enslaved the Canaanites, they ended up being the ones enslaved (Judg. 2:3; 3:5–6). The same principle has been at work throughout human history.

Even though Ephraim was the largest tribe and played a significant role in the later sections of the book of Judges, only **Gezer** is mentioned in connection with their activity, again highlighting the author's greater interest in Judah than in the northern tribes.

1:30–36 / There follows a staccato series of brief summaries of other northern tribes' activities, each having essentially the same message: "*x* tribe did not drive out *y*"; instead "*x* tribe subjected *y* to forced labor." The tribes mentioned are **Zebulun** (v. 30), **Asher** (v. 31), and **Naphtali** (v. 33), all located in the northern part of the country, later to be known generally as Galilee. Most of the cities named here have not been definitively identified. Acco, one city that has been identified, was later renamed Ptolemais; the apostle Paul stopped there on his way to Jerusalem after his third missionary journey (Acts 21:7). Overall the significant point is that all the Israelite tribes except Judah disobeyed God's command to possess the land promised them and spurned his gift by refusing to take the promised territory.

Finally, the author describes Dan's experience (vv. 34–36) but does so in a way that differs from all other presentations. **Danites** is not the subject of the sentence but the object, while the subject is the people who subjugated them, the **Amorites**. This variation serves to highlight Dan's weakness and failure to occupy its inheritance. Dan's weakness is also emphasized by two other points. They were not able to press the Amorites into forced labor, but it was left up to **the house of Joseph** to do so. Even though the cities mentioned in verse 35 were allotted to Dan (Josh. 19:21), they could not or did not even stand up to fellow Israelites ("the house of Joseph") who took from them what they wanted. Later this weakness and failure will play a key role in the development of the narrative (Judg. 18).

Thus the author makes two statements in this section. First, the Israelite tribes were in such a state of disunity that no one helped the other, and they were so consumed with self-interest that they even encroached upon each other's territory. Second, the author reveals his particular interest in the cultic centers of Bethel and Dan. It is no accident that the close of this account of the northern tribes' activities involves "the house of Joseph" (whose story of conquering Bethel opened the section) along with Dan, who, in flagrant rebellion against God's plan, will later migrate far to the north and set up an illegitimate cultic center.

The overarching message of this whole section is that tribe by tribe—with the partial exception of Judah—the Israelites consistently failed to obey the Lord's command to secure what he had promised to them as one of the covenant benefits. They committed a sin, not so much of commission as of omission. But the omission was serious, representing as it did their rebellion against God's will and unfaithfulness to their own covenant pledge to obey him. Thus they missed out on the fullness of God's blessing and also missed out on fulfilling God's calling that they would be a blessing to all the world.

We also see here an example of an important principle by which God works: Although God promised them the land as a gift, the Israelites had to take the initiative to secure it for themselves. But along with the promise and the command, God also pledged to be with them to empower and enable them to face even the most difficult—indeed humanly impossible—challenges, and succeed.

Additional Notes §2

1:22 / **The house of Joseph attacked Bethel:** Some elements from the Jericho story appear in the Bethel story. They send men to spy out the city and find a man who helps them sneak into the city, on a promise that he will be treated well (cf. Josh. 2:1–21; 6:17, 25).

1:25 / **They put to city to the sword:** This verse raises perhaps one of the most difficult issues relating to interpreting Judges and other OT books. How do we understand not only God's condoning of killing and stealing—two prohibitions in the Ten Commandments—but more so his commanding the people to "put the city to the sword"? How could the LORD be with those who committed such atrocities? There are no simplistic answers to these honest and valid questions. People in the ancient Near East (not Israel alone) had the concept of holy war, which viewed human enemies as the god's (in Israel's case, the Lord's) enemies; human beings were not just killing other human beings, but they were destroying those who opposed their God(s). This does not validate genocide and injustice but suggests that God, for whatever reasons, worked within a particular historical, theological context, taking people where they were and then moving them beyond where they were. Throughout the OT, God continued to reveal more and more of himself and his ways, until he ultimately revealed himself in Jesus, who was the perfect revelation of God (John 1:18) and who revealed some things about God that superseded earlier ideas held about God. Too many people, unfortunately even Christians, have used OT Scriptures to justify all sorts of horrible attitudes and acts against others. Just because events occurred in certain OT texts does not mean that they are to be imitated today.

1:27–28 / **But Manasseh did not drive . . . them out completely:** Boling (*Judges,* p. 60) points out that the city-states not conquered by Manasseh were all strategic centers that controlled "important commercial and military traffic." Furthermore, archaeological discoveries support the account in Judges, indicating that these city-states did not become Israelite until the time of the united monarchy under David. Gezer did not become Israelite until the time of Solomon, when the Egyptian pharaoh gave it to his daughter, one of Solomon's wives (1 Kgs. 9:15–17).

1:30–36 / **Zebulun . . . Asher . . . Naphtali:** Curiously, Issachar is missing from this list. Beth Shemesh is located in the extreme north of the country, not to be confused with the Beth Shemesh of Judah.

§3 Reproof and Response (Judg. 2:1–5)

As we move into Judges 2, we do not move into a new section. Originally there were no chapter and verse divisions in the Bible; these were added in the sixteenth century to facilitate referencing. Most of the time, interpreters divided chapters and verses correctly, but in some cases they did not. Judges 2:1–5 is an instance when they did not. Judges 2 follows closely upon Judges 1, describing God's response to Israel's disobedience. It again highlights the most important theme of the book of Judges: Israel's disobedience and unfaithfulness to the Lord, with the result they were punished by continued harassment and oppression by those they failed to drive out. The Israelites' response is simply stated: they "wept aloud and, . . . they . . . offered sacrifices to the LORD." What is the meaning of these actions?

2:1–3 / The episode begins with the statement that **the angel of the LORD went up from Gilgal to Bokim.** Who is this "angel of the LORD"? While this is the first time we encounter this figure in Judges, it is not the first time in the Bible. The "angel of the LORD" or a parallel phrase ("angel of God") appears throughout the Pentateuch in contexts that usually indicate that the phrase is synonymous with the Lord himself. Though it is conspicuously absent from Deuteronomy and Joshua, it or its equivalent appears numerous times (twenty-two) in Judges, mostly in the stories of Gideon and Samson. Often the movement of the angel of the Lord—or some similar representative symbol—signals a movement or transition for Israel. The transition in the book of Judges is that the Lord will make his presence known (Exod. 2:24) to them at Bokim (Bethel). Thus the cultic center was transferred from the periphery of the promised land, at Gilgal (Josh. 5:1–12), into the heart of the country, at Bethel.

Why do we identify Bokim with Bethel? A Greek manuscript gives us a clue to the identification of Bokim by the addition of an explanatory phrase in verse 1: "Bokim, to Bethel." This, coupled with the reference to Bethel and Bacuth (related to Hb. *bokim,* "weeping") together in Genesis 35:8, indicates that the author is referring to Bethel here in Judges 2:1 and 5. Israel's unfaithfulness causes the "house of God" to become a "house of weeping."

The angel of the Lord sounded the theme song of Judges in his message: The Lord **brought** Israel **up out of Egypt and led** them **into the land** he had pledged **to give** their ancestors, with a promise and a command (vv. 1b–2a). Then in typical prophetic fashion—particularly following the model of the lawsuit, because there had been a breach of contract (covenant)—the "angel" charged: **You have disobeyed me** (v. 2). The change from third person to first person confirms that the appearance of the angel of the Lord was a theophany. The command to break down their altars echoes the Lord's similar command to Israel at the renewal of the covenant after the incident of the golden calf (Exod. 34:10, 12–13).

The following phrase, **Why have you done this?** is more precisely translated "What is this you have done?" calling to mind the question posed to Eve in the garden of Eden after she and Adam willfully rebelled against the Lord (Gen. 3:13). The sin of Israel stands close to that of Adam and Eve, in that God's purpose of bringing restoration of *shalom* to the world through a people was at risk of ever being realized. It was a dark time for Israel, but also a dark time for the whole world, as Israel's destiny was so closely bound up with that of the world (Gen. 12:3b).

The angel then announced the appropriate punishment for Israel's sin: **I will not drive them** [the Canaanites] **out before you.** The people wanted to form a relationship with those people and their gods. Well enough, the Lord would see to it that they had ample opportunity; he would not drive them out of the land. But at the same time they must know that these people and their gods **will be thorns in** their **sides and their gods will be a snare to** them. These two images, "thorn" and "snare," vividly describe the result of sinful compromise with other gods. The thorn does not immediately cause serious damage, but it is a constant irritant that distracts and wears a person down slowly. The snare catches one off guard when he or she least expects it, imprisoning suddenly and completely. No wonder the Israelites responded as they did to the angel's message!

2:4–5 / Israel's response was twofold: they **wept aloud,** and they **offered sacrifices to the LORD.** Did their weeping express true repentance, or was it just a cry of anguish for their situation? The scene calls to mind the Israelites' crying out to God when they were enslaved and oppressed by the Egyptians, though the Hebrew word is different. Israel appears to be sorry that they will suffer such severe consequences but not truly repentant with a sorrow that would lead them down a different path than they had chosen for themselves, as the continuation of the story will reveal.

They did, however, offer "sacrifices to the LORD," which may or may not reflect a true change of heart. In this case it would seem that it did not, since their sacrificing was not accompanied by other actions that gave evidence of repentance, such as confessing their sin or "breaking down altars" (v. 2). Perhaps it made them feel like they were doing what God wanted them to do, while continuing to do what they want to do (cf. 1 Sam. 15), a condition that extends beyond the borders of biblical Israel to the wider circle of humankind, even today. Certainly God demands absolute obedience and views failure to obey him absolutely as idolatry, a violation of the first, and most important, commandment (Exod. 20:1–3; Deut. 5:6–7). No matter how much people try to rationalize their compromise, God is not fooled. Also illustrated is the principle that people reap what they sow. The Israelites suffered not because God was unfaithful to them but because they were unfaithful to him. Their prostitution to foreign gods resulted in a new enslavement, from which there was no possibility of liberation such as they experienced in Egypt. They had in effect placed themselves outside of the covenant, and no other situation was possible outside of a vital relationship with the Lord, the source of all help and blessing.

Additional Notes §3

2:1 / **The angel of the LORD:** The phrase "the angel of the LORD" in the Pentateuch is found in Gen. 16:7, 9–11; 21:17; 22:11–15; 24:7, 40; 31:11; Exod. 3:2; 14:19; 23:20, 23; 33:2; Num. 20:16; 22:16, 22–27, 31–35.

I brought you up out of Egypt: The Lord's act in liberating the Israelites from slavery is foundational to his claim over them as his people in covenant contexts (cf. Deut 1:3, 35; 6:10, 18, 23; 7:13; 8:1; 11:9, 21; 19:8; 26:3, 15; 28:11; 30:20; 31:20–23).

2:5 / **They offered sacrifices to the LORD:** The Hb. word for the type of offering here *(zebah)* is somewhat generic, referring in general to a sacrifice in which the offerer participates by eating the sacrificial meat, in contrast to a whole burnt offering, which, as its name implies, is wholly offered to the Lord by burning it completely. The term *zebah* often is used interchangeably with another term, *selamim*, "fellowship offerings," which may also be translated as "peace offerings," "covenant offerings," or even "salvation offerings." Thus the *zebah* was often a communal meal that renewed or celebrated the offerer's covenant relationship with the Lord and with others with whom one shared the meal. It was often sacrificed either in requesting help from the Lord or in celebrating the Lord's covenant faithfulness *(hesed)* in acting on Israel's behalf.

§4 Survey of Israel's Early History: Joshua to Judges (Judg. 2:6–3:6)

Here begins a new section, but not immediately a new subject. In fact, rather than carrying the story forward, the text looks back to the period immediately after the Israelites renewed their covenant with the Lord at Shechem (Josh. 24). The text picks up nearly where the book of Joshua left off. Joshua 24:28 almost word for word corresponds to Judges 2:6. The section that follows (vv. 10–19) points to the author's special concern with Israel's spiritual condition in the generation after Joshua. What we have in these verses is a prime example of "second verse same as the first." There is nothing new in this analysis of Israel's spiritual history, and the repetition of events and themes serves only to emphasize Israel's spiritual apostasy during this period.

The section also functions as a prologue to the stories of the judges, presenting the stereotypic pattern that will be followed more or less consistently throughout the next fourteen chapters of the book. Finally, in 3:1–6, the same message is communicated in another way, with a few significant variations. We might think the author was beating this into the ground, and he was. This makes him not a poor writer but a good preacher. These texts were meant to persuade, to exhort, to encourage, and to warn, not simply to tell a story or recount historical events.

2:6–9 / The account assumes knowledge of the prior events. According to both Joshua and Judges, the Israelites got off to a good start after the covenant renewal ceremony at Shechem (Josh. 24:1–27). We may be sure that the author of Judges assumed that his readers connected Joshua's dismissing the people (v. 6a) with the covenant renewal ceremony, even though he does not explicitly mention it.

Several key Deuteronomic themes appear in these verses. For one, the author highlights the theme of the land: the Israelites **went to take possession of the land.** The further modifying statement, **each to his own inheritance,** renders it more emphatic, as does the detailed account of Joshua's burial **in the land of his inheritance** (vv. 8–9). Second, there is the important theme of obedience; taking "possession of the land" was the supreme act of obedience. The command to do so picks up the constantly recurring refrain from the book of Deuteronomy, where the land is mentioned no fewer than thirty-four times and the command to possess it thirty-five times. Another Deuteronomic theme, corresponding to obedience, is purity of worship. **The people served the LORD.** Purity of worship consists of worshiping the Lord alone. Israel's basic confessional statement of faith and faithfulness is found in Deuteronomy 6:4: "Hear, O Israel: the LORD our God, the LORD is one." That "the people served the LORD" is understood to refer to exclusive worship of the Lord, in keeping with the Deuteronomic standard. Finally, the theme of leadership is also highlighted. The people served the Lord as long as they had leaders who knew the Lord; people can and will rise only to the moral and spiritual level of their leaders, a principle that will hold true throughout the book of Judges.

2:10–15 / That whole generation was **gathered to their fathers,** and **another generation grew up,** which was epitomized by two characteristics: They **knew neither the LORD nor what he had done for Israel.** The author signals the transition from one epoch to another in absolute terms. As the previous generation absolutely knew the Lord and served him faithfully, so the present generation absolutely departed from that faithful relationship. Surely the author exaggerates the scope of Israel's sin, but exaggeration as a rhetorical technique is widely used in preaching, as one can hear on any given Sunday almost any place in the world. Again, Deuteronomic literature is highly homiletical in purpose and character.

The effect of not knowing the Lord is expressed not in intellectual categories but in ethical ones: they **did evil in the eyes of the LORD** (v. 11). This emphasis upon conduct pervades biblical faith, both Jewish and Christian. Faith is not merely something that one believes, or gives intellectual assent to, but essentially something one does. The biblical concept of faith is more accurately expressed in terms of faithfulness.

What does it mean to do "evil in the eyes of the LORD"? The expression is one of the most stereotypic in the Deuteronomic History. It constitutes the opening framework of the bulk of the judges' stories (Judg. 3:7, 12; 4:1; 6:1; 10:6; 13:1), added by the Deuteronomic author to press home his point. We are not left to figure its meaning out on our own but are told exactly what is the nature of the evil: they **served the Baals, they forsook the LORD, the God of their fathers, they followed and worshiped various gods of the peoples around them, they forsook the LORD,** and they **served Baal and the Ashtoreths.** The description is replete with repetition, in keeping with the author's obsession with making sure his message was clear. Evil is conceptualized in terms of unfaithfulness to the Sinai covenant, renewed again as the people were poised to enter the promised land (Deut. 27:1–32:47) and at Shechem, under Joshua's leadership (Joshua 24). The author's present audience did not physically participate in those ceremonies, but the nature of biblical faith was such that it was as if they had been present (cf. Deut. 5:1–3).

What was the power of these Canaanite religions that they were able to draw away God's covenant people, who had experienced numerous blessings and miracles, to worship their gods— and so quickly at that? Canaanite religions, essentially fertility cults, had strong appeal in two areas: physical gratification and economic security or success. It was not only great business to worship Baal but also great fun! The Baal cult operated on the principle of sympathetic magic, so in order to ensure fertility of people, animals, and crops, a person would engage in sexual intercourse with a cult prostitute—male or female—at the local Baal shrine. The purpose was to inspire Baal to act likewise on the person's behalf and thus to ensure fertility in all areas of life. Of course, the Lord promised his people that he would supply all of their needs and even more. But they wanted to make sure that all their bases were covered, as it were, and so worshiped Baal along with the Lord. The Lord viewed this not as an expedient business move on their part but as the gravest offense they could commit against him, on a par with the sin of worshiping the golden calf (Exod. 32). He demanded exclusive worship (Deut. 6:13–15) or none at all.

The result of this turning away from the Lord was that he, **in anger,** turned away from them. He no longer protected them from their **enemies** (vv. 14–15a) but worked **against them** rather than in their behalf. Their punishment suited the sin; they had worshiped Baal in order to ensure economic security, and their punishment consisted of being **plundered** by their enemies. The author also reminded the people that they had been duly warned of the consequences of turning to other gods (see Deut. 31:17, 21), and they should not be surprised at their punishment.

The final statement is very short but not very sweet—**they were in great distress** (v. 15b). This echoes the Israelites' circumstances when they were enslaved in Egypt (Exod. 2:23; 3:7). The irony is that they found themselves once again enslaved (v. 14b) after the Lord had brought them out of Egypt, when they were in the promised land of blessing.

2:16–19 / But the story was not yet finished. **The LORD had mercy on them and raised up judges, who saved them out of the hands of these raiders** (v. 16). Anyone who thinks there is no grace in the OT has not read this text and many others. The Lord revealed his great grace and mercy again and again throughout the story of Israel. Indeed, he himself explained his own name, Yahweh (Lord), in terms of grace (Exod. 34:1–28). The Lord does punish sin, but how vast is the difference between the scope of his grace and the scope of his wrath!

This same Lord is the one who graciously raised up judges to rescue Israel from those who plundered them. But what was Israel's response? **They would not listen to their judges but prostituted themselves to other gods and worshiped them.** Moreover, **they quickly turned from the way . . . of obedience to the LORD's commands** (v. 17). Already momentum is picking up in the downward spiral toward chaos. The verb behind "would not listen" is *sm'*, which points back to Israel's fundamental faith confession, the Shema (Deut. 6:4). The very thing that made Israel the Lord's people was the fact that they heard, they listened, and they obeyed. Now, in contrast to their ancestors, they do not hear the Lord, and they do not hear those whom he has sent to help them.

Verse 18 highlights the Lord's great mercy toward Israel in raising up judges to rescue them, this time even more emphatically: **for the LORD had compassion on them as they groaned under those who oppressed and afflicted them.** We hear echoes of Israel's enslavement in Egypt (Exod. 2:23–25), even to the point of verbal correspondence. By this the author indirectly underscores the incongruity of the fact that Israel should again be enslaved and oppressed, in the promised land, where they should be experiencing *shalom*. *Shalom* was God's plan for them, but they refused his good gifts and had no one to blame but themselves.

The spiraling movement never let up but continued to move downward: **When the judge died, the people returned to ways even more corrupt than those of their fathers** (v. 19). As before, their rebellion against the Lord is described in terms of unfaithfulness to their covenant with him and refusal to repent. The first part of this statement repeats the indictment against them in verse 17, but the second part adds the element of hardening the heart against the Lord, which expresses in yet another way the accelerating movement toward apostasy.

2:20–23 / The cycle continues with the next element— **the LORD was very angry with Israel** and pledged to no longer drive out before them any of the nations Joshua left when he died. Earlier the Lord responded to Israel's waywardness by raising up judges to rescue them, but now his patience is exhausted. The level of his anger reaches the same level as he expressed after the sin of the golden calf. He calls Israel **this nation** (v. 20). Although it does not sound particularly bad in English, the Hebrew phrase is as caustic as possible. The word *goy* ("nation") elsewhere, with few exceptions, denotes Gentile nations, those who stood outside of God's covenant, who had no relationship with him. Thus the Lord essentially disowned Israel, a decision further emphasized by the reference to their having violated the covenant (v. 20) and particularly by the phrase **and has not listened to** [*sm'*] **me.** If the nation would not hear, they were not his people.

If they were not his people, God was no longer bound to care for them by driving out the Canaanites. While this repeats the idea expressed in 2:3, here a new element appears: the Lord (emphatic) **will use** the nations **to test Israel and see whether they will keep the way of the LORD and walk in it as their forefathers did.** Perhaps God was looking not for further proof of their disobedience but for their repentance, their turning back to him. The picture of God calls to mind Jesus' parable of the gracious father (Luke 15:11–32); God was ever waiting to welcome them home into fellowship with him, ever holding out the hope that this testing would produce positive results.

3:1–6 / The chapter division artificially separates the beginning verses of Judges 3 from Judges 2. But this section more logically serves as a concluding summary of Israel's circumstances and spiritual condition. It consists of five parts: a general introductory statement; a list of nations that surrounded Israel's territory; a repetition of the rationale for their being left (i.e., **to test . . .**

the **Israelites**); a second list of nations (ones that lived within Israel's territory); and a concluding commentary on Israel's apostasy. In this section the author draws from Deuteronomy 7:1–4, but with a twist. In Deuteronomy the Lord promised to drive out these nations, while Judges emphasizes that they were not driven out—one more reminder of the Israelites' failure to enter fully into the blessings that the Lord had intended for them.

The testing of Israel is an important concern to the author, for he repeats the statement three times in almost as many verses. But a narrative intrusion into the story (v. 2) introduces a completely different idea—that the Lord left the nations **only to teach warfare to the descendants of the Israelites who had not had previous battle experience.** How are we to understand this "hair-raising explanation"(Boling, *Judges*, p. 77)? Surely this is a case in which we clearly see the hand of a later editor commenting from his own particular ideology or agenda. Possibly he plays upon two meanings for "test" in Hebrew—either proving (finding out) or improving (refining, training; cf. 2 Chron. 32:31). Whatever was going on in his mind, this is a strange interpretation of Israel's circumstances.

In summary, 2:6–3:6 provides an overall perspective on Israel's history, definitely Deuteronomic in emphasis. Israel quickly turned away from its covenant commitments to the Lord and, testing to the limits the Lord's enduring patience and manifold grace, suffered the consequences of its alienation from the Source of all good. Punishment did not lead Israel back to restored relationship with the Lord; rather, the people continued to harden their hearts against the Lord. But the story is not finished. The Lord is not finished. The compassionate grace of the Lord causes him to keep reaching out to his beloved people, as we shall see in the stories of the judges, to which the author now turns.

Additional Notes §4

2:7 / **Who had seen all the great things the LORD had done for Israel:** The text says that the elders had seen all the great things the Lord had done for them, while the parallel passage in Joshua uses a form of the verb *yd'*, ("to know"), translated in the NIV as "experienced." This expresses the Hebraic concept of knowing, which is always essentially existential and intensely personal, involving the whole person. Evidence of this is the fact that the verb also carries the nuance of to engage in sexual intercourse (e.g., Gen. 4:1). Thus the elders had a firsthand encounter with the Lord and his mighty acts on their behalf.

2:10 / That whole generation was **gathered to their fathers:** This expression ("gathered to their fathers") derives from the custom of burying all the members of an extended family in a family tomb. The author's judgment on the generations that followed is revealed, among other ways, in the chiastic structure of 2:6–3:6, in which the center is v. 17 (see Hamlin, *At Risk in the Promised Land,* p. 58).

2:11 / The Israelites did evil in the eyes of the LORD: The phrase appears frequently in Deuteronomic literature (e.g., Deut. 4:25; 9:18; 17:2; 31:29; 1 Sam. 15:19; 2 Sam. 12:9; 1 Kgs. 15:26, 34; 16:25, 30; 22:52; 2 Kgs. 3:2).

2:13 / They . . . forsook the LORD **. . . and served Baal and the Ashtoreths:** Prohibitions against worship of Baal and the Ashtoreths is widespread in Deuteronomic literature. Note the promises in Deut. 7:12–15; 28:2–14, which were likely given against the backdrop and strong influence of the Baal cult.

2:17 / They would not listen to their judges: Jews still recite the Shema daily and refer to this confession as "taking upon oneself the yoke of the kingdom," expressing their submission to the Lord as their King and their readiness to do his will. In this regard, note the parallel phrases in the Lord's Prayer: "Your kingdom come, your will be done" (Matt. 6:10).

2:22 / I will use them to test Israel: This new point is rather strange, since the author has just told us that the Israelites did not obey God. Why does God need further proof of their disobedience? Many interpreters have wrestled with this question, and some have found a satisfactory answer in identifying underlying sources and redactors. For example, Boling (*Judges,* p. 75) comments that "it is necessary . . . to distinguish at least three hands at work in ch. 2, none of them tampering with the work of a predecessor, but each supplying a paragraph or two for the sake of a fuller picture." He places vv. 20–23 as the earliest strand of the section.

§5 Othniel (Judg. 3:7–11)

After not one but two extended prologues, we finally get into the stories of the judges. Othniel is the first of twelve judges, six major and six minor judges (Abimelech is an antijudge). The major judges' stories are of varying length and complexity, while those of the minor judges can hardly be categorized as stories; they are more precisely brief notices, perhaps attached to an incident that is barely remembered. The major judges' stories are clearly brought together within a common framework created by the Deuteronomic editor to drive home his message about Israel's downward spiral of sin and God's unfathomable and unfailing grace that meets their sin at every point.

One interesting feature of Othniel's story is that we do not meet him here for the first time; we have already gotten a glimpse of him in action (1:13–14), though hardly so. He is presented as the paradigmatic judge. Significantly, the elements commonly found—though not consistently—in the major judges' stories all appear in Othniel's story.

3:7–8 / The stereotypic formula occurs for the first time in a judge's story: **The Israelites did evil in the eyes of the LORD.** The evil consisted of two things: **they forgot the LORD their God and** they **served the Baals and the Asherahs.** It is clear by the elaboration in verse 7 (cf. 2:11) that the expression to "forget the LORD" means much more than a temporary lapse of memory. It, or its corollary antithetic expression "to remember the LORD," appears repeatedly and again in Deuteronomy (e.g., 4:9, 23; 5:15; 6:12; 8:2, 11, 14, 18–19; 9:7, 27; 31:21, 32:18) as a synonym for to sin, or to turn away from the Lord.

The second and third elements of the Deuteronomic framework spell out the consequence of the Israelites' turning away from the Lord: he became angry, and he **sold them into the hands of Cushan-Rishathaim, king of Aram Naharaim, to whom** they **were subject for eight years** (v. 8). It is not clear to whom this refers. To begin with, Aram Naharaim most naturally refers to a geographical area far to the north of the land of Israel. Naharaim means "two rivers," logically denoting the Tigris and Euphrates rivers, but this would put the enemy kingdom in northern Mesopotamia, far away from any possible threat to Israel. Second, Cushan-Rishathaim is problematic. "Cush" is related to Canaan according to Genesis 10:6–15, and "Rishathaim" could well be a play on the root *rs'*, or "wicked" ("doubly wicked"); thus it could be a parody on the name of an unknown Canaanite leader.

3:9–11 / Israel's response to this enslavement was that **they cried out to the LORD.** Nothing in this statement points to repentance on Israel's part. Crying out is not the same as repenting. The Israelites were not sorry enough to change their ways, only enough to beg for help. The wonder in these stories is that despite a lack of true repentance, the Lord nevertheless helped his people—an example of grace that is truly amazing.

In his amazing grace, the Lord **raised up for them a deliverer . . . , who saved them.** The root term for both deliverer and saved is the same in Hebrew *(ys')*. What had been a general statement in the introduction (2:16, 18) now becomes specified in terms of a particular person, Othniel, the son of Kenaz, Caleb's younger brother. The term "judge" has not yet appeared; it will in verse 10, in the context of the notice that **the Spirit of the LORD came upon** Othniel. The charismatic endowment of the Holy Spirit was essential for the judge to enable him or her to be capable of delivering the people against those much more numerous and much better equipped than they were. We are not given any details about how the Spirit came, only the effects of the Spirit's coming—success in battle (v. 10).

The result of this miraculous deliverance was that **the land had peace** [lit. rest] **for forty years, until Othniel son of Kenaz died** (v. 11) The statement picks up almost word for word on the assertion of Judges 2:18 and implies that the situation deteriorated quickly after the judge's death. This was the cycle, rather the downward spiral, that grew increasingly worse with each judge's term of leadership.

Additional Notes §5

3:7 / **Served the Baals and the Asherahs:** That the Asherah is portrayed as a goddess that was worshiped alongside the Baals is somewhat unusual. It was essentially a wooden pole that stood at a religious shrine, rather than a goddess. But it, or a synonym Ashterah, came to be associated with Baal's consort Astarte and thus to be worshiped as her image (1 Kgs. 18:19; 2 Kgs. 23:4). A similar dynamic can be seen in the Israelites' worshiping the bronze snake as a god in itself rather than a representative of God's powerful act on their behalf (2 Kgs. 18:4). J. A. Soggin (*Judges: A Commentary* [trans. J. Bowden; Philadelphia: Westminster, 1981], p. 45) suggests that the terms did not refer to these specific deities but stereotypically denoted polytheism in general.

3:8 / **He sold them into the hands of Cushan-Rishathaim king of Aram Nahariam:** Some scholars have suggested that the text is corrupt and the unpointed text should read *'dm*, Edom, instead of *'rm*, with *nhrym* being a secondary addition (see Soggin, *Judges*, p. 47). Boling, however, offers a more cogent hypothesis. He suggests that "the reading *'rm nhrym* is the result of a misdivision of an unpointed text (originally *'rmn hrym*, "Fortress of the Mountains") which subsequently suffered a haplography due to homoioteleuton in the *Vorlage* of LXX^A" (*Judges*, p. 81).

§6 Ehud and Shamgar (Judg. 3:12–31)

The story of Ehud is perhaps one of the oldest in the book of Judges and one of the best, from the standpoint of sheer narrative artistry. In contrast to Othniel's story, which was a bare, black-and-white etching, Ehud's story is full of rich, colorful detail; we are almost blinded by the brilliant brushstrokes of its color.

Such accolades may come as a surprise to people who are at most embarrassed and at the least puzzled that the story is even in the Bible. They are put off by its graphic character. Its sanctioning of deception and murder stretches to the limit most modern Christian sensibilities regarding proper moral conduct. Despite its David-and-Goliath storyline, the story of Ehud has not found its way into many children's Bible story books.

To appreciate the story we must put ourselves in the place of those who first told and first heard it. They were Israelites who had been enslaved by a foreign power for eighteen years, beaten down so far that they saw no way to ever rise up again and without hope of ever realizing their calling as the Lord's people in the promised land. We must also put on Hebrew glasses to appreciate the story. The story is a gold mine of standard Hebrew literary conventions, which add spice and enhance its meaning. Above all, we must approach the story with a sense of humor and laugh with those who told it and heard it in early days of Israel's history.

3:12–14 / The beginning of the story is signaled by the refrain-like statement **Once again the Israelites did evil in the eyes of the LORD.** The significant addition of one Hebrew word to the refrain, however, sounds a major theme in the book of Judges, that of increasing sin. The verb translated here adverbially as "once again" frequently carries the connotation of "to add to." Thus the Israelites increasingly did evil, or acted even more wickedly. Theologically significant is the statement that **the LORD gave Eglon . . . power over Israel.** The Lord sovereignly directs the course of human history, raising up nations and bringing them down. Moreover, not only did Eglon have power over Israel, but also he was joined by **the Ammonites and Amalekites** (v. 13), nations that lay more or less to the northeast and southwest of Moab, respectively. Together they were able to enter Israelite territory to the west of the Jordan River and take **possession of the City of Palms** (Jericho). There is irony in the notice that **the Israelites were subject to Eglon** (v. 14). The Hebrew verb *('bd)* carries the nuance of "to serve"; they did not want to serve the Lord (cf. 2:19), so they ended up serving Eglon, who, we can assume, was a much harder taskmaster.

3:15–19 / This severe crisis brought Israel to its knees, but not necessarily in repentance. The text states only that **the Israelites cried out to the LORD** (Hb. *z'q;* cf. Exod. 2:23). Out of sheer grace, the Lord responded to their cry for help and **gave them a deliverer—Ehud, a left-handed man.** The NIV places the appositional phrase "a left-handed man" immediately after Ehud's name to avoid confusion about whom it describes, but the Hebrew text places the phrase at the end, hinting by word order that there is more here than meets the eye, and it has to do with Ehud's hand. We are further drawn to focus on his hand because of a wordplay in Hebrew. Benjamin is *ben yemin* ("son of [my] right hand") and "left-handed" is *'itter yad yemino* ("bound [in] his right hand"). In other words, Ehud was a non-right-handed son of [a] right hand.

Wordplay and double entendre also play a key role in the following scene. The full impact of the Hebrew words is lost in translation, so I offer my translation: "The Israelites sent *by his hand a present* for Eglon, king of Moab." At this point, in an aside, the author lets us in on a secret. Revealing this element here is good storytelling, because it keeps our focus on Ehud's hand and heightens our anticipation of how Ehud will deliver his present. **Ehud had made** [Hb. "for him"] **a double-edged sword . . . , which he strapped to his right** [Hb. *yemino*] **thigh under his clothing.** The words "for him" could equally be translated "for himself," thus referring either to Ehud or to Eglon. Which did the author intend? Probably both. The following phrase is likewise full of double entendre (again, my translation): "He brought near the present to Eglon, king of Moab." Ehud brought the king tribute on behalf of Israel, but even as he brought it near, he also brought near the real present!

Just as the story begins to gain momentum, the author interrupts with another detail, which could appear insignificant:

"Now Eglon was a very fat man" (my translation). But the narrative intrusion serves to communicate a point that is not to be
missed; this factor will play a role in the story. The story then
quickly moves to the climactic scene, the author barely mentioning the presentation of tribute (v. 18) in order to get to the real presentation. When Ehud was alone with the king, he whispered in
the king's ear: "A secret word/thing (Hb. *dbr*) I have for you, O
king." This part of the story turns on a wordplay between the two
meanings of the Hebrew word *dabar*, further emphasized by its
position as first in the Hebrew sentence. The king assumed that
Ehud brought some **secret message,** such as a spy report, but Ehud
really had a secret thing for the king. The message *was* the thing.
The dialogue in this story, though terse, speaks volumes. The only
word the king speaks in the entire story is **Quiet.**

3:20–23 / Ehud, likewise a man of few words, speaks only
three brief sentences, the second of which repeats the first—with
one significant change: "A word/thing from God I have for you"
(my translation). God is the one who gives the word or thing, that
Eglon will soon receive. **The king rose** in excited anticipation of
the special word or thing, and Ehud moved closer to deliver it.
The pace of the scene picks up with several staccato phrases in
succession: **Ehud reached with his left hand, drew the sword
from his right thigh and plunged it into the king's belly.** But then
instead of moving forward, the author stops the motion long
enough to focus upon the sword in Ehud's left hand as it pene-
trated the king's corpulent belly, describing with gusto every gory
detail, surely to the delight of his audience: **Even the handle sank
in after the blade, which came out his back. Ehud did not pull the
sword out, and the fat closed in over it.** Such excessive description is unusual in Hebrew narrative and thus expresses the author's desire to savor every detail of the climactic moment.

3:24–25 / The next scene must have been purely for entertainment's sake, for the only thing it positively contributes to
the story is perhaps to explain how Ehud was able to get so far
away before the deed was discovered. It focuses upon the servants waiting outside the door of the upper room, presuming that
the king had not called them back in because he was **relieving
himself in the inner room.** And so **they waited** . . . and they
waited . . . and finally **unlocked** the doors. The Hebrew text of
verse 25b is extraordinary in its dramatic impact: "And they took

the key and they unlocked (or opened), and behold: their lord, fallen to the ground, dead!" (my translation).

3:26–30 / While the servants were waiting, **Ehud got away.** At **Seirah . . . he blew a trumpet** to muster **the Israelites** (Ephraimites) for battle against the Moabites. In his instructions to those who responded, he acknowledged the need for a community effort to complete the liberation process and generously shared the victory with them, thus exemplifying the theme of unity. The final notice of the story is predictable: **That day Moab was made subject to Israel, and the land had peace for eighty years.** One unusual feature is the lengthy period of peace the land enjoyed, double the stereotypic unit of forty years, which reflects Israel's more or less healthy spiritual condition. They will not enjoy such a lengthy time again, for their spiritual condition deteriorates rapidly from this time forward.

3:31 / The chapter closes with a very brief notice about a judge named **Shamgar.** It does not begin or end with the usual phrases; neither are any of the other stereotypic elements such as geographical or genealogical details in the core of the story. In fact, it is not a story. The summarizing phrase seems like no more than an afterthought or a comment added to bring the story into conformity with those of the other judges. Moreover, Shamgar is not even a Hebrew name, and **Anath** is the name of a Canaanite goddess. Finally, the author ignores Shamgar when he moves to the story of Deborah, connecting it directly with Ehud's story (Judg. 4:1).

There are three reasonable explanations for why Shamgar's story was incorporated into the book of Judges: because Shamgar is mentioned in the Song of Deborah (Judg. 5:6), the author wanted to give him a story; because Shamgar defeated the Philistines, who later became Israel's archenemy, his story was incorporated into Israelite tradition and subsequently into the book of Judges; because the author wanted to present twelve judges, so incorporated Shamgar's story to complete the roster. While the last explanation is likely correct, they may not be mutually exclusive reasons; some may be combined with others, or all three may be combined.

Additional Notes §6

3:12 / **Once again the Israelites did evil in the eyes of the LORD:** In the Hb. text there is perhaps a pun. *Wayyosipu* ("the Israelites increasingly did evil") and *wayye'esop* ("Eglon gathered together . . . the Ammonites and Amalekites"), the point being that just as Israel increased in sin, so the enemies increased in number as they joined together against Israel. The Ammonites cooperated with the Moabites against Israel on other occasions (2 Chron. 20:1); Amalek, a nomadic people from the southern desert, is consistently portrayed as extremely hostile to Israel (Deut. 25:17–19; Exod. 17:8–16). The Hebrew word *'eglon* (Eglon) shares the same root with the word for "round," so perhaps another pun is intended (i.e., he was rotund or roly-poly).

3:13 / **They took possession of the City of Palms:** Jericho was the closest city and elsewhere called the City of Palms (Deut. 34:3), but problematic is Josh. 6:21–26, which indicates that Jericho remained a ruin (cf. 1 Kgs. 16:34). Soggin (*Judges,* p. 54) suggests that the designation "City of Palms" "can easily be explained by the desire of the redactors not to create tensions between the note and the traditional theory according to which the city was destroyed by Joshua, only to be rebuilt in 1 Kgs. 16:34." The problem is even more complex than it would first appear, for 2 Sam. 10:5 implies that Jericho was rebuilt at least by the time of David. Cundall (*Judges,* p. 75) posits that Jericho was occupied by Moab but not rebuilt into a walled fortress. But it is difficult to imagine that David would have left such a strategic location unfortified. The Hebrew verb for "take possession" (*yrs;* v. 13) is the same that repeatedly designates the Israelite settlement of the promised land, thus emphasizing that Israel no longer had possession of its inheritance, a harsh statement indeed.

3:15 / **Ehud, a left-handed man:** It has been suggested that the word *'itter* ("bound, drawn up") implies that Ehud was disabled in his right hand (cf. Soggin, *Judges,* p. 50). But the same phrase describes the Benjamite warriors in Judg. 20:16, and it is not likely that all of them suffered from some physical disability. The Benjamites seem to have been famous for being left-handed.

3:25 / **There they saw their lord fallen to the floor, dead:** The translation "There they saw their lord fallen to the floor, dead" does not do justice to the word *hinneh;* it is a strong exclamatory particle that emphatically points to the object or statement that follows it. One might say, "They couldn't believe their eyes!"

3:27 / **He blew a trumpet:** Here is another wordplay: *wayyitqa'e* ("plunged") in v. 21, and *wayyitqa'* ("blew a trumpet") are both formed off the same root. This holy war against Moab was fought in two stages (the assassination of Eglon and the ensuing battle), each one with the help of the sovereign Lord, who was gracious and faithful to Israel. On the trumpet as an instrument for mustering troops, see Num. 10:9; 31:6.

3:31 / **Shamgar son of Anath:** Anath was a goddess of war (see P. C. Craigie, "Deborah and Anat: A Study of Poetic Imagery (Judges 5)," *ZAW* 90 [1978], pp. 374–81). Also G. F. Moore (*A Critical and Exegetical Commentary on Judges* [ICC; Edinburgh: T&T Clark, 1976], p. 106) comments: "Anath is represented in an Egyptian stele in the British Museum, sitting, holding shield and javelin in the right hand, while with the left she brandishes a battle axe." Cundall (*Judges,* pp. 80–81) describes Shamgar's weapon of choice: "An ox goad was a formidable [weapon]. . . . It was a long-handled (between 8 and 10 feet), pointed instrument tipped with metal, and when freshly sharpened it would have many of the qualities of a spear."

§7 Deborah and Barak (Judg. 4:1–24)

The story of the fourth of Israel's judges is full of the unexpected. Deborah is a multigifted woman whose roles parallel those of Moses. Barak behaves as anything but a hero of faith. Jael, a simple, non-Israelite woman, is privileged to deal the death blow to a powerful warrior—with highly unconventional weapons, a tent peg and hammer. Unlike other judges' stories, the narrative account is followed by a poem, the Song of Deborah, which celebrates the Lord's miraculous victory on behalf of Israel.

4:1–3 / The story of Deborah is introduced in the way we have come to expect, with only the names, places, and duration of oppression changed. The Israelites once again found themselves enslaved, this time to **Jabin, a king of Canaan.** Then the author directs our attention to two details peculiar to this story, the reference to **Sisera** and to the king's arsenal of **nine hundred iron chariots,** both of which are key elements. The Israelites suffered long and hard for their rebellion, until they finally **cried to the Lord,** the only one who could help them.

4:4–5 / The scene abruptly switches to another part of the country, **the hill country of Ephraim,** where a woman sits **under** a palm tree, judging (NIV: **leading**) the Israelites. The woman was Deborah, the lone judge who was a woman, the lone judge who was also a prophetess, and the lone judge who served in a judicial capacity before leading the people to freedom. Even the grammar of the text introducing Deborah accents her stature as a leader by departing from normal Hebrew word order (verb-subject) to place her name first in the clause: **Deborah . . . was leading Israel at that time.** From the beginning, the focus is upon her—her identity and her special role in the life of Israel. Moreover, the whole scene bears a striking resemblance to that of Moses seated in the wilderness, settling the disputes of those who likewise looked to him for justice (Exod. 18:13–16). Deborah's prophetic gifting was expressed as she gave guidance to those who sought to know God's word and will, as well as in her speaking on behalf of the Lord to commission Barak (vv. 6–7), to announce the appropriate moment for the battle and to assure Barak of the Lord's help (v. 14).

The appositional phrase translated in the NIV as **wife of Lappidoth** is ambiguous in Hebrew and thus has given rise to several translations and interpretations. For example, *lappidot* could be a noun ("torches, lightning flashes"), suggesting that Deborah was a "woman of fire." Others have proposed that because Lappidoth and Barak (lightning) are similar in meaning they were one and the same—Barak was really Deborah's husband. Some have carried it a step further, suggesting that *lappidot* was Barak's nickname. But more important than her husband's name was what she did. The Hebrew text emphatically states that she "was leading (Hb. judging) Israel at that time" and is specific that **she held court under the Palm of Deborah between Ramah and Bethel in the hill country of Ephraim.** The reference to Ramah points ahead to the great prophet and greatest judge of Israel—Samuel (1 Sam. 7:15–17).

4:6–10 / In place of the usual notice that the Lord sent or raised up such and such a judge, the text reports that Deborah **sent for Barak** and commissioned him in the name of the Lord to fight a battle, which he would win, with the help of the Lord (vv. 6–7). With a commission from the Lord and such a promise of success, how could Barak refuse? His response is surprising, if very human: **If you go with me, I will go; but if you don't go with me, I won't go** (v. 8). Granted, an army with nine hundred iron chariots would be a formidable foe, but not every commander goes to war with a prior assurance of success from the Lord of the universe. Considering Barak's response, it is amazing that the author of the book of Hebrews places Barak in his trophy cases of heroes of the faith. But Barak is not the only one in history who has chosen to focus upon the flesh and blood that he can see rather than the one whom he cannot physically see. And the Lord was not pleased with his response.

Deborah agreed to accompany Barak but added a note of rebuke: **The honor will not be yours, for the LORD will hand Sisera over to a woman.** These words must have stung Barak; to not receive the honor for the victory would have been bad enough, but for a woman to receive it in his stead would have been a bitter pill, and a shameful bitter pill at that. Naturally, we assume Deborah was speaking about herself as the honored woman, but the author is very skillfully setting the stage for a surprise ending.

4:11 / The troops were called up, the battle was ready to begin, the climactic point of the story was at hand—and the author again abruptly shifts the scene to tell us about some Bedouin named **Heber** who **pitched his tent . . . near Kedesh** (v. 11). We might find ourselves asking, Who cares? But this kind of backtracking is common in Hebrew narrative. And far from being superfluous, the information is important in setting up the events that will follow; the fact that the author draws attention to it out of place, as it were, serves to highlight its importance even more. We can see in this unusual movement of the Kenites God's sovereign hand at work, orchestrating the circumstances to use Jael in bringing deliverance to Israel.

4:12–16 / The scene again shifts to **Mount Tabor** and to **the Kishon River,** where the troops were drawn up and prepared for battle. Sisera moved to attack **when they told** him **that Barak . . . had gone up to** Mount Tabor; likewise Barak moved to attack when he was told something, the word from Deborah: **Go! This is the day the LORD has given Sisera into your hands. Has not the LORD gone ahead of you?** The ensuing battle that has taken so long to happen is described rather briefly (vv. 14b–16), as if the author tells about it only to get to what follows. He does, however, tell enough to get the point across that the victory was miraculous: **the LORD routed Sisera and all his chariots and army by the sword.** (v. 15). We are not told how the Lord routed the enemy, but the Song of Deborah provides the crucial information that a timely storm caused the chariots to bog down in the river (5:20–22), thus immobilizing Sisera's main offensive weapon. The drowning of Sisera's troops recalls the Lord's miraculous intervention under Moses' leadership when Pharaoh's army was drowned in the Reed Sea.

Amid all the clatter and confusion of horses and iron and men clashing and crashing and crying out we almost miss a lone figure running away from the scene of the battle. The text quietly notes that **Sisera abandoned his chariot and fled on foot** (v. 15). Even though Sisera's army was completely destroyed (v. 16), Deborah's prophecy had not yet been fulfilled. And so we focus upon Sisera, trailing his movement from the battlefield.

4:17–21 / There is some question, understandably, about whether verse 17 more appropriately falls within the previous division or within this one. The Hebrew text, however, is clear. The word order indicates that it belongs with this section and that the author wants to keep us focused on Sisera. The verse could be paraphrased, "Now back to Sisera, who, as you will recall, fled on foot." The specific repetition of the phrase "on foot" (Hb. *beraglayw*) sets up a wordplay that will be picked up later in the story, along with several other wordplays.

Sisera . . . fled . . . to the tent of Jael, the wife of Heber the Kenite (v. 17). Because the Kenites had **friendly relations** with Jabin, Sisera assumed that Jael was an ally and trustingly went to her tent. But the author has already told us that the Kenites were related to Moses' father-in-law, which should lead us to suspect that these Kenites have closer ties with the Israelites than with Jabin. **Jael went out to meet Sisera.** Did she know who he was? Later events indicate that she recognized him. She urged him, "Turn aside, my lord, turn aside to me (lit.). **Don't be afraid.**" Too weary to refuse, Sisera finally gave in to her effusive invitations and **entered her tent.**

The next events unfolded quickly: **She put a covering over him,** he asked for **some water,** and **she opened a skin of milk** and **gave him a drink.** Then she **covered him up** again. All of this extra care was perfectly in keeping with the protocols of Semitic hospitality (cf. Gen. 18:1–8), but more so carefully calculated to give Sisera a false sense of security. He peacefully went off to sleep, like a baby on his mother's lap, but not before he gave Jael final instructions to not let anyone know he was there (v. 20). The word rendered as **someone** in the NIV is "a man" in the Hebrew text, which highlights the irony in the story: Sisera thought he had to fear a male, but it was a woman who did him in when he least expected it. The ironic word also recalls Deborah's prophecy and signals that it is about to be fulfilled.

The author moved immediately to the most important scene, recounted deliberately and directly, with not one wasted word: **But Jael, Heber's wife, picked up a tent peg and a hammer and went quietly to him while he lay fast asleep, exhausted. She drove the peg through his temple into the ground, and**—the greatest understatement in the Bible—**he died** (v. 21). The whole deed done in one verse!

While this part of the story is so skillfully told that even in translation it captures the imagination of its audience, one who reads it in a language other than Hebrew misses some of the wonderful wordplay and assonance on which the storyline turns. For example, the text specifically describes each stage of the action with words that are similar: Jael took *(wattiqqah)* the tent peg and drove *(watitqa')* it into Sisera's temple (v. 21). Also, Jael took the tent peg and hammer in her hand *(beyadah)*, which picks up on Deborah's prophecy that God would give Sisera into the hand of *(beyad)* a woman (v. 9). The piling up of all of these accents the fulfillment of Deborah's prophecy through Jael's actions and also the hand of the sovereign Lord in bringing about the fulfillment (see 4:23).

4:22–24 / With Sisera now lying motionless on the ground and Jael standing over him, the hammer still in her hand, all movement of the story has stopped, the action frozen, as it were. But quickly it picks up again as Barak rushes by **in pursuit of Sisera**. Once again, **Jael went out to meet** a man passing by her tent. And once again she invited a man in. Just when we might begin to get a little uncomfortable, not knowing if the same fate awaited Barak, Jael added, **I will show you the man you're looking for.** So once again, a man **went in with her.**

And what did he see? Sisera—**with the tent peg through his temple.** The sequence of the words "Sisera, fallen, dead" represents Barak's process of discovery. He first recognized Sisera, then that he was fallen, and finally that he was dead. At the close of these phrases, the author directs our attention to the tent peg through his temple to emphasize how unconventionally Sisera died, and also perhaps to make another point, through wordplay. The Hebrew phrase translated as through his temple is *beraqqato*, which has similar consonants as the name Barak *(baraq)*. It would appear that the author wanted emphasize that Barak did not receive credit for the victory but rather it went to a woman, armed with a mere hammer and tent peg.

The final paragraph of the story assures that we make no mistake about who ultimately received the credit and honor for the victory: **On that day God subdued Jabin, the Canaanite king, before the Israelites** (v. 23). To make the point more emphatically and humorously, the author plays upon two Hebrew roots: *kn'* ("subdued") *kn'n* ("Canaan"). The final statement in the paragraph, which almost seems like an afterthought, adds the important information that **the hand of the Israelites grew** continuously **stronger against Jabin . . . until they destroyed him.** The miraculous victory was the beginning of a process that took some time to complete. Note also that even to the end, the accent remains on the hand. We have seen the hands of Jabin (v. 2), the hands of Barak (v. 7), the hand of a woman (v. 9, Hb.), the hand of Jael (v. 21), and now the hand of the Israelites. And—even though it is not explicitly stated—behind it all lies the hand of the Lord.

Additional Notes §7

4:2 / **The LORD sold them into the hands of Jabin, a king of Canaan, who reigned in Hazor:** This passage presents some difficulties in interpretation. Essentially the problem lies in relating this to a similar account in the book of Joshua (Josh. 11:1–15), which tells the story of Joshua successfully leading Israel against a Canaanite alliance led by Jabin, king of Hazor, who had a huge army (11:4) and a vast arsenal of chariots (v. 4). As in the Deborah-Barak story, the battle took place near a water source, but the site was "the Waters of Merom" (v. 5); also parallel is the fact that the Lord enabled the Israelites to win the battle and assured their leader of victory beforehand (v. 6). Apart from these, however, the two accounts diverge.

In the aftermath of Joshua's victory, he captured and completely destroyed by fire Hazor, the leading city-state of the alliance, and executed its king (vv. 10–11, 13). If we assume that there happened to be two kings of Hazor named Jabin, the question still remains: How could Hazor, which was completely destroyed, have within a generation regained its former glory enough to have become so formidable an adversary? The prose account does not mention Jabin again until the end (v. 23), and the Song of Deborah (Judg. 5) does not mention him at all, only Sisera (v. 26). The Song, however, is a highly poetic account and thus cannot be expected to give every detail in a straightforward way; it does refer to kings who came and fought (v. 19). Soggin (*Judges,* p. 70) argues that the reference to Jabin in Judg. 4:2 is secondary, inserted by the Deuteronomistic editor "for reasons which we cannot now establish."

4:4 / **Deborah, a prophetess:** Other women served in a prophetic role: Miriam (Exod. 15:20), Huldah (2 Kgs. 22:14), and Noadia (Neh. 6:14).

4:5 / **She held court under the Palm of Deborah:** The Palm of Deborah was so named probably not after the Deborah of Judges but Rachel's nurse Deborah, who was buried under an oak tree near Bethel (Gen. 35:8). If Deborah followed the same pattern as Moses, we can assume that she too informed the people of God's decrees and laws (Exod. 18:16), which implies that she also was a teacher. For examples of *lappidot* as torches, or flashes of lightning, see Judg. 7:16–20; 15:4–5; Exod. 20:18. Boling (*Judges,* p. 95) believes that they are one and the same: "We suggest that this explains why the name Lappidoth does not occur again in the story; tradition knew him chiefly as Baraq." But Moore (*Judges,* p. 113) disagrees: "The name has given occasion to all manner of conceits, among which we need only mention that which finds in Lappidoth . . . another name of Barak."

4:8 / If you don't go with me, I won't go: In Heb. 11:32, Barak is listed, with no mention of Deborah. Attempts have been made to make Barak live up to his legend in Hebrews. See, for example, M. Wilcock (*The Message of Judges: Grace Abounding* [Downers Grove, Ill.: InterVarsity, 1992], pp. 63–64): "So what are we witnessing when Barak refuses to set out without this woman? Not cowardice—far from it—but faith: faith, that is, which is the glorious combination of a humble confession of his own inadequacy and a sure confidence in the grace of God, known in this case through his mouthpiece Deborah. . . . The outstanding example of faith [in the book of Hebrews] is not Deborah, let alone Jael. It is Barak."

4:11 / Heber the Kenite: The NIV here reads "descendants of Hobab, Moses' brother-in-law," but other versions read "Moses' father-in-law." There is some confusion about this name in the various sources. According to Judg. 1:16, the Kenites were descendants of Moses' father-in-law, not named here but named Reuel in Exod. 2:21 and Jethro in Exod. 3:1. In Num. 10:29, Hobab is called the son of Reuel. In the present context, there are two textual variants. It seems more probable that the author here refers to Moses' father-in-law, whether or not the name is correct.

4:13 / Sisera gathered together his nine hundred iron chariots and all the men with him . . . to the Kishon River: Parallels between this and the deliverance at the Reed Sea have not been missed by Jewish commentators, who as early as the first century even rewrote the story to emphasize inherently corresponding elements and to add more. For further discussion of these interpretations, see C. A. Brown, *No Longer Be Silent: First-Century Jewish Portraits of Biblical Women* (Louisville, Ky.: Westminster John Knox, 1992), pp. 39–92.

4:22 / There lay Sisera with the tent peg through his temple—dead: I have translated the Hebrew text to more precisely communicate the dramatic impact of the words. Note that they are almost exactly the words used to describe what Eglon's servants saw when they went into his room. There are also other parallels between the two stories, one in particular being the use of unconventional weapons.

§8 The Song of Deborah (Judg. 5:1–31)

The Song of Deborah is a rare treasure in the OT, an ancient epic poem embedded in a narrative. While it shares this nearly unique character with a handful of other such texts (Exod. 15:1–18; Deut. 32:1–43; Isa. 38:10–20; Jonah 2:2–9), there is wide agreement that it is the oldest literary witness to early Israelite life and faith. Some scholars believe that it, or part of it, is contemporaneous with the events themselves, while others suggest that it was composed within a generation of the events it celebrates. That which makes the Song such a jewel also makes it difficult to interpret. Its language is frequently archaic and at times, for various reasons, unintelligible; hence the great variations between translations that are available.

The Song gives us a glimpse into the world of northern Israel prior to the monarchy. We must keep in mind, however, that it gives us only a glimpse, a glimpse that is not always distinct and clear. As poetry, it focuses on a few carefully chosen scenes and presents them not concretely but impressionistically. It speaks in lyric, rhythm, and image. It was surely intended, in the context of Judges, to be read along with the narrative, for it is otherwise quite incomprehensible. This was likely not the case for the ancient Israelites who heard and recited the Song at their campfires (5:16), watering places (5:11), and local shrines; the lack of historical setting within the Song itself indicates that its audience was sufficiently familiar with the events it celebrates.

5:1 / The Song of Deborah begins with a brief historical reference: **On that day, Deborah and Barak . . . sang this song** (cf. Exod. 15:1). The author clarifies the meaning of "that day" by juxtaposing the narrative and poetic accounts; "that day" was the day the Lord defeated Sisera. While the text as it stands implies that the Song of Deborah was the Song of Deborah and Barak, the verb "sang" is feminine singular in form (Hb. *watasar*) and the content of the Song focuses much more on Deborah than Barak. Thus it is possible that "and Barak" was a later addition, probably suggested by the reference to Barak in verse 12.

5:2–5 / The Song begins with a statement of the occasion for singing: an enthusiastic response to the muster call. Two groups respond, **the princes in Israel** and **the people,** both leaders and followers. Why would something as earthy as a response to a call to arms occasion a song of this importance? Deborah answers in lines 3–5. The people in reality are responding not to Deborah but **to the LORD.** Princes and people **willingly offer themselves** to the Lord. It is the Lord's battle against the Lord's enemies. Indeed, the Lord led them in battle (vv. 4–5). Whereas this cosmic perspective is barely hinted at in the narrative, it becomes a major theme in the Song, from the beginning (v. 2). In fact, the Song presents the battle exclusively from the cosmic perspective (vv. 19–20). This interweaving of the Lord's purposes with those of Israel is further expressed by the repeated appearance of the names **Yahweh** and **Israel** in the first section of the Song.

Imagery about Sinai in verses 4–5 suggests a connection between the present victory and the Lord's miraculous deliverance at the Reed Sea, which the Song of the Sea likewise attributes to cosmic intervention.

5:6–9 / After establishing the focus of the Song (the Lord), the author moves on to tell the story of the miracle by introducing some vignettes about what life was like in Israel before **Deborah arose** and the Lord delivered them. He paints a bleak picture: **roads were abandoned, travelers** were forced to take back roads, and **village life** had all but **ceased**—a picture of chaos. No security, no freedom, no order—in a word, no *shalom.*

But how had chaos come to power in Israel? It was no accident of history or simple happenstance. **They chose new gods.** They willfully rejected the Lord of *shalom* (Judg. 6:24) and the only source of *shalom.* The result, that **war came to the city gates** and that Israel was severely weakened (v. 8b), was inevitable. Verse 9, however, returns to a more positive note, with the promise that Israel's circumstances were soon to change. The text forms an *inclusio* with verse 2 and as such marks the closing of the first section of the Song.

5:10–13 / This section opens a window into the mustering process in ancient Israel. The whole spectrum of the population, from the richest to the poorest (donkey riders and walkers), were encouraged to respond to the call, sounded forth by **the singers at the watering places.** Apparently the singers **recite the righteous acts of the LORD** and **of his warriors in Israel,** and then the warriors assembled at **the city gates.**

5:14–18 / Then came the roll call. In this case, the list of participants and nonparticipants forms the centerpiece of the Song. It was crucial to identify who was on the Lord's side (who had shown up) and who was committed to neither the Lord nor fellow Israelites (who had stayed home). The list makes reference to all of the tribes that lived in or near the area of Canaanite hegemony, as well as others who were farther away; in general, only those who were directly affected participated in the battle, while those who were not directly affected found reasons to stay home. As human nature was, so shall it ever be.

5:19–23 / The battle is finally described in beautifully poetic language and imagery, which the NIV captures as well as possible, though the assonance of the Hebrew words is lost in translation. The author expands on the narrative's cryptic declaration that "the LORD routed Sisera and all his chariots and army" (4:15), indicating he routed Sisera through a storm and flash flood. Not by coincidence, the two most repeated words are **fought** (vv. 19–20) and **river** (v. 21). The thundering of the **horses' hoofs** as they and their riders were swept away and drowned recalls the Song of the Sea (Exod. 15:1, 4–5, 8). The section ends with an abrupt change of subject, common in oral epic, to a cursing of **Meroz,** who apparently failed to **come** to the battle; kings **came** (v. 19), but Meroz came not.

5:24–27 / Cursing turns to blessing as the subject turns to Jael, **most blessed of women.** She definitely showed up for the battle, though in her own way. The author presents a carefully crafted, stylized interpretation of the events that transpired in her tent. He eliminates several elements included in the narrative, such as all of the direct dialogue and Jael's invitation to Sisera to come into her tent, and focuses upon only two things: the bowl of milk and the killing of Sisera. While the whole scene is told with exquisite linguistic artistry, one wordplay that is particularly noteworthy revolves around the words *halmut* **(hammer)** and *halema* **(struck,** v. 26), and *halemu* ("thunder," of horses' hooves, v. 22), all of which have the same root. The juxtaposing of the two verses by this wordplay underscores the importance of Jael's role in Israel's victory, thus highlighting the miraculous, surprising way God acted on Israel's behalf. Strength made perfect in weakness! Such an affirmation would encourage not only early Israelites in difficult or seemingly impossible circumstances but also Israelites and Judahites in exile—and God's people at any time and any place.

5:28–30 / As the spotlight fades from the figure of a woman standing over the crushed foe, it moves ahead to yet another woman, **Sisera's mother,** standing at the window of her palace, eagerly looking for some sign of her son's **chariot.** His return is so long delayed that she has begun to worry; the silence of his chariot is deafening. **Her ladies** try to ease her fears by getting her to focus on the positive, and what could be more positive than all **the spoils** they are surely **finding and dividing**? She consoles herself with thoughts of the girls for the men, the beautifully embroidered garments for Sisera and for herself. If the picture of a mother waiting for her son who would never return home might evoke some degree of sympathy within us, the mother's gleeful imagining of men raping Israelite women should stifle any such feelings.

We could subtitle the Song of Deborah "A Tale of Two Mothers." What began with "a mother in Israel" (v. 7) ends with a mother in Canaan—one victorious and one vanquished, one singing a victory song and one a mourner's dirge. The reversal is complete. "The LORD brings death and makes alive; he brings down to the grave and raises up. The LORD sends poverty and wealth; he humbles and he exalts" (1 Sam. 2:6–7).

5:31 / The author does not comment on the final scene directly. Leaving us to ponder its poignant message(s), he moves to a prayer that summarizes the most important point: **May all your enemies perish, O LORD! But may they who love you be like the sun when it rises** [Hb. *ys'*, goes out; cf. v. 4] **in its strength.** The fate of enemies is contrasted with that of allies; the word "enemies" is contrasted with the phrase "those who love the LORD." How are these contrasting categories? And what does it mean to "love the LORD"? The modern western understanding of love is fraught with sentimental drivel that has nothing to do with the biblical idea of loving the Lord. The expression must be interpreted against the backdrop of covenant: To "love the LORD" means to be faithful to covenant commitment(s) to the Lord. The book of Deuteronomy, which provides the context for the Deuteronomic History, equates loving the Lord with covenant faithfulness (i.e., obedience to the Lord; e.g., 7:9; 10:12; 11:1), or obedience to God's will as revealed in the Torah. Thus the statement means that those who are in covenant relationship with the Lord and maintain that relationship through obedience to the Lord will shine "like the sun when it rises in its strength." The great strength of such persons derives not from themselves but from the Lord, who is faithful to his covenant commitments to them. Conversely, those who stand outside of covenant relationship with the Lord and who are disobedient are enemies for whom there is no hope for life, apart from the One who is the Source of life. Thus this last verse of chapter five presses home a key theme of Judges: blessings of obedience and cursings of disobedience. Moreover, it contains a wonderful promise, not only for Israel but for all of us who "love the LORD," that if we do so we will indeed shine with strength, because the Lord is our strength and song (Exod. 15:2).

Additional Notes §8

5:1 / **On that day, Deborah and Barak . . . sang this song:** In many cases, different translations of the Song reflect textual emendations proposed for the purpose of making sense of the present Hb. text. But numerous highly respected scholars caution against rushing too quickly to change the text, because our growing knowledge of Hb. lexicography continues to shed increasing light on the language of the period of the judges. One could write a whole book on the textual issues in the Song. In this brief commentary I will not delve into the complexities of Hb. and other ancient languages but refer the reader to other resources for further discussion. I will generally deal with the text of the Song according to the NIV translation.

5:4–5 / **O LORD, when you went out from Seir:** These verses correspond amazingly closely to ideas in Canaanite mythology, though Yahweh was not associated with the land of Canaan, but with the area to the south, at Sinai (e.g., Exod. 19:11; cf. Pss. 97:1–5; 68:7–8; Josh. 10:10–14). Davis (*Such a Great Salvation*, p. 83) aptly comments that "Yahweh is not stuck at Sinai. Rather, the God who decisively came to Israel in Sinai comes again and again to the aid of his people in their present troubles. The God who delivered them at the Sea of Reeds (Exod. 14) can rescue at the waters of Megiddo (Judg. 5:19); the God who came to Mount Sinai (Exod. 19–24) comes to Mount Tabor as well" (Judg. 4:14–15).

5:14–18 / **Some came from Ephraim:** The antiquity of the list is evident in that Makir had not yet moved across the Jordan River and Dan had not yet moved north.

5:30 / **A girl or two for each man:** Instead of "a girl or two for each man," the Hb. literally says "a womb, two wombs for every man." Rape in warfare has been and continues to be a common practice. But what is especially shocking is that here women accept it and even excitedly expect it. R. Alter (*The Art of Biblical Poetry* [New York: Basic Books, 1985], p. 46) comments upon the irony of this scene: "All this stands in shocking contrast to the still lingering—or perhaps even synchronous—image of the Canaanite general felled by the hand of a woman, lying shattered between her legs in a hideous parody of soldierly sexual assault on the women of a defeated foe."

§9 The Call of Gideon (Judg. 6:1–24)

The forty years of peace under Deborah's leadership passed quickly, and before long the Israelites found themselves in bondage again, this time to the Midianites. The reason for their bondage? As always, "they did evil in the eyes of the LORD." But here the intensity of Israel's enslavement was much worse than ever before, so much so that any semblance of normal life was lost. The downward spiral toward chaos hastened to its goal.

But God set aside his anger, and in his compassion he sent Israel a leader to free them from their bondage. That leader was Gideon, who appears as anything but a Herculean freedom fighter in this passage. Once again we come face to face with God's amazing grace, which ever causes him to act on behalf of his people and to use the weak and insignificant to confound the strong and mighty (Judg. 4–5; cf. 1 Sam. 2:1–10; Luke 1:52). We could say that in his weakness Gideon mirrors the people of God.

6:1–6 / The author sets the stage for the call of Gideon, beginning with the conventional notice that **the Israelites did evil in the eyes of the LORD** and so **he gave them into the hands of the Midianites.** Although the duration of the enslavement was not as long as others, the intensity was worse. The author goes into great detail, excessive detail, in these verses to describe the Israelites' plight under Midianite hegemony and hyperbolizes every detail to emphasize the extremity of their suffering, which affected every area of their lives. **The Israelites** could no longer live in their homes but instead took shelter **in mountain clefts, caves and strongholds** (v. 2). The Midianites, along with the **Amalekites and other eastern peoples,** prevented them from growing food anywhere in the country and destroyed all of their livestock (vv. 3–4). They plagued the country like **swarms of locusts. It was impossible to count the** number of **men and . . . camels** that **invaded the land to ravage it** (v. 5). The picture was indeed bleak. In fact, things became so bad that **the Israelites ... cried out to the LORD for help** (v. 6).

6:7–10 / In answer to their cry, the Lord **sent them a prophet,** recalling the story of the Israelites in Egypt under Pharaoh's heavy hand. They too cried out, and God sent a prophet, Moses. But the correspondence ends there. Moses gave the people words of hope and led them to freedom; this anonymous prophet sternly rebuked them for idolatry and for not listening to (*sm'*, "obeying") the Lord. References to idolatry and the Shema, Israel's supreme affirmation of their covenant commitment to the Lord (Deut. 6:4), imply that the Lord no longer considered Israel his people. Moreover, the prophet added to the severity of the rebuke by referring to the exodus from Egypt (vv. 8–9), to remind Israel of the Lord's claim upon them, his past miracles on their behalf (that they did not see presently), and their now broken covenant commitments to him (v. 10). The whole speech sounds very Deuteronomic and well could have been crafted by the author to express key themes with prophetic authority. The scene ends abruptly, without any indication as to how the people responded to the message.

6:11–13 / God's response, however, is expressed in the following events, by the Hebrew literary technique of juxtaposition. The text relates matter of factly that **the angel of the LORD came and sat down under the oak tree ... , where ... Gideon was threshing wheat** (v. 11). The expression "the angel of the LORD" is another way of saying the Lord himself. Here again we come face to face with the grace of God. The Lord's great compassion moved him, compelled him, to personally help his suffering people (Exod. 2:25; Isa. 59:16).

Gideon is introduced in terms of Israel's severe circumstances: He was threshing wheat **in a winepress to keep it from the Midianites.** It would be very difficult to thresh wheat in a winepress, because it is troughlike (narrow and small), rather than flat and wide like a threshing floor. Also, it could not have accommodated much wheat; Gideon probably had only very little. The angel appeared to Gideon and greeted him with words of standard greeting: **The LORD is with you** [sing.], **mighty warrior.** These words have an ironic twist, because indeed the Lord was with him, though he did not know it. The designation "mighty warrior" is also ironic, addressed as it is to a man threshing a little wheat in a winepress. Gideon affirmed that it was indeed a strange way to address him (v. 23). He responded in the first person plural, perhaps because he recognized that his personal circumstances were closely bound up with those of his people.

Gideon's response possibly reflected an awakening awareness of his destiny as a leader of his people, not unlike Moses when he first became aware of his own connection with the Israelites (Exod. 2:11). In fact, the parallels between Gideon and Moses are numerous, as we will see. The reference to the exodus (v. 13) recalls the prophet's words in verses 8–10, and also the Israelites' failure to fulfill their covenant commitments to the Lord. Why were they not experiencing the presence and power of the Lord that they should have been experiencing? In the words of the prophet, they no longer listened to the Lord. Here Gideon uses the word **abandoned,** which parallels a key theme in the Song of Moses: God would abandon Israel because they would abandon him (Deut. 32:15–26). But this reference to the Song of Moses would also have offered hope to suffering Israelites, because the Song ultimately promises that God sovereignly will free them from their enemies and reconcile both them and their land to himself (32:43).

6:14–19 / The Lord's answer to this query was to commission Gideon: **The LORD turned to him and said, "Go in the strength you have and save Israel out of Midian's hand. Am I not sending you?"** (v. 14). The Lord's commission works together with human compassion and awareness of need. But it is one thing to point out a need and another to meet that need. Gideon was not eager to get involved, partly because of his self-doubt and partly because of the magnitude of the task (v. 14): **But Lord, . . . how can I save Israel? My clan is the weakest in Manasseh, and I am the least in my family** (v. 15). Gideon again looks like Moses, hustling to come up with any excuse to avoid getting involved (Exod. 3:11–4:11). The irony is, however, that the Israelites were in need of another exodus—right in the promised land.

The Lord's answer to Gideon is almost verbatim what he had said to Moses: **I will be with you** (*'ehyeh*; Exod. 3:12). And, as implied in the story of Moses, despite this assurance, Gideon requested a sign (v. 17; Exod. 3:12), in this case, the acceptance of his **offering** (v. 18). The Israelites had fallen so deeply into apostasy that they had ceased to sacrifice to the Lord; they even had forgotten how to do it properly. This accepted offering would be a sign of the Lord's acceptance of Israel and a renewal of the covenant, as it was later revealed to be (see Judg. 6:24). So Gideon hastened to prepare the offering, **a young goat** and bread **from an ephah of flour,** and then returned to offer them to the divine figure **under the oak.** Specific mention of the oak tree possibly signifies that this was a sacred place of worship, especially because it was owned by Gideon's father, who also owned the altar to Baal (v. 25).

A theme that is beginning to come to light is the theme of bread. The Israelites were so oppressed that they could not even grow grain. When we first met Gideon, he was threshing grain in a winepress, which also demonstrated his and his people's subjugation to the Midianites. When he was commissioned by the Lord to save Israel, he made bread, more specifically, *masah* (unleavened bread), which though frequently offered with Israelite sacrifices, most readily calls to mind the exodus, especially in light of the other parallels between Gideon and Moses. This theme of bread will appear again further in the story (see below).

6:20–24 / The offering of sacrifice would have signified covenant renewal, an assumption suggested by two facts. First, the altar was called **The LORD is Peace** after the offering was presented. "The LORD is Peace" refers to the reconciliation that the acceptance of the sacrifice represented, for *shalom* in sacrificial contexts connotes reconciliation (see especially Num. 6:22–26). In this regard, note the Lord's word of reconciliation to Gideon when he recognized before whom he stood: **Peace!** Secondly, immediately afterward (that night), Gideon tore down the altar to Baal and the Asherah pole and offered a burnt offering on a new altar he had built (vv. 25–27), thus reestablishing Yahweh worship. The theme of covenant runs in a veiled way throughout the story of Gideon: as Israel was faithful to the covenant, the Lord was faithful to liberate them from bondage.

Finally, we must note a further parallel with Moses. Gideon exclaimed, **I have seen the angel of the LORD face to face!** (v. 22). A similar phrase also appears in connection with Moses: "The LORD would speak to Moses face to face, as a man speaks with his friend" (Exod. 33:11) and "No prophet has risen in Israel like Moses, whom the LORD knew face to face" (Deut. 34:10). But before the end of the story, these parallels will diverge into separate paths.

Additional Notes §9

6:13 / **If the LORD is with us:** This story not only parallels that of Moses but also has some parallels to the story of Samson (Judg. 13:2–23) and even to Abraham (Gen. 18). Perhaps the latter reminded the author's Israelite audience that they existed only because of the Lord's miraculous work, thereby fulfilling his promise to Abraham and Sarah, and also the faith or faithfulness of their forefathers and foremothers (Gen. 15:6).

6:14 / **The LORD turned to him and said:** There is interplay between "the LORD" and "the angel of the LORD," which is understandable since the "angel of the LORD" often referred to the Lord in theophanic contexts. The LXX here reads "the angel of the LORD."

6:15 / **But Lord, . . . How can I save Israel?** How many of us can see ourselves here and in Moses' story? In the case of Moses, after the Lord had answered every one of his objections, Moses became honest about his real attitude and pleaded, "O LORD, please send someone else" (Exod. 4:13).

6:19 / **Gideon . . . prepared a young goat, and . . . made bread without yeast:** Hb. *gedy 'izzim,* possibly playing on the name Gideon: *gid'on.*

We see both sides of Gideon in this passage. He is presented as absolutely obedient to the Lord and zealous in upholding the covenant, even to the point of taking a stand against his own family's and community's religious values and practices, much like Phineas (Num. 25:1–13) or Elijah (1 Kgs. 18). But, like Elijah, whose confidence could quickly be shaken (1 Kgs. 19), Gideon also was fearful and sometimes required special assurance that the Lord had called him and would help him to lead the Israelites to freedom.

6:25–27 / **That same night, the LORD** commanded Gideon to tear down his father's **altar to Baal and** its **Asherah pole** and to **build** an **altar to the LORD,** sacrificing upon it **the second bull as a burnt offering,** using the pieces of the Asherah pole for firewood (cf. Isa. 44:9–20). Clearly the author contrasts Israel's disobedience (v. 10) with Gideon's obedience: **Gideon . . . did as the LORD told him** (v. 27). In the context of Judges, with its concern for leadership that upholds covenant values, this signals Gideon's suitability to deliver and lead Israel. As a judge, he was first and foremost to be a spiritual leader, and as such he was to lead Israel, by example, to a path of listening *(sm'),* a fundamental Deuteronomic value.

But Gideon was also very human. Although he obeyed the Lord's command, he did it **at night, because he was afraid** (v. 27). He again resembles Moses, who carefully checked to see that no one was looking before he reached out to help his fellow Israelite (Exod. 2:12). One does not have to be free of healthy realism to be used by God; it is sometimes difficult, however, to distinguish between healthy realism and fear. But God was patient with him in his fear; on the same night, Gideon had received a divine message: "Do not be afraid" (v. 23). This will not be the last time Gideon manifests human fraility (vv. 36–40). In this way, his life continues to parallel that of Moses, whose self-doubt is candidly portrayed (e.g., Exod. 3:11–4:13). The Bible does not hesitate to present heroes of the faith as having clay feet and reveals that the Lord is patient with genuine human weakness and willing to accommodate reasonable needs for assurance.

6:28–32 / The author vividly describes the community's response in verse 28 as they discovered what had happened to their cult objects. The short clip of dialogue, the epitome of understatement, summarizes the essence of their questions in four Hebrew words: "Who did this thing?" (v. 29). Some unnamed informant let them know that Gideon was to blame. In Hebrew, Gideon stands in emphatic position. While they were shocked that anyone could have done "this thing," it must have been all the more unthinkable that it was Gideon, whose own family had been entrusted with the care of the shrine that stood on their property.

The next scene (vv. 30–32) is extended, with much detail and repetitions of what had already been stated, thus revealing points author sought to emphasize. **The men of the town** demanded that **Joash** hand over his **son** so they could execute him. The reference to Gideon as Joash's son, rather than by name, again reflects the people's surprise that a member of the caretaker's own family would be responsible for such an unthinkable act. They rehearsed almost word for word (for the third time!) the most important deeds that Gideon had done to deserve death (v. 30b; cf. 25–26, 28). Surely the author wanted to emphasize what Gideon had done as proof of his zeal to uphold the covenant.

The people demanded that Joash give them his son, but all he gave them was a theological lecture: So **are you** [Hb. emphatic] **going to plead Baal's cause? . . . Whoever fights** [against; my translation] **him shall be put to death by morning! If Baal really is a god, he can defend himself when someone breaks down his altar.** Joash expressed a single point—Baal is not a real god—in two different ways. He argued that if someone were to fight against Baal, he or she would be put to death (implying by the god himself) by morning. Since this encounter was **in the morning** (v. 28) and Gideon was still alive, we are to assume that Baal is not really a god. Furthermore, the fact that the altar was broken down indicated that Baal is not really a god, because he obviously did not fight for himself. Joash seems to have convinced the people that Baal could or would contend for himself, because they ceased their bid to punish Gideon. All they did was to give Gideon a new name: **Jerub-Baal,** by which he was remembered for breaking down Baal's altar. This is the fourth time the author has told us essentially the same thing, that Gideon tore down Baal's altar.

6:33–35 / Now that we have met Gideon and seen him in action, the story continues. **All the Midianites, Amalekites and other eastern peoples joined forces** and invaded Israelite territory, camping **in the Valley of Jezreel.** Gideon was made ready for the confrontation with the most important weapon: **the Spirit of the LORD came upon Gideon** (v. 34). This supernatural endowment gave him boldness and enabled him to successfully muster a contingent of men. To do so, he **blew a trumpet,** the ancient weapon of the covenant community that signaled the call to holy war (Num. 10:9). Although it was the customary means of mustering troops, it also foreshadowed the unusual method by which Gideon would overcome the enemy (vv. 7:16–22).

6:36–40 / But again the movement of events is temporarily put on hold. Gideon was not quite ready to lead the Israelites against the more numerous and better equipped (7:12) army of invaders and asked for further confirmation of his call. He devised two tests whereby he would know beyond all doubt that the Lord would **save Israel by** his **hand.** First, if he were to **place a wool fleece on the threshing floor** overnight, and if it were wet with **dew** in the morning **and all the ground** around it **dry,** he would **know that** the Lord would **save Israel by** his **hand.** The nearly identical phrases are repeated twice, expressing emphasis. Gideon was keen to know that God was committed to him and his mission. Many commentators and preachers have criticized Gideon for his "little faith" in asking for such a sign, and even a reverse sign—which would have been an even greater miracle, for wool absorbs water—but the text never denounces him for his requests. God was ready to accommodate his need for assurance.

Interpreters have often focused so much on the type of test that they have missed an important point, which focuses on the location of the test. It takes place at the threshing floor. The threshing floor, being a flat and open stone, was an obvious place to conduct such a test. But is there more to it? The Lord first appeared to Gideon threshing wheat in a winepress, presumably because Israel's plight was so severe that he was unable to thresh the grain in the normal place. Now again, Gideon met the Lord at the

threshing floor, in a foreshadowing of Israel's victory that would
enable them to return to their threshing floors—and also to have
something to thresh! Further evidence that the author intended to
communicate this message is the presence of the definite article
before "threshing floor," thus pointing it out in a special way.

Very likely another foreshadowing element is the word
"dry" (Hb. *horeb*) in verses 37, 39, and 40 (three times). This Hebrew root offers a wealth of wordplay possibilities and also ties
this text together with what follows. A form of the word *hereb*,
from a different root, means "sword" (Hb. *hereb*), which is featured
as a key element in the story of Gideon's noctural attack (7:14, 20,
cf. v. 22). The root also could be vocalized another way to produce
the word *horeb*, a synonym for Mount Sinai, especially in Deuteronomy and Deuteronomic literature (Exod. 3:1; Deut. 1:2, 6, 19;
4:10, 15; 5:2; 9:8; 18:16; 1 Kgs. 8:9; 19:8; 2 Chron. 5:10). This would
have suggested to a Hebrew audience a connection between Gideon's test and sword and Horeb, which represented the Lord's
revelation of his nature and will in the Torah and Israel's covenant
with the Lord to hear (obey).

Finally, by repeating the phrase **that night** (6:25, 40; 7:9), the
author indicates the importance of this testing by tying it together
with Gideon's tearing down of Baal's altar and his later attack
against the Midianites. Furthermore, "that night" also thematically links the impending deliverance to Passover (Exod. 12:8, 12,
42; Deut. 16:1), underscoring, along with the anonymous prophet
(Judg. 6:7–8), what the Lord had done for Israel in the exodus,
which was the basis of his claim upon Israel (Judg. 6:10) and also
his assurance of a new exodus on their behalf.

Additional Notes §10

6:26 / **Offer the second bull as a burnt offering:** The Hebrew
phrase here is difficult to interpret, hence the alternate reading suggested in the NIV footnote. But the principal reading in the NIV text,
though somewhat awkward, is sustainable by the underlying Hebrew
text.

6:30 / **Bring out your son:** Compare this episode with the story
of Samson. When the Philistines demanded that the Judahites hand him
over, communal relationships had deteriorated so extensively that they
gave him up willingly, without a fight or even a theological lecture.

6:32 / **They called Gideon "Jerub-Baal":** See Judg. 7:1; 8:29, 35. It was not unheard of for an Israelites to have a Baal name. But there was also a distinct effort to modify such names. Note, for example, that in 2 Sam. 11:21, Gideon is called Jerub-Besheth. Also, Saul's sons, Ish-Baal and Merib-Baal, are renamed Ish-Bosheth and Mephibosheth (2 Sam. 3:8; 4:4; 9:12; 1 Chron. 8:33–34; 9:39–40). Even David had a son with a Baal name: 1 Chron. 14:7. The word *bosheth* means "shame."

§11 Gideon Delivers Israel (Judg. 7:1–25)

We finally move to the confrontation. There have been numerous interruptions along the way. But these have not been superfluous interruptions; each has contributed something substantive to help craft the story in such a way that it illustrates important lessons about the Lord's work on behalf of Israel, the most important being that the Lord delivers them. This point will now be explicitly expressed, as well as dramatized in an unsual way.

7:1–3 / The two opponents were **camped** opposite each other, **Gideon and all his men . . . at the spring of Harod** and the Midianites **near the hill of Moreh,** both poised for the showdown. But once again comes an interruption. Israel was still not ready to fight the battle, not because they did not have enough troops but because they had too many. **The LORD** spoke to **Gideon** yet another time, directing him to reduce the number of troops so that **Israel** might **not boast that her own strength** had **saved her** (cf. Deut. 8:17–18). The criterion by which he was to divide them was that **anyone who tremble[d] with fear** could go home, while the rest could stay and fight (cf. Deut. 20:8). This phrase picks up and significantly expands upon the theme of fear, which again appears in verses 1–3. Israel was camped at "the spring of Harod" (Hb. *harod,* trembling); and the Midianites were camped at Moreh (Hb. *moreh*), which closely resembles the Hebrew word for "fearing" *(mora')*. Little Israel was trembling because of the "fearful" Midianites. Here was a David-and-Goliath situation.

7:4–8a / But even after twenty-two thousand left, the Israelites were not ready to fight. The Lord interrupted again to announce to Gideon that there were **still too many men** and that he would **sift them** (note the threshing imagery, 6:11) even more. Gideon was to **take them down to the water** and note how they drank, those who lapped **like a dog** and those who knelt **down to drink.** The three hundred men who lapped were "the few, the chosen." **Trumpets** and jars appear in verse 8 as if we know already what they are for; these offer a sneak preview of what is to come.

7:8b–11 / We have just heard about the Israelites' fear; now again we hear about Gideon's fear. **That night the LORD** told **Gideon** to **go down** with his troops to attack Midian, but, knowing that Gideon was still afraid, the Lord graciously offered a solution (v. 10). Gideon obeyed and **went down to the outposts of the camp** (v. 11). The use of the verb "go down" (Hb. *yrd*) subtly insinuates that a reversal was surely coming. The Midianites were already below the Israelites; they were as good as conquered. The same is in view in verses 12 (in the valley) and 13 (tumbling).

7:12–14 / The Lord allowed Gideon and his servant to eavesdrop just as one Midianite told another about his dream. Dreams were thought to be messages from God and thus would have been significant to anyone, Israelite or non-Israelite. In this case, the dream clearly previewed the certainty and totality of Midian's defeat under Gideon's leadership. As we would expect, the dream and interpretation are replete with symbolism—and also wordplay. For example, the Hebrew word for dream, *halom*, is emphasized by appearing three times in verse 13; the dream itself is about a loaf of barley bread (Hb. *lehem*), which features the same three consonants in a different order. The *lehem* rolled into Midian's camp and fell *(napal)* upon a tent so that it turned upside down and fell *(napal)* to the ground (my translation). The word *napal* is the same as the word used to describe Midian's camp in verse 12 (translated as **settled**), the ironic message being that they thought they were settled, safe and sound, but they would soon fall. Another verb that clearly denotes reversal is "turned upside down" (v. 13; translated as **overturned**).

A related, veiled reference to the theme of reversal is inherent in the notice that the number of Midianites camped in the valley **could no more be counted than the sand on the seashore** (v. 12). The Lord used the same terminology to refer to Israel's blessing in his promise to Abraham after the supreme test of his faith (Gen. 22:16–17). The close connection in that text between the promise of offspring and the land would have been noted by the author of Judges and applied to his contemporary situation: Both were presently in bondage and both would presently be liberated.

The **friend** of the man who had the dream interpreted the **bread** of the dream to refer to **the sword of Gideon . . . into** whose **hands God** had **given the Midianites and the whole camp.** The sword of Gideon was the sword of the Lord (v. 20), for the Midianites were mysteriously moved by the Lord to turn their own swords on each other (v. 22). What irony there is in the fact that the Midianites' own swords were the sword of the Lord and Gideon. The interpretation of the dream identifies Gideon with the loaf of bread, linking up with the previous references to the threshing floor and to Gideon's making bread for the angel of the Lord. Gideon's being represented by a loaf of bread points backward to those essentially negative images and forward to the restoration of normal life under Gideon's leadership.

7:15–21 / We have already mentioned Gideon's battle plan, especially the significant fact that the Israelites were to use uncoventional weapons, trusting the Lord to fight for them. The story resembles the account of the fall of Jericho (Josh. 5:13–6:25), the firstfruits of Israel's realization of the Lord's covenant promise of the land. The dynamic at work in the present story is the element of surprise and deceit. No army fights a battle in the middle of the night! The enemy troops were caught off guard, abruptly awakened by a tremendous cacophony of noise—ram's horns blasting, pots shattering, men shouting—and then immediately met by flashes of light all around. The purpose was to startle and to deceive them into thinking there were many, many more out there than three hundred men. Predictably, the Israelites were successful, because the Lord was with them, supernaturally working to accomplish his will.

7:22–25 / The Midianites were quickly and completely routed. They fled toward the Jordan River. At that point other Israelites were called out, including **Ephraim,** the largest and most influential tribe. Gideon commanded them to **Come down** [Hb. *yrd*] **against the Midianites and seize the waters of the Jordan** (Hb. *hayyarden;* v. 24). The Ephraimites responded and **took the waters of the Jordan** (v. 24). The reference to the Jordan *(hayyarden)* picks up dominant themes in this story, for it is related to the root *yrd* ("to go down") and hints at the word for fear, *harod.* The point emphasized is that of reversal: The Israelites have been raised up and the Midianites brought low. And the theme of fear ties the story together, whether it be fear of enemies, fear of the Lord, or fear of those who fear the Lord.

Additional Note §11

7:5 / **Separate those who lap the water with their tongues like a dog from those who kneel down to drink:** There is a wordplay on the Hb. words *yelek* ("he will go") and *yaloq* ("he will lap")/*malaqeqim* ("they lap"). The Lord said that he would tell "who would go" and "who would not go," which was distinguished by "who lapped like a dog" and "who did not lap." D. Daube ("Gideon's Few," *JJS* 7 [1956], p. 156) suggests that lapping like a dog could have been understood as prefiguring "lapping of the enemy's blood" (cf. 1 Kgs. 21:19; 22:38) and further (p. 158) that "these men are, in a sense, already drinking the blood of their enemies; they are destined to go into battle, just as the others, who drink like cattle, are destined for peace."

Gideon has just led the Israelites to defeat a coalition of their enemies. In a surprise attack, he and his men routed the armies and pursued them all the way to the Jordan River. Then they called in reinforcements from the tribe of Ephraim to help them in the sweeping-up effort. After a brief altercation, these took over the pursuit and executed two Midianite leaders. This would have been a good place to stop. The author could have closed the story with the stereotypic notices that the land had peace for forty years (Judg. 8:28) and Gideon died and was buried in his family tomb in Ophrah (8:32). But he did not stop there. He continued on with the story of Gideon, a story that reveals a different side of Israel's judge—the dark side, to be sure. Judges 8 begins with a positive presentation of Gideon in a peacemaking role but quickly moves into a presentation of him as cruel and vindictive and ultimately as the judge who led Israel into renewed idolatry. While Gideon is most remembered for his fearless, if unconventional, exploits against Israel's enemies and even his moments of self-doubt and need for reassurance, the events that transpired in the final chapter in his life were not so noble. But in that these underscore the reality of sinful human nature, this passage, too, is "useful for teaching, rebuking, correcting and training in righteousness" (2 Tim. 3:16).

8:1–3 / Judges 8 begins with an episode that presents Gideon as a diplomat who successfully negotiated peace with opponents from his own people, the Ephraimites. But this incident of intercommunal conflict, which in itself was rather minor and quickly resolved, was the flagship of future developments that from this point on will occur with greater frequency and greater intensity.

The Ephraimites, whom Gideon had mustered to help in pursuing the enemy across the Jordan, complained that they had been left out of the initial battle. They had a practical reason to be angry; they had been deprived of not only the glory but also—

more so—the spoils of victory. The author subtly points to the tragic irony in this intercommunal conflict by using a particular verb to tell us that Ephraim **criticized him sharply** (v. 1). This verb *(ryb)* is a form of the same verb from which Gideon's nickname, Jerub-Baal, was derived. The irony is that Gideon was contending not with Baal, the expected enemy, but with his fellow Israelites. From this point onward, the author will increasingly emphasize the theme of intercommunal conflict as he chronicles Israel's downward spiral toward chaos.

Gideon's response to his detractors is presented in chiastic form, which expresses his verbal prowess. He frames his main point with the essentially repeated query: **What have I accomplished compared to you?** (vv. 2a and 3b). Sandwiched between are dual statements, one figurative, the other literal: **Aren't the gleanings of Ephraim's grapes better than the full grape harvest of Abiezer** [i.e., Gideon]? "Into your hands, the Lord (NIV: **God**) gave Oreb and Zeeb, the Midianite leaders" (my translation). The reference to the Lord's role in the victory was a reminder that they were all part of the same covenant community under one Lord; hence what benefited one benefited the other. The Ephraimites seem to have gotten the point, because **at this, their resentment . . . subsided.**

8:4–7 / After that brief interlude, **Gideon and his three hundred men** continued to pursue the fleeing enemy, crossing **the Jordan** River and moving on to the first major town, **Succoth** (Gen. 33:17). There he made a simple, polite request: **Give my troops some bread.** Gideon is once again associated with bread, which was a symbol of Israel's experience of both enslavement and liberation. But in this context, it will represent something quite different (see pp. 187, 196). Gideon added that he was **still pursuing Zebah and Zalmunna, the kings of Midian.** Up to this point, we have not been told why Gideon was relentlessly trailing the Midianites so far from the scene of the battle. Now we know: he had a personal interest in capturing the two Midianite kings. The leaders of Succoth were not keen on feeding three hundred hungry Israelite soldiers and promptly refused Gideon's request. But they responded not with a simple no but with a pair of derogatory rhetorical questions that betrayed their skepticism that Gideon would catch the Midianite kings and pay them back with the spoils they would gain. Their derisive reponse calls to mind Nabal's retort at David's request for provisions for his men

(1 Sam. 25:10–11). As we will see, Gideon did not do as well as David did (1 Sam. 25:26–31) in his eventual response to such scornful treatment—perhaps because he did not have an Abigail to intervene. All of this continues to point to the breakdown in communal solidarity that will eventually result in the horrific events of Judges 19–21.

Gideon's response was quick and caustic: **Just for that, when the LORD has given Zebah and Zalmunna into my hand, I will [thresh] your flesh with desert thorns and briers** (v. 7). I have bracketed the words in my translation that differ from the NIV. This reading is suggested by the Hebrew verb, which occurs in Amos 1:3, where Damascus is denounced because "she threshed Gilead with sledges having iron teeth." Moore (*Judges*, p. 219) describes this graphic image: "He will throw them naked into a bed of thorns and trample them together, like grain on a threshing floor." We see here not Gideon the fearful, nor Gideon the fearless, but Gideon the frightful. Ironically, we first met Gideon while threshing, and we will once again see him in that role but with a macabre twist.

8:8–9 / Gideon moved on to the next town, Peniel (cf. Gen. 32:30–31), where he **made the same request of them** and received the same response. Likewise, his reply—as before—was similarly menacing: **When I return in triumph, I will tear down this tower** (v. 9) It is not clear why Gideon focused on the tower. But references to the tower and thorns (though a different word in Hb.) foreshadow the story of Abimelech (Judg. 9:14–15, 51–52). Indeed, there are numerous linguistic parallels with this part of Gideon's story and the following judges' stories. As we move closer to the significant turing point in the story (8:22–27), Gideon is looking more and more like his renegade son. Such attitudes and behavior did not suddenly appear, but they slowly took over Gideon, step by step. We can be sure the son learned well from the father.

8:10–12 / Gideon moved on in pursuit of the two Midianite kings. He **fell upon the unsuspecting army . . . , routing their entire army,** and **captured** the two kings (vv. 11–12). The description of the army as "unsuspecting" foreshadows the story of the Danites' brutal attack of Laish (18:27); the reference to **swordsmen** points both backward to Ehud (3:22) and forward to Abimelech (9:54; cf. 8:20). The reference to Abimelech is the more important, as several other foreshadowing words tie the two stories together. Again, the author indicates that this was the turning point in the period of the judges, that from this point on it was all downhill, though not all at once. There were still a few sparks of light in an otherwise dark period in Israel's history.

8:13–17 / Now that Gideon had accomplished his goal, would his promises, pledged in the heat of battle, be retracted? As in the case of a future judge, Jephthah, they would not. Gideon made a special point to return to the towns that had withheld hospitality from him and his army on their way to the enemy's camp, in order to fulfill his threat to destroy them. At Succoth, he detained **a young man,** who **wrote down for him the names of the seventy-seven officials** of the town. Supposedly Gideon called those men to a meeting, where he stood before them the two Midianite kings about whom they had taunted him and then **taught . . .** them **a lesson by punishing them with desert thorns and briers** (v. 16). The author did not go into as great a detail about what happened in Peniel but summarized, rather glibly, the most important points: Gideon **also pulled down the tower of Peniel and killed the men of the town** (v. 17). The punishment was more severe than originally promised (v. 9). It appears that Gideon has already begun to mutate into an egotistical tyrant.

A major interpretive issue related to this part of the story is whether or not Succoth and Peniel were Israelite towns. Of course, life is life no matter what the religious and/or ethnic background of the people involved; all were created in the image of God. But if they were Israelite, which is most likely, the sin was much worse from a covenantal perspective than if they were not. To treat fellow Israelites in such a way was a grave sin, not only against them but also against the Lord of the covenant

8:18–21 / Gideon then moved to execute Zebah and Zalmunna, the two Midianite kings. At this point, the author includes a snippet of dialogue that lets the reader in on some important information. Briefly summarized, Zebah and Zalmunna executed two of Gideon's **brothers, the sons of** his **own mother,** at Mount Tabor. These words and events point both backward and forward. They highlight the theme of reversal, particularly as in the encounter with Adoni-Bezek (Judg 1:7), whose punishment likewise was "an eye for an eye, a tooth for a tooth" justice. The reference to Mount Tabor reminds us of Deborah and Barak; and the appositional phrase "the sons of my own mother" points ahead to Abimelech (9:1–3).

§13 Gideon's Ephod and Death (Judg. 8:22–35)

These final episodes in Gideon's life reveal two sides of Israel's judge: Gideon the zealous defender of the covenant and Gideon the apostate defector of the covenant, who also led Israel down the same path. This is the first time we have met the idea, although not in the exact words, that Israel did evil in the eyes of the Lord before the judge's death (8:27), which marks a significant turning point in Israel's history. The two major judges who follow, Jephthah and Samson, will demonstrate a similar mixture of good and bad, though each of them increasingly worse.

8:22–23 / **The Israelites said to Gideon, "Rule over us— you, your son and your grandson—because you have saved us out of the hand of Midian."** Gideon got more than he bargained for in liberating Israel from the Midianites. The people wanted to acclaim him as more than their judge; they invited him to become their king. Up to this point, Israel had never raised the issue of kingship; it was unthinkable, because the Lord was their king. He became their king when they pledged absolute and unceasing allegiance to him at Mount Sinai; they existed as a people solely because of that covenant agreement. So to claim any king other than the Lord would be to deny their very existence. True, the Lord did give them flesh-and-blood leaders, but they were viewed as representatives of the heavenly king, who worked through them by special charisms imparted by the Spirit of the Lord. Many of these leaders were prophets. But ideally Israel had never confused these representatives with the true King. Thus the request signaled a serious development that revealed Israel's growing rejection of the Lord's sovereignty over them (cf. 1 Sam. 8). The reference to Gideon's son and grandson gave expression to Israel's desire for not only a monarchy but a dynastic monarchy, which they would not experience until the reign of David. At the same time, the author hints at later developments involving Gideon's sons, particularly Abimelech (Judg. 9).

Gideon demonstrated his covenant loyalty by refusing the role that was reserved for the Lord alone: **I will not rule over you, nor will my son rule over you. The LORD will rule over you.** This statement is emphatic in two ways: the words "I" and "the LORD" stand in emphatic position in the Hebrew text, and the verb "rule" is repeated three times. Ironically, Gideon referred to his son, which prophetically predicted what would happen after his death. Many scholars believe that Gideon's answer reveals the author's antimonarchic bias, which contrasts with the perspective of the last five chapters of Judges. In this case, Gideon's reply reflects the perspective of the Deuteronomic author (DTR₁), who wanted to stress the failure of dynastic kingship in Israel because of human sinfulness (see Cross, *Canaanite Myth and Hebrew Epic*, pp. 278–89). But probably the author did not have a bias against all monarchy, only against illegitimate monarchy, evaluated in terms of covenant fidelity or infidelity.

8:24–27 / Gideon answered commendably. But almost in his next breath, he set things up for Israel to step onto the slippery path to idolatry: **I do have one request, that each of you give me an earring from your share of the plunder.** This picks up on what was foreshadowed in the words of 8:21, the seemingly superfluous detail that "Gideon . . . took the ornaments off [the Midianites'] camels' necks" (v. 21). His request for the gold earrings hints at the idolatry to come, because it is nearly exactly what Aaron did in initiating worship of the golden calf in the shadow of Mount Sinai (Exod. 32:2–6). The people who had wanted to proclaim him king were only too happy to do whatever he told them (v. 25). The author's excessive detailing of the items taken from the Midianites and the process of the Israelites' donating the earrings serves to emphasize the gravity of the situation.

Gideon made the gold into an ephod (v. 27). The statement is simple, almost matter of fact, yet scandalous. The ephod was a part of the priestly vestments reserved for the high priest alone (Exod. 28:15–30); he alone was given the prerogative of determining the Lord's will on behalf of the covenant community. Thus Gideon's act was treasonous against the Lord and contradicted his affirmation that only the Lord would rule over Israel. By this act he took upon himself the role of the Lord in designating Israel's spiritual leadership and also seeking to control Israel's destiny. According to the continuation of the story, although he refused the title of king, he acted more like a king than a judge: He had many wives (8:30) and at least one concubine (8:31), and even named one of his sons Abimelech, meaning "my father is king" (8:31). L. Klein encapsulates the irony of Gideon's action in *The Triumph of Irony in the Book of Judges:* "Gideon was clothed with Yahweh's Spirit; now he clothes himself with an idolatrous ephod" ([JSOTSup 68; Sheffield: Almond, 1988], p. 65).

The result of Gideon's fashioning the ephod was predictable: **All Israel prostituted themselves by worshiping it ... and it became a snare to Gideon and his family** (v. 27; cf. 2 Kgs. 18:4). The expression "prostituted themselves" recalls the author's summarizing description in 2:17, and "snare" recalls the prophecy of the angel of the Lord at Bokim (2:3). What is so reprehensible is that these things happened during Gideon's lifetime, which represents a major turning point. From here on the downward spiral begins to accelerate very quickly toward its goal.

8:28–32 / Against the backdrop of these events, it is astonishing that **during Gideon's lifetime, the land enjoyed peace forty years** (v. 28). It would appear that Gideon made the ephod early in his period of judgeship, and yet the Lord blessed Israel with peace for forty years. Granted, this is both a stereotypic notice and number, but it is nevertheless amazing. Once again we come face to face with the Lord's amazing grace, grace that he continued to shower upon Israel when they deserved nothing more than annihilation. But even amazing grace has its limits. Not by accident is this the last time the book of Judges refers to the land's having peace. From here on, it was nothing but increasing disintegration of all normal order of every kind *(shalom)* and the triumph of chaos.

Gideon was busy during the following years; he fathered at least **seventy** plus one **sons.** We are not told of any of his other activities, because they were not important to the author. He wanted to move on to the story of Gideon's sons, particularly one already-mentioned son, named Abimelech, and so focused exclusively on these. He does, however, close the story of Gideon with the stereotypic notice that **Gideon died and ... was buried in the tomb of his father Joash in Ophrah of the Abiezrites.**

8:33–35 / With these verses, the author departs from his usual formula in presenting a judge's story, which signals a new phase in the narrative. We are alerted to look for something different. And we will not be disappointed. He notes that as soon as **Gideon died ... the Israelites again prostituted themselves to the**

Baals, more specificially, the **Baal-Berith.** This sets up an important element in the story that follows, as Abimelech and his cronies will be given money from the temple of Baal-Berith (9:4). The significance of their worshiping the Baals is emphasized by the antithetical notice that they **did not remember the LORD their God, who had rescued them from the hands of all their enemies on every side** (v. 34). Finally, the author points to the breakdown in community, expressed in the Israelites' failure to demonstrate appropriate covenant loyalty: **They also failed to show kindness** (Hb. *'asah hesed*) **to the family of Jerub-Baal . . . for all the good things he had done for them** (v. 35). Thus the stage is set for the entrance of Abimelech, who will be a fitting leader for people such as these.

Additional Notes §13

8:22 / **Rule over us—you, your son and your grandson:** In 1 Sam. 8, the Israelites demand a king in order to be like other nations (vv. 5 and 20), which, ironically, is exactly what they were not. They alone had been set apart, consecrated, from other nations to be God's people (Exod. 19:5–6); their distinction from other nations was the only thing that made them a nation. Note that according to 1 Sam. 8:18, the end result of the Israelites' being like other nations (having a king) would be a return to slavery, such as they experienced in Egypt before being set apart as a nation—a reversal of the exodus—but with no hope of God's rescuing them a second time.

8:35 / **They . . . failed to show kindness:** The Hb. expression translated in the NIV as "show kindness" is *'asah hesed,* which has a broad range of meaning. While *hesed* is most often rendered as "love," "loving-kindness," or "steadfast love" in the OT, it always denotes faithfulness to covenant obligations, whether vertical (between God and human beings, or a superior to an inferior) or horizontal (between equals).

The story of Abimelech reveals the depths of degeneracy to which Israel had fallen in their rebellion against the Lord. Abimelech, evil as he was, was able to accomplish what he did because he exploited Israel's tribal chauvinism and perverse desire for an earthly king, which gave expression to their inner rebellion against the One who already was king in Israel (8:23). Israel got what it deserved in Abimelech. Here, for the first time in Judges, the oppressing power came from within the covenant community rather than from outside. Many commentators treat the Abimelech story as an interruption or an aside. But we must take seriously the fact that structurally it stands at the center of the book and seek to understand its important function in the overall story, particularly what it reveals about Israel's wickedness and Israel's leadership, two points the author clearly seeks to communicate through this tragic story.

9:1–6 / Abimelech is first identified as a **son of Jerub-Baal,** which draws attention to Abimelech's relationship to those he murdered. Abimelech was a brother of the seventy he murdered, and the fact that they were related to him by the same father made the deed all the more nefarious (cf. 8:22–23). This son of Jerub-Baal **went to his mother's brothers in Shechem** and proposed that they place him in leadership over them, since, of course, they would rather have **just one man rule over** them than **seventy,** and who else but Abimelech, because he was their own **flesh and blood.** The Shechemites liked this plan, **for they said, "He is our brother."** Abimelech shrewdly exploited individual family loyalty to provoke a division of loyalties between members of the covenant community. But at the same time the Shechemites were vulnerable because they already had turned away from "the LORD their God" (8:34).

The Shechemites **gave** Abimelech a large sum of money **from the temple of Baal-Berith,** which he used **to hire reckless adventurers, who became his followers** (v. 4). This statement brims with irony. First, a legitimate leader should not have to hire people to follow him. Second, the Shechemites took the money from the temple treasury to pay those people, not to mention that the temple was dedicated to Baal worship. Finally, the word behind "adventurers" is very negative. The root word *(phz)* has the connotation of unrestrained lawlessness. It is used to describe Reuben's odious sin (sleeping with his father's concubine, Gen. 49:4) and false prophets who led Israel astray (Jer. 23:32; Zeph. 3:4). Zephaniah places the term in parallelism with "treacherous men" (betrayers), which also suits this context in Judges. These were not men out for a little excitement in life; they were reprehensible.

Having enlisted support from the Shechemites and scraped together a small army, Abimelech made his next move: **he murdered his seventy brothers.** It is impossible to overstate how severe was this betrayal of everything that gave order to community life and human existence in general. The author subtly emphasizes the sheer audacity of this act by referring three times in one verse (v. 5) to Abimelech's relationship to those he murdered—**his father's home,** seventy brothers, **sons of Jerub-Baal**—while only succinctly stating what Abimelech did. **One stone** is emphatic by its position in the sentence. Besides adding to the horror of the deed, it also possibly communicates two other messages: If the stone is the one on which Gideon sacrificed to the Lord to renew the covenant, it speaks to Abimelech's repudiation of Israel's covenant with the Lord; and it foreshadows the manner in which Abimelech would die (9:52), again an example of just retribution.

The following sentence forebodes an unexpected outcome. Abimelech thought he had executed all of Gideon's sons, **but Jotham, the youngest son of Jerub-Baal, escaped by hiding** (cf. 2 Kgs. 11:1–3). Alerted to an impending surprise twist to the story, we wait to hear from Jotham again. Meanwhile—in contrast to this lone figure—**all the citizens of Shechem and Beth Millo gathered . . . in Shechem to crown Abimelech king** (v. 6). We cannot miss the irony that this took place in Shechem, which was the sight of Israel's great covenant renewal ceremony under Joshua's leadership. We also cannot miss the author's message to his contemporaries. Shechem was in the heart of Samaria, the northern kingdom of Israel. Thus its leadership was illegitimate from the beginning (Jeroboam I) and guilty of every breach of covenant possible. The people of Shechem were equally guilty; as we will see, they got the leadership they deserved.

9:7–15 / In the midst of the pomp and circumstance of this parody of a coronation ceremony, Jotham reappeared. From the **top of Mount Gerizim . . .** he **shouted** out a parable to the crowd gathered below. Even the reference to the place where Jotham stood adds to the irony that pervades this whole story. Mount Gerizim was the place from which the Levites were to call out the covenant blessings, in contrast to the curses called out from Mount Ebal (Deut. 11:26–29; 27:9–26). Jotham prefaced his parable with solemn words: **Listen to** *[sm']* **me . . . so that God may listen to** *[sm']* **you,** implying that he spoke prophetically, in the tradition of a covenant prophet.

The parable concerned leadership—good leadership and bad leadership. Many commentators have viewed Jotham's parable as an example of antimonarchic tendencies in Judges. But if we look more closely at the parable, we see it is not inherently antimonarchical but has a more general point—that people foolishly accept bad leadership and get what they deserve. This point is empirically verifiable from numerous examples in human, including church, history.

The parable is prophetic. According to it, when finally the thornbush was invited to become king, it accepted but pledged to rule under the threat of punishment: If the trees did not want to **take refuge in** its **shade,** then **fire** would go **out of the thornbush and consume the cedars of Lebanon** (v. 15). The point is clear: Something insignificant and worthless as a thornbush (Abimelech) had the power to destroy something so grand and noble as the cedars of Lebanon (Shechemites).

9:16–21 / Jotham interpreted his own parable. In essence, he said that they deserved nothing better than each other and would eventually destroy each other by fire. Justice would demand their mutual destruction because they had together destroyed his father's family. They would get what they deserved, reap what they had sown. Between a leader and his or her people there is potential for mutual good or mutual evil, depending upon the quality of the people. In this case the quality of both was definitely poor.

Finally, the text states that **Jotham fled . . . because he was afraid of his brother Abimelech** (v. 21). The word order ("his brother" precedes "Abimelech") points out the incongruity that a person would have to fear his own brother. The final word of the pericope, thus in emphatic position, is "Abimelech."

Additional Notes §14

9:1 / **Abimelech . . . went to his mother's brothers in She-chem:** A major interpretive issue in the story is whether the Shechemites were Israelite or Canaanite. The evidence favors the view that the main protagonists in the story were Israelites. First, the lead in to Abimelech's story is the notice that the Israelites fell into idolatry, particularly expressed in worship of Baal-Berith, and they did not show covenant loyalty to Gideon (8:34–35); the text specifies that the Shechemites gave Abimelech money from the temple of Baal-Berith (9:4). While this does not preclude the possibility that they were non-Israelite, the immediate context implies that they were Israelite. Second, a major theme of Judges is intercommunal conflict, and the example of this story loses its impact if it is not about people who should have demonstrated covenant loyalty to one another. Third, Jotham's parable (9:7–15) clearly speaks to the Israelites' foolish desire for a foolish king and their mistreatment of Gideon's family in spite of all he did for them. Moreover, its imagery closely parallels that of another of Israel's parables, told in the context of a serious intercommunal conflict between the northern and southern kingdom (2 Kgs. 14:9; cf. 2 Chron. 25:18). Finally, Abimelech's story stands at the center of the book of Judges, indicating that Abimelech played a key role as an Israelite leader. Klein (*The Triumph of Irony*, p. 70) calls Abimelech the "anti-hero of the book of Judges." But some of the Shechemites were Canaanite, as the episode of Gaal indicates (9:26–29).

9:6 / **All the citizens of Shechem and Beth Millo gathered . . . in Shechem to crown Abimelech king:** Davis (*Such a Great Salvation*, p. 122) points out: "How ironic that this occurs by the oak of the pillar at Shechem" (RSV) where both Jacob (Gen. 35:4) and Joshua (Josh. 24:1, 26) affirmed fidelity to Yahweh; now Abimelech uses the place to sanctify his treachery under the auspices of Baal-Berith."

9:7–20 / **Listen to me so that God may listen to you:** Davis (*Such a Great Salvation*, p. 123) agrees that this is the main point: "The parable does not stress the worthlessness of kingship but the worthlessness of Abimelech; the concern is not that the worthy candidates depreciate the offer of kingship but the character of the king and his cronies, as Jotham makes clear in vv. 16–20." The two terms, "thornbush" (a close synonym) and "cedars of Lebanon," also appear together in 2 Kgs. 14:9 (cf. 2 Chron. 25:18), which likewise speaks to the issue of intercommunal conflict. The "cedars of Lebanon" were the most magnificent of all the trees, and the phrase here refers to the Israelites.

9:21 / **Abimelech:** Boling's point is well taken: "It is impossible to exaggerate the narrative's sustained contempt for Abimelech . . . ; the name occurs thirty-one times in the chapter" (*Judges*, p. 170).

§15 The Fall of Abimelech (Judg. 9:22–57)

Abimelech's story is a classic example of the principle of sowing and reaping. He who rose to power by treachery, violence, and murder in the same way fell from power. In this passage Jotham's prophetic parable about those who lead and those who follow is fulfilled with extraordinary precision.

9:22–25 / After Abimelech had governed Israel three years, God sent an evil spirit between Abimelech and the citizens of Shechem, who acted treacherously against Abimelech (vv. 22–23). The Hebrew clearly communicates the cause-and-effect relationship between the two clauses: the effect of the evil spirit's presence was that the Shechemites acted treacherously against Abimelech. The primary work of the evil spirit was to cause a breakdown of *shalom* between people; note that the evil spirit came between Abimelech and the citizens of Shechem. How ironic it is that after the Holy Spirit came upon Gideon, God worked to cause his non-Israelite enemies to turn against each other; here, an evil spirit caused Abimelech's own people, such as they were, to turn against him and him against them. In verse 24, the author continues to underscore the same theme by declaring through narrative intrusion three times Abimelech's relationship to those he violently murdered.

The author also highlights this theme in the phrase **in opposition to him** (9:25a). We are not told if the **citizens of Shechem** paid the robbers to **rob everyone who passed by,** though the text implies that they did. If so, the irony increases, for the same people had paid Abimelech to gather around himself a coterie of hoodlums. The text does not specify why this action would have adversely affected Abimelech, but it likely siphoned off revenue money he would have received from travelers (cf. Hos. 6:9).

**9:26–29 / Soon even more trouble came to Abimelech in the person of Gaal son of Ebal who, along with his brothers, moved into town. The text indicates that their arrival was orches-

trated by God in order to bring Abimelech's rule and life to an ignominious end, as well as just retribution to the Shechemites. The
illustrious brothers appear to have been Canaanite, because they
exploited the Shechemites' loyalty to their common ancestor,
Hamor (v. 28; cf. Gen. 34). These were people whom the Israelites
failed to drive out of the land and who now had come back to ha-
rass them (Judg. 2:3b). Again and again, the author emphasizes
that Gaal worked together with his brothers (vv. 26, 31, 41), which
contrasts starkly with Abimelech, who murdered all but one of his
brothers so that he could reign over Shechem, thus portraying
Abimelech as worse than even the most pagan lowlife.

Gaal and his brothers effortlessly drew the loyalties of the
Shechemites from Abimelech to themselves, which further illustrates how chaotic the situation had become; covenant fidelity
was all but dead. They rebelled against Abimelech's leadership
and led others to follow them, playing the same card Abimelech
had played—chauvinistic tribalism. Gaal boasted that if he were
in control, he would easily overthrow Abimelech's whole army
(v. 29). Through extended dialogue, the author focuses attention
on the details of Gaal's boast, which points to its importance in
the story. In many ways his words echo those of Abimelech (v. 2),
thus subtly pointing out the justice of God's ways of dealing
with Israel.

9:30–33 / **Zebul** was casually introduced in the context
of Gaal's insolent boast (v. 28). Now he enters fully into the un-
folding drama. Somehow he found out about Gaal's bravado and
informed Abimelech, suggesting a plan about how best to attack
them. His strategy—to **lie in wait in the fields** and launch their attack when **Gaal and his men come out against** them—will again
be followed in the book of Judges, but then, tragically, by Israelites
attacking Israelites (Judg. 20:32–36).

9:34–41 / The details of Abimelech's movements in the
attack recall Gideon's nocturnal attack on the Midianites. At this
point, the author pauses in his description of the action to let us
hear a conversation between Gaal and Zebul. Through dialogue,
he enhances the dramatic effect of the story, allowing it to unfold
before us. At the same time, he incorporates themes he wishes to
highlight. Somehow Gaal and Zebul both came together at **the entrance** to Shechem, at the crack of dawn. Gaal caught a glimpse of
movement in the morning shadows and rightly guessed that it
was **people . . . coming down from the tops of the mountains**

(v. 36a). But Zebul taunted him, suggesting that it was merely morning **shadows** (Hb. sing.). The conversation is about whether Abimelech and his men are or are not a shadow. The word "shadow" is the same word used by Jotham in his parable: "The thornbush said to the trees, 'If you really want to anoint me king over you, come and take refuge in my shadow (NIV: **shade**); if not, then let fire come out of the thornbush and consume the cedars of Lebanon' " (9:15; 19–20). With this one word, the author hints that the story is moving toward resolution, and the resolution will be the fulfillment of Jotham's prophetic parable.

In keeping with Jotham's prediction, Gaal and the citizens of Shechem went out and **fought Abimelech** (v. 39). Abimelech roundly defeated them (v. 40), many Shechemites died (NIV: **fell wounded**), and in the end, **Gaal and his brothers** were driven **out of** the city (vv. 40–41). The dramatic effect of the events is heightened by the use of the unusual Hebrew root, *hll* ("died"), which picks up on similar sounding roots in Gaal's impudent boast: *hll* ("festival") and *qll* ("cursed"; v. 27) and underscores the theme of just retribution.

9:42–49 / But the prophecy had not been completely fulfilled. What about the Israelite citizens of Shechem and Beth Millo (v. 20)? What about the cedars of Lebanon (v. 15)? The carnage continued. When **the people of Shechem went out to the fields** to work, Abimelech **rose to attack them** (v. 43). He did not stop until he had destroyed the city. The text specifies that Abimelech *(abimlkh)* **scattered salt** *[mlh]* **over** the city (v. 45), a sign of perpetual desolation—and also possibly pointing out the irony that the king *(mlkh)* destroyed his own city.

A few Shechemites had taken refuge in the city tower and later moved to **the stronghold of the temple of El-Berith** (v. 46). Abimelech put **branches** on **his shoulders** and **ordered the men with him** to do the same (vv. 47–48). We cannot fail to see yet another point of irony, that in this Abimelech looks and acts much like his father, Gideon (8:17–18) but with one conspicuous difference: Gideon had liberated his compatriots from foreign oppression, while Abimelech oppressed and enslaved his own compatriots.

The events move quickly toward the final fulfillment of Jotham's parable. Abimelech and his men set the stronghold on fire and burned alive **all the people** inside. Literally, fire had come out from Abimelech and consumed the citizens of Shechem and

Beth Millo (9:20). In Hebrew, the expression translated **men and women** is literally "man and woman"; the phrase ending with "woman" foreshadows the pivotal role of a woman in the final events of the story.

9:50–55 / Abimelech then **beseiged . . . and captured** the neighboring town of **Thebez.** When he attempted a repeat of what he had done in Shechem he met with more than he expected: **But . . . a woman dropped an upper millstone** [about 27 lb.] **on his head and cracked his skull** (v. 53). The statement is deceivingly simple, but its simplicity communicates powerfully. The word "but" speaks volumes and calls us back to the bigger picture, to the role of the sovereign Lord in history, such as articulated in Proverbs 19:21: "Many are the plans in a man's heart, but it is the LORD's purpose that prevails" (see also Prov. 16:9). For Abimelech, everything was going according to plan—except that God had the last word. The text does not explicitly specify that God was responsible for Abimelech's downfall, but the fact that a woman—a nameless, nondescript, nobody in this story—could have singlehandedly brought him down implies God's miraculous intervention, as it does in the story of Jael and Sisera.

This illustrious warrior, like Sisera, did not want to be remembered by the epithet, **A woman killed him** (v. 54). Such an ignominious ending was more than he could bear, so he ordered **his armor-bearer** to **draw** his **sword and kill** him. Thus Abimelech died in some ways like Sisera, in some ways like Saul would later die (1 Sam. 31:4). The analogy to both is appropriate and intentional. One was a pagan leader, the other a failed king of Israel—both equally wicked and both equally punished appropriately. In the story of Abimelech, the line between pagan and Israelite blurs almost into oblivion. Could there be a more scathing commentary on illegitimate leadership?

9:56–57 / In these final verses, the author summarizes the important lesson of Abimelech's story. Jotham's parable was fulfilled: **God repaid the wickedness that Abimelech had done to his father by murdering his seventy brothers. . . .** and **made the men of Shechem pay for all their wickedness.** The principle of sowing and reaping could not be better illustrated.

Additional Notes §15

9:23 / God sent an evil spirit: That God would send an evil spirit is not unique in biblical literature. For example, according to 1 Sam. 16:14–15; 18:10; 19:9, an evil spirit from God came upon Saul, where the evil spirit's activity was counterpart to the Holy Spirit's coming upon David (cf. 1 Sam. 16:13–14). A similar phenomenon is recorded in 1 Kgs. 22:19–23, where God dispatched a spirit, presumably evil, which orchestrated the downfall of King Ahab. The notion that an evil spirit could come from God may present theological difficulties for us, but for the ancient Hebrews, it expressed God's absolute sovereignty over all forces and all events.

The text states that the evil spirit came "between Abimelech and the citizens of Shechem"; the impact of the evil spirit was a breakdown in communal harmony. This concept is also found in NT teaching, although such attitudes and actions may not be explicitly attributed to an evil spirit. For example, many of the items in the list of the "acts of the sinful nature" in Gal. 5:19–21 have to do with interpersonal relationships, and these are contrasted with the fruit of the Spirit (Gal. 5:22–23).

9:25 / These citizens of Shechem set men on the hilltops: There is a wordplay on the root *sym*: the evil spirit came between Abimelech and the Shechemites in order to place *(lasum)* upon them the bloodguilt for the murders (v. 24); the Shechemites placed *(wayyasimu)* men against him (v. 25). By this the author again highlights the theme of *talion*, or just retribution.

9:26 / Gaal, son of Ebed, moved . . . into Shechem: Although the NIV reads "Gaal, the son of Ebed," I give preference to the alternate reading Ebal. The two divergent translations reflect variant readings in Gk. and Hb. manuscripts. The Hb. text reads *'ebed,* and one group of Greek texts reads *Iobel* and another (minor group) *Iobed* or *Iobid*. Both readings find strong support; I, however, prefer the Gk. *Iobel* (Hb. *'ebal*), because the name preserves a wordplay that the author appears to work with in the narrative. Ebal was the mountain above Shechem from which the Levites were to read the list of curses *(qllym)* that would fall upon the Israelites if they failed to keep their covenant commitments to the Lord (Deut. 27:13). It is no accident that the author specifically notes that at the grape harvest festival *(hillulim)*, Gaal and his brothers ate and drank and cursed *(wayeqalelu)* Abimelech (v. 27), playing on the similar roots *hll* and *qll*. There is also a possible wordplay on the name Gaal. The Hebrew root *g'l* means "to abhor" or "to be loathesome," while a similar root, *g'l,* means "to redeem." Gaal purported to be a redeemer, but he was only a loathesome character.

9:46 / The temple of El-Berith: El-Berith and Baal-Berith were one and the same, though some commenators disagree.

9:48 / **Quick!** The word "quick" occurs two times, here and in v. 54 (Hb.). This repetition links the two scenes and thus points out the irony of how differently these two episodes turned out. Also note the similarity to Saul's death. Moore (*Judges*, p. 268) discusses the parallels between the deaths of Abimelech and the Greek hero Hercules; in both cases, the greatest shame was to die by the hand of a woman.

Framing the Jephthah story are accounts of several minor judges, beginning with Tola and Jair and ending with Ibzan, Elon, and Abdon (Judg. 12:8–15). These, along with Shamgar (Judg. 3:31), are commonly designated as minor judges, because their stories are condensed into a few brief lines. In most cases, all we know about the judge is his tribal affiliation, his geographical location, and how many years he led Israel; sometimes we learn about his economic situation. But, strikingly, the stories make no reference to the charismatic activity associated with the major judges. While they provide interesting information for historians and biblical geographers, what is not clear is the process by which they came to be integrated into the story of Israel's judges. They may have been incorporated into the book by the Deuteronomic author in order to round out the number of judges to twelve, generally one for each tribe.

Significantly, the stories of Tola and Jair follow immediately the story of Abimelech; the author explicitly links them with the phrase "After the time of Abimelech" (v. 1). We will suggest the implications of this after we have looked more closely at the text.

10:1–2 / **Tola rose to save Israel.** The detailed information about his genealogical history and place of residence conforms to the general pattern for the minor judges. The most complete version appears in the story of Elon (Judg. 12:11–12). Tola lived in Shamir, which means "thornbush," further linking him with Abimelech (9:14–15), though the Hebrew word is not the same. The exact location of Shamir is unknown, though some scholars have suggested that it is to be identified with Samaria (Hb. *somron*).

Tola **led** [judged] **Israel** for **twenty-three years.** His lengthy term of leadership implies a period of relative stability and tranquility, which stands in stark contrast to the brief but tumultuous reign of Abimelech. The fact that he immediately followed such a leader as Abimelech again reveals God's amazing grace, still working to bring *shalom,* even in the midst of such a seemingly irreversible trajectory toward chaos.

10:3–5 / In the case of **Jair of Gilead,** who **followed** Tola, the author omits the extended genealogical details included in Tola's story but does tell us that he **led** [judged] **Israel twenty-two years.** Again, this lengthy period is indicative of relative stability, a sign of God's covenant faithfulness toward the Israelites, despite their perpetual waywardness.

The author includes some additional information about Jair's economic situation, which was evidently good: **He had thirty sons, who rode thirty donkeys** . . . and **controlled thirty towns in Gilead.** The fact that Jair had thirty sons is as much an indication of the stability of the times as a reflection of his personal wealth. That they all rode donkeys also speaks of their wealth and status, for the donkey was the transportation of choice for the rich and famous. It seems that these thirty sons each governed a town in Gilead, which likewise points to Jair's wealth and wide influence. All details together present a picture of political stability and economic prosperity, a picture that constrasts starkly with the days of Abimelech and those immediately following Jair's death (10:6–10). It would be virtually the last season of *shalom* in Israel for a long, long time.

Additional Notes §16

10:1 / **Tola son of Puah, the son of Dodo:** The expression "son of Dodo" could also be translated "son of his uncle." The LXX so renders it and even implies that the uncle is Abimelech.

10:4 / **He had thirty sons, who rode thirty donkeys:** There is clearly a wordplay between the words for donkeys (*'ayarim*) and cities (*'arim*), which explains the author's use of a rare word instead of the usual word for donkeys and also the anomalous form for cities (*'ayarim*) in the Hb. text.

§17 Jephthah: Ammonite Oppression (Judg. 10:6–18)

Jephthah is not mentioned by name, but this section sets the stage, both generally and specifically, for his entrance on the scene. The author describes Israel's deteriorating spiritual condition and interaction with God about their circumstances (vv. 6–16); more specifically, he begins to focus attention upon the events that directly led to Jephthah's rise to leadership (vv. 17–18). The obvious emphasis in this section is upon the general, spanning as it does eleven verses. To be sure, we have not encountered such a lengthy and detailed exposé of Israel's condition since the beginning of the book (2:1–3:6). But because Jephthah's story marks the beginning of the second half of the book, the author pauses to review the basic principles set out in the first half of the book, which will come to full realization as this chapter of Israel's story plunges to its climax in Judges 21.

With Gideon and Abimelech, Israel's history began to take a definite turn for the worse. One sign of this is that after Gideon, the judges' stories close not with a reference to the land having peace for *x* years but merely a notice about the length of time the judge led Israel (10:2, 3; 12:7, 9, 11, 14; 15:20). In the second half of the book, God withholds his gift of peace in response to Israel's willful rejection of the covenant relationship that would have guaranteed peace. But even in that dark period in Israel's history, the light of God's gracious presence and help never went out; God continually sought to bring his people back into relationship with himself, into the true *shalom* that he longed to give them. Even as it appeared that God's patience with Israel had been exhausted (vv. 11–14), his inexhaustible love for his people compelled him to act once again on their behalf (v. 16).

10:6 / Jephthah's story begins with the stereotypic opening statement we have already encountered many times (2:11; 3:7, 12; 4:1; 6:1): **The Israelites** increasingly **did evil in the eyes of the LORD.** The remainder of the verse details the nature of the evil. It is described in language we have come to expect—idolatry, which fundamentally is unfaithfulness to the covenant relationship, as underscored in the last part of the verse: **The Israelites forsook the LORD.** The Israelites **no longer served** the Lord, but **they served** the foreign gods named in the second part of the verse. It is clear that biblically speaking, to forsake the Lord is to serve other gods. There is no place for atheism or agnosticism; a person is on either one side or the other side of the fence (cf. 1 Kgs. 18:21).

10:7–9 / The Lord's response to Israel's apostasy was predictable: **He sold them into the hands of the Philistines and the Ammonites, who . . . shattered and crushed them.** The reference to the Philistines is strange, because thus far they have hardly been mentioned (3:31) and do not appear in any subsequent material relating to Jephthah. The reference to enemy oppression on the east (Ammonite) and west (Philistine) sides, possibly even the north, represents an increase in the scope of Israel's suffering at the hands of enemies. The Ammonites even took over territory west of the Jordan River. The point, however, is clear: As the sin increased, so the punishment increased.

10:10–16 / The intensity of the oppression finally drove **the Israelites** to cry out **to the LORD.** Their cry sounds like a cry of repentance, what the Lord was waiting to hear, all the words theologically correct. Hence we expect the Lord to do as he has done in the past, immediately raise up a judge to deliver the people. But perhaps the Lord, who knows the heart (Pss. 44:21; 66:18; Heb. 4:13), knew that their crying out was not a cry of genuine repentance, not a "sorry for" but a "sorry that." The author all but explicitly states this in the Lord's response (vv. 11–15). In the form of rhetorical question, the Lord rehearses the history of his gracious rescuing of Israel from seven nations and then sardonically concludes: **But you have forsaken me and served other gods, so I will no longer save you. Go and cry out to the gods you have chosen. Let them save you when you are in trouble!** (vv. 13–14). How could Israel worship other gods and then cry out for help to the very God they deserted?

Apparently the Israelites were moved to a level of genuine repentance. They repeated the same words, but this time they backed up their words with action: **They got rid of the foreign gods among them and served the LORD** (v. 16). It is impossible to overstate the importance of the point this accentuates, that words are easy to speak and only when accompanied by appropriate actions are they proven to be genuine. The Lord was looking not for a superficial change of words but for a true change of heart and recognized it in Israel's penitential action.

Israel's change of heart moved the Lord to a change of heart, or at least to defer to his compassionate side. The statement that **he could bear Israel's misery no longer** (v. 16) expresses God's heart for his people and his readiness to act on their behalf; action would be immediately forthcoming. The Bible clearly teaches that loving compassion is the dominant aspect of the Lord's essential nature. As he revealed his name (Yahweh, Lord) to Moses, he also revealed his nature, which was to show *hesed* (covenant love and faithfulness) to those to whom he was committed "to the thousandth generation" (Exod. 20:6; 33:19; 34:5–7). The notion that the God of the OT was only wrathful and vengeful is challenged by numerous passages, this one included.

10:17–18 / God acted by setting in motion the process of deliverance, beginning with the raising up of a deliverer. These two verses serve as a transition to that event. The Ammonite crisis reached such a point that **the Israelites assembled . . . at Mizpah** in order to challenge Ammonite hegemony over them (v. 17). Although it looks like things will continue as in the past eighteen years (v. 8), the author has alerted us that a change is coming by stating that the Lord could bear Israel's misery no longer. Thus the section closes with the leaders of Gilead searching for the appropriate leader, promising that whoever would step forward **will** also **be the head of all those living in Gilead.** Together with the Gileadites, we wait expectantly for the appearance of that leader, who is waiting in the wings to make his entrance. But he will not look like what we expect.

Additional Notes §17

10:6 / **Again the Israelites did evil in the eyes of the LORD:** The list of pagan gods in v. 6 has every appearance of being stereotypic, likely the product of the same Deuteronomic editor who wrote the introduction (2:6–3:6) and placed the individual stories within the Deuteronomic framework. There are seven gods, a symbolic number, which corresponds to the later list of seven oppressing nations from whom God liberated Israel (10:11). These gods represent the nations that surrounded Israel, though not all are included; Midian is strangely absent, while Maon is strangely present. Some manuscripts contain the word "Midian" instead of Maon.

10:11–14 / The Lord replied: The length and detail of this divine speech is significant; for in Hb. narrative convention, important points are often communicated in the form of direct speech, and how much more in the form of divine speech!

10:16 / And he could bear Israel's misery no longer: Christians, who believe that Jesus was the perfect revelation of God (John 1:18), must reject a hermeneutic that distingushes between "the God of the OT" and "the God of the NT," especially by referring falsely and pejoratively to the God of the OT as a God of wrath and vengeance.

§18 Jephthah: Surprise Leader! (Judg. 11:1–28)

The Gileadite leaders gathered at Mizpah did not find a military chief capable of leading their militia against the Ammonites. The present scene opens with the spotlight focused elsewhere, upon an Israelite warrior, first in Gilead and then in the land of Tob. The section stars a half-breed named Jephthah who was rejected and exiled by his brothers, in contrast to another half-breed, Abimelech, who rejected and murdered his brothers. In a flashback sequence, the author informs us of Jephthah's ignominious background, which would not forebode his illustrious role as Israel's next judge. But, as with Ehud, Deborah, and Gideon, God often chooses the least likely people and manifests his strength and glory through such as these (cf. 2 Cor. 12:9–10).

Our ambivalence about Jephthah's suitability to serve as Israel's judge increases as the story develops, for Jephthah later radically oversteps the boundaries of biblical faith to such a degree that we wonder how the author of the epistle to the Hebrews could have included him among the heroes of the faith (Heb. 11:32–33). But we meet Jephthah for the first time and see him in action as a negotiator, a role that he performed with exceptional skill with both Israelites and Ammonites, though successfully only with Israelites.

11:1–3 / **Jephthah** is introduced in terms of two characteristics: he was a **Gileadite** (an Israelite) and **a mighty warrior** (cf. Gideon, 6:12). These qualifications, especially the second, were sufficient to equip him to free the Israelites from Ammonite oppression. But immediately following this description, additional information introduces an element of unresolved conflict: **His father was Gilead; his mother was a prostitute.** This is one step removed from Abimelech's situation, for at least his mother had the status of a concubine. Jephthah was utterly illegitimate. And he was utterly rejected by his legitimate siblings, who **drove** him **away** (v. 2), mostly for selfish reasons, so they would not have to share their **inheritance** with him. Thus **Jephthah fled from his brothers and settled in the land of Tob** (v. 3). There, being a natural leader, he gathered around himself a group of men, in this case a gang of lowlifes, such as Abimelech had attracted.

11:4–11 / Now that Jephthah has been properly introduced, the scene returns to the conflict between Israel and Ammon and Israel's subsequent crisis of leadership. **The elders of Gilead**—who had banished Jephthah—**went to get** him **from the land of Tob** and invited him back, as their **commander.** That they would turn to him demonstrates the severity of the crisis. This element of Jephthah's story is unique in the book of Judges; in no other case does a judge become the leader as a result of being invited to do so by the Israelites. Later, the Holy Spirit's role will be acknowledged ("the Spirit of the LORD came upon Jephthah," 11:29), but this occurred only after he had been commissioned by the people to lead them in battle (11:12).

The elders had proposed to Jephthah that he become their commander (Hb. *qasin*). They were very careful about the term they used; they were looking for nothing more than a military leader. But Jephthah's response motivated them to offer more. He rightly responded with a question as to why they (Hb. emphatic), the ones who had banished him, had now **come to** him **when** they were **in trouble?** (v. 7).

Jephthah's hesitancy, whether genuine or tactical maneuvering, gained him an even better position. The elders came back with an offer he could not refuse: he would be not just their military commander but the **head** of **all** those living **in Gilead** (v. 8). Jephthah could not believe his ears, so he asked to hear the particulars again: **will I** [Hb. emphatic] **really be your head?** In their desperation, the Gileadite elders affirmed their offer in the strongest of terms, with a solemn oath (v. 10), and made good on their promise, even before Jephthah fulfilled his part (v. 11).

It appears that the elders installed Jephthah as **head and** commander in a ceremony at the sanctuary at **Mizpah;** there is a vague reference that Jephthah **repeated all his words** there (v. 11), which sounds like some sort of oath of office. This is the second time in as many verses that the author has referred in Hebrew to Jephthah's "word(s)" (Hb. *dabar*), and he will develop it into a major *Leitmotif* in Jephthah's story (vv. 28, 37). Jephthah was a smooth talker who knew how to use words to his advantage, but he also did not know when to keep his mouth shut. Later, most likely again at Mizpah (v. 29), he will speak words that should have been left unspoken.

That Jephthah repeated all his words before the Lord in Mizpah represented a significant step in Israel's history. As we already noted, the process of Jephthah's becoming judge was quite unlike that of other judges but more closely resembled the choosing of a king. Since Abimelech—perhaps even Gideon, who acted like a king, despite his refusal of the title (Judg. 8:23)—Israel had been steadily moving closer to the reality of a monarchy. As we progress to the end of the book of Judges, this reality will come more and more into view, though it will not be realized until the time of Saul (1 Sam. 10:17–25; 11:12–15).

11:12–28 / These verses present Jephthah as a skillful diplomat, attempting to negotiate peace with the Ammonites in lieu of armed conflict. His is the only story with this element, and throughout the whole dialogue (virtually monologue) Jephthah speaks and acts more like a king than does any other judge. He sent envoys in his name (v. 12), who posed the question in terms (first person singular) elsewhere used by a king (v. 13).

Jephthah argued his point from three perspectives. First, he denied that the Israelites had ever set their sights on anyone's land; they always respected international boundaries (vv. 17–19). They fought only when attacked (v. 20) and took land only when they won it in battle (vv. 20–22). Second, Jephthah brought in the theological perspective (v. 22). The God of Israel, who had proven himself greater than the Amorites' god, gave the land to them! The land in question belonged to Israel by divine right; how could or would anyone argue with that? Third, the only issue left to be resolved—which will happen shortly after all the talk dies down—is whose God is greater. Jephthah went on to play this card for all its worth (vv. 23–25), first repeating the assertion that **the LORD, the God of Israel,** had given them the land, followed by the sardonic, almost rhetorical question: And *you* (Hb. emphatic) **take it over?**

Jephthah continued by suggesting that just as the Ammonites **take what** their **god Chemosh gives** them, **likewise, whatever the LORD** their **God** gives them, Israel **will possess** (v. 24). He placed their conflict within a larger context, a much larger context—a cosmic contest between their respective gods. This was the common way of understanding such conflicts, as evidenced in numerous other biblical and extrabiblical texts (cf. 1 Sam. 4:1–6:6; 17:26, 36, 43–47) and will again be emphasized as the keynote of Jephthah's message to the Ammonite king (v. 27). Through these references, the Deuteronomic author continues to press home his polemic against idolatry and to ridicule those who worship any god but the "one LORD" (Deut. 6:4) as well as to reaffirm God's promise of the land for Israel.

Jephthah pressed harder: **Are you better than Balak son of Zippor, king of Moab? Did he ever quarrel with Israel or fight with them?** (v. 25). The words "better," "quarrel," and "fight" are especially emphatic in the Hebrew text; the occurrence of these repeated words (Hb.) in one sentence demonstrates the intensity of Jephthah's rhetoric. Balak indeed did attempt to quarrel with Israel (Num. 22–24) and soon found that he was up against more than he had bargained for. The reference to that episode in Israel's history, which included Balaam's prophecies, recalled the Lord's blessing upon the Israelites and pledge that no enemy would ultimately stand against them (Num. 23, 24).

Finally, Jephthah appealed to simple logic: **For three hundred years Israel occupied** the territory in dispute. **Why didn't you retake them during that time?** (v. 26). This question functions as his final point before resting his case with two important assertions: **I** [Hb. emphatic] **have not wronged you, but you are doing me wrong by waging war against me.** He concluded with an appeal to **the LORD, the Judge,** to **decide** [Hb. judge] **the dispute.** This is the only place in Judges where the Lord is referred to as "the Judge"; it occurs in an appropriate context, a legal dispute. The appellation here is intensive because of the definite article; it recognizes no other Judge but the Judge, the God of Israel.

To this point Jephthah presented himself rather positively, both as a take-charge leader and as a negotiator. Perhaps he was also an ambitious opportunist who would do anything or say anything to get ahead. But Jephthah's gift of verbosity would prove to be his nemesis, as the next episode reveals.

Additional Notes §18

11:3 / **A group of adventurers . . . followed him:** The Hb. phrase *('anasim reqim)* is the same as that in the story of Abimelech. What is translated "gathered" is much more graphic. The Hb. root *(htlqqt)* signifies "raked together." Note also the parallel with David, whose "militia" consisted of "all those who were in distress or in debt or discontented" (1 Sam. 22:2).

11:7 / Didn't you hate me and drive me from my father's house? Note the parallel with the earlier episode in which Israel, who had rejected the Lord, went crying to him in their trouble, and then the Lord's response to them (vv. 13–14). This is not to say that Jephthah is a type of God in this story, as some commentators have suggested; the lack of resemblance (the total opposite!) elsewhere (vv. 34–39) precludes such an interpretation.

11:12 / What do you have against us that you have attacked our country? This is the NIV rendering, but the Hb. is clearly singular: me/my country.

11:24 / Will you not take what your god Chemosh gives you? The god Chemosh is referred to as the Ammonite god, which is difficult to reconcile with other sources that name Chemosh as the national god of the Moabites. Boling (*Judges,* pp. 203–4) suggests an interesting possibility: "The Ammonites must have treated the former Moabite territory [which they occupied] as a separate entity, administratively and diplomatically. . . . Under such circumstances the jurisdiction of the god Chemosh would be generally recognized for diplomatic purposes (cf. the Mesha inscription in *ANET*³, p. 320)." Cundall (*Judges,* p. 144) notes that in the seventh century "parts of Moab and Gilead were occupied by the Ammonites which resulted in a merging of religions." Perhaps this fact testifies to the situation at the time of the author writing in the seventh century. Another difficulty is that Jephthah appears to concede that Chemosh is a real god. There is no compelling reason to think that a character like Jephthah was a strict monotheist. But in reality he affirms just the opposite, as did Gideon's father (6:31–32); if Chemosh were really a god, he would protect his interests.

§19 Jephthah: Bittersweet Victory (Judg. 11:29–40)

The Ammonites rejected a peaceful solution to their dispute with Israel, so Jephthah turned to the military option. Taking the lead at the head of the Israelite forces, he moved quickly to engage the enemy. But not before two events occurred, one indispensible and the other inconceivable. The latter caused Jephthah to be remembered not as Israel's most heroic and brilliant judge but as the most heartless and barbaric of all Israel's judges. It is difficult to pause and look at this passage, more so to scrutinize it. Would that it were not in the Bible. But it is in the Bible, and we must seek to understand its meaning and its role in the overall story of God's people. Truly these events mark a very low point in Israel's history, demonstrating that the downward spiral toward chaos has spun considerably closer to its conclusion.

11:29–31 / The passage opens on a positive note: **Then the Spirit of the LORD came upon Jephthah.** This charismatic endowment of the Spirit, as in the case of other judges, demonstrated God's choice of Jephthah as judge and equipped him for the task of delivering Israel. In every judge's story where it occurred, the event consistently marked the judge's gifting and empowering for successful leadership in battle. Thus the Spirit's coming upon Jephthah signaled the Lord's readiness to lead Israel to certain victory; everything was set in place and victory was assured.

But as Jephthah advanced to the battlefield, he made a brief stop along the way, most likely at Mizpah (v. 29), to make sure he would have no surprises. He had gone out on a limb to procure his newfound status and did not want to take any chances of losing it, so he **made a vow to the LORD.** The celebrated negotiator struck a bargain with the Lord (vv. 30–31). On the surface, Jephthah appeared to be a deeply pious person. After all, he acknowledged that the Lord was responsible for his victory; and a whole burnt offering was no small gift, inexpensive as it was. But how pious was Jephthah's vow? Would not the gift of the Holy Spirit have been sufficient to assure him of victory? Rather than go in the strength he had (Judg. 6:14), Jephthah preferred to strike a deal with the Lord, to manipulate him in order to guarantee success.

While the action was bad enough in itself, the content of Jephthah's vow made it scandalous. Much debate has focused on this vow, largely around the singular question: Did Jephthah intend a human sacrifice? Not necessarily his beloved daughter, but some*one*, as opposed to some*thing*, an animal of some sort? The Hebrew, which is ambiguous, does not help; it could equally be translated as "whoever" or "whatever." And lest we assume that a "whatever" would probably not come out of a house, we must remember that ancient Israelite houses were constructed to house livestock as well as people. So the question remains open.

From a logical standpoint, for Jephthah to have vowed to sacrifice an animal would not have been anything special, certainly not in view of the magnitude of the crisis. So he must have intended a human sacrifice. It was not unheard of to offer a human sacrifice at a time of grave national crisis (2 Kgs. 3:26–27), but what was unheard of was the Lord's being moved to action by such sacrifices. One of the important points made by the story of Abraham's offering of Isaac, the Aqedah (Gen. 22:1–14), is that the Lord neither demands, nor is pleased with, human sacrifice.

The most logical conclusion, therefore, is that Jephthah did intend a human sacrifice. But could or would Jephthah, an Israelite, a hero of the faith (Heb. 11:32), have made such a vow? It is not impossible that he could or would have done so. Biblical heroes were never perfect but were capable of committing all kinds of gross immoral acts. David, who violated almost every one of the Ten Commandments in his sin against Bathsheba and Uriah (2 Sam. 11), is a case in point. It will not do to distort the Bible's presentation of a character in a way the text does not, just to make it conform to our ideas of moral propriety. We must hear what the text says on its own terms, even if it presents theological difficulties or moral dilemmas that would easily be resolved if we made a few adjustments here and there. The text must inform our theology rather than our theology inform the text. This passage has given rise to many interpretations that start from everywhere but the text. The truth is that Jephthah was a master manipulator and a "big mouth" who did not always use the best judgment in how he used his mouth, or when he used it.

11:32–33 / What the author has been building up to since 10:17 he now describes in only two verses. He is not interested in the battle; he uses it as a foil for dealing with Jephthah's vow, to which he devotes seven out of nine verses. Jephthah's victory over the Ammonites was decisive (vv. 32–33). That, plus the fact that the same verb appears in the statement that **the LORD gave them into his hands** as in the vow, leads us to look for an impending fulfillment of the vow. The stage is set for the next scene, which we approach with anticipation, wanting to see how it turns out. Who or what will come out of Jephthah's house? Will he sacrifice it, him, or her to the Lord as a burnt offering? Will something or someone unexpectedly intervene? Will Jephthah cut another deal with the Lord?

11:34–40 / The author introduces this scene in a way that recalls the exact wording of Jephthah's vow: **Jephthah returned to his home,** certainly in triumph. Now that the Lord has clearly done his part, we watch with Jephthah to see what or who will come out of his house. The Hebrew text dramatically captures the climactic moment with merely four short words: "Behold, his daughter, coming out, toward him." The young girl emerged from the house celebrating her father's victory, unaware of the price she would pay for the victory she celebrated so heartily. "His daughter" stands in emphatic position, so all attention is focused upon her. Furthermore, the sentence does not even contain a verb, but only a participle, which further heightens the dramatic impact of the moment; the present tense draws us into the story so that we, along with Jephthah, watch the events unfold. We watch her dance toward her father, and we wonder what Jephthah will do. What will the Lord do? Surely he will not expect Jephthah to sacrifice this young girl!

Before describing the father-daughter meeting the author gives additional information that increases the poignancy of the situation: **She was an only child. Except for her he had neither son nor daughter** (v. 34). The repetition serves to emphasize the magnitude of the tragedy.

To most effectively communicate the indescribable pathos of the father-daughter meeting, the author at this point changes from narrative to dialogue; he remains in this mode until the subject matter becomes so profane that he must allow us to step back from the odious reality. Jephthah first expressed his absolute horror by an appropriate action, commonly associated with shock or grief: **He tore his clothes** (cf. Gen. 37:29; 2 Sam 13:19, 31), accompanied by a great, agonizing wail (considerably stronger than the NIV's **Oh!**). His second word named the unnamable: **My daughter!** His daughter had come out to meet him! While probably Jephthah had intended to offer a human sacrifice, he surely did not intend for it to be his beloved daughter. Some household servant, yes, but his daughter, no. Would he keep his promise?

We are not kept in suspense very long, for immediately Jephthah bellowed: "You have dealt me a terrible blow! *You* have been my bane, because *I* opened my mouth to the LORD and I cannot return it" (v. 35, my translation). Jephthah's statement that he "opened his mouth to the LORD" means that he **made a vow to the LORD,** as the NIV correctly renders it. I have rendered it literally to point out that the Hebrew focuses upon Jephthah characteristically opening his mouth. He had made a vow to the Lord, and such vows were believed to be impossible to nullify, since the word spoken represented the deed done.

Next—finally—the girl opened her mouth! She responded to what her father had not explicitly stated; she understood what he had not been able to bring himself to articulate. Her words are significant, for through them she reveals her character. She begins with one word, corresponding to Jephthah's first word ("My daughter"), accenting relationship—**My father!** Then she pledged her willing submission to what neither could openly declare: "You have opened your mouth to the LORD. Do to me what came out of your mouth after the LORD worked vengeance for you against your enemies, [that is] from the Ammonites" (v. 36). I have translated the verse literally in order to indicate the force of the Hebrew, particularly the continued repetition of the word "mouth." Jephthah's daughter did not specify what came out of her father's open mouth, but it is clear that she knew exactly what he had vowed. Her reluctance to speak openly about the content of the vow reveals her awareness of what it meant to her.

The girl revealed her understanding by proposing **one** last **request,** which presents her as a daughter who has learned well from her father how to bargain (v. 37). This is a difficult text to understand, especially for those from a modern western cultural context. Things have changed considerably from the ancient biblical culture, in which the epitome of fulfillment—the only means of fulfillment—for a woman was to marry and to bear children.

Moreover, to have children also ensured that a woman and her husband would be remembered for posterity and even may have impacted the parents' circumstances in the afterlife.

The final word of the father-daughter dialogue came from the father's mouth—one simple word, "Go." Then **she returned to her father** and he did **as he had vowed** (v. 39). The text speaks volumes by its very silence. It refrains from saying what the father did in order to communicate more dramatically, more forcefully what he did.

The silence of the text has provided a basis for some interpreters to rationalize Jephthah's action by reading into the text what they thought it should say or wanted it to say. Some, understandably, cannot accept an Israelite judge practicing human sacrifice; and even more, the Lord by silence allowing it. Thus the view has developed that Jephthah merely dedicated his daughter for perpetual service at the sanctuary, which entailed perpetual virginity. While it would be nice to think that this was what Jephthah did, it does not read out of the text (exegesis) but into the text (eisegesis) what modern ears would like to hear. The truth is that Jephthah offered his daughter, his one and only daughter, as a burnt offering.

The section closes by emphasizing—by repetition—that Jephthah's daughter was a virgin (v. 39) and communicating the further information that her communal mourning became the basis for a yearly custom in which her death was mourned for four days (v. 40). What this refers to is not clear. Some commentators have hypothesized that it preserves a vestige of some ancient Israelite agricultural myth, acknowledging the dying and rising of a god or goddess, but the lack of any reference to such a festival in biblical literature seriously challenges this interpretation. We do not have enough information to enable us to understand the significance of this commemoration.

Additional Notes §19

11:34 / **Who should come out to meet him but his daughter:** Here again is a wordplay, this time foreshadowing what was sure to happen. The Hb. word for "his house" is *beto* and "his daughter" is *bitto.* This story significantly parallels Abraham's offering of Isaac as it has been interpreted in Jewish tradition and in classical literature (see Brown, *No Longer Be Silent*, pp. 93–139, for details).

11:35 / You have made me miserable and wretched: A wordplay upon *kr'* ("to sink to one's knees under a blow") and *'kr* ("bane") intensifies the force of Jephthah's declaration and by a similar root (v. 33) further connects the events with his subduing *(kn')* the Ammonites. Also there is a wordplay with the root *sub* ("return") in vv. 31 and 34.

§20 Jephthah: Civil War in Israel and His Death (Judg. 12:1–7)

This final episode in the Jephthah cycle depicts the most serious breakdown in communal relations to this point in the book. While there have been signs of friction brewing (5:15b–17, 23; 8:1–3; 11:1–3), here the breakdown reaches crisis proportions and ultimately eventuates in full-blown civil war. The Ephraimites, the largest and leading tribe, complain that Jephthah had not included them in the battle against Ammon. But Jephthah has little patience left to stroke inflated Ephraimite egos and does nothing to diplomatically resolve the crisis. There is a great difference of style between him and Gideon, who in a similar crisis was able to negotiate a peaceful settlement by skillful diplomacy. The fact that Jephthah does not attempt to solve the crisis diplomatically, given his past performance, and the fact that the Ephraimites are so eager to resort to armed conflict because of injured egos, exposes a community steadily slipping into chaos.

12:1–3 / The men of Ephraim called out their forces. No sound was made, no voice was raised in objection to the sacrifice of Jephthah's daughter. Even she succumbed to her fate in silence. This new episode begins with the word we expected to find earlier: called (Hb. shouted). The sound came from far away, across the Jordan River, in the territory of Ephraim. But it did not censure Jephthah for his unspeakable deed. It was much more narcissistic; it "called out" troops to war—to war against their own fellow Israelites, for having slighted them at the time of the previous battle. Although this crisis was somewhat analogous to the one Gideon faced with the same tribe (8:1–3), a major difference is that here the Ephraimites confronted with more than words; they had weapons of war ready to be deployed against their "brothers." The author does not need to tell us explicitly that things had deteriorated significantly; beginning the new episode with this word and juxtaposing the two episodes is enough to clue us in that the moral climate was grave indeed.

It is not clear how long after the battle with the Ammonites the Ephraimites mustered for battle. The text implies that they waited two months (11:37, 39), as does Jephthah: **Why have you come up today?** (12:3, Hb. emphatic). If this were true, it further reveals the level of breakdown of *shalom,* because the Ephraimites could only have been seeking a pretext for war.

Jephthah as much as accused them of this in his reply (vv. 2–3), which highlighted the lack of communal solidarity that has grown ever more acute as the book of Judges progresses. Even his reference to the Lord underscored this flaw in the national character and should have called the Ephraimites back to their ancient covenant commitments to the Lord and to their fellow Israelites. But then as now it was difficult to think about covenant commitments when self-interest was at stake.

12:4–6 / The Ephraimites' contemptuous insults finally drove Jephthah to war. Even the content of the insult, with its "us versus them" dynamic, underscores intercommunal conflict: "From Ephraim you Gileadites are renegades, from Ephraim and Manasseh" (v. 4). The following events are full of irony. This is the third time in the book of Judges that the waters of the Jordan River have played an important role. The first was at the time of Ehud, who delivered Israel from the Moabites and, along with Ephraimites (3:27), captured the fords of the Jordan so that no one was able to cross (3:28); the wording in that account and here in Judges 12 is strikingly similar. The second incident occurred at the time of Gideon, who commanded the Ephraimites to take the waters of the Jordan, which they did (7:24). In both cases the Ephraimites were the victors. But here it is another story. Here they were the vanquished (12:5).

Finally, the litmus test to identify the Ephraimites involved speaking a word (12:6), which has been a consistent theme in the Jephthah cycle. Anyone who wanted to cross the Jordan River was required to pronounce one word, *shibboleth,* that would identify him as either Gileadite or Ephraimite. The word probably was not chosen because of its meaning but because of the *sh* phoneme, which was unpronounceable to the Ephraimites. Accentuating the linguistic divisions between Israelites further points to the lack of societal cohesion.

The civil war was disastrous for Ephraim; in fact, they probably never fully recovered from its devastating effects. This would not be the last time Israelite swords would be deployed against fellow Israelites, and the later episodes will be even more devastating. The collapse is coming, now more swiftly than ever.

12:7 / The text merely notes the length of Jephthah's administration—**six years**—without reference to what has appeared in every story up to this point, except Abimelech's: the land had peace. After Gideon (8:28), the land no longer enjoyed the Lord's gift of peace, even under the leadership of those he had raised up. The time of Jephthah, the subsequent minor judges (12:8–15), and Samson (chs. 13–16) was truly a transitional time for Israel, one from which there was no turning back. They had set their course to chaos by their resolute waywardness.

Additional Notes §20

12:2 / **I and my people were engaged in a great struggle with the Ammonites:** Jephthah says he is an *'is rib,* which links him with Jerub-Baal (Gideon) and points out the contrast between this episode and that in which Gideon dealt diplomatically with the Ephraimites (Judg. 6).

12:5 / **You Gileadites are renegades from Ephraim and Manasseh:** NIV; my translation is based on the word order of the Hb. text, because it highlights the emphatic elements. Technically, however, it does not come from the MT but from a reconstructed Hebrew *Vorlage* behind the LXX; the Hb. is unintelligible. The Ephraimites accused the Gileadites of being "renegades from Ephraim." As the events unfolded, it was the Ephraimites who became the renegades (12:5); for the same Hb. word *(pelite)* stands behind what is translated both as "renegades" and "survivors."

§21 Other Minor Judges (Judg. 12:8–15)

Following Jephthah's story is a second series of minor judges, this time three. Their stories are placed here intentionally to communicate something the author wants to underscore. While they admittedly do not make the best stories for preaching texts, nevertheless these too are inspired Scriptures that are profitable for our instruction (2 Tim. 3:16). Each one's story stereotypically follows the established pattern for minor judges with little variation, mostly those that describe the judge's economic status.

12:8–10 / The first judge is **Ibzan of Bethlehem.** Lest we think that he was a forerunner of King David, we must realize that this Bethlehem was most likely located in the territory of Zebulun, though Ibzan was probably an Asherite. As in the case of the other minor judges (with the exception of Shamgar), the author focuses on his administrative role rather than charismatic savior role. We do not even know if he and the others were endowed with the Holy Spirit as were the major judges.

Ibzan's virility as father of **thirty sons and thirty daughters** (v. 9) contrasts starkly with Jephthah, which, in a society that viewed children as a covenant blessing from the Lord, powerfully affirmed God's continued blessing upon Israel despite its continued waywardness. Additionally, that he was able to arrange marriages for his thirty daughters indicated that he was a man of means. All implied that he lived during a time of relative peace and prosperity in order to be able to engage in normal social functions such as these, which underscores the Lord's continued gracious provision for Israel.

The reference to Ibzan's giving his sons and daughters **in marriage to those outside his clan** is puzzling, for the author's audience would not have viewed this positively. Yet there is no censure.

12:11–12 / **Elon, the Zebulunite led Israel for ten years.** We are given virtually no details about his life or administration, only his pedigree and the fact that **he died and was buried in Aijalon in the land of Zebulun.** His clan is mentioned in Genesis 46:14 and Numbers 26:26.

12:13–15 / **Abdon** was the fourth and last of the minor judges. He was an Ephraimite, **from Pirathon,** later cited as the hometown of one of David's "mighty men," Benaiah (2 Sam. 23:30; 1 Chron. 11:31; 27:34). He **had forty sons and thirty grandsons, who rode on seventy donkeys.** This would probably not be the main characteristic we would point out in introducing a judge, but in that culture it communicated that Abdon was blessed by the Lord and had a wide area of influence and jurisdiction. The reference to the sons and grandsons, who, it is implied, represented their father and grandfather in administering numerous towns, possibly hints at the coming dynastic monarchy, beginning with David.

Perhaps the most important message from these stories is not found in each one individually but rather in the three as a whole. These three brief vignettes, probably added to round out the number of judges to twelve, canonically serve a larger purpose—demonstrating that the life of faith, or "unfaith," does not always move exactly in a straight line from point *a* to point *b*. Israel was on a collision course toward chaos, but there were some turns in the road. Despite the fact that the Lord was angry with Israel, he did not withdraw his blessing from them all at once. He continued to hold out his arms inviting them to return to him and to his way of life in the fullest sense of the word.

Samson is admittedly the most problematic of all Israel's judges. Any honest interpreter would have to acknowledge that he or she would rather skip over some parts of his story; evidence that most do ignore it is the fact that few sermons are preached on every verse in Judges 13–16. Small wonder. Samson does not conform to our idea of how a biblical hero should act. This arrogant, duplicitous, womanizing trickster is hardly an exemplary model of biblical morality. Moreover, his story itself, on the whole, does not follow the familiar pattern we have come to expect in the book of Judges. Samson was born under supernatural circumstances, his advent heralded by the angel of the Lord. He was a miraculous though unsolicited gift to Israel, who handed him over to the enemy to save their own necks. He died while singlehandedly fighting that enemy. He neither led an army nor definitively conquered the enemy so as to inaugurate an era of peace for Israel. Yet the author of Judges has chosen to incorporate the cycle of Samson stories into his chronicle of premonarchic Israel's history—with good reason, as we will see.

13:1 / The Samson cycle begins like the episodes of other major judges, with the notice that **the Israelites** sinned, and thus **the LORD** punished them through **the Philistines for forty years.** The period of Israelite enslavement is striking—twice the longest so far in the book (cf. 4:3)—indicating that the situation was gravely deteriorating, and ever more quickly. Elements present in the Samson cycle foreshadow later developments in Judges 17–21, so the cycle serves as a transitional link between the two major divisions of the book.

13:2–5 / After these standard elements, the story takes an unexpected turn. Rather than hearing about how God raised up Judge X, we are instead led to the Danite town of Zorah, where we are introduced to an Israelite man, Manoah, and immediately informed about a personal crisis: He **had a wife who was sterile and**

remained childless. It may appear strange that at such a time of national crisis, the author should take off on a caveat about one family's problem. But it is not strange in Hebrew narrative; merely juxtaposing the personal problem with the statement of the national problem would communicate that the two elements were closely connected, the solution to one entailing the solution to the other.

By this point, those familiar with biblical literature know that the author has set the scene for a story about the miraculous birth of a son who will play an important role in Israel's history. The elements are so stereotypic as to constitute a type scene (cf. Gen. 15:2–3; 16:1ff.; 17:15–16; 25:21; 30:1–2; 22–24; 1 Sam. 1:1ff.). It signals a new thing God is doing for Israel, and we anticipate the birth of the boy and the subsequent deliverance of Israel. Hence the first words of verse 3 are not surprising, and at the same time they are: **The angel of the LORD appeared to** the woman. We have been cued to expect some miraculous event, but we would not have expected the angel to appear to the woman! She has not been properly introduced; we do not even know her name. Yet, the angel of the Lord appeared to the woman. This surprising development speaks volumes about God's valuation of men and women as equals and at the same time is a harbinger of future surprising developments in the story.

The angel's message is also expected—at least in part. He solemnly announced to the woman what she already knew: **You are sterile and childless.** Good that he did not stop there! The next word is the wonderful little word, "but," that introduces statements which affirm in all kinds of ways that "It ain't over till it's over": **But you are going to conceive and have a son.** It is impossible to overstate the impact of these words in a culture in which a woman's value was measured by her ability to bear children, especially male children (cf. Gen. 30:1; 1 Sam. 1:1–11).

The angel then provided a list of instructions about the woman's prenatal care. She was not to **drink . . . wine or other fermented drink** (beer) and not to **eat anything unclean,** the reason being that she **will conceive and give birth to a son** (v. 5). The repetition serves to emphasize the point and also has another purpose. The Hebrew word for "conceive" *(harah)* closely resembles the word for **razor** *(mora),* the important element in the clause announcing the son's Nazirite status (v. 5b); hence, the reference unmistakably links Samson's miraculous birth with his being set apart to God from birth. Once he violates his Nazirite vow, he forfeits his purpose for living. The angel closed his message by announcing the purpose for the boy's birth, that he would begin to deliver **Israel from the . . . Philistines.** The word "begin" points to a momentous development; for the first time Israel's deliverer will not deliver them completely.

13:6–8 / **The woman went to her husband and told him** everything, except for two points. She omitted reference to the razor, but the detail was understood if he was to be a Nazirite from birth. She also eliminated the reference to his beginning to deliver Israel. Finally, she added one element, stating that he would **be a Nazirite . . . until the day of his death.** The mention of death in the midst of rejoicing over birth ironically foreshadows Samson's destiny. Manoah responded with a prayer, an indication of his faith and piety. He prayed that **the man of God** would return **to teach** them **how to bring up the boy . . . to be born,** linking by wordplay the subject of teaching *(horah,* cf. *torah)* with conceive *(harah)* and razor *(morah).*

13:9–14 / In response to Manoah's prayer, **the angel of God came again to the woman,** which is especially striking, because he came in response to Manoah's prayer. In contrast to many other biblical stories, here the woman is portrayed as taking the lead, as she is later (v. 23). While this is understandable, since she is so intimately involved with the process, the text goes beyond what is demanded by the story line.

When all three—man/angel, wife, husband—finally met, Manoah immediately began to fire questions at the man, all of which were reasonable in light of the highly unusual circumstances of the boy's birth. In response to a query about the boy's lifestyle, the angel repeated the essential details of the Nazirite regimen. This is the third time we have heard the same information, which emphasizes the disparity between what the Lord planned for Samson and what he turned out to be.

13:15–23 / Manoah responded as would any good Middle Easterner; he invited the man to be their guest for a meal. The angel refused the meal but suggested that it be offered up as a burnt offering to the Lord. By this he hinted that he and the Lord were one and the same, but Manoah did not get the hint, as the narrative intrusion (v. 16b) informs us. Instead he asked the man/angel his name, to which he responded, **Why do you ask my name? It is beyond understanding** (v. 18). Manoah **sacrificed** the offering, and **the angel of the LORD ascended in the flame.** At this, husband and wife fell **with their faces to the ground** (v. 20), an appropriate response to the wholly otherness of the Lord.

13:24–25 / The angel's promise was fulfilled. A son was born, whom the mother **named . . . Samson.** His growth to maturity is expressed in terms that elsewhere in Scripture refer to a significant figure's impending rise to prominence (cf. 1 Sam. 2:26; Luke 1:80; 2:52). The chapter closes with the first hints of Samson's readiness to begin his work: **the Spirit . . . began to stir him** (v. 25).

Here is a good point to introduce discussion of a theme that runs throughout Samson's story and appears repeatedly in Judges 14–16. This theme plays upon the Hebrew root *r'h,* which in different forms can mean, among others, to see, to appear, to show, or appearance. The root first occurs in verse 3, and others are found in verses 10, 19, 20, 21, 22, and 23. The same theme finds expression in the related word "eye(s)." While it occurs only once in Judges 12 (v. 1), it will become increasingly important in the chapters that follow, especially as it interacts with forms of the root *r'h.*

Additional Notes §22

13:3 / **The angel of the LORD appeared to her:** The NIV reads "to her," but the Hb. specifies "the woman," which is more emphatic. We should read it as if it were punctuated "the *woman*"(?!).

13:5 / **The boy is to be a Nazirite, set apart to God from birth:** According to Num. 6:3–21, a Nazirite was someone who had made a special vow to the Lord, dedicating himself or herself to a higher degree of ritual holiness for a limited period of time. Nowhere does it indicate that a person could be a lifetime Nazirite or that the mother would be required to follow the guidelines while carrying the child. Samson was a unique figure in the OT. Samuel was dedicated to the Lord from his birth, and he was a Nazirite, but nowhere does it state that he was a Nazirite from birth. In the NT, John the Baptist appears to have been a Nazirite from birth. The text states that he was filled with the Holy Spirit from his mother's womb and that he should abstain from wine and fermented drink (beer) (Luke 1:14–15).

13:15 / **We would like you to stay until we prepare a young goat for you:** The allusion to Abraham was surely intentional (Gen. 18:1–10) and underscored the contrast between Abraham's son, Isaac, and their son, Samson. Although the parents were pious like Abraham and Sarah, the son was no Isaac!

13:18 / **Why do you ask my name? It is beyond understanding:** The Hb. word for "beyond understanding" is *peli'*, also frequently rendered "wonderful," in the sense of "wonder-full." A form of the word appears in Gen. 18:14, the story of the angel's annunciation to Abraham and Sarah: "Is anything too wonderful (NIV: hard) for the LORD?" (see also Isa. 9:6; Jer. 32:17, 27). Truly the Lord's name (i.e., the Lord's essence) is beyond human understanding. We must constantly be reminded that we mortals are not God but are mere creatures, although created in the image of God. But God is and will always be for us creatures wholly other, beyond human capacity to understand and human ability to control.

§23 Samson's First Encounter with a "Foreign Woman" (Judg. 14:1–20)

After the dazzling introduction of this wonder-man in Judges 13, we anticipate seeing him in action. He was grown, the Spirit was stirring him, the Israelites had been in bondage to the Philistines for forty years. Surely it was time for some action. We want to see what he can do, and we know that the stage is set for the performance. That is why Samson's first moves are so surprising, and frankly, disappointing. We expected a little more than a spoiled brat who orders his parents around and has no regard for family values. With Samson, the quality of Israel's leaders reaches an all-time low. But God—once again, strange and improper as it may seem to us—will use even a Samson to accomplish his purposes.

Even the structure of this chapter reveals the moral and spiritual deficiency of our hero. It divides into five sections, each introduced by the verb "went down" (Hb. *yrd*): verses 1–4, 5–6, 7–9, 10–18, and 19–20 (Davis, *Such a Great Salvation*, p. 170). The verb frequently appears in negative contexts, under the influence of its prototype, the Israelites' going down into Egypt (Genesis 42–46), leaving the land of God's covenant promise and hence abandoning the covenant it represented. So Samson's "going down" communicates subtly yet clearly that his actions were less than exemplary.

14:1–4 / In biblical literature, a figure's first words and first actions are always significant, for they reveal one's character. The is true of Samson, whose first actions were revealing: he **went down to Timnah and saw there a young Philistine woman.** His first words, spoken to his parents, were equally revealing: **I have seen a Philistine woman in Timnah; now get her for me as my wife.** Both times the Hebrew text has the sequence: a woman, in Timnah, Philistine. This word order accentuates the word "woman" (which will be Samson's Achilles' heel) and the fact that she was a Philistine. Samson waited until the end to divulge her ethnic identity, because it was unacceptable to marry outside of the circle of Israelites, especially to marry someone from the occupying power.

Three of the first five words in the Hebrew text introduce or develop important themes in the Samson cycle: went down, saw, woman. Samson's eye problem plays a key role in the saga, particularly in combination with the other theme word "woman." The two proved to be a deadly combination for Samson.

The theme of seeing is even more prominent than it appears on the surface. Commentators have noted that the dual themes of knowing and ignorance also play important roles in the Samson cycle. So much of the episodes involve interaction between clued-in-one(s) and those who haven't a clue, those who think they know and don't, those who don't know and want so desperately to know that they will do whatever it takes. The word "see" has both a physical and a perceptual connotation; to see is to know, to not see is to be ignorant. Therefore, we could say that the theme of seeing overlaps with knowing and ignorance and thus extends its influence to a major part of the episodes.

Samson's request was a demand, revealing his lack of respect for his parents and for family traditions, based upon God's word. When they expressed concern that the woman was a Philistine, he rudely and crudely ordered: "Her get for me, because she is right in my eyes" (v. 3)! I have rendered the Hebrew literally in order to indicate emphasis on "her" and the attitude he displays throughout. Samson wanted what he wanted when he wanted it. Samson's stated reason for wanting the woman is revealing and at the same time ironic: "she is right in my eyes" (my translation). It points not only to the theme of seeing/eyes in the Samson cycle but also ahead to the refrain of the epilogue (Judg. 17–21): "Every person did what was right in his/her own eyes" (my translation).

The section closes with a narrative intrusion, letting us in on what no one in the story knows, not even Samson: **The LORD** was using this situation to work out his own purposes for Israel, to deliver them from **the Philistines**, who were ruling over them. Who would not be amazed at such a declaration? The Lord ultimately works good out of sinful human actions (Gen. 50:20; Rom. 8:28). Such a reality does not fit into a neat theological box, but God is not known for dancing to our tunes. We may not be comfortable with it; we may not be able to understand it or be able to explain it, but nevertheless it is God. The text does not say that God approved Samson's activities, only that he used them to fulfill his will. While on one hand it is disturbing, on the other hand it should be comforting to know that God can bring ultimate good out of anything, usually in spite of human weakness.

14:5–6 / Samson's parents apparently gave in to his demands, because this scene features the three of them going down **to Timnah,** presumably to arrange the marriage. On this journey Samson's strength was first revealed, but only to himself and to us, for the incident appears to have occurred without his parents' knowledge. On the way, **suddenly a young lion came roaring toward him.** Simultaneous with the lion's rushing to Samson **the Spirit of the LORD** rushed **upon him . . . so that he tore the lion apart . . . as he might have . . . a young goat.** Samson returned to his parents but did not tell them what had happened—why, we are not told. Perhaps it is because as a Nazirite, he should not have been in a vineyard (13:14; cf. Num. 6:3–4), as it would have violated his Nazirite vow. We can say that his parents' ignorance is crucial for the setting up of the next events (14:8–9).

14:7–9 / Samson continued on his journey; he **went down and talked with the woman, and** she was right in his eyes. The important phrase is repeated (see v. 3), and along with it, the important theme of seeing. When **he went back** with his parents to Timnah **to marry** the woman (v. 8), something happened that would prove to be the beginning of the fulfillment of the narrator's words (v. 4). He **turned aside to look at** [Hb. to see] **the lion's carcass.** In the carcass was a swarm of bees and honey. Samson scraped the honey out with his hand, ate some along the way, and then **gave** some to his parents, who also ate it (cf. Gen 3:6). Samson **did not tell** his parents about the source of the treat. They remained ignorant of his violation, by contact with a carcass, of his Nazirite status.

14:10–18 / The incident with the honey set the stage for the next events, the transition to which is again signaled by the verb "to go down." The text unmistakably implies that in yet another way Samson violated his Nazirite vow. The word for feast is *misteh,* from the root word "to drink." Wine and beer were standard fare at wedding feasts, and it is impossible to imagine that Samson did not join in the drinking. As the feast was at the bride's home, he probably also would have eaten unclean food. Little by little, Samson did everything to annul his Nazirite status. The only element left is the cutting of his hair.

When Samson **appeared, he was given thirty companions,** also Philistines. Our hero was well on his way to assimilation—important to note now, but discussed later. To spice up the festivities, Samson proposed a wager between himself and the thirty young men. He would tell a riddle, and if they could solve it within seven days (the length of the wedding festivities), he would give them each a new outfit. But if they could not, they would each give him an outfit; obviously Samson's new wardrobe would have thirty outfits to their one—not a bad deal. The thirty young men were game to try it.

So Samson told them the riddle (v. 14). The theme of knowing/ignorance comes into play here. Samson knew the answer and we know; the focus was on their not knowing and desire to know. They tried to find out for seven days. Finally, in their desperation, they turned to the woman and laid it all upon her. The joke was no longer funny; it was time to get serious. The intensity of the dialogue builds toward the crisis point and centers upon forms of the Hebrew root "to tell" *(ngd)*, which appears eight times in verses 11–17 (also two times in vv. 6 and 9). The Philistines demanded that she **coax** her **husband** to tell her the answer. The Hebrew root behind the word "coax" *(pth)* can also mean to entice or deceive in Deuteronomic literature (see, e.g., Deut. 11:16: "Be careful, or you will be enticed to turn away and worship other gods"). They backed up their demand with threats to **burn** her and her **father's household to death** (v. 15).

With that kind of incentive, the woman pulled out all the stops to get Samson to reveal the answer. She pressed him relentlessly, throwing **herself on him** and wailing day and night (cf. Num. 11:13). Finally, under this intense, incessant pressure, he broke down and told her (v. 17), whereupon predictably she immediately went and **explained the riddle to her people.** The repeated reference to "her people" emphasizes again the otherness of the Philistines and calls into question whose side Samson was on.

At zero hour, the Philistine men told Samson the riddle, and Samson realized that his wife had let out the secret. The theme of knowing/ignorance creates irony: Samson knew, and they did not; but he did not know that his wife would let them know what she knew. His name may have meant "sun," but he was not very bright. But he did have a smart comeback, the force of which is difficult to render in English (v. 18).

14:19–20 / Now the narrator's words (v. 4) will be fulfilled, for when Samson saw that he had been duped, he became so angry that **he went down to Ashkelon** and **struck down thirty ... men,** and took their clothing to the men in Timnah. He did this because **the Spirit of the LORD came upon him in power** in the same way the Spirit had done right before he tore apart the young lion (v. 6). The text states three times that the Holy Spirit empowered Samson (14:6, 19; 15:14), in contrast to only once in the case of the other judges.

Samson's abrupt departure from the wedding feast would have disgraced the woman and her family; in order to save face, her father quickly gave her to Samson's **friend who had attended him.** But Samson did not know what her father had done (15:1–2).

Additional Notes §23

14:2 / **He said to his father and mother ... "Now get her for me as my wife":** Samson's mother is specifically included in all the conversations, pointing to her value and perhaps subtly censuring Samson, for we cannot help but think of her role in Judg. 13 and what we expected of her son.

14:3 / **Must you go to the uncircumcised Philistines to get a wife?** The phrase "uncircumcised Philistines" is highly pejorative (cf. Judg. 15:18; 1 Sam. 14:6; 17:26, 36; 31:4; 1 Chron. 10:4).

14:4 / **Get her for me. She's the right one for me:** The woman is a person, hence, a "who" and not a "what," a "her" and not an "it"; but in Samson's case my carefully chosen words are, unfortunately, appropriate. Note also that the author reminds us that the Philistines were more than just next-door neighbors; they were ruling over Israel; therefore, Samson's eye for Philistine women was all the more scandalous.

14:5 / **Suddenly a young lion came roaring toward him:** Samson appears to have been alone at this point, though a textual variant says "when they came"; the text does not tell us how, if he was traveling with his parents, he could have gotten the honey without their knowledge, but it is not impossible that he did.

14:6 / **The Spirit of the LORD came upon him in power:** While the NIV does not use the term "rushed upon" here, the same verb is similarly translated in other accounts of the Spirit's empowering presence, especially in Deuteronomic literature (1 Sam. 10:6, 10; 11:6; 16:13; 18:10).

14:8–9 / **In it was a swarm of bees and some honey, which he scooped out with his hands:** There is a wordplay between the forms of the Hb. root "went down" *(yrd)* and "scraped" *(rdh);* that the author used this unusual root *(rdh)* demonstrates that the wordplay was intentional. Samson's touching a carcass to scrape the honey represented his "going down," spiritually speaking.

14:10 / **Now his father went down to see the woman:** The NIV (following the Hb. text) states that "his father went down to see the woman," followed by the notice that "Samson made a feast there." The reference to the father is anomalous. But the Gk. text reads, "Samson went down to see the woman," which surely is the better reading and would again point to the theme of Samson's going down and seeing, linking it with "woman."

14:11 / **When he appeared:** A textual variant accounts for different translations. One says "When he appeared" and the other "Because they feared him," the variants understandable in light of the similarity between the Hb. words behind "appeared" and "feared." The word "appeared" is the harder reading in this context and thus is to be preferred. The number "thirty" appears frequently in Judg. (10:4; 12:9, 14; also in 2 Sam. 23:13; 1 Chron. 11:15).

14:15 / **On the fourth day:** There are two variant readings, one "fourth day" (so NIV) and one "seventh." The seventh day is the harder reading, as well as more dramatic (at zero hour), and is thus likely the correct reading.

14:18 / **If you had not plowed with my heifer, you would not have solved my riddle:** Samson's comeback plays upon the Hb. words *hrs* and *hrs.* Some commentators have suggested emending the text here, but the emendation would destroy the wordplay and render the specific wording of Samson's comeback unexplainable.

§24 Samson's Vengeance on the Philistines (Judg. 15:1–20)

The saga continues with the conflict between Samson and the Philistines heating up and expanding to affect a larger number of people. Samson's burning anger led him to some unusual and radical actions, which he justified as doing unto them what they had done to him (v. 11). There are also some surprising developments within the Israelite camp. Admittedly shocking is the role of the Judahites. Whereas Judges 1 presents them as zealots who alone of all the Israelites obediently drove out the Canaanites, by this point they had succumbed to their enslavement and sought to avoid any move that would upset the status quo, even if that entailed handing over to the enemy one of their own. The theme of intercommunal conflict stands out in this episode, as Israelite betrays Israelite in the interest of self-preservation. Also, on a more positive note, we are introduced to a different side of Samson as he finally relates to the Lord in a personal way.

15:1–2 / After a while, during the **wheat harvest**, Samson decided **to visit** the woman he thought was his wife. He showed up at the door of her father's house with a goat and announced, **I'm going to my wife's room.** But her father refused him entry and informed him that, because he had understood that Samson had divorced her, the woman had been given to his best man. He offered instead her younger sister as a consolation prize.

15:3–8 / Samson was not interested in substitutes. He vowed revenge and declared that it was righteous revenge, as people are prone to do. In announcing what he would do, he used the phrase *'oseh ra'ah* ("do evil"), which plays upon the word *mere'* ("best man"); in other words, because his best man was given to his wife, he was justified in doing evil to the Philistines.

Samson's revenge was, to say the least, peculiar. He captured **three hundred foxes**, tied their tails together **in pairs, . . .**

fastened torches to them, **lit the torches and let** them **loose** into the Philistines' fields of ready-to-be-harvested wheat. It is easy to understand why he wanted to burn their crops at harvest time, but why by tying burning torches to foxes' tails? Besides the fact that he could thereby inflict a much greater harm, not to mention the sheer entertainment factor, the theme of fire is one that we frequently encounter in the Samson cycle. Before he was born, his parents came to realize the presence of the Lord in the fire of their sacrifice (13:20). The Philistines had threatened to burn Samson's wife and family alive if she did not persuade Samson to reveal the riddle (14:15); ironically, this is exactly what they did after Samson burned their crops (15:5). Samson's anger burned (14:9); later the ropes that bound him "became like charred flax" (15:14) and the thongs "snapped . . . as easily as a piece of string snaps when it comes close to a flame" (16:9). Thus the theme of fire runs throughout the Samson cycle. The references to torches *(lappidim)* in the foxes' story (15:4–5) also pick up on this theme. Moreover, Samson's name meant "sun," which likewise evokes images related to the theme of burning.

Samson again vowed revenge on the Philistines. But he did not think of it in terms of a communal issue, as did the other judges; rather, the pronouns are singular (v. 7). This aspect of personal vendetta rather than communal vindication is consonant with Samson's self-absorbed personality and will appear again at the end of the story (16:28). In verse 8, we find another example of Samson's going down, but this time to hide from the Philistines (cf. 1 Kgs. 19:3–5).

15:9–13 / In pursuit of Samson, the Philistines dragged the Judahites into the conflict. They **went up and camped in Judah, . . . near Lehi,** seeking to apprehend Samson and extradite him to their own territory. The involvement of the Judahites gave opportunity to indicate how low Israel had fallen. They did not hesitate to hand him over to the Philistines, but not before they gave him a lecture reminding him that **the Philistines** were **rulers over** them and casitgating him for upsetting the status quo (v. 11). This is not the Judah we met in Judges 1. Forty years of subjugation had taken its toll. It was much easier to go along with the circumstances and not rock the boat. Although Samson was not the paragon of virtue, he at least was willing to fight the subjugating power—God's enemy—even if the fight was mostly in his self-interest. Although we cannot condone much of Samson's attitudes, style, and methods, we can be thankful that he, if not anyone else, stood up to the power that sought to annihilate God's covenant people.

Samson's only request was that they (Hb. emphatic), his fellow Israelites, not kill him (v. 12), a statement that speaks volumes about the degree to which communal solidarity had broken down. They promised they would not; they would only **tie** him **up with two new ropes** and **hand** him over to the Philistines. This reference to tying him up with new ropes foreshadows the experience with Delilah (16:10–12) and sets us up to suppose that he will likewise extricate himself from that tight situation when it occurs.

15:14–17 / The Judahites took Samson captive and led him to the Philistines camping nearby at Lehi, which means "jawbone." As the contingent neared the Philistine camp, these rushed toward Samson, shouting a war cry, not unlike the lion (14:5). Also not unlike the lion episode, **the Spirit of the LORD came upon** Samson **in power** and **the ropes** fell off **his arms like charred flax** (v. 14). He found a **fresh jawbone of a donkey** and with it **struck down a thousand men.** Several aspects of this episode are unusual. To begin with, a donkey's jawbone is a bizarre weapon. Moreover, Samson again violated his Nazirite vow by touching a carcass to get the fresh jawbone. The fact that he singlehandedly struck down a whole military contingent with it is nothing short of miraculous. Samson's clever little ditty composed for the occasion (v. 16) recalls similar witty compositions (14:14, 18) and plays upon the Hebrew root *hmr,* which means both "donkey" and "heap."

15:18–20 / The next scene recalls Elijah's experience after his great victory over the prophets of Baal (1 Kgs. 19:3–5). After soaring up to the heights of triumph, he almost immediately fell to the depths of despair. In this experience—which reveals Samson the weak, Samson the dependant, Samson the mere mortal—we for the first time see him personally relating to the Lord. Not since Judges 13 has the name of the Lord appeared, except for references to "the Spirit of the LORD." Samson has shown no evidence of any personal faith, in contrast with his parents. But now it was time for his parents' faith to become his own. In desperation, Samson **cried out to the LORD.** Interestingly, Samson's is the only judge's story that does not contain the element of the Israelites crying out to the Lord. Instead, only

Samson cried out to the Lord. Possible implications of this are discussed below.

God's miraculous provision of water from "the rock" is pregnant with symbolism from Israel's wilderness experience (Exod. 17:6; Num. 20:11; Isa. 48:21) and likewise Elijah's (1 Kgs. 19:6, 8), parallels that would not have been lost on an ancient Hebrew audience. Significantly, an exact translation of the Hebrew phrase for the NIV statement that **his strength returned and he revived** is "his spirit returned," which also suggests numerous figurative analogies. For one, the ambiguity between Samson's spirit and the Holy Spirit is such that the author could have intended to refer to one or the other—or both. Also, the word *sab* means either "return" or "repent." Was Samson in some way returning to the Lord in calling upon him? Another intriguing possibility is suggested by the dual meanings of the Hebrew root *'yn*, "spring" or "eye." Was this wild man with an eye problem beginning to see at En Hakkore? We can see that Samson's life had some high points of spiritual insight as well as low points, the implications of which we will discuss in the next section (pp. 252–59).

The final notice in the chapter (v. 20) is strange. Unlike other judges' stories, it appears well before Samson's death and is repeated at the end of the Samson cycle. Canonically, its appearance in this context perhaps intimates that Samson should have stopped here. From this point on, it was all downhill for our hero.

Additional Notes §24

15:1 / **Her father would not let him go in:** Commentators agree that the father would have understood Samson's actions at the wedding feast as tantamount to divorcing her (cf. Deut. 24:3).

15:11 / **Don't you realize that the Philistines are rulers over us?** The state of mind in Judah recalls the stories I have heard from all over Central and Eastern Europe about life before the end of communism. People were taught to think alike and act alike; they were taught to conform and to obey. When freedom came, they had to learn a whole new way of life, mentally as well as physically. The effects of years of subjugation continue to have their hold on people in numerous ways. A Jewish proverbial statement, "It's not enough to get the Jews out of the captivity but also to get the captivity out of the Jews," applies appropriately in many contemporary situations.

15:16 / **With a donkey's jawbone I have made donkeys of them:** The NIV rendering preserves a wordplay but does not literally translate the phrase. A more exact translation is "With the jawbone of a donkey, a heap, two heaps . . ." (cf. Boling, *Judges,* p. 239; I arrived at this independently). Davis (*Such a Great Salvation,* p. 184) refers to Moffatt's ingenious rendering: "With the jawbone of an ass I have piled them in a mass!"

15:19 / **Then God opened up the hollow place in Lehi:** This verse calls to mind imagery from Deut. 32, where the rock is a symbol of the Lord (vv. 15, 18, 30–31; note especially v. 36: "The LORD will judge his people and have compassion on his servants when he sees their strength is gone."

When Samson drank, his strength returned and he revived: Repentance in Hb. thought is essentially relational; one turns around and moves toward God, instead of moving away from God. That is why the result or effect of repentance is expressed in terms of reconciliation. The most accurate dramatization of this concept in the Bible is the story of the gracious father (the prodigal son) in Luke 15:11–32.

§25 Samson's Downfall and Death
(Judg. 16:1–31)

Few stories in the Hebrew Bible have more recognition factor than the story of Samson and Delilah. It is a gripping, poignant drama brought to life by a gifted artist who has skillfully combined plot and characterization to present a classic story whose elements, if not the whole, have been told and retold in many cultures through all varieties of media, whether story, song, art, or film. But as we turn to this famous story, we must remember that it is part of a whole and thus be careful to place it in its literary context. It stands as the climactic point of both the Samson cycle and Judges 3–16, that is, the stories of all twelve judges. As we analyze the story from this perspective, we will discover that, rich as it is on its own, it becomes a gold mine of themes and images picked up from earlier pericopae and woven into the fabric of this story by a master storyteller. Many of these gold nuggets are not readily discernible in translation but are so obvious in Hebrew that no native speaker could fail to detect them. While they are interesting enough in themselves and fun to play with, more importantly, they provide important keys to meaning that the inspired author sought to communicate, truths about Israel and Israel's God.

16:1–3 / Samson must have returned home after the events of Judges 15. But the beginning of Judges 16 finds him going out again, this time **to Gaza,** which is astonishing considering that by now he was on the Philistines' most-wanted list. Even though the text does not use the verb to "go down" *(yrd),* this was a case of "going down" spiritually from where he had been after his experience at En Hakkore. Samson was his old self again, succumbing to his two points of greatest vulnerability, his eye problem and foreign women problem: **He saw a prostitute.** The next words come as no surprise: **He went in to . . . her.** Most likely, this prostitute—no Rahab (Josh. 2:1–21)—somehow notified the authorities that Samson was with her (v. 2).

Samson's indiscretion provided opportunity for another demonstration of his strength, which enabled him not just to get away but to do it in a way that made the Philistines look like bumbling idiots (v. 2). It is not clear how he managed to escape with the city gates without their detecting it! But crystal clear is the point the author sought to communicate through inserting this episode here. Samson's downfall did not occur in a linear fashion but was a slow process with ups and downs, strength and weakness, decisions to sin and demonstrations of the Spirit's power. Also, the story serves to tie the previous stories together with the following story, starring Delilah. In this way the author built suspense toward the climax of the whole Samson cycle and highlighted the incredible irony and tragedy of Samson's demise. All along we can see what Samson did not see, we know what he did not know, and watching unfold before our eyes what we know is surely coming helps us to see with new eyes what we had failed to see within ourselves.

The author ties these threads together largely by means of imagery and wordplay. We have already noted the occurrence of the verb "to see" *(r'h)* and "to tell" *(ngd)*. In addition, Samson went to Gaza *('aza)*, which shares the same Hebrew root with **strength** *('oz)*. His second escapade with a foreign woman, in Gaza, concluded with a colossal show of strength; the major focus of the episode is Samson's strength. In this regard it is especially ironic that the one who left Gaza in such a blaze of glory will go down (16:21) once more, but in disgrace and debility.

16:4 / Samson was not as smart as he was strong, or perhaps he just liked to live life on the edge. He next **fell in love with a woman in the Valley of Sorek** (v. 4). It was then that he reached a very low point in his life, highlighted by the reference to the woman's coming from the Valley (Hb. depths) of Sorek, rather than the customary city name. Sorek in Hebrew means "choice vines"; the irony is self-explanatory: she was out of bounds for a Nazirite like Samson (Num. 6:3; Judg. 13:14). But that did not deter him.

Her name was **Delilah.** There have been numerous suggestions as to the etymological derivation of the word, but most convincing are those that account for the message of the pericope. The root *dll* is found also in Judges 6:6, with the meaning to lay low or impoverish. From this root come other derivatives such as *dl:* "weak, poor, helpless," all pointing to what Delilah will soon do to Samson. Also, very intriguing is a possible other connection. A similar root is *dlh*, thrum or loom (particularly the hanging threads of a warp), and likewise *dl*, referring to hair woven in tapestry (BDB, p. 195), both possibly drawing attention to one of Samson's trick answers (16:13) to her query about the secret of his strength and also to the genuine answer, Samson's hair. Moreover, Delilah was the third of Samson's women; thus, according to Hebrew narrative convention, we expect her to be the most important.

16:5 / **The rulers of the Philistines,** presumably of the five cities (Gath, Ekron, Ashkelon, Ashdod, and Gaza), made Delilah an offer she could not refuse. They told her that if she would **lure** Samson so she could "see" (*r'h;* in this case, "know") **the secret of his great strength,** in order that they might **tie him up and subdue him,** each one would give her eleven hundred shekels of silver, an enormous amount of money. The word "lure" *(patti)* is found also in the story of the Timnite woman (14:13). The word "subdue" *('nh)* means to "humble" or "subdue," more or less synonymous with *dll*.

16:6–9 / Delilah, of course, agreed. So she asked him point blank to tell *(ngd)* her the source of his great strength, and we have a case of "second verse same as the first." It is a wonder that Samson did not see what was going on, especially when she asked him so directly to tell her how he could **be tied up and subdued** (v. 6). Samson, however, was not biting; he put on his best dramatic face and told her, **If anyone ties me with seven fresh thongs that have not been dried, I'll become as weak as any other man.** The word "seven" almost always has carries a special meaning in the OT, and it will appear again in the story (16:13). The expression "weak as any other man" is even more significant, for it is repeated each time Samson tells Delilah how to subdue him, whether he is telling the truth or lying. The expression for "to be weak" *(haliti)* comes from *hll*, which also means "to profane," hence, to "deconsecrate." The key to making Samson weak was to take away that which distinguished him from other human beings, that is, his "set apartness" unto the Lord, expressed in his uncut hair. But Delilah did not know that, so she bound him with seven fresh thongs, which he broke **as easily as a piece of string snaps when it comes close to a flame.** One for Samson, zero for Delilah.

16:10–12 / Delilah tried a second time to discover Samson's secret. And a second time he deceived her. And a second time, he easily broke free. Two for Samson, zero for Delilah.

16:13–14 / Delilah tenaciously came back a third time. Knowing that the number three often holds special significance in the OT, we expect Samson to tell the truth this time. In fact, we are really ready for it, because Delilah is also the third woman Samson was involved with and the third one to betray him. And he moved perilously closer to the truth in referring to **the seven braids of** his head. The loom would have been well secured in the ground; thus, Samson's pulling it completely out of the ground with his hair was an amazing feat of strength. Three for Samson, zero for Delilah.

16:15–17 / Determined not to lose this war of wills, Delilah made yet another bid, the fourth one. Knowing it is her fourth attempt has already prepared us for a significant turn of events. The author further prepares us by departing from the pattern established in the other three scenes, adding the comment that Delilah nagged Samson and **prodded him day after day until he was tired to death** (v. 16). This notice calls to mind a previous episode in which another foreign woman badgered Samson until he finally told her another secret—even the same verb *(hesiqa)* is used—and thus signals that a similar incident is about to occur. It is clear that in this case the impact would be much worse for Samson, because the narrator comments that "he was tired to death" (lit. his life was shortened to die). The reference to death recalls Samson's mother's prophetic words about Samson's Nazirite vow (13:7). All of these factors focus our attention on the impending twist the story will soon take. It was not long in coming, for the next verse states that Samson told Delilah everything: **I have been a Nazirite set apart to God since birth,** with "Nazirite" standing in emphatic position in the Hebrew. Moreover, Samson's reference to his "mother's womb" (NIV: birth) again recalls his mother's prophetic word about his death.

16:18–22 / Two prominent themes reappear in these verses, one that Delilah saw, and two, that Samson told *(ngd)* her all that was in his heart. She called the Philistine rulers, who **returned with the silver in their hands** (v. 18). Delilah's crass cupidity stands out above all, emphasized by its placement at the end of the sentence. She enlisted the help of one of the Philistines to cut off Samson's **seven braids of . . . hair** while he was sleeping with his head on her lap (v. 19). Even as he slept, unknowingly, he began to become as weak as any other man; **and**—notably—**his strength left him.**

The next events are predictable yet poignant. Samson awoke as usual and thought the game was still going, but he did not know that "his strength had left him." The next words, which echo the statement about his hair, are among the saddest in the whole Bible: **He did not know that the LORD had left him.** Why was the departure of Samson's hair so intricately tied up with the departure of the Lord? There was nothing magical about his hair. Its power lay in what it represented—his special relationship to the Lord, that he was not like every other man but set apart to the Lord, distinct and different. With the cutting of his hair, he lost that special distinction and relationship; he became like everyone else. Perhaps the greatest tragedy with Samson is that he disdained that special relationship. The Lord had awesome plans for his life, and for Israel through him (13:6). The Lord did not plan for Samson to be like any other man, because if he were like any other man he could not accomplish that for which he had been created. But Samson failed to appreciate or to live up to his full potential. He did not live out his imagehood; he did not bring *shalom* and *sedeqa* to his world.

The Philistines seized Samson, **gouged out his eyes, and** caused him to go down (lit.) **to Gaza.** Ironically, Samson returned to Gaza, this time in weakness rather than in strength. There is also great and tragic irony in the fact that the Philistines gouged out Samson's eyes, which had been a major source of his weakness and led to his downfall (cf. Matt. 5:28–29).

The final words (v. 22) of this episode are tantalizing. They begin again with the word **but,** this time not "but God," rather but **the hair.** Yet another classic example of "It ain't over till it's over." The Philistines thought they had subdued Samson when they clamped the bronze shackles on his hands and feet. But they failed to notice that his hair, sign of the Lord's presence and empowering, **began to grow.** This is the third time the verb "begin" is used with Samson. First, he would begin to deliver Israel. Second, he began to be weak/humbled. Third, his hair began to grow. However, this new beginning in Samson's life will be shortlived.

16:23–25a / **Now the rulers of the Philistines assembled . . . to celebrate** their victory, which was perceived as the victory of their god Dagon (cf. 1 Sam. 4–5), over the God of Israel. **When the people saw** Samson, **they praised their god.** The verb *r'h* picks up on the theme of seeing and highlights the poignancy of the scene before us: The Philistines saw the one whose eye problem was why he stood before them. There is great wordplay in the Philistines' hymn of praise. One example is found in the notice that the people praised *(wayehalelu)* their god for delivering into their hands **the one who . . . multiplied our slain** *(halalenu)*.

16:25b–30 / They called for Samson to be brought out of the prison so they could have some fun with him; he who loved playing games with the Philistines was now the object of their amusement. Samson performed before a capacity crowd that day, including all of the rulers of the Philistines (16:23). The author uses excessive detail in describing the crowd who saw (Hb. *r'h*) Samson that day in order to underscore the scope and impact of the following events. It also sets up a scene with one lone, seemingly weak figure standing before hordes of the mighty and powerful. But in reality, Samson did not stand alone—he called out (Hb. *qr'*) **to the LORD** (v. 28). This was the second time in the whole cycle that Samson prayed, and the last time. His desperation is evident, for he spoke three names of God in the one brief prayer. Samson prayed only for **revenge for** his **two eyes.** Once again, and significantly at the end of the story, is a reference to Samson's eyes, source of his weakness and ultimately responsible for his death. Samson's final plea, that he might *die* (my emphasis) **with the Philistines** (v. 30), picks up on the theme first introduced in his mother's words (13:7), repeated in 15:18 in the context of his other prayer and in 16:16, and now brought to fulfillment as the temple crashes down upon him and the crowd.

16:31 / Perhaps it is ironic that in the last scene of Samson's story, there is another "going down," forming an *inclusio* with the beginning of Samson's term of office as judge of Israel. But this time it was his **family** who **went down**—to get his body in order to give it a proper burial in the family tomb.

Now that we have scrutinized Samson's story in greater depth, some further comments are in order. A number of interpreters have pointed out that Samson is to be viewed on two levels, as the last of the twelve judges and as a mirror of Israel. He more than any other judge embodied the tragedy that was Israel at that time—born by an act of God, set apart to God from birth (Exod. 19:4–6), blessed to be a blessing; and yet continually repudiating that special relationship and calling, squandering those gifts. This special relationship with God was expressed in terms of Samson's Nazirite status, particularly represented by the relationship between his hair and his strength. There was nothing magical in his hair. Its power lay in what it represented—Samson's set-apart status. Note that each time Samson referred to how he could be subdued, he repeated the same phrase: "I will weaken and become like any other man." We watched Samson's strength fall away as his hair fell to the ground (16:19). No longer set apart, no longer different from other men, he became no more than a slave and as good as dead.

A similar idea appears more explicitly in another Deuteronomic passage we have already referred to: 1 Samuel 8. The Israelites demanded a king (vv. 5–6). Why? Because they wanted to be like other nations (vv. 5, 20). Samuel warned that they would pay a very high price to be like other nations. They would lose their freedom and become slaves again, as they had been in Egypt. But the second time would be different in one way: When they cried out in their distress, the Lord would not answer them (v. 18). This poignant statement closely resembles the Lord's response recorded in Judges 10:6–14, which stands at the center of the book of Judges. The fact that the author chose to place Samson's story— with these parallels—as the last of the judges' indicates his desire to communicate a similar message. His message was directed against an Israel who had abandoned the Lord as their king and thus had become like any other nation, weak, enslaved—and ultimately dead. We can reasonably place this in the context of Judah's last days, when the northern kingdom had fallen; and they, having already become enslaved, were about to suffer the same fate. They had still had the opportunity to repent, as Jeremiah prophesied until the end. The example of Samson was held out to them as a warning and as a call to repentance. Would they heed the call?

Additional Notes §25

16:1 / **He went in to spend the night with her:** The NIV translation implies sexual intercourse, but the Hb. text is more graphic in its simplicity. Essentially the same phrase is found in 15:1, when Samson announced he was going in to his wife. Here is admittedly a difficult text; Samson was no model of morality. Note the process of sinning this episode represents: first the seeing and then the doing. It recalls the process of the first sin in the garden of Eden, where Eve saw the fruit and then took it and ate it (Gen. 3:6).

16:3 / **He . . . carried them to the top of the hill that faces Hebron:** Some commentators, understandably, have been reluctant to accept the text as it stands, for Hebron is about forty miles from Gaza—uphill! Consequently it has been suggested that there was another Hebron (which no one has identified) in the vicinity of Gaza or that the preposition "to" ("to the top of the hill") should rather be translated "toward." Neither of these solves the problem; there appears to be an element of folklore present.

16:4 / **He fell in love with a woman in the Valley of Sorek:** The text does not specify that Delilah was a Philistine but strongly implies it.

16:13 / **Weave the seven braids of my head:** This is the first time we have heard anything about how Samson's hair, that had never been cut, was coiffured. It is difficult to imagine how he could have managed such a lot of hair. The Hb. root *sb'*, here translated "seven," also stands behind the word for "oath," hence possibly hinting at Samson's Nazirite vow or oath, although he did not swear an oath. Another wordplay that likely ties this passage together with the story of Samson's Timnite wife turns on the words *mahlpot* ("braids"), which closely resembles *halipot* ("changes of clothing"; 14:12, 13, 19). Also note that the wedding feast lasted seven days.

16:19 / **Having put him to sleep on her lap:** Delilah did not act very differently from Jael. What makes Jael a heroine and Delilah a hussy? Obviously, from Israel's perspective, Jael was on the right team. As we have seen even currently in our world, one person's terrorist is another person's freedom fighter. At the same time, it appears that Delilah acted not out of ideological convictions but from pure greed.
    And so began to subdue him: The NIV reads **and so [she] began to subdue him,** which represents the Hb. text, as well as some Gk. manuscripts. According to the LXX, however, Samson is the subject and the verb is intransitive, as I have rendered the phrase. I believe this reading is more consistent with the main point of the story, repeated again and again, that Samson became weak as any other man.

§26 Micah's Idolatry (Judg. 17:1–13)

With the completion of the Samson cycle we also have completed the second major section of the book of Judges (3:7–16:31). This central core section is framed by two others, an introduction (1:1–3:6) and an epilogue (17:1–21:25); and as the introduction divides neatly into two parts (1:1–2:6; 2:7–3:6), so does the epilogue (17:1–18:31; 19:1–21:35). The epilogue does not evidence the recurring refrain that characterized the accounts of the major judges. In fact, there is no mention of judges. Instead, the stories are clustered around a different refrain: "In those days, there was no king in Israel, what was right in each person's eyes, he/she did" (17:6; 18:1; 19:1; 21:25). I have translated very literally from the Hebrew to indicate where the emphasis lies: "no king" and "what was right in each person's eyes." Individualism reigned supreme; there was no order, no communal solidarity, no *shalom*.

In these final chapters, the disintegration of *shalom* increases exponentially, in scope and in degree. By the time we come to the end of the book, Israel has just about come to the end of its existence as God's covenant people, entangled in a morass of syncretistic worship and social chaos. Had they not taken draconian measures to deal with the national crisis described in Judges 20–21, who knows what would have been the outcome? But the fact that Israel did somehow continue, and a Samuel was born (1 Sam. 1:20), and then a David (1 Sam. 16), is again evidence of God's profoundly amazing grace.

17:1–4 / Somewhat surprisingly, this new section begins not with the refrain but with the first part of Micah's story. The author interjects the refrain as a narrative intrusion at verse 6 and then proceeds to finish the story. It appears that he wanted to *show* us how bad things had become before *telling* us. We do not have to look very far into Micah's story to see enough to get the message.

The story begins with a brief introduction and then a confession—a son stole eleven hundred shekels of silver (a very large sum) from his own mother. Perhaps because he was afraid of the curse she had pronounced upon the thief, he owned up to what he had done and returned the money to her. The linking of mother to son calls to mind the story of Samson, but Micah's mother was miles apart from Samson's mother. Her immediate response upon recovering the silver was to pronounce a blessing upon her son in the name of the Lord (v. 2) and then to announce that she would **solemnly consecrate** her **silver to the Lord**. Admirable indeed! But the sentence continued: **for my son to make a carved image and a cast idol.** How could a person dedicate silver to the Lord to make an idol? Besides violating the first and second commandments, those who made idols stood at the top of the list of those cursed, according to Deuteronomy (Deut. 27:15). The theme of blessing/cursing is ironically played out. The mother retracted her curse but gave the money for her son to make idols, which thereby brought upon him a curse.

17:5–6 / Micah also had a shrine *(bet 'elohim)*. He set it all up as a "real nice worship center," complete with appropriate articles and priest—who happened to be his son; but what did it matter if he was not a Levite? If we find ourselves wondering if all this was kosher, the author offers a clue: "In those days there was no king in Israel; every one what was right in his/her own eyes did" (Hb.). It was illegitimate worship and illegitimate leadership: it was chaos.

17:7–13 / Enter one young Levite. He was from Bethlehem, at least most recently, and was out looking for "whatever he could find" (Hb.), underscoring his confused lack of purpose and direction. This Levite somehow ended up at Micah's door, and Micah welcomed him. He offered to pay his expenses plus some pocket money, even treat him as a son, if he would be his very own priest, an offer the young Levite could not refuse (v. 12b). Micah was elated, assuming that he now had a special connection with the Lord. Now he knew God would bless him.

It is easy to look at this as just another story that happened to "them," "back then," "over there," and miss what it reveals about human nature and about God. Micah wanted to be in control; he worked hard to do everything just right, and he expected everything to go his way. In the same way, human nature seeks to control everything, including God. But there is no magic formula that will guarantee blessing; God will not be put into the flimsy, human boxes we construct. In spite of his self-satisfaction, Micah betrayed his lack of truly knowing the God of Israel by his faulty assumption that he could control him by having the right setup and personnel, by saying the right things and pushing the right buttons. The following episode reveals that Micah was thoroughly mistaken.

Additional Notes §26

17:1 / **A man named Micah:** Micah is first introduced by his full name, as *mikayehu* ("Who is like Yahweh?"), perhaps to point out the irony that someone with such a solidly Yahwistic name could have moved so far away from Yahwistic worship.

17:2 / **The LORD bless you, my son:** Possibly his mother blessed Micah in order to cancel out the curse she had pronounced upon the thief, not knowing that it was her son (Cundall, *Judges*, p. 183).

17:3 / **He returned the eleven hundred shekels of silver to his mother:** Further links between this story and Samson's are the sum of eleven hundred shekels of silver (16:5) and the role of the Danites (13:2; 18).

17:6 / **Right in his own eyes:** The similarity of the Hb. expression "right in his eyes" *(yasar be'eynayw)* here and in 14:3 is another link between this story and Samson's.

17:7 / **A young Levite from Bethlehem:** The Levite was a *ger* in that he lived *(gar)* among people who were not blood relatives. According to Judg. 18:30, this Levite was already where he should not have been. He was a Gershom (Hb. *gersom;* cf. Exod. 2:22) Levite, whose allotted cities were in the north of the country in Issachar, Asher, Naphtali, and Manasseh (Josh. 21:6).

17:13 / **Now I know that the LORD will be good to me:** I use the word "connection" very intentionally. The connection Micah thought he had was a parody of the covenant relationship he could or should have had with God.

§27 The Danites Take Their Own Inheritance (Judg. 18:1–31)

The road to chaos winds its way through Judges 18 but now widens increasingly (cf. Matt. 7:13–14) to encompasse an entire Israelite tribe. The Danites were a small tribe who were never able to secure their allotment of territory in the land of Israel. Judges 1 describes their containment by the Amorites (1:34; cf. Josh. 19:40–46) and the Joseph tribe's encroachment into their territory. The story of their migration from the area originally allotted to them to a new place of their own choosing reveals a degree of social and moral chaos that we have not met before in Judges.

18:1–2a / The story begins with the refrain that appeared in 17:6, although the second part is absent. We have seen that the phrase "there was no king in Israel" was intended as a double entendre, referring to both a human king and to the Lord (cf. Judg. 8:23). Thus the following statement becomes more meaningful—and ironic. That the **Danites** were **seeking a place of their own . . . because they had not yet come into an inheritance** is ludicrous. Why had they not come into an inheritance? Because of their sinful disobedience (Judg. 2:2–3; 20–23). Now they added to their sin by playing God and seeking a place themselves. The irony is further expressed by the story's unmistakable parallels with Israel's movement into the land under Moses and then Joshua. The scene of the Danites dispatching five men to spy out the land is a parody of the original account and would be humorous if not so sadly sick.

18:2b–6 / Zealously enthusiastic and expectant about their mission, the spies entered the promised land—of **Ephraim**! We do not know why they ended up spending the night at Micah's **house;** perhaps it was fate, because they deserved each other. The text is ambiguous about whether they met the Levite before they went to Micah's house or after they were already there. At any rate, **when they were near** the **house, they recognized the voice of the . . . Levite** and stopped by. We are not told how they recognized the voice of the Levite; possibly his accent betrayed him as not a native Ephraimite (cf. Judg. 12:5–6; Luke 22:59).

The Danites fired off three questions that underscored their surprise that the Levite was at Micah's house. Levites were supposed to serve at communal places of worship, not private residences. The Levite's answer, understandably devoid of any reference to the Lord, was that he was there because Micah paid him well. This response sets up the later development described in verses 19–20. The spies next asked him to **inquire of God** about the success of their **journey.** The Hebrew highlights the irony in verse 6: "if our way we are walking on will be successful." They were going their own way instead of God's way, and they wanted God to tell them if they would be successful? Who needed a priest to tell them the answer to that question? But this points out the depths of their apostasy, that they could do what they wanted and think that God was with them. Do we see a shorn Samson here in Micah's house?

The Levite was no better. He had already demonstrated that he had no commitment to the Lord he was supposed to serve but could and would do anything for the right price. In this case, he conveniently told the Danites what they wanted to hear: Their **journey** had **the LORD's approval.** What had become of the Lord's will expressed in Joshua 19:40–46? Would the Lord have blessed their defiant action?

18:7–10 / The spies moved on, all the way to the very far north, so far that they moved outside the boundaries of the land of Israel. But no matter, they had found the place of their dreams! At **Laish, . . . the people were living in safety, . . . their land lacked nothing, they were prosperous,** and—most importantly, they would be an easy take. Once back home, they recommended immediate action (v. 9). There is so much irony here it is difficult to know where to begin. For one, the Danites went outside the boundaries, outside the order established by the Lord, outside of *shalom* and into chaos. Moreover, the contrast between the Danites and the people of Laish, who were not Israelites, makes the Danites look even worse; the people of Laish were everything the Danites could have been had they chosen to submit to the Lord, to live out their imagehood. Verbal parallels with and echoes of the spies' mission in Numbers 13 (vv. 26–29) add to the farce. The spies' motivational speech to their fellows to not **hesitate to go there and take it over,** because **God has put** it in their **hands**—not to mention that the **people** were **unsuspecting**—all sounds wonderful, until we realize that, in spite of their claim to have divine approval, they were being motivated to disobey God. One wonders why they did not demonstrate that same level of zeal in taking what God had actually given them. Perhaps the pacifistic nature of the Laishites had something to do with it; there was nothing in the report about giants and walled cities (cf. Num. 13:28–33).

18:11–13 / The Danites were easily convinced. **Six hundred** of them put on their **battle** gear and **set out.** After camping the first night at **Kiriath Jearim** (renamed **Mahaneh Dan**), they headed for Micah's house. This time they did not stop there in order to spend the night.

18:14–21 / The reason they did stop by immediately became apparent. It was Micah's cache of idols. That the author wanted to focus attention upon these is obvious; the entire inventory—**an ephod, other household gods, a carved image and a cast idol**—is laboriously rehearsed four times in verses 14–20 (except that "the cast idol" is omitted in v. 20). The spies who had seen them on their earlier journey again gave a good report about their discoveries, and it was not difficult to convince the others that these were just what they needed for their new place. While six hundred Danites stood watch at the city gate, the five men entered the Levite's quarters at Micah's house. The text of the NIV states that they **greeted** the Levite, which is an accurate dynamic equivalent translation. But the Hebrew captures the irony: "They requested for him *shalom.*" *Shalom* carries, among others, the connotation of success or prosperity. Thus the men's greeting foreshadowed what was soon to come for the Levite, although in his case it was only in crassly material terms, not true *shalom,* which was possible only within the context of a right relationship with God. The Levite initially put up some resistance to the robbery but quickly changed sides when he was invited to go along with the idols and be the Danites' priest. When they put the offer in terms he could relate to—it would be more lucrative to **serve a** whole **tribe . . . than just one man's household**—he bit the bait. In fact, he took the idols himself.

18:22–26 / The next scene is so pathetic, it would be humorous if not so tragic. Micah and a few neighboring men gave chase to the Danites, who were such a large group, including "little children" and "livestock," that Micah's posse was easily able to catch up with the migrating mob. As they drew near, Micah and the others yelled out at the Danites, whereupon they retorted, **What's the matter with you that you called out your men to fight?** The absurdity of this question is surpassed only by its audacity. Micah pitifully complained, "The gods I made you took, and my priest, and you went away, and what do I have left, and what is this that you say to me, 'What's the matter with you?' "(v. 24, my translation).

The author ridicules idolatry so artfully that there is no need to comment directly; the scene of Micah standing before the Danite mob, whining that they had taken his gods that he had made (cf. Isa. 44:9–20) and his priest speaks for itself. The author also subtly makes the point that Micah got what he deserved, for Micah's story began with the verb "take" (*lqh*, 17:2) and ended with the statement that the Danites took (*lqh*) his god and priest (18:24, 27). Justice was served, the biggest guys won, and Micah was left to go home empty-handed.

18:27–31 / Meanwhile, the Danites moved on to Laish. Verse 26 states that they went their way, referring both to the question the Danites asked the Levite in 18:5 (NIV: our journey), and even to the Levite himself in 17:8 (NIV: on his way). How appropriate that both, who had chosen to go their own way, were now on that way together. Their own way took them to Laish, which **they attacked . . . and burned** (v. 27) and **rebuilt as Dan.** It also took them to the high place of the city, where they **set up for themselves the idols** and installed the illegitimate priesthood. Perhaps most shocking is the fact that the Levite of this story, Jonathan, son of Gershom, was a grandson of Moses. It is so shocking that those who compiled the Hebrew edition of the text inserted an "n" within the name Moses to change it to Manasseh (cf. 2 Kgs. 21).

Most interpreters point out that this story represents a scathing criticism of one of the two central shrines of the later northern kingdom. The shrine, established long before Jeroboam set up the golden calf in Dan (1 Kgs. 12:25–30), was born not out of *shalom* and *sedaqa* but out of chaos and injustice, and as such it could lead only to destruction. Hence, the notice that the illegitimate cult continued at Dan **until the time of the captivity**

of the land (v. 30). Repeatedly, the Deuteronomic History pinpoints idolatry as the reason for the destruction first of the northern kingdom (731 B.C.E.) and then of the southern kingdom (586/7 B.C.E.).

Additional Notes §27

18:1 / In those days Israel had no king: In this introduction to Judg. 18, I use the word "road" deliberately, because it describes the process in apostasy (lit. to "stand away from"). This was not a happenstance, a slipping here and there; it was willful rebellion, a road freely and deliberately chosen.

18:7 / They saw that the people were living in safety . . . unsuspecting and secure: The point is emphasized by the piling up of phrases that describe the vulnerability of Laish.

18:9–10 / Don't hesitate to go there and take it over: They even use the same verb (*lareset*, "to possess one's inheritance") and proclaim that **God has put** it **into** their **hands** (v. 10)!

§28 Atrocities in Gibeah (Judg. 19:1–30)

Judges 19–21 constitute the final episode of the story of the judges. Even though we must divide them for the sake of analysis, they are intended to be read as one unit. These chapters have not found their way into many Sunday school books or sermons or onto the "top ten Christian books" list. They are difficult to read and more difficult to interpret. They portray human nature at its worst, and even worse than worst, because the main players were God's covenant people. They did the unthinkable, and they did it to each other. This story candidly and graphically portrays what happened "when there was no king in Israel" (19:1, 12; 21:25) and "everyone did what was right in his/her eyes" (21:25). It carries us along the final turns in the downward spiral toward chaos—disorder reigns, societal breakdown is complete, and God is virtually silent.

19:1–2a / The narrator intrudes into the story to set the scene for the coming events. He reminds us that **in those days Israel had no king,** referring on one level to an earthly king (premonarchy) and on another level to the Lord, under whose sovereignty they were ultimately supposed to be. The repeated refrain links this episode with those that precede (17:6; 18:1) and follow (21:25), and serves as a framework for the narrative in Judges 19–21. In the same way, the next words **Levite who lived** (Hb. *ger*) call to mind the previous passage (17:7), as do geographical references to **the hill country of Ephraim** and **Bethlehem in Judah;** possibly this was one reason the author juxtaposed the stories.

19:2b–10 / As the central characters move onstage, we first hear about the Levite's concubine but do not see her. She is absent, having run away from her husband and gone **back to her father's house in Bethlehem.** The Levite went to retrieve her, "to speak to her heart" (NIV: **persuade her**), an intention that expressed loving commitment to the woman (cf. Hos. 2:14[16]). The word "heart" thematically appears in various idiomatic expressions throughout the story. It would seem that the husband's mission was successful, for the woman **took him into her father's house** (v. 3), an action that then set up the following scenes starring the Levite and the father. The concubine was, significantly, silent, in keeping with her role throughout the drama. She virtually disappeared for five days and then reappeared—in the same category as the servant, the donkeys, and the baggage (vv. 9–10).

The scenes at the father's house are all about hospitality. The father's generosity may appear exaggerated or overbearing to a western audience, but his actions are perfectly consistent with the experience of people from most of the two-thirds world, especially Middle Eastern countries. Hospitality was and still is a most important cultural value, and any deficiency in fulfilling one's obligations was/is looked upon as grossly shameful, even sinful. Thus what might be interpreted as the author's needlessly dragging out the story with endless repetitions and detail would have been in biblical culture a key element. The lavish hospitality of the father will contrast strikingly with the deficient, indeed twisted, hospitality of a town just a few miles to the north of Bethlehem, even as Abraham's hospitality contrasted with that of Sodom in a story that closely parallels the present one (Gen. 18–19). In the Bethlehem scene, verbs related to eating, drinking, and spending the night appear repeatedly (vv. 4, 5, 6, 7, 8, 9, 10) and will play an important role in the scenes to come as well.

19:11–15 / The next scene finds the Levite and company beginning their journey, curiously, quite late in the day. The strangeness of this action forebodes stranger things to come. It grew darker and darker as they moved away from Bethlehem, and as they arrived at Jebus, the next closest town (about six miles north), the day was nearly over. It was not yet dark; that came later: **the sun set as they neared Gibeah in Benjamin** (v. 14). The contrast between the light in Bethlehem, where the accent was upon the day, and the darkness in Gibeah is striking.

The scene at Jebus is full of irony. The Levite refused to **spend the night** there because it was **an alien city, whose people** were **not Israelites** (v. 12). He would rather **go on to Gibeah ... or Ramah** in the dark than to risk the danger of lodging among foreigners, who were other than they. The author calls attention to this response by communicating it through direct speech, with a hint that things are not always as they appear. **So they went on.**

9:16–21 / They arrived at Gibeah in Benjamin, just north of Jebus, as night was coming on. (The Hebrew text places the detail about the timing before the location, indicating that it is a significant point.) In accordance with established social custom, they went to the city square and waited to be invited home for the night. There was no question that someone would ask them; after all, these were no aliens, these were bona fide Israelites. The next phrase should be set off by itself (contra NIV), because it is very strong in Hebrew: "But no one took them into his home for the night." There no one in the city who took seriously his covenant obligations! In a story that has many obvious parallels to Genesis 19, here too we hear echoes . . . echoes of Abraham's relentlessly haggling with the angel of the Lord, trying to persuade him to not destroy the city if such and such a number of righteous men could be found living in it. The fact that the Lord did destroy Sodom demonstrates that there were not even ten righteous adult males in the city (Gen. 18:32).

That evening, **an old man** came into town, on his way home from work. He too was providentially **from the hill country of Ephraim.** The author underscores by repetition (vv. 14 and 16) that the people of Gibeah were Benjamites, that is, fellow Israelites. The old man asked a few questions that provided opportunity for the author to emphasize certain details, some of which we did not know before. The mention of Bethlehem calls to mind the lavish hospitality offered there, which contrasts with and thus underscores the inhospitality of the Gibeahites. To further highlight the contrast, the Levite also states that they had all the provisions they would need for their journey (v. 19). The father had even sent them off with what he could—food and drink—but the one thing he could not provide was safe lodging. The Levite referred to the one thing they lacked as he repeated the important phrase: **No one has taken me into his house** (v. 18).

Apparently—only apparently—there was one righteous man in town, for the old man welcomed him into his **house,** but not without the disturbing comment, **Only don't spend the night in the square.** There is real irony in the wording of his invitation. Besides the hint that it might not be safe in the square, the invitation literally states, "*Shalom* to you" (sing.). While it is understandable that the old man would make the agreement with the other male in the scene, the wording still ominously foreshadows the events that would transpire that night. As it turned out, the woman was not included in the offer of *shalom.*

19:22–24 / The donkeys were fed, the men's feet were washed, they had something to eat and drink and **they were enjoying themselves.** But from then on, the similarities to the Bethlehem episode ceased as the *shalom* abruptly disintegrated. A roar of shouting broke into the quiet conversation, and frenzied pounding on the door signaled the end of the cozy two-man (lit.) party. The men of the city demanded that **the old man . . . bring out** his male guest so they might **have sex with him.**

This barbaric breach of hospitality was immediately censured by the old man. He emphasized how unthinkable it was by addressing the men as "my brothers" (NIV: **my friends**). They were not aliens but fellow Israelites who clamored outside his door that night! Indeed there are numerous parallels between this and the story of Sodom. But in the end, the one difference that places them miles apart is that this was an Israelite town and an Israelite people. As such their action was a grave violation of the covenant that had brought them into existence and held them in existence—not to mention a sin against the Lord of the covenant. Surely this was the zenith of the Israelites "doing evil" (The NIV's "vile" is the same as "evil" in Hb.) in the eyes of the Lord, the end point of the spiral.

But was it the zenith? Was it the end point? "Think about" and "consider" (v. 30) the next events. The man, who up to this point seemed good, offered instead his own **virgin daughter and his** [the Levite's] **concubine.** We would like to think that in the heat of the moment he temporarily lost his sanity, but other biblical stories reveal a distinct prejudice against women, who were treated more as property than as human beings. The old man was no different; he invited the ravenous mob outside to **use** (Hb. rape, abuse) **them and do . . . whatever** they wished. Here the old man revealed his prejudice, which mirrored the prejudice of his culture. The wicked men of Gibeah could do what they wanted with the women, **but to this man** [Hb. emphatic] **don't do such a disgraceful thing.** It was disgraceful to the man, but not to two women. The Hebrew text of the last phrase ("whatever is good in your eyes") echoes the refrain of the epilogue: "Each man did what was right in his own eyes."

19:25–30 / One of the challenges to interpreting this story is that it is difficult to know who is bad and who is good. Those who first appear as good turn out to be bad, and those who

first appear to be bad turn out to be bad. It was all a reflection of
the confusion and chaos at that time in Israel's history.

And chaos won a major victory that night. The Levite **took**
[Hb. seized, grasped hold of] **his concubine and** threw **her outside to** the mob. The subsequent events were inevitable: **They
raped her and abused her throughout the night, and at dawn sent**
her away. The Hebrew verb is *slh* ("send away"), much stronger
than the NIV's **let her go.** The verb graphically implies that they
used her and then threw her away. The Hebrew in this part of the
story is full of assonance, especially the three words "abused"
(*wayyit'allelu*), "that night" (*hallayla*), and "rising of the dawn"
(*ba'alot*). The assonance plays upon sounds related to the word
"night." This was indeed a dark time in Israel's existence.

The Levite's conduct was hardly better than that of the men
of Gibeah. When **morning** came, he **opened the door of the house**
to continue on his way . . . and nearly stepped on his concubine,
who was lying motionless at the threshold. He responded not by
"speaking to her heart" (v. 3) but by barking a command: **Get up;
let's go.**

Then, one of the most poignant statements in all the Bible:
But there was no answer. In Hebrew, this is two words, words
similar to "there was no king" and "there was no one" (vv. 15, 18).
Lying on the threshold was graphically, tragically, the end result
of all the "there was no" in the story. Interpreters have long debated whether the woman was dead or unconscious from the
night from hell. Recognizing that Hebrew narrative often speaks
volumes by what it leaves unsaid, it is most likely that the woman
was dead. The author made his point—and more emphatically—
by silence.

The Levite was also silent. Without comment, he put her on
his donkey and set out for home. But, unlike his concubine, he
was not silent for long. Once home, he **took a knife** and seized or
grasped hold of (cf. v. 25) **his concubine** and **cut** her . . . **into twelve
parts and sent** her **into all the areas of Israel.** Here again is the
verb *slh*, now the second time the woman was sent away (cf. v. 25).
Also noteworthy is the fact that while the NIV states that the Levite
sent them (the parts), the Hebrew clearly says "her." Referring to
the pile of parts as "her" forces us to recognize that she was a
human being and that no act of violence, no matter how atrocious,
could take that away from her. The woman remained a whole
("her") even as her body was ruthlessly chopped into pieces.
The first step to social chaos is to dehumanize, and the first step to

shalom is to humanize. At the risk of taking the point too far, could we say that this little (part of a) word reveals how God saw the woman—in spite of, over and above, all of society's efforts to convince themselves that what happened did not matter because she was just property anyway.

The Greek text, which is to be preferred in this case, tells us that with the pieces the Levite sent messengers, who called Israel to a searching of soul. They asked: "Has such a thing ever happened since Israel went up from Egypt until today?" And they challenged: "Give attention (Hb. put your heart) to this! Speak!" The Levite called upon the people of Israel who still had any sense of moral integrity to do the speaking; it is no wonder that the Levite himself did not offer advice! And so the scene closes with the people of Israel gaping in shock over what had arrived in the mail, pondering how to respond to such a heinous violation of covenant commitments they had made as God's people.

Additional Notes §28

19:1 / **A Levite who lived . . . in the hill country of Ephraim:** Hebrew narrative often juxtaposes material on the basis of analogy. There is evidence that this story is from an earlier period than its position in the book would indicate. Phinehas, who was the grandson of Aaron (Num. 25:10–13), was the high priest. The author probably placed the story at the end for ideological reasons, to present a picture of Israel at its worst before moving into the story of the united monarchy in 1 Sam. It was not unusual for authors to arrange material according to an overarching purpose rather than according to strict chronology, as pointed out in the introduction.

Took a concubine: A concubine, for which we in the modern western world have no corresponding category, had a higher status than a mistress or slave but less than a wife. She did have some legal rights, and her offspring were generally considered legal heirs. In this case, the Levite does not appear to have a wife, so she could have been essentially the same as a wife. Commentators differ in their opinion about this matter. Ultimately, either view is an argument from silence and therefore unprovable. At any rate, her exact status is not important to the storyline.

19:2 / **But she was unfaithful to him:** A textual variant here has elicited much discussion, with strong arguments in favor of each. While the Hb. text states that the woman "played the harlot" (*znh*), the Gk. text indicates that she ran away because "she was angry" with her husband, for which the underlying Hb. verb is *znkh*, which differs from *znh* in only one small part of a consonant. The harder reading is "was angry" (*znkh*) and best accounts for the variants. Given Judges' portrayal of Israel as a people who continually "prostituted themselves" (*znh*, 2:17), it is easy to see how the word could have been changed to *znkh*, while at the same time it is difficult to account for a change to "was angry" in light of this *Leitmotif* in Judges. In that culture, for a woman to have taken any action independent of her husband would have been viewed as prostitution. One reason this argument is important is that interpreters have pointed to the fact that the woman "played the harlot" to justify her husband's and the Gibeahites' abuse. In keeping with the human tendency to blame the victim, they conclude that she deserved what happened to her as punishment for her sin.

19:3 / Her husband went to her to persuade her to return: The Hb. word *leb* is repeated in vv. 5, 6, 8, and 9 (Hb.) and will appear again in v. 22 (Hb.), also in a context of hospitality but with a very different outcome.

19:13 / Let's try to reach Gibeah . . . and spend the night: While the word "night" appears in the story in English translation (NIV: spend the night), it does not in Hb., which is literally "to lodge." But the meaning is the same. Note that the words in the Bethlehem scene are all about morning and day, while the references to the night begin as the scene at the father's house draws to a close (vv. 8–9).

19:15 / No one took them into his home: The expression in Hebrew is *'en* ("there was no") man, which calls to mind the refrain of the epilogue that *'en* ("there was no") king in Israel. Spiritual chaos and social chaos go together.

19:18 / I am going to the house of the LORD: The Levite's statement that he was on his way "to the house of the LORD" is strange. The LXX reads "to my house," which is the more likely reading in this case.

19:20 / You are welcome at my house: The word that stands behind "welcome" here is *shalom*. Semantically, the word *shalom* has a wide range of connotations besides peace. In addition to peace, security, health, and order, it also—very graphically in light of the present context—denotes wholeness.

19:22 / Some of the wicked men of the city surrounded the house: The syntax of the Hb. text communicates the abruptness with which the *shalom* was terminated. The NIV says some of the wicked men of the city, but the Hb. is ambiguous; it is the translator's call as to whether the author referred to all of the men or just some of them. The phrase most naturally means "the men of the city." Moreover, the appositional phrase *bene beliyya'al* (translated as "wicked men" in v. 22) parallels the phrase *bene yemini* ("men of Benjamin," v. 16), which clearly refers to all the men of the city. My translation is also supported by later developments in the story, where it is assumed that it was all the men (20:12–13).

So we can have sex with him: Some translators have been unwilling to render this phrase in all its candor, and thus we find such readings as "that we may get acquainted with him." Admittedly, the Hb. verb *(yd')* can carry that nuance, but it is clear in this context that it referred to having sexual relations with him.

19:25 / So the man took his concubine and sent her outside to them: The text is ambiguous as to whether it was the Levite or the old man who threw the woman outside; the Hb. most naturally favors the view that it was the Levite.

§29 Civil War in Israel (Judg. 20:1–48)

The book of Judges begins with war and ends with war. We would be mistaken, however, if we assume that the book's structure is cyclical, since we have apparently come full circle back to where we started. While Judges 1 and 20 do share some common features, the major difference is not to be ignored. Judges 1 portrays a holy war against foreign peoples, and Judges 20 deals with holy war against a tribe of Israelites, fellow members of the covenant community. The similarity between the two chapters, juxtaposed as they are at the beginning and ending of the book, serves to underscore the tragic irony of the entire story, that Israel never figured out who the real enemy was and thus expended a great deal of energy and many resources fighting the wrong battles. What would have been the outcome had they directed their zealous efforts against the nations they should have obliterated in the beginning, rather than against each other, so that the whole nation came frightfully close to the brink of oblivion?

Judges 20 tells the story of this shocking civil war in great detail, not once but twice, revealing how momentous the conflict was for the people of Israel. Even if we take the Hebrew term 'elep to mean a "military contingent" rather than "thousand," there were still many, too many, killed on both sides. One would have been one too many! In such a war, there are no winners, as the Israelites finally came to realize. Everyone loses when societal disintegration reaches the scope and depth that gave rise to this war; it was the inevitable endpoint of "each person doing what was right in his/her eyes," which was the ultimate "evil in the eyes of the LORD."

20:1–7 / The Israelites united in reponse to the atrocities at Gibeah. The text emphasizes their unity by piling up words and phrases related to the subject. In verse 1 alone, there are five: **all the Israelites, from Dan to Beersheba, from . . . Gilead** [Transjordan tribes], **as one man,** and **assembled in Mizpah.** Verse 2 mentions twice: **all the people** and *all* (Hb.) **the tribes of Israel**. The general scene recalls the Israelites' unity before the Lord at Mount Sinai and was thus meant to call people back to the covenant—with the Lord and each other—that brought them into existence.

The assembly took on the character of a tribunal as they invited the Levite to **tell** his **awful** story (v. 3). He willingly obliged (vv. 4–7), but his story differed in some details from the narrator's account. He maintained that the intention of **the men of Gibeah** was **to kill him,** and he conveniently forgot to mention that he gave them his **concubine,** whom they **raped.** After presenting his case, he called for a verdict from the assembly.

20:8–13a / The theme of unity continues to be highlighted in the Israelites' response: **All the people rose as one man,** pledged, not to go home until they had given the Gibeahites what they deserved **for all . . .** the **vileness done in Israel** (v. 10). **All the men of Israel got together and united as one man against the city** (v. 11). They jointly called upon the Benjamites to hand over the men of Gibeah. After the story of Samson, whom the Judahites extradited without batting an eye (15:9–13), and in the present climate in which it was every person for himself or herself, we naturally expect the Benjamites to comply with the majority decision.

20:13b–17 / But the Benjamites surprise us. They refused. Moreover, they began preparations to go to war against the rest of the Israelites. The author goes into great detail in describing the strength of the Benjamite army (vv. 14–16) and then the whole three-day civil war, thus specifying the gravity of the crisis this represented to the Israelite people. He mentions that the Benjamites had **seven hundred chosen men who were left-handed,** a description that calls to mind Ehud, the left-handed judge from Benjamin (3:15) who spectacularly delivered Israel from Moabite oppression, but the recollection is a faint, foggy memory in light of present developments. The Benjamin of Judges 20 is only a shadow of what it was at the other end of the downward spiral.

20:18–22 / The author continues to tie events together with events in the beginning of the book. This scene closely parallels 1:1, in that the Israelites were about to go to holy war and thus inquired of God for guidance about what to do. In both passages they asked, **Who of us shall go first to fight?** But the ironic twist comes at the end of the query in Judges 20. Unlike Judges 1, where the declared adversary was the Canaanites, here it is **the Benjamites.** The Israelites not only had failed to rid the promised land of Canaanites, but presently were engaged in holy war against each other.

Likewise, in both passages, the Lord responded, **Judah shall go first.** But again unlike Judges 1, Israel was badly defeated in the ensuing battle (v. 21); it is no accident that the promise of success that accompanied the naming of Judah in Judges 1 is absent here. Not only Benjamin had done what was evil, but also the Israelites as a whole had turned each one to his/her own way (Isa. 53:6). The Lord's pledge to turn his hand against Israel in battle (2:15) applied to all battles, whether against foreigner or fellow Israelites.

20:23–25 / Defeat in holy war signified sin in the soldiers (cf. Josh. 7). Therefore Israel's response to the failure was to turn to the Lord. They **wept before the LORD** and again asked for guidance. Two points stand out in the question they asked. First, they did not presumptuously assume that they were to continue the conflict; they genuinely asked for guidance. Second, they attached the descriptive phrase **our brothers** to **Benjamites.** By this little phrase, the author reminds us of the incongruence and tragedy of these events.

The LORD answered that they were to **go.** So with a word from the Lord, the Israelites went back for more on the second day. Again the results were the same—the Benjamites mercilessly mowed them down. The author departs from his usual wordiness in this chapter and quickly summarizes the day's battle, apparently more interested in focussing upon the Israelites' response to a second devastating defeat in two days.

20:26–28 / The magnitude of the crisis drove all the children of Israel (Hb.), **all the people,** to their knees. At **Bethel** they not only wept but **fasted . . . and presented burnt offerings and fellowship offerings** (renewing, affirming, celebrating covenant) **to the LORD.** The reference to "all the children of Israel" (or, Jacob) at Bethel recalls the patriarch's experience there, which gave it its name (Gen. 28:10–22), hence recalling all Israel's common origins as God's people. Next, the narrator intrudes directly into the story to give a few important details about **the ark of the covenant** and the name of the high priest, Phinehas (vv. 27–28). Focus upon the ark of the covenant is vital, in the fullest sense of the word, because the ark represented God's covenant commitments to Israel, as well as theirs to God and each other. Significant, too, is the reference to Phinehas; for he had already proven himself as "zealous for the honor of his God" in purging evil from the people of Israel (Num. 25:7–13).

God, ever gracious, responded in a new way to the Israelites' inquiry about going out again for battle: **Go, for tomorrow I will give them into your hands.**

20:29–48 / Armed with this new promise, Israel set out on the third day to battle. Because of the promise and because the number three holds special significance, we expect this battle to be decisive in favor of Israel. And Benjamin was roundly defeated, nearly to the point of annihilation. The author describes the battle with exceptional detail, not once (vv. 29–36a) but twice (vv. 36b–48).

In holy war, the object was total destruction of the enemy and all they possessed. The Hebrew word for this, *herem,* essentially means "devoted." The person or object was totally devoted to God/god so that profane (nonsacred) use was prohibited, hence destroyed. This was what the Israelites had been commanded to do to the Canaanites but did not; and this is what they intended to do to the Benjamites and nearly succeeded. Only a handful—600 out of 25,100—survived because these **fled into the desert** (v. 47). But **the men of Israel . . . put all the towns . . .** of **Benjamin . . . to the sword . . . and . . . set** them **on fire** (v. 48).

The reference to setting the towns on fire recalls two biblical passages. Israel was instructed to punish by *herem* the "wicked ones" (Hb. men of Belial; cf. Judg. 19:22) in the community (Deut. 13:13–16), to "completely burn the town and all its plunder as a whole burnt offering to the LORD your God" (v. 16). The expression "whole burnt offering" is translated from the Hebrew *kalil,* the same root word that appears in Judges 20:40: "The whole burnt offering *(kelil)* of the city was rising toward heaven" (my translation). The message communicated through this clear analogy would not have been lost on a Hebrew audience. Second, the sight of smoke rising from "all the towns" of Benjamin recalls a similar scene viewed by Abraham after the destruction of Sodom and Gomorrah (Gen. 19:28). The tragic irony of all this, that the destruction of the towns of Benjamin, a tribe of Israel, corresponded to the destruction of Sodom and Gomorrah, cannot be overstated.

Additional Notes §29

20:1 / **All the Israelites from Dan to Beersheba:** This is a phrase that came to designate all of the land of Israel. Dan was at the extreme north and Beersheba at the extreme south; implied in this was also all that lay in between the two points.

Assembled before the LORD in Mizpah: There were several Mizpahs in the OT; this is most logically the one in Benjamin (1 Sam. 7:5–13; 10:17–25; 2 Kgs. 25:22–26; Jer. 40:6–41:18).

20:5 / **The men of Gibeah came after me . . . , intending to kill me:** Are these "clarified details" or just attempts at exoneration? Some interpreters have suggested that the language is ambiguous: "they raped my concubine and she died," not specifying whether she died from Gibeahite abuse or her husband's, that is, his taking the severely wounded woman on a journey home. The most logical assumption is that she died from Gibeahite abuse.

20:29–48 / **Then Israel set an ambush around Gibeah** (v. 29): Some commentators believe the repeated version in vv. 36b–48 reflects two different sources underlying the account. But Hb. narrative convention frequently gives the same information twice, once in summary fashion and then in detail. Note the parallels with the story of Abimelech (9:32–34, 39–40).

§30 Israel Preserved Intact (Judg. 21:1–25)

Just when it looked like one crisis was averted, another came to light. It is, however, not surprising, for that is how it is when chaos prevails, when "what is right in a person's eyes, he/she does" (21:25). At the end of the book of Judges, the Israelites do not seem to be able to extricate themselves from the miry bog that they have gotten themselves into. Though they appear to call out to God for help, they still rely on their own absurd solutions that only make matters worse. We will see in this chapter that the same people who fought a holy war because some Gibeahite men kidnapped an Israelite woman and ravished her until she died, themselves murdered all of the women of Benjamin and all the married women of Jabesh Gilead, not to mention having kidnapped four hundred unmarried women from there and masterminded the kidnapping of two hundred girls from Shiloh. So who was the bad and who was the good? Again, if we find it difficult to decide, it is because they all were the bad. And the grace of the story, here and in all of the book of Judges, is that God—the supreme Judge and King (8:23; 11:27)—saved Israel from self-inflicted extinction.

21:1–4 / While dramatic tension eases at the end of Judges 20, it builds up again immediately at the beginning of Judges 21. We are first informed of an incident that took place before the war began and has now come back to haunt Israel: **The men of Israel had taken an oath.** These words are disquieting if not frightening, for they recall another oath taken before holy war, by a judge named Jephthah (11:30–31), an oath that obliged him to sacrifice his only daughter in return for victory over the enemy. This story is both like Jephthah's and not like it. Like Jephthah's vow, it was impossible to undo; but unlike Jephthah, who "did to [his daughter] as he had vowed" (11:39), the Israelites found a way around their vow. But their way around turned out to be much more destructive, in terms of scope, than Jephthah's vow.

With a little distance from the frenzied heat of battle, the Israelites began to question the wisdom of their oath not to **give** any of their daughters **in marriage to a Benjamite.** Passion had given way to compassion; they realized that if they honored their vow, Benjamin would die out with the death of the six hundred survivors. In their consternation, they cried out to the Lord (vv. 2–4). Although it is not stated explicitly, the text implies that they blamed God for what had happened; they did not ask for help but only expressed in very strong terms **(weeping bitterly)** their grief over the sure loss of **one tribe from Israel.** This was neither the first time nor the last time people would cry out to God with the question Why? In Israel's case, we know the answer that they could not seem to see. Deception and confusion go hand in hand with chaos.

21:5–9 / Significantly, God remained silent. But no matter, the Israelites came up with their own solution. They remembered a second oath—literally "the great big oath" (Hb.)—they had vowed before the war: **anyone who failed to assemble before the LORD at Mizpah should certainly be put to death.** The psychological gymnastics of this passage would be humorous if they were not so tragically universal. They weighed the vows according to first and second most important, and of course "the bigger one" was deemed more important, especially since a group had not shown up, the men of Jabesh Gilead.

Why had they not joined the other Israelites in the holy war against Benjamin? There appears to have been a special relationship between Benjamin and Jabesh Gilead that may have been based on their having a common maternal ancestor, Rachel (Gen. 30:23–24; 35:18). Their special relationship is demonstrated in stories about Saul, a Benjamite and first king of Israel (1 Sam 11:1–11; 31:11–13; 2 Sam. 2:4–7). The relationship was so strong that we might speculate that Saul's maternal ancestor may have come from Jabesh-Gilead.

21:10–14 / Satisfied with the solution, the assembly dispatches twelve thousand soldiers to carry out *herem* against Jabesh Gilead. They **kill every male and every woman who is not a virgin.** Every woman who is a virgin (four hundred women) **they take to the camp at Shiloh in Canaan.** The scene closes with representatives of the tribal **assembly** meeting with **the Benjamites** to offer them *shalom*—plus four hundred wives. The tragedy is staggering: genocide of almost an entire clan to replace wives that had just been destroyed, all that so a tribe would not be wiped out? Where is the *shalom* in this? It looks more like chaos!

21:15–17 / The solution was good, but not good enough. The Israelites were able to pick up only four hundred virgins from Jabesh Gilead (v. 14b). This time they did not cry out to the Lord, but they **grieved for Benjamin, because the LORD had made a gap in the tribes of Israel** (v. 15). They clearly attributed the situation to the Lord. So what to do, **so that a tribe of Israel will not be wiped out** (v. 17)? Verses 15 and 17 form an *inclusio* that frames the statement of the problem, which was how to provide two hundred more wives for the Benjamites. The gravity of the crisis is communicated by the fourfold repetition of the phrase (with minor variation), here and in verses 3 and 6, that a tribe in Israel would not be obliterated. In accordance with Hebrew narrative convention, the repetitions with variation each time serve to underscore the issue of Israel's continual existence as a whole *(salem)* people.

21:18–24 / The Israelites were essentially back to square one, or at least square two. They as much as declare this by restating the problem: How can Israel be preserved intact if one tribe cannot continue because of our vow not to give our daughters to Benjamites? The solution was not long in coming. They instructed the Benjamites to **hide in the vineyards** at the **annual festival of the LORD in Shiloh,** and at the right time to **rush from the vineyards** and each man grab (NIV: **seize;** cf. 19:25, 29) **a wife from the girls** who were dancing in celebration and thanksgiving to the Lord. Then they were to take them off **to the land of Benjamin** (vv. 20–21). This solution yielded them two hundred wives, just what was needed.

The assembly knew that this solution was not kosher, so they also informed the Benjamites what the assembly would say when the girls' fathers or brothers disputed their right to do this. They suggested they look the other way because the Benjamites were in dire straits; they did not get wives **for them during the war.** Moreover, they could not be accused of breaking the oath, because technically *they* (Hb. emphatic) **did not give** their **daughters to them.** The two hundred Benjamites did as they were told. They all **caught** wives . . . **and carried** them **off** . . . **and rebuilt** their **towns.** Likewise, **the Israelites . . . went**

home . . . each to his own inheritance—and everyone lived happily ever after.

21:25 / The story could have ended there. But it did not. The narrator, who has stood in the shadows during these last events, now moves into the spotlight. He has the last word. He solemnly speaks: **In those days Israel had no king; everyone did as he saw fit.**

Additional Notes §30

21:1 / **The men of Israel had taken an oath:** This was an absurd oath, as likewise was the solution they concocted. H. J. M. Nouwen (*Show Me the Way: Readings for Each Day of Lent* [New York: Crossroad, 1994], p. 74) notes that the word "absurd" is related to "the Latin word *surdus,* which means 'deaf,' " while the word "obedient" comes from the Latin word *audire,* which means "listening." He comments: "A spiritual discipline is necessary in order to move slowly from an absurd to an obedient life, from a life filled with noisy worries to a life in which there is some free inner space were we can listen to our God and follow his guidance. Jesus' life was a life of obedience. He was always listening to the Father, always attentive to his voice, always alert for his directions." This remarkably parallels the Hb. concept of Shema, "Hear, O Israel." Regarding the kidnapped women of Shiloh, P. Trible (*Texts of Terror: Literary-Feminist Readings of Biblical Narratives* [Philadelphia: Fortress, 1984], p. 83) comments, "The kidnapped women were as good as raped also." This is not to justify what the men of Gibeah did or to minimize it, but only to point out how low the downward spiral has reached by this point.

21:3 / **O LORD, the God of Israel . . . why has this happened to Israel?** This all too accurately reflects the human propensity for denial, which goes back to the garden of Eden story and causes people to blame God for everything, from natural disasters to children dying of starvation. The classic expression of blaming God for what humans in freedom have chosen is Isa. 63:17: "Why, O LORD, do you make us wander from your ways and harden our hearts so we do not revere you?"
Why should one tribe be missing from Israel today? That the preservation of all Israel was critical is indicated in the threefold reference to Israel in v. 3.

21:9 / **They discovered that no one from Jabesh Gilead had come to the . . . assembly:** This sounds remarkably similar to the reproof in the Song of Deborah, specifically directed against Reuben, Gilead (Judg. 5:17), Dan, and Asher. This was pointed out to me in a private correspondence from R. Hubbard.

21:12 / **They took them to the camp at Shiloh in Canaan:** The specification that Shiloh was in Canaan continues to interest interpreters. Boling (*Judges*, p. 292) believes that the reference to Canaan points to the fact that the story was very early, as early as, if not earlier than, the material at the beginning of the book of Judges, where references to Canaan appear more frequently. Furthermore, he suggests that "by allowing the notice about the location to stand intact, the late redactor signals the irony of the situation. Conditions in the land, after all was said and done, had not changed very much."

21:23 / **Each man caught one and carried her off to be his wife:** There is great irony here, because the Hb. expression for "to marry" is "to take a wife." In this context, it takes on new meaning; for that is exactly what the Benjamites were instructed to do.

§31 Excursus: The Story of Judges

The story of Judges leads into the story of Samuel and Saul and most importantly David; and its author thus prepares his audience for the personalities and events that follow. Places such as Dan, Shiloh, Ramah, Mizpah, Bethel, Gibeah, and Jerusalem will again serve as settings for the continuing saga of Israel. It is striking that quite a number of the key places and personalities, especially in these final chapters, relate closely to the period of Saul's leadership. Some scholars have suggested that this is precisely what was intended by the author of Judges, that he intentionally told the story of Benjamin's (more specifically, Gibeah's) atrocities in order to undercut Saul's leadership and to thus promote the ascendency of the Davidic dynasty.

Be that as it may, three theological truths are unmistakably evident in the overall presentation of this period in Israel's history. One is the terrible consequences of peoples' turning their backs on God and their covenantal commitments. The second is that in spite of human failing and willful rebellion, God is gracious. Even the fact that there was a Samuel or a Saul or a David, that God had not wiped out all the tribes of Israel by the end of the period of the judges, is a miracle that must not be overlooked or taken lightly. All of which points to a third unmistakable theological truth, that God is sovereign. In spite of Israel's repeated failure to live up to its covenant commitments, which led them down the path to chaos rather than to *shalom,* God, nevertheless and in spite of Israel, brought good out of it all. Chaos led to destruction and exile—but not death. Even out of exile, a new Israel was formed, one which had studied and learned the lessons from their history, and returned to the Lord. These then returned to the Land with a vision of a world ordered by the Lord God of Israel, when not only would the children of Abraham, Isaac, and Jacob experience *shalom* and *sedaqa,* but through their witness, the Lord's *shalom* and *sedaqa* would reach to the ends of the earth (Isa. 43:10; 45:22; 49:6). Of course, human nature being what it is, good resolve was not always realized. There continued to be ups and downs along the way. But even so, the Lord's covenant love compelled him to continue to pursue his beloved, to "speak to her heart" and to offer his *shalom* to those, both far and near (Isa. 57:19), who would receive it.

Ruth

Michael S. Moore

Introduction: Ruth

The book of Ruth is a bright light in a dark world. It is no accident that it appears where it does in Scripture. Ruth follows Judges because this story so subtly yet so clearly challenges the brooding stories that darken and defile the pages preceding. Many early students of Ruth were convinced that Judges and Ruth should be read in tandem, one book engaging the other, one book illuminating the other. Contemporary students tend to ignore this interpretive tradition, yet to read Ruth against its self-stated backdrop, "the days when the judges ruled" (1:1), is to enter into a fascinating world of subtle parallels, striking contrasts, and unexpected surprises. Positioning this story against these stories is an editorial invitation to consider how the conflicts challenging Elimelech's family covertly comment on the conflicts challenging other families at a turbulent time in Israelite history.

Canonical Context

In the Masoretic Hebrew canon (MT), Ruth appears in the third section called *Ketubim* ("Writings") and is one of the five *Megillot* ("scrolls"), the other four being Song of Songs, Ecclesiastes, Lamentations, and Esther. Doubtless the book finds a home here because of a felt need to connect Scripture more intentionally to Israel's liturgical calendar. Thus Esther is read at Purim, Song of Songs is read at Passover, Qoheleth is read at the Feast of Tabernacles, Lamentations is read at the Ninth of Ab, and Ruth is read at *Shavuoth*, the Feast of Weeks (Exod. 34:22).

The canonical tradition of placing it in *Ketubim*, however, is fluid and indeterminate. The Talmud, for example (*b. B. Bat.* 14b), preserves a different order, one more chronological, where Ruth (written by Samuel) is followed by Psalms (written by David), then Proverbs (written by Solomon). The LXX, one of several Greek translations based on a Hebrew text tradition "predating by several hundred years the complete manuscript on which our

Hebrew Bible is based,"[1] situates it after Judges, in the section of Scripture the Hebrews called Former Prophets (Zech. 1:4, *han-nebi'im hari'shonim*).[2]

Further, though there will always be those who argue for the absolute priority of MT's canonical order,[3] such discussions usually fail to reckon seriously with the research generated by the discovery and publication of all the known Dead Sea Scrolls. Based on this new textual data, it is becoming increasingly clear that MT, like LXX and perhaps Syr, grew out of a fluid canonical situation characterized by several "text types."[4] Knowing what we now know about the fluidity and flexibility of the Qumran canon in the second century B.C.E., we can now state unequivocally that

> it is . . . no longer possible to posit that Ruth was moved to the Prophets by hellenized Jews whose canon is reflected in LXX. . . . Different arrangements of the Prophets and the Writings arose among different elements of the Jewish community and existed side-by-side until the time of Jerome.[5]

Therefore, when we take all four of these factors into account—self-contextualization within the era of the judges, antiquity of LXX witness, late canonical fluidity, and Talmudic witness—at the very least we must conclude that there is no longer any convincing reason for reading Ruth solely against the backdrop provided by the *Megillot*. What this means, practically speaking, is that all the old arguments for the priority of one canonical context (MT) over another (LXX) are no longer relevant. On the contrary, LXX's canonical order is just as interesting, just as legitimate, and just as authoritative as the one in MT. Since the present commentary series is based on the NIV, which, like most English Bibles, follows LXX's canonical order, this commentary will explore Ruth's literary artistry, theological message, and pastoral impact within the context of this canonical order.

Canonical-Historical Context

Immediately prior to Ruth, the book of Judges closes on a despondent note. The last major section, Judges 17–21, is a grim collection of vignettes linked into a suspenseful, even terrifying anthology. Taken together, these stories illustrate what the narrator thinks is the major reason for Israel's political, social, and spiritual chaos: "In those days there was no king in Israel" (Judg. 17:6;

18:1; 19:1; 21:25). This sweeping observation, repeated no fewer than four times in five chapters, carefully repositions these stories under a single ideological umbrella. For this narrator, the absence of a king is not a factor; it is the factor responsible for Israel's slide into moral apathy, religious apostasy, and criminal violence.[6]

Each story explores a different element of this chaos. In Judges 17, an Ephraimite named Micah hires an unemployed Levite to establish an idiosyncratic priesthood, literally in his own backyard. Why? Because "there is no king in Israel" to stop him. In Judges 18, a gang of Danites convinces this same Levite to abandon Micah and bless their fratricidal conquests. Why? Because "there is no king in Israel" to stop them. In Judges 19, another Ephraimite hides in a stranger's house while a gang of thugs rapes and murders his concubine outside, publicly, in the streets of Gibeah. Why? Because "there is no king in Israel" to protect her. With each story the narrator patiently builds his argument. Only kings have the authority to police apostate cults. Only kings have the power to enforce the law. Only kings have the ability to punish criminal sexual behavior. Tribal authority is too weak. Israel needs a king. What can anyone say to such an obvious conclusion?

As Ruth begins, the narrator of Ruth seems to agree with the narrator of Judges. Ruth 1:1–15 seems to take up where Judges 17–21 leaves off. A famine ravages Judah. A father dies. His survivors remain childless. His firstborn son dies. His remaining son dies. His widow grieves. Within the span of five short verses a dark world comes miserably into focus looking every bit as anguished, every bit as severe, and every bit as hopeless as the world just encountered.

But looking more closely at this world, there is something different about it. Difficult to see at first, its contours become clearer and clearer as the story unfolds. In Judges 17–21, the major characters balk in the face of challenge. In Ruth, they persevere. In Judges, most of the priests, landowners, husbands, wives, and warriors simply abandon their responsibilities. In Ruth, people usually shoulder their responsibilities, however burdensome. In Judges, men treat women insensitively, shamefully, even violently. In Ruth, men treat women like partners on a common mission.

And there is no king here, either. No king appears in either text. Having been led by the narrator of Judges to believe that the one and only source of Israel's agony is kinglessness,

Ruth is a surprise. In other words, to read Ruth in its canonical-historical context is to raise an unavoidable question: If kinglessness is not the determining factor behind Israel's chaos (as the narrator of Judges would have us believe), then what else might be responsible for it?

Other Approaches

Ruth can be fruitfully explored from a variety of angles. Historical approaches ask questions about dating and authorship and ancient Near Eastern context. Historical questions often lead to theories about whether the book comes from a premonarchic period (*b. B. Bat.* 14b has Samuel as the author), a monarchic period,[7] a postmonarchic period,[8] or an extended period covering all three eras.[9]

Literary approaches remind us that we are reading a book of timeless beauty and amazing intricacy. Ruth is a work of chiastic symmetry in which the first beginning scenes of emptiness are balanced by the last concluding scenes of fullness.[10] The action in the story is driven not by traditionalist male heroes but by the assertive deeds of the two female heroines, Naomi and Ruth.[11] Ruth is indeed the quintessential example of the Hebrew short story:

> The hallmarks of Israel's artistry in short stories stand out: a terse setting of the *mise en scène*, effortless transitions between episodes that often signal what is to come, a lingering over actions in a manner both ceremonious and suspense-building, fluent dialogue, and repetitions of key terms and nuanced wordplays that link episodes.[12]

Yet to read Ruth in its canonical-historical context is to review and re-capture a message in the book that would otherwise be lost. The narratives in Judges 17–21 and Ruth 1–4, for example, both end in climactic courtroom scenes, an observation that seems obvious from a canonical-historical perspective, yet one seldom even noted by contemporary commentators. Comparing and contrasting these scenes, it would seem, would help us greatly to appreciate each narrative's distinctive theological intentions. At Mizpah, for example, Israel's leaders wrestle with the problem of what to do with the Benjamites, a tribe in trouble because of its refusal to hand over the Gibeahite murderers of the Levite's concubine (Judg. 20:1–11). This crime generates a major crisis, yet no one in Mizpah seems to know what to do about it. Israel's eventual response, its crisis management strategy, is so poorly conceived and so clumsily implemented that a civil war breaks out and Benjamin is brought to the brink of annihilation.

Not so in Ruth. In Bethlehem, another council convenes to deal with another potentially explosive situation, the problem of Elimelech's inheritance. Particularly delicate is the problem of how a Moabitess is to be incorporated into that inheritance. Yet the solution here is markedly different from the one arrived at in Mizpah. The social, legal, and political dimensions of this problem are in many ways just as flammable here as they are there, yet the solution here leads to restoration and healing, not war and devastation. Why are these two situations so structurally similar, yet possessed of such radically dissimilar outcomes?

The only way to answer such questions is to examine Ruth carefully against its canonical-historical context. True, Ruth can be profitably read as a romantic novella, as a human comedy, as a response to nativistic fear about intermarriage, as a messianic preamble, as a Yahwistic response to ancient Near Eastern fertility myths, and many other ways.[13] All these approaches have genuine merit, bear legitimate exegetical fruit, and teach us important lessons from the book of Ruth. Yet they remain inadequate, not because they are mistaken or misguided but because they cannot answer the questions just posed. In short, contemporary approaches to Ruth tend to focus solely on the book's internal structure and contents. Only rarely is sufficient attention given to the book's external context, particularly its canonical-historical context.[14]

Sociohistorical Context

One of the most pertinent contributions of a canonical-historical approach to Ruth is the insight it can bring to understanding the volatile state of Israelite society during a chaotic period in Israelite history. Scholars have thoroughly investigated this transitional period from several angles and in several interesting ways, yet the focus so far has been on macrodiachronic concerns. Older historians tend to focus on the larger historical questions, for example, on whether there are twelve actual tribes in premonarchic Israel, on whether these tribes are organized into a tribal league, and on whether Israel's sociopolitical shift from judges to kings might better be described as progressive or regressive.[15]

Today there is a great deal more emphasis on a close literary, or microsynchronic, interpretation. This interpretational shift is having an enormous impact on biblical studies generally, not just research on Ruth. Recent interest in the book's gender roles, for example, is rather unexplainable apart from some understanding of this shift. Today in many circles gender is not simply an issue, it is the issue attracting readers to the book of Ruth, and not only because the book has two female heroines. More and more scholars are arguing that the present sociopolitical climate demands that the book be more relevantly read in congruence with contemporary concerns. Older scholarship says almost nothing about gender justice in Ruth or anywhere else in Scripture. Contemporary scholarship, however, is honestly attempting—in some cases, courageously attempting—to interpret the book with a keener eye to contemporary as well as ancient cultural concerns.

Two major obstacles, however, stand in the way of progress. First, too many interpreters, regardless of their sociopolitical presuppositions, fail to employ critically defensible research methods in their study of Ruth. The result, in many cases, is shallow politicization instead of convincing interpretation. Too often the air over Ruth is breezy and speculative, whether the discussion has to do with Ruth's alleged sociopolitical beliefs or her "strategy" for deconstructing "traditional" gender roles, or even her "sexual orientation."[16]

Second, too many ignore the book's all-important canonical-historical context. Interpretations that do this—which abandon historical, literary, and canonical controls—tend to be embarrassingly narcissistic. T. Frymer-Kensky makes this point quite forcefully, reminding us that "in some areas the Bible does not offer extensive discussion of matters that people need to consider."[17] In other words, we still know very little about gender roles in the ancient Near East, especially in Syria-Palestine. For all of the speculation, from the left as well as the right, the present dearth of information about gender roles in the ancient Near Eastern texts at our disposal ought to lead us to more circumspection and less speculation, not only about gender but about the entire sociopolitical shape of the book:

> To attempt to transplant gender roles, the roles of parents and children, polygamy, monogamy, celibacy, and a host of other specific features of the Israelite family into contemporary cultures would be naïve.[18]

This having been said, however, we can and should observe how particular women function in these particular texts and try to formulate from this comparative study some specific questions about their gender roles. Here the canonical-historical approach can be of great value. Take, for example, the roles enacted by the Levite's concubine versus those enacted by the Moabite Ruth. The Levite's wife is a "concubine" (*pilegesh,* Judg. 19:1).[19] Ruth, however, is a "foreign woman" (*nokriyyah,* 2:10), a Moabite widow who eventually becomes the "wife" (*'ishah,* 4:10) of an Israelite "nobleman." What do these ancient terms mean? What social roles do they signify? One does not have to know the Hebrew language to see that these are different kinship terms. And since anthropologists are agreed that kinship terms are better studied as parts of dynamic continuums rather than in static categories, perhaps one of the least speculative things we can say is that the terms "concubine" and "foreign wife" refer to gender roles relatively close together on the Israelite social continuum, somewhere between the extreme poles of "female slave" (*shipkhah*) and "Israelite wife" (*'ishah*).

Why is it important to see this? Because, like a reverse image, the similarities on the social continuum starkly highlight the dissimilarities on the moral continuum. Each of these women lives in the same geographical area (Bethlehem), moves about within the same social circles, and enacts roles relatively close together on the Syro-Palestinian societal continuum. Yet each experiences a vastly different fate. One follows an unprepared, foolish man on an ill-conceived journey, and is raped, murdered, chopped into pieces, and sent to Israel's tribal leaders. The other follows her Hebrew mother-in-law home and finds there a compassionate nobleman who protects her, marries her, and restores through her the heritage of her Hebrew husband.

Varying presuppositions lead to varying interpretations. This commentary will not attempt to read the book solely within synchronic sociopolitical parameters, nor will it seek to ignore Ruth's powerful social message. Instead, by focusing on the book's neglected canonical-historical context, we will attempt to interpret Ruth as a "word to the real world, which God has pronounced in history, and with which he addresses us today by the intermediation of human authors."[20]

Theological Themes

Interpreted in its canonical-historical context, then, the book of Ruth appears to be a masterfully crafted response to the politics of despair in Judges. Ruth's short-story structure is the perfect vehicle for subverting this despair. No prophetic oracle, no priestly torah, no psalmic lyric can match the short story for subtlety, ambiguity, and memorability. Character by character, episode by episode, Ruth is a well-crafted, entertaining story, but in its context it is something much more. In its context, Ruth is a sharp chisel in the hands of a master sculptor, methodically chipping away at Israel's hopelessness until a marvelous theology of hope begins to emerge. The structure of this theology remains hidden and covert, never becoming as visible as, say, the theology of Isaiah or Deuteronomy or the Psalms. Yet Ruth does have a theological message, and one way to expose it is to filter its contents through the following polarized lenses: the wandering and restoration lens, the religion and ethics lens, and the chaos and kindness lens.

Wandering and Restoration

Hebrews are wanderers. In fact, the very word "Hebrew" probably means "wanderer" (from *'abar*, "to cross over, wander"). This "wandering" begins with Abraham's decision to leave Ur and climaxes in Moses' return from Egypt (Gen. 12:1–4; Num. 10:11–36:13). It continues through David's flights from Saul and climaxes again in the exiles of Assyria, Babylon, and Persia (Jer. 2:1–3; Ezek. 20:33–38). For rabbinic Jews, this theme continues into the Talmud, where the rabbis discuss, among other things, the final destinies of those who "wander" in the wilderness behind Moses (*b. Sanh.* 110b). For Christians, it transforms into something universally inclusive in the NT letter to the Wanderers/ Hebrews. All believers in the one God, as the NT writer puts it, are "strangers and exiles upon the earth" (Heb. 11:13). Israel, the one who wrestles with God (whether person or nation or faith community), is an organism forever on the move, constantly facing all sorts of spatial, temporal, ethnic, social, political, religious, theological, and spiritual boundaries. Wandering is a profoundly biblical theme. Every wanderer tends to ask the same questions: "Is it my fate to wander forever? Am I ever going to find my way home again?"

Powerful echos of this theme reverberate throughout Judges 17–Ruth 4. In particular, three Bethlehemites find themselves forced to wander through their personal wildernesses. A Levite wanders north to find work (Judg. 17:8–9). A concubine wanders north to find "home" (19:1). An Ephrathite wanders east to find food (Ruth 1:1). All three have to make painful decisions about when and where to pull up stakes. All three have to cope with life on the road, packing and unpacking, pushing and pulling, setting up and setting out.

Wanderer 1 sets out, as the text ambiguously puts it, "to wander to whatever [place] he might find . . . to make his way" (Judg. 17:8). The path he chooses, however, leads to territory as morally ambiguous as it is religiously uncharted. Soon dissatisfied, he throws in his lot with a band of Danites, enticed away by offers of more money and greater prestige. Nowhere does he pray or inquire of Yahweh before making these decisions, even though this is his purported function as a religious functionary. Never does he find his way home.

Wanderer 2 sets out to follow her husband to a new land and a new life (Judg. 19:1). Soon, however, the marriage fails, and she returns to her father. Four months later, her husband arrives in Bethlehem to take her home. Three times her father begs them not to leave, sensing something ominous on the road north. But his advice is ignored, and the resulting tale is one of the Hebrew Bible's most grisly horror stories, a terrifying nightmare about cowardice and rape and murder and war. No one here even comes close to making it home.

Wanderer 3 sets out to save his family from famine. Elimelech the Ephrathite makes a painful decision to leave the safety of his ancestral inheritance to scratch out a living in Moab. The text does not tell us much about this exile, but like Jacob's in Padan-Aram (Gen. 28:5–31:55) or Joseph's in Egypt (39:1–40:23), this one, too, is hard and difficult. Unlike Wanderers 1 and 2, however, Wanderer 3 eventually does find his way home, or at least his name does. Though every male in his family dies, including himself, two of the surviving three widows stubbornly refuse to let death have the last word. Ruth and Naomi set out to make sure that the family name does not perish. Playing on the Hebrew word for "return/restore" *(shub)* the narrator of Ruth guides us step by step through their journey home. Naomi decides to "return" to Judah (Ruth 1:7). She pressures her daughters-in-law to "return" to Moab, but they refuse: "No, we will 'return' to your people" (1:10). She insists a second time, "Return!" (1:11), then a third time, "Return!" (1:12). Finally Orpah does "return," and Naomi seizes on this to pressure Ruth into doing the same (1:15). Ruth, however, refuses to give in to Naomi's depression (1:16) and accompanies her "home" to the land of Judah, the land of Naomi's ancestors. Arriving in Bethlehem, Naomi announces, "I went away full, but Yahweh 'returned' me empty." Ruth's new co-workers begin to call her "the returnee" (2:6). Finally, after Obed is born, the people describe Naomi's grandson as the "life-returner" (4:15).

Religion and Ethics

For all their gloom and doom, the stories in Judges are quite religious. Compared with Ruth, they might seem otherwise, but even a cursory reading shows this to be so. In Judges 17, for example, Micah builds a shrine, stocks it with an assortment of religious icons, then hires the aforementioned Levite to serve it, both as "priest" and as "father." One of his reasons for doing this is basic: he wants to secure Yahweh's "favor" (*yatab*, Judg. 17:13).

Micah overtly calls the icons in this shrine his *'elohim* (18:24), a very important yet ambiguous term in this context. NIV translates this term "gods," but the MT reads "my gods" (KJV, NRSV). Most often *'elohim* refers to the one God, but sometimes it can refer to the world of unseen "daemons," that is, those mysterious beings that animate the earliest layers of the Balaam traditions, the dialogues of Job, and many other ancient Near Eastern texts.[21] Micah believes that his cult will enable him to contact the unseen world (17:13). Soon afterward, the Danites ask his Levite-priest to foretell the future, and he manipulates the *'elohim* to divine an answer (18:5). Divination occurs not only here but also in Judges 20, when the warriors from the non-Benjamite tribes go up to Bethel and inquire of Yahweh: "Who of us shall go first to fight against the Benjamites?" Yahweh's reply—"Judah shall go first"—is probably ascertained by the same divinatory techniques used earlier by Micah's Levite (20:18).

Nothing overtly religious, however, ever occurs in Ruth. No one divines the future. No one bargains for priests. No one steals *'elohim*-icons from vulnerable landowners. No one manipulates the *'elohim*. This needs to be noted carefully. In place of Micah's hollow religiosity stands Boaz's solid integrity. In place of the tribal elders' divination stands Naomi's Yahwistic faith. In place of the Danites' cruelty stands Ruth's compassion.

Doubtless there is some kind of traditional Yahwism beneath all this, yet in marked contrast to its canonical-historical context Ruth has little to say about it. On the one hand, Ruth epitomizes the best of Yahwism, quietly radiating a message of inclusion in a world segregated by ethnic prejudice. Every Hebrew in Bethlehem accepts Ruth for who she is, a *nokriyyah* ("foreign woman").[22] On the other hand, tolerance for foreigners never translates in this Hebrew short story to abandonment of responsibility, particularly family responsibility. The book of Ruth may begin by focusing on a foreigner's character, compassion, and faith. But it ends by focusing on the restoration of an Israelite family, not a Moabite individual.

Religious activity does not translate into moral integrity, and the canonical-historical approach to Ruth makes it easier for us to see this as we examine the loyalty of Ruth's characters versus the fickleness of Judges' characters. Micah's Levite abandons his employer without batting an eye—yet one cannot even imagine Ruth doing such a thing (Judg. 17:11; 18:20; Ruth 3:11–13). The concubine's husband drags her foolishly and needlessly into harm's way—yet one cannot imagine Boaz being so stupid (Judg. 19:9–22; Ruth 2:8–9). The Levite's concubine abandons her husband (even though she is not an *'ishah*, "wife," she is still obligated to stay with her *'ish*, "husband")—yet Naomi refuses even to abandon the name of her husband (Judg. 19:2; Ruth 3:2–5). In light of all the similarities, this fundamental dissimilarity is striking. "Behind this desacralized narrative stands a different conception of reality."[23]

In short, the book of Ruth quietly subverts the shallow religiosity of its context. Ruth is much more than a "lovely little composition" (Goethe) or a "quiet, out-of-the-way contrast" (Peterson). Instead, in its context, Ruth is an "autonomous text" permitting us to see a world which refuses to "allow itself to be absorbed" by the world all around it.[24] This book, like no other book in the Bible, challenges Israel to rethink the depth of its character, the goals of its mission, and the identity of its *'elohim*.

Chaos and Kindness

Perhaps the most overlooked comparison has to do with the notion of kindness in both Judges and Ruth. Ruth's term, *hesed*, is justifiably hailed by interpreters as one of the book's most important themes. The parallel term in Judges, however (*khanan*), is virtually ignored. No one, to my knowledge, has ever systematically compared these synonyms for kindness within their common canonical-historical context.

In Judges 21, Israel drives Benjamin to the brink of extinction. Not only this, but Israel, in typical Near Eastern fashion, vengefully issues a ban against any Hebrew man's giving his daughter to marry a Benjamite. Mercifully, this mistake is soon realized (must Benjamites now intermarry with non-Israelites?), and Israel's leaders backpedal hard to correct themselves. An exception clause is hastily drafted, permitting the Benjamites to receive four hundred virgins from the town of Jabesh Gilead. However, since this number is not nearly enough, they have to backpedal again and permit the Benjamites to seize even more brides from a nearby Shiloh festival. Should the Shilonites protest this legal rape policy, Israel's leaders prepared to respond with the following rationale:

> Do us a "kindness" by helping them, because we did not get wives for them during the war, and you are innocent, since you did not give your daughters to them. (Judg. 21:22)

In short, kindness in Mizpah is a character trait rooted neither in divine promise nor in personal conviction. Instead, kindness is a poker chip, something of a necessary political evil. Kindness is something expected of innocent bystanders after not one but several hundred of their least powerful citizens are institutionally raped by a paternalistic elite.

In Ruth, the family of Elimelech also teeters on the brink of extinction. Famine, death, and depression have taken a huge toll. Things are so bad that Naomi starts to talk about changing her name (from Naomi, "sweet," to Mara, "bitter"). She becomes so depressed that Elimelech's daughter-in-law has to confront her openly (1:16–17). Yet as soon as Boaz enters the picture, Naomi dares to do something that no character in this context ever really does. She dares to worship. She dares to trust in Yahweh—not manipulate the *'elohim*. She dares to imagine, even before anything is planned or dreamed or attempted, that there *is* a way out of her dilemma:

> May he be blessed by Yahweh, who does not abandon his "kindness" to either the living or the dead. (Ruth 2:20)

Kindness for Naomi is no poker chip to be cashed in at the threatening of one's tribal purity. Kindness is no awkward expectation, no it's-easier-to-ask-for-forgiveness-than-permission kind of thing. No, kindness is a gift. Kindness is something rooted in personal character and integrity. Kindness is something that grows out of faith in the promises of Yahweh, the God of Naomi's ancestors, the God to whom she now slowly (re)turns with chastened heart and hopeful countenance. It is only after she opens her heart to Yahweh's kindness that things start changing in her life. The narrator wants us to see this clearly. It is only after her faith revives that she begins to strategize with Ruth about the future. It is only after she interprets what she has experienced as the kindness of Yahweh that she begins to plan a face-saving way for Boaz to do what near-kinsmen are supposed to do: raise up heirs for deceased male relatives. Astonished by God's kindness, Naomi dares to dream of a new life months before Obed is born, decades before David is born, centuries before Jesus is born.

Boaz speaks of kindness as well, but it is difficult to tell what he means by it. One reader, commenting on the introductory description of him as a "man of standing" in 2:1, identifies Boaz as belonging to a "class of able-bodied and fully empowered citizens,"[25] but such identifications need updating badly in light of more recent anthropological research into what "family" and "clan" actually signify.[26] Another reader sees him as a "fatherly" man, a voice through whom the narrator articulates the book's "main theme": "faith has its rewards."[27]

Perhaps. We simply note that as soon as he realizes why Ruth has come to him, he exclaims,

> The LORD bless you, my daughter. This "kindness" is greater than that which you showed earlier. (Ruth 3:10–11)

Evidently somewhere between crass manipulation and spiritual regeneration, kindness for Boaz is something that enables him to experience the joy-filled wonder of discovering, on a public threshing floor of all places, that Yahweh intends to place a beautiful woman in his life. The only appropriate response is that he be a man who can "live up to the privilege of his responsibilities."[28]

Summary

In its context, Ruth is less a romantic novella than a subversive challenge, less a messianic preamble than a pastoral parable. In its context, Ruth's major theological themes—the yearning for home, the hunger for integrity, the hope for kindness—all come into clearer focus, project a sharper image than they would other-wise. Ruth is a very bright light in a very dark world.

Changing the metaphor, Ruth is a challenge to hear as well as see. Not only does each character bring a different "voice" to the "performance," each listener brings a different ear to the biblical "score."[29] One reader hears the "melody line" of a broken woman trying to find her way "home." Another resonates to the "alto part" sung by the loyal daughter-in-law who seeks to sing along-side her. Another gravitates to the "bass line" of the benevolent patriarch who wants only to support his fellow "singers."

But this is not all. Soon this trio is joined by a larger orches-tra in which the powerful countermelodies of justice and compas-sion blend and blur into the grander harmonies of a canonical symphony. Drawn in and nourished by this music, discerning lis-teners may discover that Ruth can be a quiet interlude in the midst of this symphony—a place where Maras of all sorts can learn to re-sing the simple melodies of childhood, a place where prima don-nas can relearn the pleasant essentials of harmony, a place where creative artists find a new voice, even after long hours of unwill-ing silence.

Notes

1. M. Peters, "Septuagint," *ABD* 5:1102.

2. R. G. Boling, *Judges* (AB 6A; Garden City, N.Y.: Doubleday, 1975), pp. 277–79; G. Gerleman, *Ruth* (Neukirchen: Neukirchener, 1981), p. 1; and D. Jobling, "What, If Anything, is 1 Samuel?" *SJOT* 7 (1993), pp. 25–30 all give preference to LXX's canonical order.

3. For example, R. Beckwith, *The Old Testament Canon of the New Testament Church* (Grand Rapids: Eerdmans, 1985), pp. 119–22, 183–87.

4. J. VanderKam, *The Dead Sea Scrolls Today* (Grand Rapids: Eerd-mans, 1994), pp. 121–58; L. Schiffman, *Reclaiming the Dead Sea Scrolls* (New York: Doubleday, 1994), pp. 161–80.

5. F. Bush, *Ruth, Esther* (WBC 9; Dallas: Word, 1996), pp. 8–9.

6. E. F. Campbell (*Ruth* [AB 7; Garden City, N.Y.: Doubleday, 1975], p. 36) sees only Judg. 19–21 as a unit, but P. Satterthwaite (" 'No King in Is-rael': Narrative Criticism and Judges 17–21," *Tyn Bul* 44 [1993], pp. 75–88) offers several substantive arguments for viewing all of Judg. 17–21 as a coherent narrative unit. M. K. Wilson ("As You Like It: The Idolatry of Micah and the Danites," *RTR* 54 [1995], pp. 73–85) thinks that Judg. 17–18

forms a logical sequel to Judg. 1–16. Whereas in Judg. 1–16 the accent falls on the incorrigibility of Israel with respect to idolatry, in Judg. 17–18 the narrator describes the psychology of idolatry.

7. Campbell, *Ruth*, p. 24; R. Hubbard, *The Book of Ruth* (NICOT; Grand Rapids: Eerdmans, 1988), p. 35.

8. J. Vesco, "La date du livre de Ruth," *RB* 74 (1967), pp. 235–47.

9. G. Glanzman, "The Origin and Date of the Book of Ruth," *CBQ* 21 (1959), pp. 201–7.

10. S. Bertman, "Symmetrical Design in the Book of Ruth," *JBL* 84 (1965), pp. 165–68.

11. P. Trible, *God and the Rhetoric of Sexuality* (Philadelphia: Fortress, 1978), pp. 166–99.

12. N. Gottwald, *The Hebrew Bible: A Socio-Literary Introduction* (Philadelphia: Fortress, 1985), p. 555.

13. These are the interpretations (in order) of H. Gunkel, *Reden und Aufsätzen: Ruth* (Göttingen: Vandenhoeck und Ruprecht, 1913), pp. 65–92; P. Trible, *God and the Rhetoric of Sexuality*, p. 195; J. Vesco, "Ruth"; *Ruth Rabbah* (London: Soncino, 1983); and W. Staples, "The Book of Ruth," *AJSL* 53 (1936–37), pp. 145–57.

14. Gunkel (*Ruth*, p. 81) notes the contrasts between Boaz and Mr. So-and-So in 4:1–6 as well as that between Ruth and Orpah in 1:14–15, but such observations do not intend to enunciate the book's canonical-historical message.

15. J. Holbert, "The Bible Becomes Literature: An Encounter with Ruth," *Word and World* 13 (1993), pp. 130–35; L. Perdue, *The Collapse of History: Reconstructing Old Testament Theology* (Minneapolis: Fortress, 1994), pp. 7–11.

16. I. Ljung, *Silence or Suppression: Attitudes Towards Women in the Old Testament* (Stockholm: Almqvist, 1989); J. Berquist, "Role Dedifferentiation in the Book of Ruth," *JSOT* 57 (1993); R. Alpert, "Finding Our Past: A Lesbian Interpretation of the Book of Ruth," in *Reading Ruth*, ed. J. A. Kates and G. T. Reimer (New York: Ballantine, 1994), pp. 91–96.

17. T. Frymer-Kensky, *In the Wake of the Goddesses: Women, Culture, and the Biblical Transformation of Pagan Myth* (New York: Free, 1992), p. 213.

18. L. Perdue, "The Household, Old Testament Theology, and Contemporary Hermeneutics," in *Families in Ancient Israel*, ed. L. Perdue et al. (Louisville, Ky.: Westminster John Knox, 1997), p. 254.

19. K. Engelken uniformly translates *pilegesh* as "secondary wife" (*Frauen im Alten Israel. Eine begriffsgeschichtliche und sozialrechtliche Studie zur Stellung der Frau im Alten Testament* [Stuttgart: Kohlhammer, 1990]).

20. Commission biblique pontificale, "L'interprétation de la Bible dans l'Église," *Bib* 74 (1993), p. 466.

21. See M. Moore, "Job's Texts of Terror," *CBQ* 55 (1993), pp. 662–75.

22. See M. Moore, "Ruth the Moabite and the Blessing of Foreigners," *CBQ* 60 (1998), pp. 203–17.

23. G. Gerleman, *Ruth,* p. 10.

24. E. van Wolde, "Texts in Dialogue with Texts: Intertextuality in the Ruth and Tamar Narratives," *BibInt* 5 (1997), pp. 1–28.

25. W. Rudolph, *Das Buch Ruth, Das Hohe Lied, Die Klagelieder* (KAT XVII/1–3; Gütersloh: Gütersloher Gerd Mohn, 1962), p. 48.

26. N. Steinberg, *Kinship and Marriage in Genesis* (Minneapolis: Fortress, 1993); C. Meyers, "The Family in Early Israel," in *Families in Ancient Israel,* ed. L. Perdue et al. (Louisville, Ky.: Westminster John Knox, 1997), pp. 13–41.

27. Gunkel, *Ruth,* p. 79.

28. E. Peterson, *Five Smooth Stones for Pastoral Work* (Grand Rapids: Eerdmans, 1980), p. 104.

29. F. Young, *The Art of Performance: Towards a Theology of Holy Scripture* (London: Dartman, Longman, & Todd, 1990).

§1 Judah's Famine and Elimelech's Death (Ruth 1:1–3a)

1:1 / The story of Ruth has a specific historical context, **the days when the judges ruled** (lit. when the judges judged). The act of repeating a seminal Hebrew root twice *(shepot hashopetim)*, however, immediately implies that Ruth's opening line attempts to do more than just situate the book historically. Hebrew, like English, repeats words for emphasis (GKC §117p). Ruth, in other words, is very much a story about *mishpat* ("justice," from *shapat*, "to judge, rule").

The crisis pressuring Elimelech is **famine in the land,** a terrifyingly common reality in the ancient Near East. Not only does it drive people from their land (Gen. 12:10; 26:1; 46:1; Exod. 16:3), but also it forces them to mortgage it away (Neh. 5:3). Precisely how long one can retain ownership while absent is an oft-debated question among the rabbis (e.g., *b. B. Qam.* 60b). Famine can be personified as a terrifying demon, as in Job 5:20, where famine is the first of seven evils, much like the Sibitti, the "gang of seven" in Mesopotamian myth.

Elimelech, like the Levitical priest (Judg. 17:7) and the doomed concubine (Judg. 19:1) in the immediate context, is **from Bethlehem in Judah.** "Beth-lehem" is actually two words *(bet lekhem)* and means "house of bread," an ironic name for a city plagued by famine. NIV translates the keyword *gur* as **to live for a while,** but a better choice would be "to wander" or "to sojourn." Elimelech is no weekend tourist but a *ger*, a "resident alien," a wanderer dependent upon the hospitality of homeborn Moabites for protection and privilege. As such, he follows in a long line of resident Israelite aliens, including Abraham (Gen. 12:10), Lot (19:9), and Joseph's brothers (47:4).

The place of this wandering is **the country of Moab** (lit. the fields of Moab). MT reads "fields"; 4QRuth[a], LXX, Syr, and Tg read "field." Israel and Moab sustain a love-hate relationship over many years, a fact attested by biblical and inscriptional sources.

David, for example, both protects and attacks Moab, depending on his situation (see 1 Sam. 22:3–4 vs. 2 Sam. 8:12). The Moabite stone celebrates a number of military victories over Israel by Mesha, king of Moab, during the time of Omri (*KAI* 181.5–20; see 2 Kgs. 3:1–27).

1:2 / **Elimelech** ("my God is king") is a name pregnant with irony in light of the focus on human kingship preoccupying the end of Judges (17:6; 18:1; 19:1; 21:25; see Introduction). Cognate names are found on second-millenium texts from Egypt and Canaan. **Naomi** means "pleasant, sweet," and is related to a word meaning "ardent desire" (e.g., "to gaze on the *no'am* of Yahweh," Ps. 27:4) or "mysterious grace" (Zech. 11:7, 10). Here at the story's outset, life is indeed pleasant for Naomi. Only her children's names foreshadow trouble. **Mahlon** is related either to a Hebrew word for "sickness" *(khalah)* or perhaps an Arabic word for "sterile" *(makhil)*. **Kilion** probably means "failing" (Deut. 28:65). Some rabbis called these men "the leaders of [their] generation" *(prnsy hdwr, b. B. Bat.* 91a). That they are here called **Ephrathites from Bethlehem** may refer to their genealogy, their geographical origin, or both.

1:3a / **Elimelech . . . died.** In ancient Near Eastern societies patriarchal death always triggers socioreligious crisis. Thus the death of Elimelech, **Naomi's husband,** is difficult to overemphasize. One could even argue that in many ways it is the book's primary conflict. Like other patriarchal stories, everything that follows is a reaction to it, directly or indirectly. Jacob's competition with Esau, for example, remains muted and embryonic until Isaac dies (Gen. 27:1–39). The concern underlying Joseph's revelation to his brothers is summed up in a single question, "My father . . . is he still alive?" (Gen. 45:3, my translation).

Patriarchal death is also one of the major themes of Canaanite myth. In the legend of the patriarch Kirta, for example, Kirta's illness triggers a series of desperate responses. The lords of Ḥubur, his neighbors, offer sacrifice. Ilhu and Titmanat, his children, perform the requisite appeasement rituals. El, the father of the gods, convenes a divine council and even sends an angelic messenger to cure Kirta. Naomi's husband's death is just as devastating as any other patriarchal death in the ancient Near East.

Additional Notes §1

1:1 / **The days when the judges ruled:** B. Porten ("Historiosophic Background of the Scroll of Ruth," *Gratz College Annual of Jewish Studies* 6 [1977], pp. 69–78) suggests that the book of Ruth is a microcosm of Genesis: both books emphasize famine; both employ the divine epithet Shadday; and both speak of marriages where the survival of posterity is in doubt.

Famine in the land: On the Sibitti, the "gang of seven" demons in ancient Mesopotamia, see L. Cagni, ed., *L'epopea di Erra* (Roma: Istituto di Studi del Vicino Oriente, Universita di Roma, 1969), tablet 1, lines 32–38. On Jewish attitudes about fraternizing with Moabites and other foreigners, see D. R. G. Beattie, "The Targum of Ruth—A Sectarian Composition?" *JJS* 26 (1985), pp. 228–29.

To live for a while: For a discussion of *gur,* see C. Bultmann, *Der Fremde im antiken Juda. Eine Untersuchung zum sozialen Typengriff ger und seinem Bedeutungswandel in der alttestamentlichen Gesetzgebung* (Göttingen: Vandenhoeck und Ruprecht, 1992), pp. 9–22. For a recent translation of the Mesha inscription (Moabite stone), see J. A. Dearman, ed., *Studies in the Mesha Inscription and Moab* (Atlanta: Scholars, 1989), pp. 93–95.

1:2 / **Elimelech:** The name *Ilimilku* appears in the Amarna correspondence from Egypt (*Die El-Amarna Tafeln* [repr.; ed. J. Knudtzon; Aalen: Zeller, 1964] letter #286, line 36). *Ilmlk* is also the name of a scribe at Ugarit (J. C. L. Gibson, *Canaanite Myths and Legends* [Edinburgh: T&T Clark, 1977], p. 102, line 60). On **Kilion,** the proper name *Ki-li-ya-nu* is attested at Ugarit and listed in the glossary of C. H. Gordon, *Ugaritic Textbook* (Roma: Pontificium Institum Biblicum, 1965) no. 1238. On the **Ephrathites,** H. Cazelles argues ("Bethlehem," *ABD* 1:712) for an origin in an Ephraimite clan who eventually settled in Judah. Should this be so, this perhaps would illuminate why so much of the activity in the context takes place in or around Ephraim.

1:3a / **Elimelech . . . died:** J. Sasson downplays the impact of Elimelech's death in *Ruth: A New Translation with a Philological Commentary and a Formalist-Folklorist Interpretation* (Sheffield: Sheffield Academic Press, 1989), p. 201. But the father's house *(bet 'ab)* is the basic unit of Israelite society (C. J. H. Wright, "Family," *ABD* 2:763–66), and Sasson downplays this as well. On the legend of Kirta, see Gibson (*Canaanite Myths and Legends,* pp. 97–102).

§2 Naomi's Survival (Ruth 1:3b–5)

1:3b / In response to the trauma of his death, Elimelech's family has more to do than just grieve over him. In a real sense the survivors have to grieve their own death. The text underlines this not once but twice. Twice Naomi is **left** alone (*tisha'er*, 1:3, 5), and the narrator uses a word for "survival" (*sha'ar*) that is designed to transmit the depth of Naomi's devastation.

The Canaanite myth of *Aqhat* uses a word, cognate to Hebrew *sha'ar*, that similarly describes the pain of bereavement. In this contemporary story, Aqhat is the son of Danil, a patriarchal character like Elimelech. Anat, the divine sister/wife of Baal, complains bitterly to El that Aqhat will not give her his magical bow and arrows (probably a coded symbol for the secret of eternal life). She becomes so enraged at him that she plots his doom, striking when Aqhat is *"left alone (shar)* in the mountains" (Gibson, *Canaanite Myths and Legends*, p. 112, line 15). Afterward, Danil reacts to his son's death by cursing the divine world (very much like Naomi's reaction in 1:20–21).

The canonical context helps us to contrast Naomi's bereavement with that of other Israelites. Israel, for example, grieves over the Benjamites who survive (*notarim*, Judg. 21:7) the tribal war after the rape of the Levite's concubine. Having survived, they now find themselves desperately needing new wives. Two elements are carefully repeated here in Ruth: survival and wives. Note also that Benjamin's crisis occurs because he has refused to hand over a pack of murderers. The war that ensues, though brutal and vicious, is at least explainable (perhaps even justifiable—"eye for an eye," Lev. 24:20). Naomi's loss, however, is patently unexplainable. No one ever tries to explain to this widow what has happened to her.

Some commentators later argue that Naomi is "left alone" because of her "sin" of fraternizing with "foreign peoples" (*Tg. Ruth* 1:5). Others argue, with regard to the story in Judges 20–21, that Benjamin suffers because he has foolishly listened to "the counsel of the serpent" (*b'tyw shl nkhsh, b. B. Bat.* 17a—referring to the serpent who tempts Eve). In other words, the ancients try to explain these losses via legal and mythological means. No explanation, however, is ever provided for Naomi. This widow never learns why her fate is to be the same as that of her criminal cousins in Gibeah.

1:4 / After Elimelech's death, Naomi's first survival plan is to start where she is, in Moab, and arrange marriages for her sons to **Moabite women, one named Orpah and the other Ruth.** The Judean famine makes it difficult, if not impossible, for her to arrange marriages that are endogamous, or within the same clan. Elimelech's family now lives in Moab, not Judah.

"Orpah" may be related to a Canaanite word for "neck" (*'arap*, as in the famous expression "stiff-necked," Exod. 32:9; Deut. 9:6). "Ruth" likely comes from the verb *rawah* ("replenish/restore") as in the stock phrase *gan raweh* ("replenished/well-watered garden," Isa. 58:11; Jer. 31:12). A few scribes connect it with the verb "to see" (*r'th, Ruth Rab.* 2.9), but Rabbi Johanan, in a wonderful turn of phrase, suggests that Ruth receives her name "because there issued from her David, who replenished *(rywhw)* the Holy One with hymns and praises" (*b. B. Bat.* 14b). Naomi's plan, however, fails. Mahlon and Kilion both die without producing a single male heir, even after **ten years** of marriage.

1:5 / The text discreetly refrains from lingering over the pain of this childlessness, but this is doubtless the final blow for Naomi. Childlessness takes as huge a toll on Naomi as it does on Abraham (Gen. 15:2), Sarah (16:2), and Hannah (1 Sam. 1:10), other childless progenitors. The narrator is saying that Naomi is trying, under incredibly difficult circumstances, to preserve the fading memory of her dying family. Hurdle after hurdle gets in her way. Blow after blow strikes her down. That she continues to try again and again to resurrect Elimelech's name, despite such harsh and unforgiving circumstances, is nothing less than remarkable.

Additional Notes §2

1:3b / **She was left:** C. Barth discusses death's ability to intimidate the living in *Die Errettung vom Tode in den individuellen Klage-und*

Dankliedern des alten Testaments (Basel: Zollikon, 1947), pp. 87–94. D. N. Fewell and D. M. Gunn (" 'A Son is Born to Naomi!' " *JSOT* 40 [1988], pp. 99–108) see Naomi as a scheming manipulator whose only goal is power and position.

B. Batto (*Slaying the Dragon: Mythmaking in the Biblical Tradition* [Louisville, Ky.: Westminster John Knox, 1992], p. 11) points out that bereavement and grief are central to the human dilemma, regardless of religion, economics, ethnicity, or any other distinguishing characteristic.

1:4 / **They married Moabite women:** On endogamous versus exogamous marriage, see the discussions in N. Steinberg, *Kinship and Marriage in Genesis,* pp. 12–17; and S. Kunin, *The Logic of Incest: A Structuralist Analysis of Hebrew Mythology* (Sheffield: JSOT Press, 1995), pp. 56–61.

§3 Naomi's Decision (Ruth 1:6–13)

1:6 / Having failed in her first attempt to salvage Elimelech's heritage, Naomi decides to leave Moab. Verses 6–13 give us three reasons for this decision: the lifting of the famine in Judah, her desire to deal honestly with her widowed daughters-in-law, and her feeling that she is too old to be of further use.

First, Naomi hears that Yahweh has **come to the aid of his people.** The word translated "come to the aid" is *paqad* (lit. to visit). In the Talmud, this word denotes the peculiarities of marital life (*b. Yeb.* 62b), which, as every spouse knows, is not a pleasant visit all the time. Yahweh's visit can be compassionate and merciful, but *paqad* does not always have such connotations, particularly in Ruth's canonical-historical context. In Judges 21:3, for example, Yahweh's visit to Benjamin is hostile:

> "O LORD, the God of Israel," they cried, "why has this happened to Israel? Why should one tribe be so visited *(lehippaqed)* in Israel today?" (my translation)

The same word appears in both Ruth and Judges, yet the contrasts are striking. One visit ends a protracted period of suffering (Ruth); the other begins a painful period of questioning (Judg.). One visit cripples an entire tribe (Judg.); the other begins a process of national rejuvenation (via David, Ruth 4:22). Nowhere is Yahweh's mysterious sovereignty more evident than in these two passages. Yahweh's visits, in other words, come totally at Yahweh's discretion. Yahweh and Yahweh alone decides whether they are to be peaceful or hostile, beneficent or malevolent.

1:7 / **She left the place where she had been living and set out on the road.** Unlike the Danites (Judg. 18:5) and the Mizpah council (20:18), Naomi conspicuously refrains from going to diviners to find out whether her newly chosen "road" *(derek)* is correct or not. Naomi is not one to spend time on psychics. Her decisions do not depend on the whims of *'elohim*-diviners.

1:8 / Naomi's concern for her daughters-in-law is too deep to watch them suffer (see 1 Tim. 5:11). **Go back, each of you, to your mother's home,** she urges. Some scholars imagine an anthropological counterpart to the father's house (*bet 'ab,* Judg. 6:15, 27). Yet "mother's home" may imply no more than that the fathers of these women may have had multiple wives. Resolving this question (see Additional Notes) is not nearly so important as the fact that Naomi tells them to go home. The concubine in Judges 19:2, for example, returns to her father's house after the collapse of her marriage, yet parental gender has nothing to do with the point of the story. So it is here as well. In fact, Boaz later commends Ruth for leaving her mother and father (2:11).

Naomi underlines her concern via two hope-filled statements. The first is, **May the LORD show kindness to you, as you have shown to your dead and to me.** Evidently she is impressed with these Moabite women. Out of deep concern for their welfare she pronounces the first of several statements that, taken together, articulate a marvelous theology of hope in Ruth. To Naomi's grace under pressure (1:9), Boaz later adds a hope-filled blessing (2:12), followed by the blessings of the Bethlehem council (4:11) and the Bethlehem women (4:14).

1:9 / Naomi's second wish is for Yahweh to **grant that each of you will find rest in the home of another husband.** Here we come to the core of her concern. Naomi wants her widowed daughters-in-law to find "rest" *(menukhah)*. Her feelings about this are so strong, she repeats them again in 3:1, "My daughter, should I not try to find a home ('rest,' *manoakh*) for you?"

One need look only at the story of the Levite and his concubine (Judg. 19:25–28) to realize how rare rest was "in the days when the judges ruled" (1:1). To most people who suffer, rest is an "eager longing":

> There came over me an eager longing for the blessings of calm and retirement . . . so that I could not submit to be thrust into the midst of a life of turmoil. . . . If any of you has been possessed by this longing, you know what I mean, and will sympathize with my feelings. (Gregory Nazianzus, *Oration* 2)

Naomi wants her loved ones, her remnant, to experience rest. The possibility that they might wind up as abused concubines somewhere is very real.

She kissed them and they wept aloud. These are tears of anguish, not only for the dead but also for the impending pain of separation. These women have gone through a lot together. Their weeping parallels that of the Israelites who weep before Yahweh after the demise of Benjamin (Judg. 20:26; 21:2).

1:10 / The first response of the daughters-in-law is swift: **We will go back with you to your people.** The ease with which they propose leaving their home is unsettling, particularly since they live in a world where many believe that "whoever lives outside the land" (lit. is attracted to foreignness) is like "one who has no God . . . (and) worships the stars" (*b. Ketub.* 110b). Xenophobia, however, is not a peculiarly Israelite sin. Doubtless there are Moabites who feel just as much antipathy toward Naomi as later Bethlehemites do toward Ruth.

1:11 / At any rate, Naomi confronts their resistance: **Return home, my daughters. Why would you come with me? Am I going to have any more sons, who could become your husbands?** Most commentators see this as simple exaggeration. C. H. Spurgeon, however, sees Naomi's words as setting before Orpah and Ruth "the trials which [await]" (*Morning by Morning: Daily Readings for the Family or the Closet* [New York: Sheldon and Co., 1866], Dec 15 a.m.). Jerome sees Naomi as a "lonely woman . . . deprived of her protectors" (Letter to Paula, #39, §5). Perhaps the most we can say is that Naomi no longer envisions a relationship with them beyond that of mother-in-law/daughter-in-law.

1:12 / Naomi voices her most insurmountable problem: **I am too old to have another husband.** Apparently she feels that apart from a maternal role in their lives she has nothing to offer them. Naomi does what a lot of despairing older people do. She defines herself more by what she does than by who she is. Role reversal is always upsetting, but particularly for elderly people. **Even if I thought there was still hope for me** is a telling line, an unguarded glimpse into the soul of someone rapidly succumbing to the quicksands of depression. "Hope" *(tiqvah)* grows out of a term for patient waiting (note the rare synonym "wait," *sabar,* in the next verse) and should probably be imagined less as bright-eyed optimism than determined anticipation.

1:13 / **Would you remain unmarried for them?** (lit. would you bind yourselves to not having a man?). This is the only place in the Bible where this root occurs *('agan).* In rabbinic literature, the *'agunah* is the forsaken wife. Legally forbidden to re-marry, she is a problem for the rabbis because they generally do not permit divorce, even in cases where the husband is mentally ill and/or death cannot be established. Some rabbis try to ease this situation (mitigating, for example, the strict laws of evidence and accepting hearsay testimony), yet the plight of an *'agûnâ* is always a desperate one (*b. Git.* 3a; *b. Yeb.* 122b). There is no way of knowing whether Naomi has all this in mind, yet the fact that she raises the specter of *'agûnâ*-life at all seems calculated to convince these widows to stay in Moab and rebuild their lives.

No, my daughters. It is more bitter for me than for you. The versions disagree significantly on how to read this sentence. LXX, followed by RSV, ignores the comparison, reading "it is bitter to me for your sake." Syriac concurs, adding, "I am more bitter than you." Targum embellishes the opposite way: "my soul is not bitter." Vulgate reads the comparison as internal rather than external: "Why would you have your distress press down on me any more?" NIV and NJPS follow the MT, while NRSV moves the comparison into the past tense. Obviously the earliest interpreters of Ruth significantly disagree over how to interpret this statement.

In the canonical-historical context, Micah's friends overtake the Danite brigands who kidnap his priest (Judg. 18). Defensive and angry, the Danites warn, "Don't argue with us, or some hot-tempered men will attack, and you and your family will lose your lives" (18:25). In other words, the Danites seem to be saying, "If you think things are bad now, just wait . . . things could get a lot worse!"

The Hebrew phrase "hot-tempered" employs the same word Naomi uses here for "bitter" (*mare nepesh*, lit. bitter-souled), so a comparison of the two does not seem unwarranted. Both Naomi's and the Danites' warnings speak of dire consequences. Both come from the lips of persons emotionally upset. The Danites, however, warn Micah about the corrosive power of bitterness on a warrior's soul; Naomi warns Orpah and Ruth about the power of bitterness on a widow's soul.

Naomi then traces the cause of her bitterness to a single, in-exorable source: "the LORD's hand has gone out against me!" Targum immediately euphemizes this to "a plague before Yahweh has gone out against me"—Tg gags at the very thought that Yahweh might be personally responsible for human suffering. "The LORD's hand" (*yad yhwh*) is found, however, forty times in the Hebrew Bible, usually in reference to a mysterious, unpredictable power:

> Whenever Israel went out to fight, the hand of the LORD was against them to defeat them, just as he had sworn to them. (Judg. 2:15)

In other words, while Naomi is left alone as a widow, in no way is she alone in her feelings about Yahweh. Like many other Israelites, Naomi believes—or at least part of her believes—that Yahweh is just as responsible for disaster as he is for salvation (see, e.g., Isa. 45:7). As a good Yahwist, she refuses to look for an easy way out by, say, blaming her predicament on one of the *'elohim*.

In verses 8–13 Naomi repeats the same command three times: **Return** *(shobenah)*. This contrasts visibly with the threefold plea of the concubine's father ("Stay!" Judg. 19:5–9). The irony is almost palpable between these two passages. Here a Bethlehemite mother-in-law pleads with her foreign daughters-in-law to return home. There a Bethlehemite father-in-law pleads with an out-of-town son-in-law not to return home. Both parent figures fear for the safety of those in their care. One tries to reason with a son-in-law who is sorely lacking in common sense. The other tries to persuade a loyal daughter-in-law to become something she will not.

Additional Notes §3

1:8 / **Mother's home:** C. Meyers thinks there is some anthropological significance to this phrase in " 'To Her Mother's House': Considering a Counterpart to the Israelite *bet 'ab"* (in *The Bible and the Politics of Exegesis;* ed. D. Jobling et al.; [Cleveland: Pilgrim, 1991], pp. 42–44). Steinberg, however *(Kinship and Marriage in Genesis,* p. 14), thinks this is an example of overinterpretation. In a thorough study of the Genesis genealogies, I. Fischer argues for the "complete insignificance" of the "female descendants" mentioned in Gen., in spite of the "great significance attributed to (individual) mothers" *(Die Erzeltern Israels: Feministisch-theologische Studien zu Genesis 12–36* [Berlin: Walter de Gruyter, 1994], p. 71).

1:12 / **I am too old:** L. Jarvik and G. Small discuss geriatric role reversal in *Parentcare: A Commonsense Guide for Adult Children* (New York: Crown, 1988), p. 6.

1:13 / **The LORD's hand:** On the significance of this biblical phrase, see J. J. M. Roberts, "The Hand of Yahweh," *VT* 21 (1971), pp. 250–51.

§4 Orpah's Decision and Ruth's Decision (Ruth 1:14–22)

1:14a / Then Orpah kissed her mother-in-law good-by. By deciding to follow Naomi's advice, Orpah does nothing immoral or unethical; she merely demonstrates that she has a "weaker nature" (Gunkel, *Ruth*, p. 68). Some commentators, however, find this explanation itself weak and condemn her for "turn[ing] her back on her mother-in-law" (*Ruth Rab.* 2.9). J. Wesley, for example, sees in her a type of spiritual lukewarmness:

> She loved Naomi, but she did not love her so well as to quit her country for her sake. Thus many have a value for Christ, and yet come short of salvation by him, because they cannot find in their hearts to forsake other things for him (*Notes on the Bible: Ruth* [Albany, Ore.: Ages Software, 1996], p. 829).

From a literary perspective, however, Orpah's character is merely a foil for Ruth's character. This is as common a literary technique as the juxtaposition of a text like Ruth alongside a text like Judges 17–21 is a common canonical technique.

1:14b / But Ruth clung to her. Ruth's loyalty to Naomi contrasts more sharply with the unfaithfulness of the Levite's concubine (Judg. 19:2) than with any unfaithfulness on Orpah's part. Both the Levite's concubine and Ruth listen to practical advice from older parent figures. Both refuse that advice. Yet death comes to one and not the other. Why? Is it appropriate to argue that Ruth acts solely out of love while the concubine acts solely out of ignorance? The text is conspicuously silent. Probably there is as much anxiety in Ruth as there is loyalty in the concubine, regardless of the narrators' attempts to portray these characters unidimensionally.

1:15 / Your sister-in-law is going back to her people. C. Jung argues for an organic link between ethnic identity and individual personality, that what we are as individuals is organically connected to who our ancestors were. A Jungian reading of this text might therefore suggest that Naomi is challenging Ruth to rediscover herself by rediscovering her people, to forget the last ten years of her life and start over again. Perhaps. What we can say is that every people defines its identity by focusing on its idiosyncrasies, focusing on a particular form of societal organization, and focusing on a common enemy. As a general rule, the relationship between individual and group is more complex in eastern than it is in western cultures, though this should not be overstated. Naomi seems to be pleading with Ruth to give in to the cultural status quo and follow the path of least resistance: "Go back to your own people."

Many commentators blanch at the inclusion of the comment **and her gods,** but Naomi is probably not referring here to the tribal-national deities of Transjordan. Instead she may mean the household gods or the icons representing the ancestral dead (the mysterious *'elohim*). The majority of Hebrews, like their Canaanite neighbors, always revered such icons. The story of Micah clearly illustrates this (Judg. 18:24).

1:16 / In short, neither mother's house, nor native people, nor ancestral *'elohim* can lure Ruth away from Naomi's side. Even Naomi cannot. Ruth is amazingly ready to walk away from everything important and meaningful in her world. Her response to Naomi is one of Scripture's greatest declarations of interdependence. It consists of three parts: a negative refusal, a poetic comparison, and an oath.

The negative refusal, **Don't urge me to leave you,** is translated in the LXX with a probably ingressive aorist infinitive, "Stop urging me" (this is not the same word translated "leave" by NIV in 1:3, 5). The word for "urge" appears to be a pun on the Hebrew root *paga'*. At root it means "encounter" and can refer to several kinds of "encounter," good and bad. In Judges 18:25, for example, the Danites warn Micah of possible "attack" *(paga')*. In Ruth 2:22, Naomi warns Ruth not to leave Boaz's property, lest she suffer possible attack *(paga')*. Here Ruth warns Naomi not to encounter her too severely.

Next is the poetic comparison, **Where you go I will go, and where you stay I will stay.** Male-female intimacy is obviously not the context, yet these couplets continue to be a perennial favorite at weddings. "Stay" here means "stay the night" *(lun)* and ironically parallels the plea of the old man from Gibeah, "Don't stay the night *(lun)* in the square!" (Judg. 19:20, my translation). *Lun* appears in several stories to signal fearful apprehension before chaotic powers (Gen. 19; Judg. 19). **Your people will be my people and your God my God.** There is no way of knowing what Ruth means precisely by God *('elohim)*. While many translations (including NIV) singularize and capitalize *'elohim* as "God," it is just as likely that Ruth speaks to Naomi as Naomi earlier spoke to her, as one Syro-Palestinian to another, using theological language more at home in the polytheistic world of Mesha, Balaam, and Micah (Judg. 17–18) than in the monotheistic world of the Mishnah or the NT. As a general rule, the interpreters who insist on associating *'elohim* with Yahweh here tend to be the same interpreters who insist on positing a conversion from polytheism to monotheism in Ruth.

1:17 / Where you die I will die, and there I will be buried. Recent research on ancient Near Eastern beliefs about the afterlife significantly heightens our appreciation for Ruth's faith. Choosing to be buried outside of one's ancestral estate *(nakhalat 'elohim,* 2 Sam. 14:16) is highly unusual for Syro-Palestinians because such decisions are believed to impose grave danger to the everlasting security of one's extended family, living as well as dead.

Finally Ruth takes an oath, **May the LORD deal with me, be it ever so severely, if anything but death separates you and me.** In Judges 21:1, many Israelites take an oath not to give their daughters in marriage to surviving Benjamites. Here a Moabite swears allegiance to a Hebrew in the very name of Yahweh. The Judges narrative illustrates the complete inadequacy of ethnic and racial categories for determining the parameters of covenant loyalty. The story of Ruth, however, quietly demonstrates the power of love to transcend these boundaries. The first vision is preservative; the second is transformative. The first looks inward; the second looks outward. D. Senior says it well: "At its best moments [Israel] recognized signs of deep solidarity with the non-elect nations . . . outside the bounds of its covenant" (D. Senior and C. Stuhlmueller, *The Biblical Foundations for Mission* [Maryknoll, N.Y.: Orbis, 1983], p. 213).

1:18 / Like Job, Ruth suffers innocently, unjustly, and unfairly. Unlike Job, however, Ruth does not become bitter (see Job 17:6–9). Augustine would agree that human determination

can be powerful but would also insist that it pales in comparison with God's grace (*Treatise on Perfection in Righteousness,* §10).

1:19 / **When they arrived in Bethlehem, the whole town was stirred.** The Hebrew root for "stirred" (*hom/hamam*) denotes significant social upheaval (1 Sam. 4:5; 1 Kgs. 1:45). Some lexicographers think that the Hebrew word for "the deep" (*tehom,* Gen. 1:2) derives from this same root. "Upheaval," at any rate, sums up well not only this incident but also the incidents that precede it. In Judges 18, for example, the Danites throw the hamlet of Laish into such traumatic upheaval that it never fully recovers. In Judges 19–21, the rape of the Levite's concubine throws all Israel into civil war. Bethlehem's upheaval here is similar, yet Naomi and Ruth come to heal, not to conquer; to replenish, not to destroy.

1:20–21 / Naomi's response to her old friends' astonishment (Can this be Naomi?) makes two proposals: that she be allowed to change her name and that God be held responsible for her suffering.

Don't call me Naomi . . . call me Mara. It is not uncommon, at moments of great stress, for Hebrews to change their names. Joseph, for example, signifies his increasing Egyptianization by becoming Zaphenath-Paneah (Egyptian for "the god speaks and lives," Gen. 41:45). Saul signifies his awareness of God's international love by changing his name to Paul (Acts 13:9). Though her friends seem not to take her seriously (2:1; 3:1; 4:17), Naomi ("sweet") becomes Mara ("bitter").

After this dramatic declaration, Naomi bravely homes in, by means of parallel couplets, on what she thinks is the source of her suffering. Couplet 1 reads:

The Almighty has made my life very bitter.
I went away full, but the LORD has brought me back empty.

Couplet 2 reads:

The LORD has testified against **me** (NIV: **afflicted**);
The Almighty has brought misfortune upon me.

Each couplet parallels the personal name of Israel's deity, Yahweh ("the LORD"), with a more generic Syro-Palestinian divine name, Shadday (*shdy,* "the Almighty"). Yahweh is Israel's revealed deity (Exod. 3:15). Shadday, however, is more like a mysterious Force, sometimes benevolent (Eliphaz's position), sometimes malevolent (Job's position). Shadday may well be, as Gunkel argues, "the divine name in an older religion, (later) subsumed to Yahweh in Israel" (*Ruth*, p. 70).

The second couplet reverses the order of the first (scholars call this a chiasm because, when diagrammed, this reversal looks like the Greek letter *chi* [X]). I am in basic agreement with the NIV translation of couplet 1 but would argue that the first verb in couplet 2 (Hb. *'anah*) is deliberately polysemantic. The Hebrew *'anah* can mean either "to afflict" (Tg, Rashi, KJV, ASV, RSV, NASV) or "to testify" (LXX, Syr, Vg, NIV, NJPS, NRSV). I think the author uses a polysemantic term to convey the multidimensional depth of Naomi's pain. Thus we feel not only her sense of legal impotence (testimony) but also her sense of theological abandonment (affliction).

1:22 / **Ruth the Moabitess** is the oft-repeated title of the heroine who helps to replenish Elimelech's family. If, according to Deuteronomy 23:4, Moabites are to be excluded from the assembly of Yahweh, some rabbis ask, how can David be allowed to enter Yahweh's assembly when he descends from a Moabitess (*b. Yeb.* 76–77)?

Additional Notes §4

1:14a / **Orpah kissed her mother-in-law good-by:** M. Sternberg discusses the use of foils in *The Poetics of Biblical Narrative* (Bloomington: Indiana University Press, 1987), p. 479. M. Fishbane discusses canonical intertextuality in *Biblical Interpretation in Ancient Israel* (Oxford: Clarendon, 1985), pp. 322–26.

B. Miller-McLemore ("Returning to the 'Mother's House': A Feminist Look at Orpah," *Christian Century* 108 [1991], pp. 428–30) imagines Orpah as a type of the "woman caught in the middle." Whereas Ruth and Naomi are types of women in culture and against culture, Orpah is a type of the woman caught between cultures, a woman on the threshold between progressive and traditional female roles.

1:15 / **Back to her people:** C. Jung advances his theories in *Memories, Dreams, Reflections* (New York: Random House, 1961), pp. 26–98. B. Morris dismisses Jung as a "mystagogue" in *Anthropological Studies of Religion* (Cambridge: Cambridge University Press, 1987), p. 174. H. Lewis discusses the irresistability of tribal morality in *A Question of Values* (San Francisco: HarperCollins, 1990) 87–88. J. Rogerson discusses the temptation to overstate the distinctions between eastern and western cultures in "Corporate Personality," *ABD* 1:1156. T. Lewis carefully researches the use of *ilū* ("gods") for "the deceased" in a number of ancient Near Eastern texts, then proposes that such is the case in 2 Sam. 14:16; see "The Ancestral Estate *(nakhalat 'elohim)* in 2 Samuel 14:16," *JBL* 110 (1991), pp. 602–3.

1:16 / **Where you stay I will stay:** D. Penchansky discusses the parallels between Judg. 19 and Gen. 19 in "Staying the Night: Intertextuality in Genesis and Judges," in *Reading Between Texts: Intertextuality and the Hebrew Bible* (ed. D. N. Fewell; Louisville, Ky.: Westminster John Knox, 1992), pp. 77–88.

Your God my God: Mesha, king of Moab, refers to the god Chemosh on line 3 of the Moabite stone, then to the goddess 'Ishtar-Chemosh on line 17 (*KAI* 181.3, 17). Balaam is introduced on the plaster texts from Tell Deir 'Alla (J. Hackett, *The Balaam Text from Deir 'Alla* [Chico, Calif.: Scholars, 1984], p. 25) as a "seer of the gods" *(hzh 'lhn)*. A. G. Hunter ("How Many Gods Had Ruth?" *SJT* 34 [1981], pp. 427–36) wonders whether Ruth's loyalty to Chemosh continues in Judah. A. Steinsaltz, however, follows *Tg. Ruth* to argue that Ruth converts to Yahwism (*On Being Free* [Northvale, N.J.: Aronson, 1995], p. 123).

1:17 / **Where you die I will die:** On the Israelite belief in a connection between land and afterlife, see H. Brichto, "Kin, Cult, Land and Afterlife—A Biblical Complex," *HUCA* 44 (1973), pp. 1–54. On the relationship between the *'elohim* and the teraphim, see K. van der Toorn, "The Nature of the Biblical Teraphim in the Light of the Cuneiform Evidence," *CBQ* 52 (1990), pp. 203–22.

1:20–21 / **The Lord has** testified against/**afflicted:** On the rancorous debate between Eliphaz and Job, see Moore, "Job's Texts of Terror," pp. 662–75.

My argument for polysemanticism is more thoroughly presented in M. Moore, "Two Textual Anomalies in Ruth," *CBQ* 59 (1997), pp. 234–43.

§5 Naomi's Reality (Ruth 2:1–2a)

2:1 / Now Naomi had a relative on her husband's side, from the clan of Elimelech, a man of standing, whose name was Boaz. Jewish tradition is full of fables about Boaz. The Talmud identifies him as the minor judge Ibzan (Judg. 12:8) and reveres him as a patriarchal figure on the level of a Kirta or a Danil in Canaanite myth (*b. B. Bat.* 91a). According to the Talmud, he becomes a widower on the very day Ruth arrives in Israel and is rich enough to throw lavish wedding parties for every one of his sixty children (*b. B. Bat.* 91a). Christian tradition similarly conventionalizes him. Spurgeon sees him as a type of Christ, often referring to Jesus as "our glorious Boaz" or "our bounteous Boaz" (*Morning by Morning*, March 19 p.m.; *Till He Come: Communion Meditations and Addresses* [London: Passmore and Alabaster, 1896], p. 116).

Here, however, Boaz's character is merely sketched in broad strokes. First, he is a "relative" (lit. a known one, *moda'*, Qere), a term found only once elsewhere (Prov. 7:4). The Greek equivalent chosen by LXX, *gnōrimos*, means "well-known," even "famous." Second, he is "from the clan of Elimelech" (i.e., Elimelech's extended village/kinship-protection group). "Clan" is not an adequate translation of Hebrew *mishpakhah*, for on one hand *mishpakhah* connotes much more than a mere grouping of blood relatives; on the other, *mishpakhah* is less significant sociologically than the *bet 'ab* (lit. house of the father). Third, he is a "man of standing," a "noble man" (*gibbor khayil*), a rather stock epithet for famous men like Jephthath (Judg. 11:1), Saul (1 Sam. 9:1), and David (1 Sam. 16:18).

This same adjective (*khayil*, "noble") also denotes the Danite party of spies (Judg. 18:2), the 43,000 Benjamites who die in battle, and the 12,000 hired assassins who slaughter Jabesh Gilead (Judg. 18:2; 20:44, 46; 21:10). Introducing Boaz via this same adjective therefore raises an important question: How is Boaz like or unlike these 55,005 men? Is his nobility to be understood solely in military terms? Or does the narrator have another kind of nobility in mind?

2:2a / Hunger drives Ruth to ask Naomi for permission to **go to the fields.** The NIV does not overtly translate it, but MT uses an untranslatable particle *(nah')* to signify that Ruth is formally asking Naomi for permission (inexplicably, NIV translates *nah'* as "please" in 2:7 but not here). Her goal is to **pick up the left-over grain** (lit. ears of grain, *shblt*). In Israelite society the poor have a legal right to glean at harvest time (Lev. 19:9–10; Deut. 24:19). To the average U. S. citizen, this might seem to be a quaint tradition. The problem of hunger, however, is central to the plot of this story.

In the Canaanite myth of Aqhat, for example, Danil (a Boaz-like figure) inspects his famine-stricken land and finds upon it a single, blighted "ear of grain" *(shblt).* Dismounting from his donkey, he kisses it hungrily and cries out,

> Oh please *(án)* may this ear of grain *(šblt)* shoot up in the devoured land. (Gibson, *Canaanite Myths and Legends,* p. 116)

Note the parallel use of the term *shblt* alongside a particle for "permission." The difference between these stories is that Ruth asks permission of Naomi to glean from a land already visited. Danil, however, asks the gods to replenish a land still unvisited. Ruth's world, like Danil's, is a fragile place.

Additional Notes §5

2:1 / **Whose name was Boaz:** On Boaz's patriarchal "equivalence" to Kirta and Danil, see Gibson, *Canaanite Myths and Legends,* pp. 82–122. D. M. Gunn and D. N. Fewell, "Boaz, Pillar of Society: Measures of Worth in the Book of Ruth," *JSOT* 45 (1989), pp. 45–59, reconceptualize Boaz as a weakling reluctant to take initiative.

From the clan of Elimelech: N. Gottwald discusses the sociological significance of *mishpakhah* in *Tribes of Yahweh* (Maryknoll, N.Y.: Orbis, 1979), pp. 257–94. N. P. Lemche discusses the primacy of the *bet 'ab* in *Early Israel* (Leiden: E. J. Brill, 1985), p. 269.

2:2a / **Pick up the leftover grain:** On the global dynamics of hunger see R. Sider, *Rich Christians in an Age of Hunger* (Downers Grove, Ill.: InterVarsity, 1977); G. Riches, *First World Hunger: Food Security and Welfare Politics* (New York: St. Martin's, 1997).

§6 Ruth's Ministry (Ruth 2:2b–7)

2:2b / Ruth's goal, however, is not just to **find favor** in the **eyes** of someone with enough economic wherewithal to save her life. Keats inimitably expresses the greater depth of her pain in his *Ode to a Nightingale:*

> Thou wast not born for death, immortal Bird!
> No hungry generations tread thee down;
> The voice I hear this passing night was heard
> In ancient days by emperor and clown:
> Perhaps the self-same song that found a path
> Through the sad heart of Ruth, when sick for home,
> She stood in tears among the alien corn.

Ruth seems to be coming to a theological realization, however unfocused, of a need for grace. Whether it is a need for human or divine grace is impossible to say. Whether this is the first or the hundredth time she has sensed this need is also impossible to say. We have no evidence for imagining overt religious activity in her life (in contrast to, say, Micah in Judg. 17). We only know that what she requests is not *hesed* but *khen* ("favor," a derivative of the same root in Judg. 21:22). Unlike the Mizpah leaders arrayed against Benjamin, however, Ruth asks for favor to serve, not to manipulate.

Naomi responds to Ruth's request with two short words: *leki bitti,* **Go ahead, my daughter.** With these words, Naomi does more than just give Ruth permission. She confesses her willingness to change. Elimelech, Mahlon, and Kilion, her previous sources of sustenance, are all dead. Whether she likes it or not, she has a different life now, a harder life. Granting permission to Ruth to glean alongside the rest of the institutionalized poor is the point where Naomi hits rock bottom.

2:3 / **So she went out and began to glean.** Rabbi Eleazar interprets the chain of verbs in this verse ("she came," "she went," "she gleaned") as a sequence of back-and-forth trips over several days (*b. Shabb.* 113b). **As it turned out** is NIV's translation of a rather rare verb (*qarah*) plus its cognate noun (*miqreh;* cf. the similar doubling of the root *shpt* in 1:1). A morphologically faithful translation might be something like "her chance chanced" or "her fate fated." Perhaps the emphasis here on coincidental randomness is a subtle response to the mechanical dependence on divination in Judges 20:18, 23, 28.

2:4 / **The LORD be with you! The LORD bless you!** Harvest is a time of celebration, especially after a famine. "The valleys are mantled with grain; they shout for joy and sing" (Ps. 65:13). "Bless" (*barak*) links Boaz to a number of other international blessers in the Hebrew Bible (Melchizedek, Balaam, and Jethro). Later liturgists adopt this greeting as a model for all greetings, especially those intended for synagogue worship (*b. Ber.* 63a).

2:5 / Upon seeing Ruth, Boaz immediately asks his foreman, **Whose young woman is that?** Boaz is surprised or at least bemused that Ruth is unprotected—not because he is oppressively paternalistic but because he is responsibly patriarchal (see §15). Like Naomi, he takes his leadership responsibilities seriously. Later rabbis, fearful that he might be perceived as a little too interested in Ruth, fall all over themselves to explain Boaz's intentions:

> He perceived a wisdom in her behavior. She gleaned two ears of corn, but not three. . . . He perceived a modesty in her, the standing ears [she gleaned] standing; the fallen ears [she gleaned] sitting. (*b. Shabb.* 113b)

At least one rabbi, however, sees her entrance as erotically arousing (*Ruth Rab.* 4.4).

2:6 / **She is the Moabitess who came back from Moab with Naomi.** (lit. a young woman [*na'arah*], a Moabitess is she). With this response, placed in the mouth of the **foreman,** the narrator quickly communicates three things: by calling her a *na'arah,* he deftly positions her near the middle of the Israelite social continuum; by calling her a Moabitess, he has Boaz learn of her status as a foreigner; and by calling her "the returnee" (*hashabah;* NIV translates "who came back"), he underlines the themes of wandering and returning.

2:7 / Vital character information is often conveyed through dialogue. By listening in on the foreman's dialogue we learn bits and pieces about Ruth, but only from a distance. The effect of this technique is to bring Ruth close, yet still keep her at arm's length, veiled and mysterious. From the foreman we learn, first, that Ruth respects his authority: **Please let me glean.** This is the second time Ruth asks for permission to glean (first from Naomi [2:2], now from Boaz's foreman). Second, we see her wait patiently until this permission is granted. MT puts the place of her gleaning as the already harvested grain stacks, the **sheaves,** but this is problematic. P. Joüon rightly points out that Boaz does not give her permission to glean from the sheaves until 2:15 (*Ruth: Commentaire Philologique et Exégétique* [Rome: Institut Biblique Pontifical, 1953], p. 49). "Stalks" therefore seems to be the better reading, especially since this involves no emendation of the text but only a slight revocalization (*'amirim*, "stalks," instead of *'omarim*, "sheaves").

NIV translates the next line as **she went into the field and has worked steadily from morning till now,** but this too is problematic. First, "into the field" is not in MT. There is no indication that Ruth has yet entered a field. Second, the second verb in the line is "she has stood" *(ta'amod)*, not "has worked steadily." MT says only, "She has come and she has stood." It is important to be precise here because otherwise we cannot decide whether Ruth starts to glean before or after the giving of Boaz's permission. I am inclined to think that it is Ruth's dignified patience (waiting while others work) that so impresses Boaz's foreman, not her strong work ethic.

The final words of 2:7 constitute a major textual problem (Campbell does not even translate the last fourteen words of 2:7). Several readings have been proposed. D. Lys catalogues some nineteen of them under four headings: "Ruth takes a little rest"; "Ruth does not take a little rest"; "Ruth takes only a little rest" (NIV); and "Ruth scarcely takes any rest." I am inclined to follow Lys's translation of 2:7's final clause and read: "This [waiting area] has been her dwelling. The house [shady shelter?] means little."

Should this translation be plausible, the portrait would contrast sharply with the one in Judges 18. Here a hungry foreigner waits patiently for permission; there a gaggle of well-fed Israelites jockeys for power. The Danites roam the countryside looking for an inheritance upon which "to settle" (*lashebet*, Judg. 18:1). Ruth, however, refrains from "settling" (*shibtah*) until she is given permission. In Judges, the Danites desperately seize an entire town as their "rightful" inheritance. Ruth, by contrast, patiently trusts that things will work out in their own good time.

Additional Notes §6

2:2b / **Go ahead, my daughter:** Ambrose gives Ruth the credit for much of Naomi's new attitude in *Concerning Widows* in *Nicene and Post-Nicene Fathers* (Albany, Ore.: Sage, 1996) 785. P. Hiebert emphasizes widowhood's awful finality in " 'Whence Shall Help Come to Me?' The Biblical Widow," in *Gender and Difference in Ancient Israel* (ed. P. L. Day; Minneapolis: Fortress, 1989), p. 130.

2:5 / **Whose young woman:** R. L. Maddox ("The Word of God and Patriarchalism: A Typology of the Current Christian Debate," *Perspectives in Religious Studies* 14 [1987], pp. 197–216) examines whether patriarchalism is structured into or challenged by Scripture.

2:7 / **She said, "Please let me glean":** On the various functions of dialogue in Hb. narrative, see S. Bar-Efrat, *Narrative Art in the Bible* (Sheffield: Almond, 1989), pp. 64–77.

On gleaning among the sheaves Joüon's opinion is followed by Rudolph, *Das Buch Ruth*, p. 46.

Into the field: On the textual problems in 2:7 see Campbell, *Ruth;* D. Lys, "Résidence ou repos? Notule sur Ruth ii 7," *VT* 21 (1971), p. 498; Moore, "Two Textual Anomalies in Ruth," pp. 238–40.

§7 Boaz's Character (Ruth 2:8–12)

2:8 / When Boaz calls Ruth **my daughter,** he is assuming Elimelech's place as the responsible patriarch of the family. He does not merely raise up children for the deceased, however. He also protects, nourishes, and restores two displaced widows whose connection to the kinship structure has been severed. Fleshing out this role, Boaz uses a series of action verbs over the next few verses, each an unexpected gift delicately laid at the feet of a surprised Moabitess: *Listen to me . . . Don't go . . . Don't glean elsewhere . . . Don't go away . . . Stay here . . . Watch the field . . . Follow along . . . Go and get a drink . . . Come over here . . . Have some bread . . . Dip it in the vinegar . . . Stay with my workers.*

MT has a question: "Will you not listen, my daughter?" NIV closely follows Syr and translates as an imperative command, **Listen to me,** preceded by a particle of permission *(n'),* "my daughter, please listen to me" *(brty n' shmy' lky).*

From the outset Boaz makes it clear to this widow that her wandering days are over: **Don't go away from here** (lit. "you shall not wander," *'abar*). One can only imagine the impact these words must have had on Ruth's heart.

The verb translated **stay** is the same verb translated "cling" in 1:14 *(dabaq).* Boaz wants Ruth to cling to him as tightly as she now clings to Naomi. To hyperegalitarians this undoubtedly sounds patronizing, but Boaz is under no obligation to do a thing for this foreign widow. To shepherd Ruth into the fold of his **servant girls** is an act of grace. Boaz is trying to help Ruth, not manipulate her. His intention is to move Ruth away from the precarious role of "foreign woman" *(nokriyyah)* toward the more socially centrist role of "young (servant) girl" *(na'arah).* Boaz is no Gibeahite gangster.

2:9 / Boaz explains his actions by assuring Ruth, **I have told** (lit. Have I not commanded?) **the men not to touch you.** Apparently Boaz has the authority to enforce such commands, in contrast to Nabal's relationship with his employees (1 Sam. 25:17).

He warns the *na'arim* ("young men") not to touch the new *na'arah* ("young girl"). The word for "touch" *(naga')* can refer to criminal assault as well as other kinds of touching (contrast Deut. 21:5 and 1 Sam. 10:25). Here it refers to sexually inappropriate touching. It cannot refer to touching in general because Ruth is later instructed to drink from the community **water jars.**

From a canonical-historical perspective, Boaz stands out against an uninspiring crowd. His is the only male character in Judges 17–Ruth 4 who consistently demonstrates compassion, integrity, and moral courage in the face of challenge. Others pretend to such traits but uniformly fail to incarnate them. Micah, for example (Judg. 17:1–13), takes his mother's money under strange circumstances and uses it to finance a "house of the gods" *(bet 'elohim)*. His intentions seem noble, but his methods are suspect. His response to the Danites, moreover, is to whine and sulk. The Bethlehem Levite agrees to serve Micah as priest but abandons his post as soon as a better offer comes along (Judg. 17:7–13; 18:20). The Danites are dutifully labeled "noble" men *(bene khayil,* Judg. 18:2), but are more interested in enticing employees than in helping widows (Judg. 18:1–31). The Ephraimite Levite says he is "going to the house of the LORD" (Judg. 19:18) but soon surrenders his own wife to a gang of murderers (Judg. 19:1–30). Boaz stands head and shoulders above all the men in the canonical-historical context.

2:10 / At this, she bowed down with her face to the ground. Ruth, like the Levite's concubine, "falls down" (see this same word, *napal,* in Judg. 19:25), but not in forced submission to a violent male. Ruth falls before this male out of deep respect, much like Abigail, the wise woman of Tekoa, the Shunammite, and the Syrophoenician woman (1 Sam. 25:23, 41; 2 Sam. 14:4; 2 Kgs. 4:37; Mark 7:25; Eph. 5:25–28).

With the question, **Why have I found such favor in your eyes that you notice me—a foreigner?** the narrator resolutely keeps our attention focused on two themes. The first is favor. Ruth wants to know (as do we) why Boaz lavishes upon her such undeserved favor. The narrator uses here the same word used by the narrator of Judges in describing the "favor" *(khen)* sought by Israel's leaders (Judg. 21:22). There seems to be a subtle wordplay here involving the synonyms *khen* and *hesed*. At the outset of the chapter Ruth dreams predominantly of human favor (2:2). Boaz, however (as will become clear in 2:12) wants to extend to her a "grace" *(hesed)* far deeper than anything she has ever yet experienced.

The second part of Ruth's response also involves wordplay. The word for "notice" *(nakar)* and the word for "foreigner" *(nokriyyah)* share the same consonantal root in Hebrew *(nkr)*. In Israel, a foreigner is someone who is noticeable. This root is common to several Semitic languages. An Akkadian inheritance text, for example, allows the passing down of inheritance rights "to any of my children . . . but not to a foreigner" *(na-qa-ri)*. An Aramaic text discussing funerary details carefully distinguishes between the corpse of a son and the corpse of a "foreigner" *(nkry)*.

Apart from the sheer joy of writing great literature in a wonderfully flexible language, the narrator's point is that Ruth is grateful. Ruth knows who she is—a foreigner, a stranger, a person easily recognized by her speech, her customs, and her beliefs. She also knows that foreigners, widows, and sojourners are usually forced to live on the fringes of society. Thus she is grateful that Boaz's behavior contrasts so sharply with, say, the behavior of the Levite from Ephraim:

> When they were near Jebus and the day was almost gone, the servant said to his master, "Come, let's stop at this city of the Jebusites and spend the night." His master replied, "No. We won't go into an alien city *('ir nokri)*, whose people are not Israelites. We will go on to Gibeah." (Judg. 19:11–12)

There are several levels of irony here. First, it is ironic that the city deemed foreign by this Ephraimite is the same city later transformed into Israel's capital by the great-grandson of the *nokriyyah* Ruth. Indeed, the interplay between Israel and non-Israel is a subject of endless fascination in the Bible, the Targumim, the Talmud, and the midrashim. Second, how ironic it is that Jebus proves, if only by default, to be more Yahwistic in its morality than is Gibeah, presumably an ethnically purer city. Third, the genuine compassion of Boaz contrasts sharply with the hypocritical nativism of the concubine's husband. To illustrate this in contemporary language, it is much easier for a white male judge, John B. Scott, to fine a poor black woman, Rosa Parks, for disorderly conduct (refusing to give up her seat to a white man) than it is to challenge the evils of a racist legal system. Likewise is it easier for a Levite to look down his nose at Jebusite foreigners than it is to protect his concubine from Israelite harm.

2:11 / I've been told all about what you have done for your mother-in-law. The book's characteristically emphatic grammar *(hugged huggad)* might well be translated, "It has been explained and reexplained to me." Boaz has done his homework. Evidently he has gathered information about this Moabitess from a number of sources, not just his foreman. Fully aware of her non-Hebrew origins, Boaz demonstrates a broader vision of community than do the majority of his peers. He has already determined in his heart to welcome her into the Bethlehemite community. He is impressed by the fact that Ruth has **left** her **father and mother** and her **homeland** to **live with a people** she **did not know before.** He knows that Ruth is serving Naomi at great personal risk. He knows how dangerous it is to leave (*'azab,* 1:16) one's "homeland" (*moledet*).

2:12 / **May the LORD repay you for what you have done. May you be richly rewarded.** The word translated "repay" in NIV is the verbal form of the well-known noun *shalom,* usually translated "peace" in English Bibles. In its verbal form (*shalem*) it can be rendered "to complete," "to make whole," "to restore," "to make good," or "to pay back." Thus the versions vary significantly. LXX, for example, uses a contractual term from the world of economics (*apotino*) to explain Boaz's repayment. Vulgate translates *shalem* with *reddere,* a term which can sometimes be translated "to render" or "to translate" ("May the Lord 'translate' your foreignness").

Syriac, however, uses a word (*pr'*) which goes in a different direction altogether. In some contexts *pr'* can mean "to spring up, to bud (like a flower)." There is a more precise cognate to MT *shalem* in Syriac (*shlm*), but the Syr translator of Ruth still chooses *pr',* evidently to focus more on Ruth's spiritual growth than the legalities of her agreement with Boaz.

Boaz attributes this to **the LORD, the God of Israel, under whose wings you have come to take refuge.** Boaz wants Ruth to understand that the *'elohim* to whom she has bravely yet ignorantly pledged her allegiance (1:16) is a deity unlike any other. Ancient Near Eastern deities are often given the epithet "rewarding god" (*'lh' shkr*). Boaz, however, wants Ruth to know that Yahweh is more than this. Yahweh's "wings" provide "refuge." The Canaanite goddess 'Anat, for example, has wings which "lift up" and "vibrate" whenever she takes to flight, yet 'Anat cares little about refuge. Perhaps Boaz's speech is rooted in a childhood memory of the wings of the cherubim solemnly enfolded over the ark of the covenant (Exod. 37:9).

What makes Yahwism so different from other ancient Near Eastern religions is its proven ability to transform human character. Boaz does more than just talk about Yahweh's protection; he becomes Ruth's protector. He does more than just visualize *hesed;* he incarnates it.

Additional Notes §7

2:8 / **My daughter:** A. Phillips ("The Book of Ruth: Deception and Shame," *JJS* 37 [1986], pp. 1–17) believes that one of this book's primary intentions is to chastise societies who ignore their widows.

2:10 / **Foreigner:** Informed discussions of *nokriyyah* appear in C. Maier, *Die "fremde Frau" in Proverbien 1–9: Eine exegetische und sozialgeschichtliche Studie* (Göttingen: Vandenhoeck und Ruprecht, 1995), pp. 252–69; and L. Stager, "Archaeology, Ecology and Social History: Background Themes to the Song of Deborah," in *Congress Volume: Jerusalem 1986* (ed. J. Emerton; Leiden: E. J. Brill, 1988), pp. 229–30. Fred Gray, Rosa Parks's attorney, tells her story in his memoir, *Bus Ride to Justice* (Montgomery, Ala.: Black Belt, 1995), p. 56. The Akkadian inheritance text is cited from *CAD* N, 191. The Aramaic text is cited from *DNWSI* 732.

2:12 / **May the Lord repay:** On *shalem,* see BDB 1022. On Syr *pr',* see PSSD 463.
Under whose wings: The epithet "rewarding god" (*'lh' shkr*) is found at Palmyra (*DNWSI* 1135). F. I. Andersen, "Yahweh, the Kind and Sensitive God," in *God Who Is Rich in Mercy: Essays Presented to Dr. D. B. Knox* (ed. P. T. O'Brien and D. G. Peterson; Homebush West, Australia: Lancer, 1986), p. 82, sees Yahweh as much more than a "rewarder of good deeds." Anat's wings are described in Gibson, *Canaanite Myths and Legends,* p. 132.

§8 Excursus: Yahweh, God of Grace

Boaz's speech records something rather rare in ancient Israelite literature. Here an Israelite bears witness to a non-Israelite about the very character of God. If Ruth is like most other Syro-Palestinians, she is a polytheist. Presumably what she knows about Yahweh is the direct result of her husband's family's influence. Perhaps it is the evidence of this influence that encourages Boaz to be so direct with her. Predictably, some rabbis overinterpret this encounter and attempt to transform Boaz, as they do many other biblical characters, into a messianic "prophet" (*b. Shabb.* 113b). Careful attention to the canonical-historical context, however, shortcircuits such extremism.

Judges 17–18, for example, preserves a story about a typical cult center in Iron Age Palestine. The narrator of Judges calls it a "house of the gods" (*bet 'elohim*, Judg. 17:5). The icons inside this house are themselves called *'elohim* (18:24), The magicoreligious specialists who use them are called *kohanim* and *'abot* ("priests" and "fathers," 18:19). Recent research on these *'elohim*-icons affirms that the best way to understand their cultural role is to view them holistically, as part of a much larger socioreligious network involving kinship, cult, land, and afterlife beliefs. That varying beliefs about the *'elohim* are anchored deep in Syro-Palestinian culture well explains why so many Israelites, in spite of attempts to police them, go on worshiping these deities at high-place sanctuaries (1 Kgs. 3:2; 12:31; 13:2).

In 1967, a team of Dutch archaeologists found the remains of a sanctuary very much like Micah's only twenty miles east of Shechem. Its present-day Arabic name is Deir 'Alla (probably ancient Succoth). Inside the Dutch found plaster fragments containing an oracle of Balaam, presumably the same Balaam who speaks in Numbers 22–24. The first line of this inscription identifies Balaam as "a seer of the gods" (*khzh 'lhn*). Subsequent lines record the sinister plans of a group of *'elohin* who are intent on destroying Balaam's people. The Deir 'Alla texts shed a great deal of light on Ruth's polytheistic world.

Another archaeological discovery sheds even more light. In Moab, Ruth's homeland, the Mesha inscription (see above on 1:1) describes Chemosh as a god who "gets angry" *('np)*, who "returns" land *(shwb)*, who "replenishes" himself *(ryt)*, who "speaks" *('mr)*, who shares power with a female consort ('Ishtar), who receives "devoted things" from worshipers *(khrm)*, and who "drives away" enemies *(grsh)*. In other words, Ruth's national god looks very much like the Yahweh who is worshiped in popular Israelite circles, even down to the detail of having a goddess-consort (as on the inscriptions found at Kuntillet 'Ajrud and Khirbet el Qôm).

These inscriptions tell us a great deal about the substance and context of Ruth's religious world. Doubtless Ruth learns from her husband's family that Yahweh is the imageless deity responsible for humbling Egypt under Moses (Exod. 12:33), the God who leads Israel safely through the sea (Exod. 14:29), the God who confounds the plans of Balak the Moabite (Num. 24:10). Boaz, however, wants to emphasize a side of Yahweh that even Naomi seems to have forgotten: that Yahweh is a God of kindness as well as judgment, a God of refuge as well as war.

Additional Note §8

I discuss the traditional tendency to transform biblical characters into prophets in "Balaam the Prophet?" *RQ* 39 (1997), p. 104. On the *kohanim* ("priests") as peculiar magicoreligious specialists, see T. Fahd, *La divination arabe* (Leiden: E. J. Brill, 1966), pp. 92–97. On the Deir 'Alla texts, see J. Hoftijzer and G. van der Kooij, eds., *Aramaic Texts from Deir 'Alla* (Leiden: E. J. Brill, 1976), pp. 184–88. The Moabite descriptions of Chemosh are cited from *KAI* 181.5, 8, 12, 14, 17, 19. D. N. Freedman discusses the relationship of Yahweh to his "a/Ashera" in "Yahweh of Samaria and His Asherah," *BA* 50 (1987), pp. 241–49.

§9 Ruth's Introduction to Bethlehem
(Ruth 2:13–19)

2:13 / For the third time (see 2:2, 10) Ruth mentions "favor": **May I continue to find favor in your eyes, my lord. Though I do not have the standing of one of your servant girls** is a sensitive political statement acknowledging the reality of a delicate situation. Not only does she address Boaz as "lord" (*'adon*), she also refers to herself, in spite of Boaz's earlier suggestion, as "servant girl" (*shipkhah*) instead of "young woman" (*na'arah*, 2:5).

This situation is similar to the one in the Gibeahite square (Judg. 19). In Ruth, an older man takes a young female stranger under his wing. In Judges 19, an older man shelters a young female stranger out of what looks to be fatherly concern for her safety. In Ruth, Boaz gathers information from several sources before speaking to Ruth. In Judges 19, the old Gibeahite immediately and frantically interrogates the Levite and his concubine, even before he finds out who she is (19:17). In Ruth, the house means little (2:7). In Judges 19, the house means everything (the Levite complains, "No one has taken me into his house," 19:18). In Ruth, Boaz promises and delivers a "reward" (*shalem*). In Judges 19, the old Gibeahite promises but fails to deliver "peace" (*shalom*, 19:20).

2:14 / Boaz continues his litany of grace-filled imperatives: **Come over here. Have some bread and dip it in the wine vinegar.** These are not mere dining instructions. Boaz wants to introduce Ruth to Bethlehem society, starting with his own workers. He insists that Ruth be treated no differently from any other worker. Wesley sees compassion for the poor here: "It is no disparagement to the finest hand to be reached forth to the needy" (*Notes on the Bible: Ruth*, p. 832). But this is not a text about the nobility of serving the poor. What Boaz gives to Ruth is justice (see 1:1). Doubtless aware that nativistic segregation is a problem (Judg. 19:11–12),

Boaz wants his fellow Bethlehemites to rise above passive tolera-tion and actively accept Ruth.

2:15–16 / After this first meal together, Boaz leaves fur-ther instructions for his workers: **Don't embarrass her. . . . Pull out some stalks for her . . . leave them for her to pick up, and don't re-buke her.** Two of these commands—"Pull out some stalks . . . leave them for her"—are positively framed. Two others—"Don't em-barrass . . . don't rebuke"—are prohibitive. There would be no need for Boaz to be so direct were the potential for abuse not so pervasive. When the Danites find the sleepy village of Laish, for example, they realize that there is "no one in the land to 'molest' them" (*kalam;* NJPS; NIV softens this to "embarrass"). For men like this, tolerance is often taken as a license to abuse. Boaz realizes this. Thus he uses this same word *(kalam)* to warn anyone who molests Ruth that there will be a price to pay.

2:17–18 / The action shifts back to Ruth. Earlier she in-sists on accompanying Naomi back to Judah. Lingering beside Boaz's field, she waits respectfully for permission to glean. After meeting Boaz, she **gleaned, gathered, threshed, carried, brought out,** and **gave** of her harvest to Naomi, gladly and gratefully. This string of verbs echoes Boaz's string of verbs.

2:19 / Whereas Boaz uses imperatives and Ruth uses declaratives (1:16–17), Naomi continues to rely on interrogatives. Questions bubble out of her pell-mell: **Where did you glean today? Where did you work?** Finally learning of Ruth's meeting with Boaz, Naomi pronounces a blessing, the first of several in the book: **Blessed be the man who took notice of you!**

Additional Note §9

2:19 / **Where did you glean?** Peterson ("The Pastoral Work of Story-Making: Ruth," in *Five Smooth Stones for Pastoral Work,* pp. 97–105) argues that Naomi's mode of speech is primarily interrogative.

§10 Naomi's Surprise (Ruth 2:20–23)

2:20 / After Naomi finds out the identity of this "man" (well after the sneak preview given to the reader in 2:1), she joyfully pronounces another blessing, this time directly invoking Yahweh's name: **The LORD bless him!** This blessing compares readily with the blessing pronounced by Micah's mother:

Naomi: The LORD bless him! (Ruth 2:20)

Micah's mother: The LORD bless you! (Judg. 17:2)

Whereas Micah's mother blesses the recovery of her silver so that it can be used to build "a carved image and a cast idol" (Judg. 17:3), Naomi blesses Yahweh for revealing to her that God has been at work all along, even in her darkest hour. Both mothers desire to bless the accomplishments of their children. The difference is in their theologies. One sees Yahweh as God. The other sees the *'elohim* as God. Micah's mother desires only to make sure that her son has the resources necessary to construct a "house of the gods" *(bet 'elohim)*. Mahlon's mother surrenders herself to Yahweh.

Yahweh **has not stopped showing his kindness** *(hesed)*. Though she may be tempted to believe otherwise, Naomi still believes in a God of *hesed*. Perhaps it's been decades since she's heard the name Boaz, yet she recognizes it. Hearing it enables Yahweh's *hesed* to steal quietly back into her heart. Josephus sees God's *hesed* as something only intermittently revealed to Israel (*Antiquities of the Jews* 2.7.1). Origen sees it as divine "condescension," the incarnation being the best example (*Against Celsus* 5.12). Calvin imagines *hesed* as something against which "sinners . . . have no defense" (*Institutes* 27). Augustine sees it as something "better than life," referring to it often as the reason for his own conversion (*Confessions* 11.29).

It is important to see that Naomi includes **the dead** family members (Elimelech, Mahlon, Kilion) as well as **the living** (Ruth,

Orpah). In spite of everything that has happened, her convictions about family remain unshakeable. Like all Syro-Palestinians, Naomi believes in an innate, mysterious connection between kin, cult, land, and the unseen world. Outside of the prophetic and apocalyptic texts, this statement is about as close to a resurrection faith as one can find in Scripture. The locus of this faith is the family. The means for reigniting it comes from family. Thus the corollary exclamation: **That man is our close relative; he is one of our kinsman-redeemers.**

2:21 / **He even said to me, "Stay with my workers until they finish harvesting all my grain."** Literally, Boaz instructs Ruth to cling to his young men. This is the third appearance of the verb "cling." Ruth clings to Naomi while Orpah returns to Moab (1:14). Boaz instructs Ruth to cling to his young girls, subtly moving her away from the fringes toward the center of Bethlehemite society (2:8). Now Ruth reports Boaz's words to Naomi, repeating this word a third time (2:21). Like all patriarchs, Boaz's instinct is to shelter those who are most vulnerable. Jacob does the same thing when he takes his family to meet Esau, carefully sheltering Rachel at the back of the caravan (Gen. 33:1–3). One Canaanite patriarch, Pabil, even tries to protect his family via economic payoffs to their enemies:

> Take silver and yellow metal, gold fresh from the mine,
> And perpetual slaves, triads of horses and chariots. . . .
> Take . . . the peace-offerings . . . and go away . . . from my house.
> Stay far away from my court. (Gibson, *Canaanite Myths and Legends*, p. 85)

2:22 / **It will be good for you, my daughter, to go with his girls, because in someone else's field you might be harmed.** Naomi understands what Boaz is trying to do and supports him wholeheartedly. Ruth's long-term welfare stands behind her own desire for Ruth to find a home (1:9; 3:1). Like Boaz, Naomi knows what the world is like, a violent place filled with "hot-tempered men" (Judg. 18:25).

2:23 / **So Ruth stayed close to the servant girls of Boaz to glean until the barley and wheat harvests were finished. And she lived with her mother-in-law.** Ruth 1 and 2 end with Ruth and Naomi seemingly alone against the world and a summary reference to harvest time in Bethlehem.

Additional Notes §10

2:20 / **To the living and the dead:** On the connection between kin, cult, land, and afterlife, see H. Brichto, "Kin, Cult, Land and After-life—A Biblical Complex," *HUCA* 44 (1973), pp. 1–54.

2:21 / On the Kirta myth, see the commentary on 1:3a.

2:22 / **You might be harmed:** R. Girard has given a great deal of thought to the problem of violence in the Bible, especially in *La Violence et le Sacré* (Paris: B. Grasset, 1972).

§11 Excursus: The Redeemer as Cultural Gyroscope

The word translated "kinsman-redeemer" in 2:20 (NIV) is the participial form of the verb *ga'al,* some form of which is repeated no fewer than twenty-one times in Ruth. This alone makes it one of the book's most important concepts. Some lexicographers divide it into separate semantic categories: *ga'al* I ("to redeem") and *ga'al* II ("to defile"). Others see a common root, "to cover," in the sense of "to cover positively" or "to protect/redeem" versus "to cover negatively," in the sense of "to stain/defile." This dispute remains unresolved because there is little cognate evidence outside of the Hebrew Bible to which we might profitably turn for lexicographical perspective. Syr consistently translates *go'el* ("redeemer") as "the one who asks for the inheritance" *(tb' yrtwt')* in Ruth, preferring to put more emphasis on the product than the agent of redemption.

In the Bible, there are at least five basic functions of the *go'el*-redeemer: he acquires the alienated property of a kinsman (Lev. 25:25); he purchases property in danger of being lost to a stranger (Jer. 32:6–15); he redeems relatives who have been reduced to slavery (Lev. 25:47–55); he avenges relatives' wrongful deaths (Num. 35:17–34); and he is obligated to support a relative's widow (Ruth 4:4–10).

Anthropologically, the function of the *go'el* is to restore societal equilibrium. In ancient Israel, where internal tribal controls are stronger than external legal constraints, the *go'el* functions as a cultural gyroscope (L. J. Luzbetak). Whenever and wherever there is a breach in the cultural fabric, the *go'el* serves as the restorative agent.

Reading Ruth anthropologically goes a long way toward resolving one of the book's most celebrated problems, namely, whether Ruth's marriage to Boaz is better defined as "redemption" (Hb. *ge'ullah*) or as "levirate" (from the word *levir,* "husband's brother," the Latin translation of Hb. *yabam,* Deut. 25:5).

L. M. Epstein sees only the *ge'ullah* here ("redemption marriage"), dismissing all allusions to the levirate as later interpolation. J. G. Frazer hypothesizes a continuum in which Canaanite polygamy and polyandry slowly evolve into the Israelite institutions of levirate and *ge'ullah,* positioning Ruth's marriage somewhere in the middle. M. Burrows sees here "a transitional stage between redemption-marriage as an affair of the clan and levirate-marriage as an affair of the family." J. Sasson argues for disentangling *ge'ullah* from Ruth's marriage because the *ge'ullah,* in his opinion, is of interest to the narrator of Ruth only insofar as it pertains to Naomi's fate.

None of these solutions is completely satisfying. Some conclude too much from too little evidence; others make antiquated distinctions between clan and family (see the discussion on *mishpakhah* at 2:1). Very few approach the problem from an anthropological perspective. Manslaughter, murder, war, death, widowhood, slavery, and poverty are all agents, indications, or results of disequilibrium. The *go'el* is the agent of (re)equilibrium. Sociolinguistic debates over terminology (levirate versus *ge'ullah*) will continue to remain irresolvable as long as they fail to get at what H. H. Rowley calls "the wider duties devolving on the next-of-kin" ("The Marriage of Ruth," in *The Servant of the Lord and Other Essays on the Old Testament* [Oxford: Blackwell, 1965], p. 179).

Boaz is the cultural gyroscope of Elimelech's family. "Redeemer" can still appropriately translate the Hebrew *go'el* as long as it is adequately defined. The English word "redeem" comes from a Latin verb, *reddere,* which means "to give/buy back" and is a term fundamentally rooted in law and economics. *Ga'al,* however, is a Hebrew word designed to denote the process of restoring the created order, including, but not limited to, the legal, socioeconomic, and theological aspects of that order. Thus Yahweh himself is the quintessential *go'el,* the compassionate Redeemer who delivers Israel from every distress (Ps. 78:35; Isa. 52:3).

Additional Note §11

This excursus is a condensed revision of M. Moore, "*Haggō'ēl:* The Cultural Gyroscope of Ancient Hebrew Society," *RQ* 23 (1980), pp. 27–35. Among other lexica, BDB 145–46 and KB 162–63 divide *ga'al* into *ga'al* I and *ga'al* II. A. Johnson, "The Primary Meaning of *ga'al*," VTSup 1 (1953), pp. 73–74, argues for a single root meaning. J. Unterman has a summary discussion in "The Social-Legal Origin for the Image of God as Redeemer of Israel," in *Pomegranates and Golden Bells: Studies in Biblical, Jewish, and Ancient Near Eastern Ritual, Law, and Literature in Honor of Jacob Milgrom* (ed. D. Wright, D. N. Freedman, and A. Hurvitz; Winona Lake, Ind.: Eisenbrauns, 1995), pp. 399–405.

On the anthropological notion of cultural gyroscope see L. J. Luzbetak, *The Church and Cultures* (Pasadena: William Carey Library, 1970), p. 221. On the debated relationship between levirate and *ge'ullah,* see L. M. Epstein, *Marriage Laws in the Bible and the Talmud* (Cambridge: Harvard University Press, 1942), pp. 86–87; J. G. Frazer, *Folklore in the Old Testament* (3 vols.; London: Macmillan, 1919), 2:304; M. Burrows, "The Marriage of Boaz and Ruth," *JBL* 59 (1940), p. 453; and J. Sasson, "The Issue of *ge'ullah* in Ruth," *JSOT* 5 (1978), pp. 52–64.

§12 Naomi's Strategy (Ruth 3:1–4)

Naomi is Ruth's mother-in-law (*khamot*, 2:23). This feminine form of *kham* ("father-in-law") is widely perceived by lexicographers to be a nominal derivative of the unattested verb **khamah*. Cognates of this word appear in extrabiblical literature (Arabic *khamay*, "to protect, defend"; OSA *ḥmh*, "sacred precinct, protective association"), and the root idea seems to be protection, shelter, or refuge. An Arabic attorney, for example, is a *muḥamin* ("protector"), while an Egyptian "protector" is a *ḥmy*. Hebrew *khamot* stands in this same semantic field, as does the term *khomah* ("wall"). Naomi sees herself as Ruth's wall of defense.

3:1 / Naomi returns to her earlier concern (see 1:9), **My daughter, should I not try to find** [lit. seek] **a home for you?** assuming the responsibility of "seeking out" (*baqash*; see Ezek. 34:16) for Ruth a place of rest (see *menukhah* in 1:9). Not only does she believe that Ruth needs a home, she also believes it to be her responsibility to help her find it. Underscoring this parental concern, Tg translates this line, "I swear I shall not rest (*l' 'nykh*) until the time when I claim for you a resting place (*nykh'*), in order that you might be happy" (*Tg. Ruth* 3:1).

3:2 / **Is not Boaz, with whose servant girls you have been, a kinsman of ours?** In the Syriac Bible, Naomi calls Boaz *mkhkwmtn* ("our kinsman"). What makes this interpretation so interesting is that this is not the same Syr word for "kinsman" in 2:1, though the Hebrew word is the same in both texts (*moda'*). The root of the Syr word here is *khkm*, which means "to know," particularly "to know sexually." The *mkhkwmt* is the cultural gyroscope responsible for knowing a widow in order to raise up seed for the dead. Syr's interpretation brilliantly gets to the heart of Naomi's realization. Finding Boaz may seem serendipitous (see 2:3), but not for Naomi. Naomi sees the hand of Yahweh at work. The same hand that once afflicted or testified (1:21) now heals and restores. Doubtless Ruth would have found one of Elimelech's kinsmen sooner or later ("Is there a man in Israel who has no kinsmen?" *b. Qidd.* 21a), yet to find one so quickly astonishes Naomi.

Tonight he will be winnowing barley on the threshing floor. Since one of the most pivotal scenes of the book takes place on a threshing floor *(goren)*, one might imagine it to be a very private encounter. Yet Israelite threshing floors are very public places. People stream through them constantly, buying and selling goods of all sorts, not just threshed grain. In fact, so central are they to Israelite commerce, the idiomatic way to ask "Where can I find that?" in Modern Hebrew is still ". . . from the threshing floor or the wine press?" Festivals are celebrated there (Deut. 16:13–17). Prostitutes ply their trade there (Hos. 9:1).

Naomi is asking Ruth to go to a very public place and take a very public risk. Ruth's intentions could easily be mistaken for those of any streetwalker (Hos. 9:1). This is probably why Boaz tells his men afterward not to "let it be known that a woman came to the threshing floor" (3:14).

3:3 / Complementing the verbal command sequences of Ruth (1:16–17) and Boaz (2:8–14), Naomi now issues a command sequence of her own (3:3–18): *Wash . . . Anoint . . . Put on . . . Go down . . . Do not make known . . . Know . . . Go . . . Uncover . . . Lie down . . . Wait.*

The command **Wash and perfume yourself, and put on your best clothes** seems clear enough, yet *Ruth Rabbah* cannot resist the temptation to translate "wash yourself clean of your idolatry," anoint yourself with "good deeds," and put on "Sabbath clothes" *(Ruth Rab.* 5.12). **Go down to the threshing floor.** MT (Ketib) can be read as "I will go down" *(yrdty)*, especially since early scribes correct to *yrdt* (Qere, "you go down"). Reading the first person ketib, *Ruth Rabbah* even has Naomi awkwardly add, "my merits will descend with you" *(Ruth Rab.* 5.12). Yet *yrdty* is probably an older second person feminine form (Syr, Tg, and Vg all translate as second person). In other words, Ruth is alone when she meets Boaz at the threshing floor.

Sexual connotations often orbit around the Hebrew term for "know" *(yada')*, but nowhere is this more subtle than in the instruction **Don't let him know you are there,** particularly in light of the canonical-historical context. The perigee, or lowest point, of this orbit occurs when a gang of violent men taunt and terrorize a frightened old Gibeahite, demanding that he "bring out the man who came to your house so that we might 'know' him" *(neda'ennu,*

Judg. 19:22). The apogee, or highest point, occurs when Naomi delicately cautions her daughter-in-law not to let herself become known too quickly by Boaz, their newly discovered kinsman (Syr *mkhkwmt,* from *khkm,* "to know sexually"). One kind of knowledge is destructive and violent. The other is patient and gentle.

3:4 / Instead of **Uncover his feet and lie down,** the Syriac reads, "you shall draw near and lie down near his feet" *(wtqrbyn wtdmkyn lwt rglwhy).* The word for "feet," as is well known, can be a euphemism for "genitalia" (1 Sam. 24:4; Isa. 6:2). Syr would have Ruth "uncover" nothing (the verb is conspicuously absent in Syr). Targum has Naomi add, "and you shall request counsel from him" *(wth' sh'yl' mynyh 'yt').* Both options are more politically correct than textually precise. Both deal with the sexual tension in this encounter by euphemizing it. Naomi does not tell Ruth to uncover "his feet" (Hb. *raglayw)* but rather the "place of his feet" (MT *margelotayw).* This is a rare term found only four times in the Hebrew Bible (three of which are in this chapter, 3:4, 7, 8). In Modern Hebrew this word denotes "the place for the feet, the bottom," for example, of a bedstead.

The versions offer little interpretive help. LXX reads "you shall uncover the things (?) near his feet" *(apokalupseis ta pros podon autou),* a translation that does little more than recognize the problem, not resolve it. Syr reads "his feet" *(rglwhy),* as does Tg *(ryglwy),* even though the more closely equivalent term *(mrglwtyw)* is readily available in Tg's lexicon. In sum, Naomi tells Ruth to do something risky, but precisely how much of this can be characterized as sexual should remain an open question.

Additional Notes §12

3:1 / **Mother-in-law:** On *khamot* ("mother-in-law"), see the article on *khomah* in *TDOT* 4:267 and BDB 327. On *mukhamin* ("defender"), see *Dictionary of Modern Written Arabic* (ed. H. Wehr and M. Cowan; Ithaca, N.Y.: Cornell University Press, 1966), p. 209. On *khmy,* see *Wörterbuch der Ägyptischen Sprache* (ed. A. Erman and H. Grapow; repr.; Leipzig: J. C. Hinrichs, 1963), 3, p. 80.

My daughter: O. Loretz ("The Theme of the Ruth Story," *CBQ* 22 [1960], pp. 391–99) emphasizes that Ruth is a story about the preservation of Elimelech's family in the face of powerful destructive forces.

S. Niditch ("The 'Sodomite' Theme in Judges 19–20: Family, Community, and Social Disintegration," *CBQ* 44 [1982], pp. 365–78) reads Judg. 19–21 as the story of a domestic dispute that escalates into civil war.

3:2 / **Kinsman:** On Syr *mkhkwmt* see PSSD 264.

Threshing floor: On the idiom "from the threshing floor or the wine press?" see R. Alcalay, *The Complete Hebrew-English Dictionary* (Jerusalem: Masada, 1981), p. 385.

3:3 / **Then go down:** On *yrdty* as an old second person feminine, see *GHB* § 42b and GKC § 44h.

3:4 / **Uncover his feet:** G. Gerleman (*"Brglyw* as an Idiomatic Phrase," *JSS* 1 [1959], p. 59) suggests that *brglyw* (Job 18:8; Judg. 5:15) does not mean "by his feet" but "on the spot, instantly." For Modern Hebrew *margelot,* see Alcalay, *Hebrew-English Dictionary,* p. 1491.

§13 Ruth's Submission (Ruth 3:5–6)

3:5–6 / Ruth's response to Naomi is clear and straightforward. **I will do whatever you say.** Notice Ruth does not say, "I will do whatever Boaz says," even though Naomi has just told her, "He will tell you what to do." In point of fact, Ruth will soon be telling Boaz what he needs to do. **So she went down to the threshing floor and did everything her mother-in-law told her to do.** Ruth's behavior here stands in direct contrast to her earlier behavior. In Moab, Naomi commands her to return to her mother's house (1:8), and Ruth politely disregards her (1:14), eloquently arguing against her mother-in-law's strategy (1:16–17). Here, however, she readily submits to Naomi's command. Why? One could argue that circumstances have changed. Ruth is no longer standing on her own turf. Does the strangeness of her new surroundings, her new life, and her new role somehow contribute to a newfound docility? Are there other factors to consider?

Naomi faces a profound conflict. She believes in a God, Yahweh, who commands her, like every other Hebrew, to "be fruitful and multiply" (Gen. 1:28). Yet having lost every male in her family, this seems impossible. Her approach to this conflict, however, is not to use Ruth as "bait" in a scheme to blackmail Boaz with the threat of "public scandal" (D. N. Fewell and D. M. Gunn, *Compromising Redemption: Relating Characters in the Book of Ruth* [Louisville, Ky.: Westminster John Knox, 1990], p. 78). Hers rather is the classic approach of the ancient Near Eastern wise woman. Though she is never called a wise woman, Naomi does what all wise women do: she is a mediator. This is a very ancient female role, habitually enacted as early as the thirteenth century B.C.E. by Anatolian wise women (the ᴬᴸŠU.GI priestesses).

In ancient Anatolia, wise women enact mediatorial roles in order to resolve conflicts of all sorts—spiritual, theological, sociological, economic, political, and psychological. Conflict resolution for them is saturated in the rituals of homeopathic magic: If an abstract evil can be transferred into a concrete image of clay or wax, then the action taken to deal with the image somehow deals with the evil itself. To destroy, expel, or curse a homeopathic image is therefore to destroy, expel, or curse the evil that it contains. Parallelism lies at the heart of homeopathic magic.

Parallelism also lies at the heart of Hebrew mediatorial counseling, only here the efficacy of the healing process depends more on logic than magic. In 1 and 2 Samuel, for example, three wise women make effective use of parallelism. The wise woman of Tekoa has David make a decision in the imaginary world (*parable*, 2 Sam. 14:4–11) before leading him to make a decision in the real world (*praxis*, 14:12–24). The wise woman of Abel engages Joab with proverbial and metaphorical speech (*parable*, 2 Sam. 20:18–19) before taking action to resolve a military conflict (*praxis*, 20:22). Abigail deftly parallels words of wisdom (1 Sam. 25:24–31) with swift action (25:18–23) to stop a range war between David and her husband.

Parallelistic patterns of *parable + praxis* also shape the counseling strategies of Esther, Judith, and Naomi. In contrast to Mordecai's classically prophetic approach, Esther chooses not to confront Haman directly. Instead she diplomatically manipulates him into a false sense of confidence (Esth. 5:1–8; 7:1–5), then hangs him on his own gallows (7:6–10). The apocryphal story of Judith takes the pattern of *parable + praxis* to baroque extremes. Like the wise woman of Tekoa, Judith spins a web of words in a powerful, hypnotic way (8:11–27; 8:32–34; 9:2–14; 11:5–19). Like Ruth, she "makes herself beautiful," arraying herself "in all her finery" (10:4; 12:15). Like the warrior Jael, she knows exactly when to take swift action (13:6–10; see Judg. 4:17–22).

So Naomi and Ruth do the same thing. Naomi plans *(parable)* and Ruth implements *(praxis)*. Naomi wants Boaz to make a decision about Ruth *(parable)* so she can help him make a decision about Elimelech's heritage *(praxis)*. That Ruth is willing to participate is no sign of desperation, anxiety, codependency, or lust. Nor is she driven simply by what Gunkel calls "the heroism of faith" *(Ruth,* p. 76). Naomi and Ruth are enacting time-honored roles, and they know exactly what they are doing.

Additional Note §13

3:5–6　/　For further study, see M. Moore, "Wise Women in the Bible: Identifying a Trajectory," in *Essays on Women in Earliest Christianity*, vol. 2 (ed. C. D. Osburn; 2 vols.; Joplin, Mo.: College Press, 1995), 2:96–101. V. Haas and I. Wegner (*Die Rituale der Beschwörerinnen* [SAL]ŠU.GI [Corpus der Hurritischen Sprachdenkmaler I/5; Roma: Multigrafica Editrice, 1988], pp. 1–4) describe in detail what [SAL]ŠU.GI priestesses do.

§14 Boaz's Leadership (Ruth 3:7–18)

3:7 / Harvest is a joyful time, especially after a famine, and so, **when Boaz had finished eating and drinking** he **was in good spirits.** As Gunkel puts it, "Erntezeit ist Segenzeit" ("harvest-time is blessing-time," *Ruth,* p. 71). Boaz heartily celebrates the barley harvest until he finds himself in "good spirits" (lit. "his heart became happy," *wayyitab libbo*). Often in Northwest Semitic marriage contracts this idiom is used to emphasize that the parties to the marriage are acting out of free will rather than compulsion. Significantly, this same idiom appears in Judges 19:9, where the Levite's father-in-law, in a vain attempt to keep him from leaving, begs him to "let your heart become happy." The parallels are telling. One man, Boaz, joyously celebrates the end of a tragic time, the Judean famine with all of its attendant miseries, while the other, the Levite's father-in-law, hollowly celebrates his daughter's departure with a heart full of anxiety.

He went over to lie down at the far end of the grain pile. The word translated "grain pile" in NIV *('aremah)* can denote a mound of anything, not just grain. One poet languidly describes the abdomen of his lover as "a mound *('aremah)* of wheat encircled by lilies" (Song 7:3). **Ruth approached quietly, uncovered his feet and lay down.** The word for "quietly" *(ballat)* elsewhere describes David's stealth in approaching Saul at a delicate private moment (1 Sam. 24:5). Syr humorously has Ruth wait until Boaz starts "snoring" *(bmkhly').*

3:8 / That nothing more takes place until **the middle of the night** implies that Ruth has to lie down next to Boaz for more than just a few minutes. Anyone who has ever camped outside in a strange place will identify with this scene. This may be one of the longest nights of Ruth's life. **Something startled the man** (lit. "the man trembled," *kharad*). Like Isaac (Gen. 27:33), Elihu (Job 37:1), and Saul (1 Sam. 28:5), Boaz trembles. Perhaps Boaz is startled by a Job-like nightmare experience: "You will lie down, with no one to make you tremble" (*kharad,* Zophar to Job in 11:19, my translation). Targum poetically speculates that Boaz's "trembling" *(rtt)* is the trembling of "tenderness" *(rkk)* but quickly adds that Boaz feels no "erotic desire" for Ruth *(yts ryh, Tg. Ruth* 3:8). Perhaps Boaz is startled by Ruth's elbow in his ribs!

3:9 / When Boaz asks **Who are you?** Ruth does not call herself a "foreign woman" *(nokriyyah,* 2:10), nor does she call herself a "young girl" *(na'arah).* Instead, she discreetly says, **I am your servant Ruth,** using a more centrist term, "your servant" *('amatekah).* What comes out of her mouth next, however, is anything but discreet. Laying aside Naomi's instructions to let Boaz do the talking (3:4), she immediately blurts out, **Spread the corner of your garment over me.** MT reads "Spread your wing *(kanap)."* Syr reads "Spread the 'wing' of your cloak" *(ks' . . . bknp' dmrtwtk).* Targum departs altogether, reading, "Put your name over your servant" *(Tg. Ruth* 3:9). NIV follows Syr in sacrificing metaphorical imagery for supposed clarity.

Reading with MT, however, Ruth picks up Boaz's earlier metaphor ("under whose wings *[kenapayw]* you have come to take refuge," 2:12) and refashions it to suggest to this *go'el* that it is his responsibility to become Yahweh's wing. Like the wise woman of Tekoa, Ruth proves that she is not inexperienced in traversing the path between *parable* and *praxis* (see 2 Sam. 14:4–24 and §13).

Ruth's tête-à-tête with Boaz sharply contrasts with the incident in Judges 19:22–30. Reading these texts in tandem, one cannot help but note how this passage counteracts and subverts its canonical-historical counterpart. Here a woman initiates a risky nocturnal encounter with a well-respected community leader. There a mob plots homosexual, then settles for heterosexual, rape. Here a woman covers herself with her best clothes. There a mob covers all the exits of escape. Here a woman lies down and waits for a man to open the door. There a gang surrounds a man's home, pounding violently on the door. Here a woman moves quietly and discreetly. There a gang bellows loudly and publicly. Here a man tries to protect a woman's reputation. There a gang "toys with" a woman *('alal;* NIV: abuses). Here an older man makes tender promises. There a younger man makes crude demands ("Get up! Let's go!"). Interpreted in its context, the book of Ruth challenges the simplistic militance prevalent among some that "patriarchal sexuality" is *the* reason for "eroticized violence" against women (A. Gilson, *Eros Breaking Free: Interpreting Sexual Theo-Ethics* [Cleveland: Pilgrim, 1995], p. 127).

3:10 / Boaz responds, **The LORD bless you, my daughter.** Gunkel wonders whether Boaz duly appreciates Ruth's struggle to overcome "her natural female shyness," but this is another extremist stereotype (*Ruth*, p. 77). Ruth has many character traits, but shyness is not one of them. When Boaz says, **This kindness is greater than that which you showed earlier,** he presumably has in mind Ruth's earlier *hesed* toward Naomi. Targum, however, thinks that Boaz is referring to Ruth's conversion (*Tg. Ruth* 3:10). By "this kindness" Boaz refers to Ruth's decision not to **run after the younger men, whether rich or poor.** Boaz is pleased by the fact that Ruth has decided to put the needs of Elimelech's family ahead of her own.

3:11 / Recognizing that it takes a strong faith not only to leave one's homeland but also to approach a strange man in a public place, Boaz immediately assures her, **Don't be afraid.** As E. W. Conrad points out, biblical characters often hear this assurance formula under times of stress. (See *Fear Not, Warrior: A Study of 'al tirâ' Pericopes in the Hebrew Scriptures* [Chico, Calif.: Scholars, 1985], pp. 76–78.) **All my fellow townsmen know** (lit. all the gate of my people, a characteristically Hebraic idiom). **You are a woman of noble character.** Boaz feminizes the title *('eshet khayil)* by which he himself is introduced (*gibbor khayil*, 2:1). "The same word *(khayil)* describes the greatness of possessions and the uprightness of character" (Gunkel, *Ruth*, pp. 70, 78). Ruth is the only female character in Judges 17–Ruth 4 to be pronounced an *'eshet khayil* (see "worthy woman" in Prov. 31:10).

3:12 / Boaz tries to communicate to Ruth something of the complex world of Israelite kinship networks (see §11): **there is a kinsman-redeemer nearer than I.** That there can be a multiplicity of kinsman-redeemers in any family clan, some nearer than others *(go'el qarob)* seems possible not only from a practical perspective but also from a legal one (note the priestly instructions about "the nearest redeemer" in Lev. 25:25, *go'alo haqqarob*). What makes Boaz stand out against his contemporaries, however, is that even though he knows his legal place (*not* the "nearest redeemer") he still commits to helping Ruth. Inevitably some scholars will argue that his intentions are to take advantage of Naomi's loss in order to seize Elimelech's land. It seems wiser, however, to examine him alongside his canonical-historical contemporaries before guessing at his motives (§15).

3:13 / **Stay here for the night.** Boaz goes into protection mode because he does not want Ruth to navigate her way home unaccompanied. Doubtless there are other inebriated men sleeping on this threshing floor who might want to spread their skirt over this unescorted young woman.

That Boaz makes the observation **if he wants to redeem, good; let him redeem** at this point in their encounter seems proof that this is no infatuated youngster easily swept away by emotion. Boaz seems willing to let Israel's social security system run its course apart from any personal involvement on his part. Perhaps this is not the first time he has had to deal with a situation like this. The Talmud is full of sticky cases where men like Boaz regularly have to decide how to apply biblical law to real life. In one case, for example, a man promises his neighbor, "This field which I have mortgaged to you shall be consecrated after I have redeemed it" (*b. Ketub.* 59b). As anyone who has ever bought or sold property will attest, something can always go wrong before closing. Thus the rabbis advise the buyer not to overcommit too soon. Similar wisdom is called for here. It is one thing for Ruth to appeal to Boaz for help. It is quite another to ignore the societal, legal, and economic institutions responsible for handling such requests.

Deuteronomic law allows for the possibility that the nearest relative may not be willing (*lo' khapats;* cf. Deut. 25:7). Boaz wants Ruth to understand this clearly. **But if he is not willing, as surely as the LORD lives I will do it.** By sealing this promise with an oath Boaz takes yet another unnecessary risk. The taking of oaths is no light matter in ancient Israel. Even foolish oaths have to be honored (see Jephthah's oath in Judg. 11:35).

3:14–18 / From this point on Boaz takes the lead in providing closure to this encounter. First, he nips rumors: **Don't let it be known that a woman came to the threshing floor.** Second, he shares with Ruth for the second time (2:14) from the bounty of his harvest. **"Bring me the shawl you are wearing and hold it out." When she did so, he poured into it six measures of barley** [lit. six barlies]. **Then he went back to town.** Syr reads "then *she* packed up and went to town" (*wshqlt w'tt-ᵯndynt'*), followed by Vg, but NIV is doubtless correct. Third, he sends Ruth back as a messenger to inform Naomi that her **empty-handed** days are over (*reqām,* v. 17; see the identical term in 1:21). Naomi's response to Boaz's action is to tell Ruth to **wait . . . until you find out**

what happens. For the man will not rest [lit. "remain inactive," *shāqat;* not the same root for "rest" in 1:9 and 3:1] **until the matter is settled today.**

Additional Notes §14

3:7 / **Good spirits:** On the use of *wayyitab libbo* ("his heart became happy"), see R. Westbrook, "The Phrase 'His Heart Is Satisfied' in Ancient Near Eastern Legal Sources," *JAOS* 111 (1991), pp. 220–22.

3:11 / **Fellow townsmen:** LXX reads "tribe *(phule)* of my people." Syr reads "generation of my people" *(shrbt' d'my).* Vg combines these options to read, "all of the people who live inside the gates of the city."
Woman of noble character: A. Wolters, ("Proverbs XXXI 10–31 as Heroic Hymn: A Form-Critical Analysis," *VT* 38 [1988], pp. 446–57) sees "noble woman" *('eshet khayil)* and "noble man" *(gibbor khayil)* as contrapuntal terms.

3:12 / **Kinsman-redeemer nearer than I:** Boaz's "mercenary motives" are hypothesized by Gunkel, *Ruth,* p. 79, and Fewell and Gunn, *Compromising Redemption,* p. 75.

3:13 / **Let him redeem:** W. Brueggemann (*Theology of the Old Testament* [Minneapolis: Fortress, 1997], pp. 173–76) lists *ga'al* ("redeem") as a "verb of deliverance" designed to "enunciate Yahweh's resolved capacity to intervene decisively against every oppressive, alienating circumstance."

3:16–18 / **Barley:** K. Nielsen (*Ruth: A Commentary* [OTL; Louisville, Ky.: Westminster John Knox, 1997], p. 80) thinks it "no coincidence that both chapters 2 and 3 end with gifts of grain," because "the book uses the need for grain . . . as a leitmotif, and alongside this, the need for an heir."

§15 Excursus: On Patriarchal Leadership

Although Boaz enacts a role as prototypical husband, what he does for Ruth on this threshing floor is best understood, perhaps, by comparing it with the behavior of the other father figures in the immediate context: the Levite's concubine's father (Judg. 19:2–10) and the old Gibeahite (19:16–26). Each of these father figures tries to do what is best for his children yet fails miserably. The goals of the Levite's father-in-law, for example, are hazy. Does he want to keep his daughter home indefinitely? Is it his intention to persuade his son-in-law to stay in Bethlehem? Does he know something about the bad reputation of the Gibeahites? And what about his methods? Is he trying, like other biblical characters, to wear down his house-guest with food and drink (like David with Uriah, 2 Sam. 11:12–13)? Or is he simply unable or unwilling to make a decision?

The old Gibeahite faces a fierce challenge. He has to make a split-second decision before a violent mob pounds down his door. Boaz, by contrast, has only to deal with a perfumed young woman. In one sense it seems unfair to compare these two men. Yet the contrasts are telling. Whereas Boaz projects every confidence that he is the man to help Ruth, the Gibeahite seems bewildered. At no time does he appear to understand how futile it is to negotiate with a street gang. Like Neville Chamberlain, the British prime minister who underestimated Adolf Hitler, he seems to rely only on the rightness of his cause:

> The owner of the house went outside and said to them, "No, my friends, don't be so vile. Since this man is my guest, don't do this disgraceful thing. Look, here is my virgin daughter, and his concubine. I will bring them out to you now, and you can use them and do to them whatever you wish. But to this man, don't do such a disgraceful thing." But the men would not listen to him. So the man took his concubine and sent her outside to them. (Judg. 19:23–25)

This is a classic case of good intentions substituting for leadership. First, the Gibeahite tries to address a lust-driven mob as "my friends" (lit. my brothers, *akhay*), attempting to converse civilly with a group the narrator himself calls the "sons of Belial" (19:22). Then, after begging them not to be "vile" (*ra'a'*) and "disgraceful" (*nebalah*), he himself does something vile and disgraceful. In place of the Ephraimite male they want to know, he offers them the man's wife. He chooses to sacrifice the most defenseless person in his house—the opposite of what faithful patriarchs do.

By contrast, Boaz's vision of pastoral care utterly astonishes Ruth. Boaz, as Andersen puts it, " 'does *hesed*'; he does not merely *appear* to be like a man who 'does *hesed*' " ("Yahweh, the Kind and Sensitive God," in O'Brien and Peterson, eds., p. 82). Unlike the Levite's father-in-law, Boaz convinces a council of his peers to let him take a foreign widow "under his wing." Unlike the old Gibeahite, Boaz courageously takes a stand. The father figures in Judges become examples of failure in a depressing string of failure stories (Judg. 17–21), while Boaz becomes a role model for future generations.

Additional Note §15

Penetrating discussions of "postmodern male bewilderment" appear in E. Cose (*A Man's World* [San Francisco: HarperCollins, 1995], pp. 7–14), D. Blankenhorn (*Fatherless America* [New York: Basic Books, 1995], pp. 3–9), and G. Gilder (*Men and Marriage* [Gretna, La.: Pelican, 1993], pp. ix–x). On leadership issues generally, see W. Bennis and B. Nanus (*Leaders: Strategies for Taking Charge* [New York: HarperCollins, 1997], pp. 82–87).

§16 Boaz's Transaction (Ruth 4:1–8)

4:1 / Boaz does not go directly to Elimelech's kinsman's house, nor does he summon him to his own. Instead, he goes to **the town gate. When the kinsman-redeemer he had mentioned came along** (lit. "wandered by," *'abar*), Boaz says, **Come over here, my friend, and sit down.** The narrator portrays this all-important meeting like the chance meeting of Ruth and Boaz in 2:3, but events only seem to happen by chance in Ruth. Boaz's patient anticipation at Bethlehem's gate contrasts sharply with the Levite's anxious sitting in the Gibeahite town square (Judg. 19:15).

We never learn the personal name of Elimelech's kinsman. Boaz addresses him only as Mr. So-and-So (*peloni 'almoni*; 1 Sam. 21:3; 2 Kgs. 6:8). LXX translates this idiom with the Gk word *kruphios* ("secret, hidden"), but the rationale for this is unclear (perhaps *kruphios* has a colloquial connotation). In Syr, Mr. So-and-So voices a response, "What?" (*mn'*). Sasson sees *peloni 'almoni* as an example of farrago (onomatopoeic wordplay like "hodge-podge" or "helter-skelter"; *Ruth*, p. 106).

4:2 / It is not surprising that **Boaz took ten of the elders of the town.** In Israel, all important social, legal, and religious questions are decided by "the elders at the gate" (Deut. 22:15). Elders appear in connection with five important Deuteronomic laws: blood redemption (19:12), expiation of murder by an unknown assailant (21:1–9), rebellious sons (21:18–21), defamation of virgins (22:13–21), and levirate marriage (25:5–10). The common denominator seems to be that these are domestic cases involving family law (judges, not elders, habitually deal with cases involving criminal law). Rabbinic tradition institutionalizes Boaz's choice of ten as the optimum number for such councils (*b. Ketub.* 7a–b).

4:3 / **The piece of land that belonged to our brother Elimelech.** According to MT, LXX, Syr, Tg, and Vg, Boaz's first words to Mr. So-and-So focus on the problem of land. NIV, KJV, NKJV, ASV, NASV, RSV, NRSV, and NJPS, however, all defer this clause to the end of the sentence, replacing it with the secondary clause, **Naomi, who has come back from Moab.** The ancient versions follow MT's order, yet contemporary English versions (with the notable exception of NEB) characteristically reshape this encounter to make it look like Boaz is more interested in Naomi (see 3:9). He may well be, but this is not the tack he takes with the elders. Instead, this farmer wants to talk to his neighboring farmers about land and inheritance rights, subjects dear to their agrarian hearts. In rural economies, questions about absentee land ownership cannot be left indefinitely open (Neh. 5:3; *b. B. Qam.* 60b).

Boaz convenes this meeting to resolve three separate, related problems: the reincorporation of Elimelech's land into Bethlehem's social economy, the preservation of Elimelech's name, and the redemption of Naomi from poverty. Gathering his thoughts under the keyword "sell" *(makerah)*, Boaz melds all three of these concerns into one package. Like a good salesperson, he speaks to the needs of his customer.

4:4 / The NIV's rendering, **I thought I should bring the matter to your attention** (lit. uncover your ear), misses the deliberate Hebrew wordplay: Boaz wants the *go'el* to *galah* ("redeemer to uncover"). Note here the two-part sales strategy. In stage one, Boaz affably dangles the prospect of economic windfall before the eyes of Mr. So-and-So, then walks him through the formulaic language of the proposed contract, gently reminding him that **no one has the right** to buy Elimelech's land **except you, and I am next in line.** Finally he closes the sale by urging everyone present, including the elders, to remember that time is of the essence. Anxious clients are waiting for a decision. To this, the kinsman immediately responds, **I will redeem it.**

4:5 / In stage two, however, Boaz deftly adds, **On the day you buy the land from Naomi and from Ruth the Moabitess, you acquire** (reading Qere *qanitah*) **the dead man's widow, in order to maintain the name of the dead with his property.** This, finally, is the fine print, the catch shrewdly worded in three preconditions. First, although this is a land transaction, fundamentally it has to do with preserving the connection between the land and "the name of the dead" (Lev. 25:25–28). Second, though this deal is economic, fundamentally it is socioeconomically intended to satisfy the fraternal obligation of Elimelech's kinsmen to his widow (Deut. 25:5–10). Like an unnamed royal official in Elisha's time,

Boaz feels duty-bound to help manage the property-retrieval problems of a desperate Israelite woman (2 Kgs. 8:6).

Third, and most remarkably, Boaz insists that "Ruth the Moabitess" be included as a part of the package. Unlike the previous two conditions, this one goes well beyond the traditions of Mosaic law. Why include Ruth? Why specifically mention the fact that she is a Moabitess? Is it because Boaz wants Naomi's land for himself, and so, by inserting this precondition last, he reckons that Mr. So-and-So will gag on the deal? (Gunkel thinks so, calling this "pure peasant-farmer thinking," *Ruth,* p. 79.) Is it because he has genuinely fallen in love with Ruth and does not want to lose her (*Ruth Rab.* 7.9)? Or is it because he knows that Naomi is unable to bear a child for the continuance of Elimelech's line (1:12)?

And what about Mr. So-and-So? Does he subscribe to a nativistic interpretation of Deuteronomy 23:3–5 ("No Moabite shall enter Yahweh's assembly . . .") like the one in *Targum Ruth,* or is he more attracted to the flexible interpretation taken by the Talmud on this biblical passage (*b. Yeb.* 76–77)? Is his commitment to the Yahwistic vision of "blessing the nations" as hollow as that of his contemporaries (Judg. 19:12), or is he as visionary as the later prophets with regard to "foreigners" (e.g., Isa. 56:6–8)? The text does not say. The beauty of great literature is that it allows readers to ponder such questions repeatedly and reflectively.

Whatever Boaz's motives or Mr. So-and-So's predilections, this is more than just fine print. Interpreted against its canonical-historical context, stage two of Boaz's proposal is a bold attempt to apply the tenets of Hebraic Yahwism to the needs of a desperately vulnerable family. Boaz believes that his God, Yahweh, is a god of justice (see 1:1), a God determined to save the landless as well as the landed, foreigners as well as Israelites, women as well as men. Historical debates over legal forms (levirate versus *ge'ullah*) and literary debates over genre (novella versus short story) too often obscure this truth.

4:6 / Hearing these preconditions, Mr. So-and-So reexamines his options and replies, **I cannot redeem it.** He fears that Boaz's proposal might **endanger** (lit. destroy, *shakhat*) **my own estate** ("inheritance," *nakhelah*), though he never says why. **You redeem it yourself. I cannot do it.** Rabbi Samuel ben Nakhman argues that Mr. So-and-So balks because he does not want his seed to be "contaminated" (*Ruth Rab.* 7.7). Whether this is true or not, the canonical-historical irony is that here we have an individual kinsman in possession of an inheritance *(nakhelah)* fearing for its endangerment, while in Judges we have a wandering tribe, the Danites, frantically searching for an inheritance *(nakhelah,* Judg. 18:1).

4:7 / **Now in earlier times.** The word translated "earlier times" *(lepanim,* "formerly") often introduces geographical (e.g., Deut. 2:10, 12, 20; Josh. 11:10; 14:15; Judg. 1:10, 11, 23) and anthropological parentheses (e.g., 1 Sam. 9:9; Ruth 4:7). This particular parenthesis gives us a glimpse into the distant past. Every culture formalizes the exchange of goods, the moment in a business transaction when **the redemption and transfer of property** becomes **final** (lit. when every word is validated, *leqayyem kol dabar*). Legal corpora preserving such transactions can become very complex over time. Fishbane has definitively shown this to be true in Israelite law.

One party took off his sandal and gave it to the other. Rudolph links the laws in Deuteronomy 25:9 and Ruth 4:7, points to the allegedly late Aramaized form of *leqayyem* ("validated"), and dates Ruth to the postexilic period *(Das Buch Ruth,* pp. 26–29). Hubbard, however, sees these customs as unrelated and of no value in dating the book *(The Book of Ruth,* p. 27).

4:8 / **So the kinsman-redeemer said to Boaz, "Buy it yourself." And he removed his sandal.** Those who closely link this custom with the one in Deuteronomy 25:9 tend to argue that Mr. So-and-So is the party removing his sandal. Those who see no linkage tend to see Boaz as the party removing his sandal ("it is usual for the purchaser to give the pledge," *Ruth Rab.* 7.12). In lieu of clear ancient Near Eastern parallels, Gunkel cites a transaction from Indian myth *(Ruth,* p. 81, n. 1, cites this Indian sandal-ceremony from A. Holtzmann, *Indische Sagen* [Stuttgart: Krabbe, 1854], p. 344):

> "So draw off the gold-embroidered shoe
> As a sign that you have transferred to me
> Your inheritance, the lordly power."
> So Rama took off his shoe and gave it to him.

It seems more fruitful to leave aside the legal debates and probe instead the remarkable parallels between the council scene in Mizpah (Judg. 20) and the council scene in Bethlehem (Ruth 4). Granted, there are substantive differences between these two scenes. (1) The Bethlehem council of ten elders is dwarfed by the much larger intertribal council at Mizpah. (2) The Bethlehem council responds to a famine-induced death in another country, while the Mizpah council investigates a murder within Israel. (3) The Bethlehem council assembles spontaneously, while the Mizpah council convenes urgently. (4) At Bethlehem a distant kinsman (Boaz) brilliantly unveils the truth in stages, while at Mizpah a parallel figure shamelessly manipulates the truth (the Levite from Ephraim).

Yet these type-scenes still hold several foundational characteristics in common. First, each council scene describes in some detail the assembling of representative authorities (elders in Ruth; rulers in Judges [lit. corners, *pinnot*]). Second, each council listens to a difficult case involving a Bethlehemite woman (Naomi in Ruth, the Levite's concubine in Judges). Third, each council listens to a kinsman-figure lay out the facts of each case via direct discourse (shrewdly by Boaz; solicitously by the Levite). Fourth, each council scene comes to a dramatic point of climax. In Judges, the chaos brewing in chapters 17–19 comes to climax when the Levite demands that the Mizpah council announce its *'etsah* ("counsel, decision," Judg. 20:7). In Ruth, the *hesed*-mercy growing in the heart of Boaz quietly climaxes when Boaz reaches down and unties his sandal (Syr reads "unharnesses his foot").

The council scene in Ruth does not just parallel its counterpart in Judges 20; it contests it, quietly but firmly challenging the integrity of its procedures, the purpose for its convening, the motives of its participants, and the wisdom of its decision.

Additional Notes §16

4:2 / **Elders:** K. Whitelam (*The Just King: Monarchical Judicial Authority in Ancient Israel* [Sheffield: JSOT Press, 1979], pp. 51–61) summarizes the differing roles of judge and elder. G. A. London ("Homage to the Elders," *BA* 50 [1987], pp. 70–74) argues, from an examination of animal remains in Early Bronze IV tombs at Jebel Qa'aqir (near Hebron), that elders sometimes receive special burial honors. For a look at how elders function in nonurban cultures generally, see the classic study of J. G. Peristiany, ed., *Honour and Shame* (Chicago: University of Chicago Press, 1966).

4:5 / **You acquire:** Bush (*Ruth, Esther,* pp. 227–29) offers several compelling reasons for preferring Qere *qanitah* over Ketib *qenotka.*

Name of the dead: C. Wright ("What Happened Every Seven Years in Israel?" *EQ* 56 [1984], pp. 193–201) thinks that the social provisions discussed in Deut. are for "Hebrews" in the social rather than the ethnic sense (i.e., landless persons who sell their services for hire). The provisions in Lev., however, are only for ethnically Israelite landowners, in Wright's view.

4:7 / **Transfer of property:** Hittite laws §§ 3–6, 7–8, 9–10 (cited in *ANET* 189–91) all have earlier and later, more complex versions. Fishbane cites numerous Israelite examples of legal corpora growing over time in *Biblical Interpretation in Ancient Israel,* pp. 170–97.

Become final: For the translation of *leqayyem* as "validated," see *GHB* § 80h.

Sandal: C. M. Carmichael ("A Ceremonial Crux: Removing a Man's Sandal as a Female Gesture of Contempt," *JBL* 96 [1977], pp. 321–36) argues that the drawing off of the sandal signifies the man's withholding conception and sees a connection between this ceremony, the law in Deut. 25:5–10, and the story of Onan in Gen. 38. In Carmichael's view, Mr. So-and-So's nonaction is intertextually equivalent to Onan's nonaction.

§17 Bethlehem's Joy (Ruth 4:9–13)

4:9–10 / Today you are witnesses. Boaz brings final closure to this scene with an antiphonal liturgy much like the ceremony at the end of Joshua (Josh. 24:22). Boaz's part begins and ends with the refrain *'edim 'attem hayyom* (lit. "Witnesses are you today!"). Sandwiched between is a formal summary detailing the day's accomplishments: (1) Boaz's acquisition of **all the property of Elimelech, Kilion and Mahlon;** (2) Boaz's acquisition of **Ruth the Moabitess, Mahlon's widow,** as his **wife** (*'ishah*)—not "concubine" (*pilegesh*), "young girl" (*na'arah*), "slave girl" (*shipkhah*), or "foreign woman" (*nokriyyah*); (3) Boaz's acquisition of all these things "from the hand of **Naomi**" (Naomi's name appears last, not first in Boaz's speech, as in 4:3); (4) his promise to "raise up," like a flag over reconquered territory, "the name of the dead over his inheritance" (*lehaqim shem hammat 'al nakhalot;* note the same phrase, *lehaqim shem,* "to raise up the name," in Deut. 25:7). Not bad for a day's work!

4:11–13 / We are witnesses. The single word *'edim* is the antiphonal response of the **elders and all those at the gate.** Perhaps the best way to catch the flavor of this is to imagine Boaz's repetitive *'edim . . . 'edim* as the "Hip, Hip . . . ," and the *'edim* of the council as the answering "Hooray!" Everyone loves a happy ending. Bethlehem is ready for one. Elimelech's is not the only family to have suffered. To see at least one family overcome the ravages of famine, death and childlessness is . . . well, inspiring. People everywhere have a deep-rooted need to be inspired, a truth obvious to anyone who has ever tried to be a pastor (Spurgeon, *Morning by Morning,* Jan 18 a.m.):

> Ah, toil-worn labourer, only think when you shall rest for ever! Can you conceive it? . . . *Here,* my . . . fair flowers fade, my dainty cups are drained to dregs, my sweetest birds fall before Death's arrows, my most pleasant days are shadowed into nights, the floodtides of my bliss subside into ebbs of sorrow.

But *there,* everything is immortal . . . , the crown unwithered, the eye undimmed, the voice unfaltering, the heart unwavering, the immortal being wholly absorbed into infinite delight.

Oh happy day!

The marriage of Ruth and Boaz inspires the people of Bethlehem. Responding to Boaz, the patriarchal council offers up no substantive summary of its own but three joyous toasts that, like Boaz's speech, come packaged within opening and closing *inclusios.* These *inclusios* take a simple phrase—**May the LORD give**—and artistically embellish it into a tapestry of celebration.

First, "may the LORD" **make** Ruth as fertile as **Rachel and Leah.** Perhaps it is impossible for overpopulated postmoderns to relate to this, but this is the prayer of every Israelite. Children are a blessing, never a curse. Children come from God, not from human parents. Children are a privilege, never just a responsibility (Pss. 127–128). Second, may the LORD give . . . **offspring** (lit. seed) just like **Perez,** the son born to their ancestor **Judah** via the Canaanite woman **Tamar.** One of the great ironies of being a Jew is that Judah himself has children by a *nokriyyah,* Tamar (Gen. 38:1–30). Ruth is not the only foreign woman to participate in Israel's messianic history.

With these words the Bethlehem council extends to this couple the *hesed* of Yahweh. Included among the toasts are complimentary words about Boaz's **standing** (*khayil;* cf. 2:1) and the hope that he might someday become **famous,** but this is not their primary message. These people are survivors. They have to live and work and raise their families in a brutal environment under harsh conditions. Everyone in this tiny village wants this couple to make it—to experience new life, to experience the same saving vision that animates their ancestors.

Additional Note §17

4:12 / **Tamar . . . Judah:** For intertextual analyses of Ruth and Gen. 38, see K. Nielsen, *Ruth,* 95–99, and van Wolde, "Texts in Dialogue with Texts," pp. 8–28.

§18 Naomi's Commission (Ruth 4:14–17a)

4:14–15 / Three times an unidentified group of Bethlehemite women speaks about or directly to Naomi in the book of Ruth. The first is in 1:19, "Can this be Naomi?" The second is here, in 4:14, **Praise** (lit. "blessed," *baruk;* see §12) **be to the LORD, who this day has not left you without a kinsman-redeemer** (see §11). **May he become famous throughout Israel! He will renew your life and sustain you in your old age. For your daughter-in-law, who loves you and who is better to you than seven sons, has given him birth.** The third is in 4:17, "Naomi has a son."

Structurally, the narrator underlines three key moments in the story by inserting the words of these women like a *choros* in a Greek play, though not in the rigid, black-or-white, tragic-versus-comic style commonly found in Attic playwrights. Many commentators overlook or dismiss the role played by this *choros,* but the narrator of Ruth uses this literary technique to articulate vital characterization questions (1:19), link important themes to specific characters (4:14), and bring closure to the story proper (4:17).

By far the densest of these moments occurs here, in 4:14, where the Bethlehemite *choros* reprises three important themes, linking each to a major character in the story. The first phrase, "who this day has not left you," focuses on Yahweh and reprises the theme of abandonment (see the discussion of *sha'ar* in 1:3, 5). MT literally reads "who has not caused to cease for you" (*'asher lo' hishbit lak).* The key word is *shabat,* the verbal form of *shabbat* ("sabbath"), a polysemic term in Ruth (see 2:7).

Second, the phrases "kinsman-redeemer, become famous, renew your life" and "sustain you in your old age" appear to be future characteristics of Obed, but they may just as easily be descriptions of Boaz or Yahweh. "Become famous" is a reprise of the council's ebullient toast to Boaz (4:11). In Israel, Yahweh is always the primal "renewer" (*meshib,* Jer. 28:3, 4) and life-"sustainer" (*kalkel,* Gen. 45:11).

Third, the final focus of this *choros* is on Ruth. Whatever roles Boaz, Yahweh, and Naomi might play in this drama, Ruth is ultimately the person responsible for giving **birth** to Obed. In this sense Ruth is the hero of the story, the person ultimately responsible for bringing order out of chaos (Sasson, *Ruth*, p. 202). Without her willingness to love Naomi, without her willingness to abandon her homeland, without her willingness to beg publicly, without her willingness to approach Boaz . . . there would be no celebration. Ruth gives Israel much more than a fertile womb. Ruth's life challenges the corrupt values of a sick culture. In Ruth's world, women are more expendable than men (Judg. 19:24; 21:12, 23), yet this woman proves that a destitute foreign widow can be of far more value to Israel than **seven** of its finest **sons.**

4:16–17a / Then Naomi took the child, laid him in her lap and cared for him. After Obed's birth, Naomi's new role becomes that of "nurse" (*'omenet*, "supporter," from *'aman*, "to support"). **And they named him Obed.** Several theories have been advanced to explain this name. Josephus (*Antiquities of the Jews* 5.9.4) tries to define it by focusing on the Hebrew verb *'abad* ("to serve"), from which Obed (*'obed*) is probably derived:

> Naomi was herself a nurse to this child, and by the advice of the women called him "Obed," as being to be brought up in order to be subservient to her in her old age, for "Obed" in the Hebrew dialect signifies a "servant."

Wesley agrees, arguing that Obed is a "servant" given to Naomi "to nourish and comfort and assist" her, adding that this is a "duty children owe to their progenitors" (*Notes on the Bible: Ruth*, pp. 836–37). From a canonical-historical perspective, the name Obed ("Servant") should be interpreted as Ruth's final renunciation of Judges' self-absorbed narcissism.

Additional Notes §18

4:14 / The women said: Aristotle discusses the functions of the Greek *choros* in *Politics* (New York: The Modern Library, 1943), line 1276b.

Who has not left you: For the polysemantic possibilities of *shabat*, see Moore, "Two Textual Anomalies in Ruth," p. 242.

4:15 / **Your daughter-in-law:** Sasson relies on V. Propp's *Morphology of the Folktale* (trans. Laurence Scott; Austin, Tex.: University of Texas Press, 1968) to designate Ruth as the hero of the story. C. Bremond has a good critique of Propp in "The Narrative Message," *Semeia* 10 (1978), pp. 5–55.

4:17a / **Obed:** Sasson (*Ruth,* pp. 175–78) lists several theories on the origin of this name.

§19 Yahweh's Promise (Ruth 4:17b–22)

4:17b–22 / He was the father of Jesse, the father of David. This, then, is the family line of Perez:

> Perez was the father of Hezron,
> Hezron the father of Ram,
> Ram the father of Amminadab,
> Amminadab the father of Nahshon,
> Nahshon the father of Salmon,
> Salmon the father of Boaz,
> Boaz the father of Obed,
> Obed the father of Jesse,
> and Jesse the father of David.

Without warning, the narrator tells us who Obed really is: David's grandfather! With this revelation, the entire symphony modulates into another, higher key. The yearning for a king in the book's canonical-historical context is finally addressed. This little genealogy transforms the book from a beautiful story into a powerful sociopolitical apology for Yahwistic leadership. Little does Boaz realize that by showing Ruth *mishpat*, he is fulfilling the patriarchal promise to bless the nations. Little does Naomi realize that by refusing to despair, she herself is reenacting the matriarchal faith of her ancestors. Little does Ruth realize that by pledging her allegiance to Naomi's God, she opens a door to joy "amid the alien corn."

Additional Note §19

4:17b / **He was the father:** K. Nielsen (*Ruth*, pp. 21–28) argues the intriguing hypothesis that, far from being an appendix or an afterthought or an introduction to a now lost *Book of Obed* (the hypothesis of Sasson), the Davidic genealogy in 4:18–22 is instead the foundation upon which everything else in the book depends. That is, the story of Ruth,

Naomi, and Boaz is written to explain and defend the genealogy, not vice versa.

Nielsen posits a rather involved political scenario to support this hypothesis: David's enemies—the family of Saul, or the "circles supporting the traditions of Samuel"—want to see him defamed as a "foreigner." The author of Ruth, a staunch supporter of David, writes in "conscious reaction to the smear campaign" against David, dashing out this piece of art somewhat like Mozart's famous composition *Eine kleine Nachtmusik*— never imagining, with Mozart, that such an off-the-cuff composition might someday overshadow the "more important" person for whom it was composed.

As interesting as this hypothesis is, it would be easier to accept were Nielsen to offer a few concrete examples of other "dueling-genealogies" representing other socio-political factions, biblical or extrabiblical; make more of an effort to engage, explain and refute the dominant literary theorists who view the genealogy, with good reason, as secondary (e.g., Rudolph, Joüon, Bertman, Campbell, Sasson); and give more attention to the book's canonical-historical context (see the too-facile discussion on pp. 19–21, particularly the claims for canonical "originality" on p. 20, n. 29).

For Further Reading

Commentaries on Joshua

Boling, R. G. and G. E. Wright. *Joshua*. AB 6. Garden City, N.Y.: Doubleday, 1982.

Butler, T. C. *Joshua*. WBC 7. Waco: Word, 1983.

Drucker, R. *Yehoshua/The Book of Joshua*. Brooklyn, N.Y.: Mesorah, 1982.

Gray, J., ed. *Joshua, Judges and Ruth*. New ed. CB. London: Nelson, 1967.

Hess, R. S. *Joshua: An Introduction and Commentary*. TOTC. Downers Grove, Ill.: InterVarsity, 1996.

Howard, D. M., Jr. *Joshua*. NAC. Nashville: Broadman & Holman, 1998.

Miller, J. M. and Gene M. Tucker. *The Book of Joshua*. CBC. Cambridge: Cambridge University Press, 1974.

Nelson, R. D. *Joshua*. OTL. Louisville, Ky.: Westminster John Knox, 1997.

Soggin, J. A. *Joshua*. Trans. R. A. Wilson. OTL. Philadelphia: Westminster, 1972.

Woudstra, M. H. *The Book of Joshua*. NICOT. Grand Rapids: Eerdmans, 1981.

Commentaries on Judges

Boling, R. G. *Judges: A New Translation with Introduction and Commentary*. AB 6A. Garden City, N.Y.: Doubleday, 1975.

Bruce, F. F. *Judges*. In *The New Bible Commentary Revised*. Ed. D. Guthrie et al. London: InterVarsity, 1970.

Cundall, E. E. and L. Morris. *Judges: An Introduction and Commentary, on Judges, Ruth*. TOTC. London: Tyndale, 1968.

Fewell, D. N. "Judges." Pages 67–77 in *The Women's Bible Commentary*. Ed. C. A. Newsom and S. H. Ringe. Louisville, Ky.: Westminster John Knox, 1992.

Gray, J. *Joshua, Judges and Ruth*. CB, new ed. London: Nelson, 1967.

Hamlin, E. J. *At Risk in the Promised Land: A Commentary on the Book of Judges*. Grand Rapids: Eerdmans, 1990.

Keil, C. F. and F. Delitzsch. *The Book of Judges*. Trans. J. Martin. 10 vols. Vol. 2. Grand Rapids: Eerdmans, 1973.

Moore, G. F. *A Critical and Exegetical Commentary on Judges*. ICC. Edinburgh: T&T Clark, 1976.

Soggin, J. A. *Judges: A Commentary*. OTL. Trans. John Bowden. Philadelphia: Westminster, 1981.

Wilcock, M. *The Message of Judges: Grace Abounding*. Downers Grove, Ill.: InterVarsity, 1992.

Commentaries on Ruth

Bush, F. W. *Ruth, Esther*. WBC 9. Dallas: Word, 1996.

Campbell, E. F. *Ruth*. AB 7. Garden City, N.Y.: Doubleday, 1975.

Hubbard, R. *The Book of Ruth*. NICOT. Grand Rapids: Eerdmans, 1988.

Nielsen, K. *Ruth: A Commentary*. OTL. Louisville, Ky.: Westminster John Knox, 1997.

Bible Atlas and Historical Geography

Aharoni, Y. *The Land of the Bible: A Historical Geography*. Rev. ed. Trans. A. F. Rainey. Philadelphia: Westminster, 1967.

——— and M. Avi–Yonah. *The Macmillan Bible Atlas*. Rev. ed. New York: Macmillan, 1977.

Beitzel, B. J. *The Moody Atlas of Bible Lands*. Chicago: Moody, 1985.

Rasmussen, C. G. *Zondervan NIV Atlas of the Bible*. Grand Rapids: Zondervan, 1989.

Other Works

Ackerman, J. S. "Prophecy and Warfare in Early Israel: A Study of the Deborah-Barak Story." *BASOR* 220 (1975), pp. 5–13.

Aharoni, Y. Pages 240–53 in *The Land of the Bible*. Trans. A. E. Rainey. Philadelphia: Westminster, 1967.

Albright, W. F. Pages 252, 273–88, 311, 321 in *From the Stone Age to Christianity*. Garden City, N.Y.: Doubleday/Anchor Books, 1957.

Alt, A. *Essays on Old Testament History and Religion*. Trans. R. A. Wilson. Sheffield: JSOT Press, 1989.

Alter, R. *The Art of Biblical Narrative*. New York: Basic Books, 1981.

———. *The Art of Biblical Poetry*. New York: Basic Books, 1985.

Andersen, F. I. "Yahweh, The Kind and Sensitive God." Pages 41–88 in *God Who Is Rich in Mercy: Essays Presented to Dr. D. B. Knox*. Ed. P. T. O'Brien and D. G. Peterson. Homebush West, Australia: Lancer, 1986.

Auld, A. G. "Judges 1 and History: A Reconsideration." *VT* 25 (1975), pp. 261–85.

———. "Review of Boling's *Judges*. The Framework of Judges and the Deuteronomists." *JSOT* 1 (1976), pp. 41–46.

Bal, M. *Death and Dissymmetry: The Politics of Coherence in the Book of Judges*. Chicago: University of Chicago Press, 1988.

Bar-Efrat, S. *Narrative Art in the Bible*. JSOTSup 70. Sheffield: Almond, 1989.

Bartlett, J. R. *Jericho*. CBW. Grand Rapids: Eerdmans, 1982.

Batto, B. *Slaying the Dragon: Mythmaking in the Biblical Tradition*. Louisville, Ky.: Westminster John Knox, 1992.

Bauckham, R. "The Book of Ruth and the Possibility of a Feminist Canonical Hermeneutic." *BibInt* 5 (1997), pp. 29–45.

Beattie, D. R. G. *Jewish Exegesis of the Book of Ruth*. Sheffield: JSOT Press, 1977.

———. "The Targum of Ruth—A Sectarian Composition?" *JJS* 26 (1985), pp. 222–29.

Bellis, A. O. *Helpmates, Harlots, and Heroes: Women's Stories in the Hebrew Bible*. Louisville, Ky.: Westminster John Knox, 1994.

Bernstein, M. J. "Two Multivalent Readings in the Ruth Narrative." *JSOT* 50 (1991), pp. 15–26.

Bertman, S. "Symmetrical Design in the Book of Ruth." *JBL* 84 (1965), pp. 165–68.

Blankenhorn, D. *Fatherless America*. New York: Basic Books, 1995.

Blenkinsopp, J. "Ballad Style and Psalm Style in the Song of Deborah." *Bib* 42 (1961), pp. 61–76.

———. "Structure and Style in Judges 13–16." *JBL* 82 (1963), pp. 65–76.

Brenner, A., ed. *A Feminist Companion to Judges*. Sheffield: Sheffield Academic Press, 1993.

Brettler, M. "The Book of Judges: Literature as Politics." *JBL* 108 (1989), pp. 395–418.

Brichto, H. "Kin, Cult, Land and Afterlife—A Biblical Complex." *HUCA* 44 (1973), pp. 1–54.

Bright, J. *The Authority of the Old Testament.* Grand Rapids: Baker, 1967.

———. Pages 128–60 in *A History of Israel.* London: SCM, 1972.

Brown, C. A. Pages 39–139 in *No Longer Be Silent: First-Century Jewish Portraits of Biblical Women.* Louisville, Ky.: Westminster John Knox, 1992.

Brown, F., S. R. Driver, and C. S. Briggs, eds. *A Hebrew and English Lexicon of the Old Testament.* Repr., Oxford: Clarendon, 1962.

Brueggemann, W. *Cadences of Home: Preaching among Exiles.* Louisville, Ky.: Westminster John Knox, 1997.

———. *The Land: Place as Gift, Promise, and Challenge in Biblical Faith.* Philadelphia: Fortress, 1977.

———. *Theology of the Old Testament.* Minneapolis: Fortress, 1997.

Burrows, M. "The Marriage of Boaz and Ruth." *JBL* 59 (1940), pp. 445–54.

Childs, B. S. "Judges." Pages 254–62 in *Introduction to the Old Testament as Scripture,* Phildelphia: Fortress, 1979.

Clark, G. R. *The Word ḥesed in the Hebrew Bible.* Sheffield: JSOT Press, 1993.

Cohen, S. J. D., ed. *The Jewish Family in Antiquity.* Atlanta: Scholars, 1993.

Coogan, M. D. "A Structural and Literary Analysis of the Song of Deborah." *CBQ* 40 (1978), pp. 143–66.

Coote, R. B. *Early Israel: A New Horizon.* Minneapolis: Fortress, 1990.

——— and K. W. Whitelam. *The Emergence of Early Israel in Historical Perspective.* The Social World of Biblical Antiquity Series 5. Sheffield: Almond, 1987.

Coxon, P. W. "Was Naomi a Scold? A Response to Fewell and Gunn." *JSOT* 45 (1989), pp. 25–37.

Craigie, P. C. "Deborah and Anat: A Study of Poetic Imagery (Judges 5)." *ZAW* 90 (1978), pp. 374–81.

———. "A Reconsideration of Shamgar ben Anath (Judges 3:31 and 5:6)." *JBL* 91 (1972), pp. 239–40.

Cross, F. M. *Caananite Myth and Hebrew Epic: Essays in the History of the Religion of Israel.* Cambridge: Harvard University Press, 1973.

————., ed. *Symposia Celebrating the Seventy-Fifth Anniversary of the Founding of the ASOR (1900–1975).* Cambridge, Mass.: ASOR, 1979.

Cryer, F. *Divination in Ancient Israel and Its Ancient Near Eastern Environment: A Sociohistorical Investigation.* Sheffield: JSOT Press, 1994.

Daube, D. "Gideon's Few." *JJS* 7 (1956), pp. 155–61.

Davis, D. R. *Such a Great Salvation: Expositions of the Book of Judges.* Grand Rapids: Baker, 1990.

Dearman, J. A., ed. *Studies in the Mesha Inscription and Moab.* Atlanta: Scholars, 1989.

Dillard, R. B. and T. Longman III. *An Introduction to the Old Testament.* Leicester: England: Apollos, 1995.

Dotan, T. "What We Know About the Philistines." *BAR* 8 (1982), pp. 20–44.

Dumbrell, W. J. "In Those Days There Was No King in Israel; Every Man Did What Was Right in His Own Eyes: The Purpose of the Book of Judges Reconsidered." *JSOT* 25 (1983), pp. 23–33.

Edelman, D. V., ed. *The Triumph of Elohim: From Yahwisms to Judaisms.* Grand Rapids: Eerdmans, 1996.

Englander, L. A. and H. W. Basser. *The Mystical Study of Ruth: Midrash HaNe'elam of the Zohar to the Book of Ruth.* Atlanta: Scholars, 1993.

Epstein, L. M. *Marriage Laws in the Bible and the Talmud.* Cambridge: Harvard University Press, 1942.

Eslinger, L. *Into the Hands of the Living God.* BLS 24. JSOTSup 84. Sheffield: Almond, 1989.

Fee, G. D. and D. Stuart. *How to Read the Bible for All Its Worth.* Grand Rapids: Zondervan, 1982.

Fewell, D. N. and D. M. Gunn. *Compromising Redemption: Relating Characters in the Book of Ruth.* Louisville, Ky.: Westminster John Knox, 1990.

————. " 'A Son Is Born to Naomi!' " *JSOT* 40 (1988), pp. 99–108.

Finkelstein, I. *The Archaeology of the Israelite Settlement.* Jerusalem: IES, 1988.

Fishbane, M. *Biblical Interpretation in Ancient Israel.* Oxford: Clarendon, 1985.

Fretheim, T. E. *Deuteronomic History.* IBT. Nashville: Abingdon, 1983.

Frymer-Kensky, T. *In the Wake of the Goddesses: Women, Culture, and the Biblical Transformation of Pagan Myth.* New York: Free, 1992.

Gibson, J. C. L., ed. *Canaanite Myths and Legends*. Edinburgh: T&T Clark, 1977.

Glanzman, G. S. "The Origin and Date of the Book of Ruth." *CBQ* 21 (1959), pp. 201–7.

Globe, A. "Judges 5:27." *VT* 25 (1975), pp. 362–67.

Gooding, D. W. "The Composition of the Book of Judges." Pages 70–79 in *Eretz-Israel, Archaeological and Geographical Studies,* vol. 16, *H. M. Orlinsky Volume*. Jerusalem: IES, 1982.

Goody, J., ed. *The Character of Kinship*. Cambridge: Cambridge University Press, 1973.

Gottwald, N. K. *The Hebrew Bible: A Socio-Literary Introduction*. Philadelphia: Fortress, 1985.

———. *The Tribes of Yahweh*. Maryknoll, N.Y.: Orbis, 1979.

Grant, R. "Literary Structure in the Book of Ruth." *BSac* 148 (1991), pp. 424–41.

Gros Louis, K. R. R. "The Book of Judges." Pages 141–62 in *Literary Interpretations of Biblical Narratives*. Ed. K. Gros Louis, J. Ackerman, and T. Warshaw. Nashville: Abingdon, 1974.

Gunkel, H. *Reden und Aufsätzen: Ruth*. Göttingen: Vandenhoeck und Ruprecht, 1913.

Hals, R. M. *The Theology of the Book of Ruth*. Philadelphia: Fortress, 1969.

Hawk, L. D. *Every Promise Fulfilled: Contesting Plots in Joshua*. CBI. Louisville, Ky.: Westminster John Knox, 1991.

Hiebert, P. " 'Whence Shall Help Come to Me?' The Biblical Widow." Pages 125–41 in *Gender and Difference in Ancient Israel*. Ed. P. L. Day. Minneapolis: Fortress, 1989.

Hoftijzer, J. and G. van der Kooij, eds. *Aramaic Texts from Deir 'Alla*. Leiden: E. J. Brill, 1976.

Holbert, J. C. "The Bible Becomes Literature: An Encounter with Ruth." *Word and World* 13 (1993), pp. 130–35.

Holladay, W. L. *The Root Šûb in the Old Testament*. Leiden: E. J. Brill, 1958.

Huffmon, H. B. "Priestly Divination in Israel." Pages 355–59 in *The Word of the Lord Shall Go Forth: Essays in Honor of D. N. Freedman*. Ed. C. L. Meyers and M. O'Connor. Winona Lake, Ind.: Eisenbrauns, 1983.

Johnson, A. R. "The Primary Meaning of *gā'al*." *VTSup* 1 (1953), pp. 67–77.

Klein, L. *The Triumph of Irony in the Book of Judges*. JSOTSup 68. Sheffield: Almond, 1988.

Koopmans, W. T. *Joshua 24 as Poetic Narrative*. JSOTSup 93. Sheffield: JSOT Press, 1990.

Landers, S. "Did Jephthah Kill His Daughter?" *BR* 7 (1991), pp. 28–31, 42.

Lemche, N. P. *Ancient Israel: A New History of Israelite Society*. TBS. Sheffield: JSOT Press, 1988.

Lévi-Strauss, C. *The Elementary Structures of Kinship*. Boston: Beacon, 1969.

Lewis, T. J. "The Ancestral Estate *(nakhalat 'elohim)* in 2 Samuel 14:16." *JBL* 110 (1991), pp. 597–612.

Licht, J. *Storytelling in the Bible*. Jerusalem: Magnes, 1978.

Longman, T., III. *Literary Approaches to Biblical Interpretation*. Grand Rapids: Zondervan, 1987.

Malamat, A. "Charismatic Leadership in the Book of Judges." Pages 152–68 in *Magnalia Dei: The Mighty Acts of God: Essays on the Bible and Archaeology in Memory of G. Ernest Wright*. Ed. F. M. Cross, W. E. Lemke, and P. D. Miller Jr. Garden City, N.Y.: Doubleday, 1976.

Mayes, A. D. H. "Deuteronomistic Editing of Judges." Pages 58–80 in *The Story of Israel between Settlement and Exile: A Redactional Study of the Deuteronomistic History*. London: SCM, 1983.

———. "The Historical Context of the Battle Against Sisera." *VT* 19 (1969), pp. 353–60.

———. "The Period of the Judges and the Rise of the Monarchy." Pages 285–331 in *Israelite and Judean History*. Ed. J. H. Hayes and J. M. Miller. London: SCM, 1977.

———. *The Story of Israel Between Settlement and Exile: A Redactional Study of the Deuteronomistic History*. London: SCM, 1983.

McConville, J. G. *Grace in the End: A Study in Deuteronomic Theology*. SOTBT. Grand Rapids: Zondervan, 1993.

McKenzie, J. L. *The World of the Judges*. Englewood Cliffs, N.J.: Prentice Hall; London: G. Chapman, 1966.

Mendenhall, G. E. *The Tenth Generation*. Baltimore: Johns Hopkins University Press, 1973.

Meyers, C. *Discovering Eve: Ancient Israelite Women in Context*. New York: Oxford University Press, 1988.

———. "The Family in Early Israel." Pages 13–41 in *Families in Ancient Israel*. Ed. L. Perdue et al. Louisville, Ky.: Westminster John Knox, 1997.

Mitchell, G. *Together in the Land: A Reading of the Book of Joshua.* JSOTSup 134. Sheffield: JSOT Press, 1993.

Mobley, G. "The Wild Man in the Bible and the Ancient Near East." *JBL* 116 (1997), pp. 217–33.

Murray, D. F. "Narrative Structure and Technique in the Deborah-Barak Story, Judges 4:4–22." Pages 155–89 in *Studies in the Historical Books of the Old Testament.* VTSup 30. Ed. J. A. Emerton; Leiden: Brill, 1979.

Nelson, R. D. *The Double Redaction of the Deuteronomistic History.* JSOTSup 18. Sheffield: JSOT Press, 1981.

Noth, M. *The Deuteronomic History.* JSOTSup 15. Sheffield: JSOT Press, 1981.

Penchansky, D. "Staying the Night: Intertextuality in Genesis and Judges." Pages 77–88 in *Reading Between Texts: Intertextuality and the Hebrew Bible.* Ed. D. N. Fewell. Louisville, Ky.: Westminster John Knox, 1992.

Perdue, L. G. "The Household, Old Testament Theology, and Contemporary Hermeneutics." Pages 223–57 in *Families in Ancient Israel.* Ed. L. Perdue et al. Louisville, Ky.: Westminster John Knox, 1997.

Peterson, E. "The Pastoral Work of Story-Making: Ruth." Pages 73–112 in *Five Smooth Stones for Pastoral Work.* Grand Rapids: Eerdmans, 1980.

Polzin, R. M. *Moses and the Deuteronomist: A Literary Study of the Deuteronomic History, Part One: Deuteronomy, Joshua, Judges.* New York: Seabury, 1980.

Rowley, H. H. *From Joseph to Joshua: Biblical Traditions in the Light of Archaeology.* London: Oxford University Press, 1950.

———. "The Marriage of Ruth." Pages 171–94 in *The Servant of the Lord and Other Essays on the Old Testament.* Oxford: Blackwell, 1965.

Sasson, J. *Ruth: A New Translation with a Philological Commentary and a Formalist-Folklorist Interpretation.* Sheffield: Sheffield Academic Press, 1989.

Satterthwaite, P. " 'No King in Israel': Narrative Criticism and Judges 17–21." *TynBul* 44 (1993), pp. 75–88.

Segert, S. "Paronomasia in the Samson Narrative in Judges XIII–XVI." *VT* 34 (1984), pp. 454–61.

Simpson, C. A. *Composition of the Book of Judges.* Oxford: Basil Blackwell, 1957.

Trible, P. *Texts of Terror: Literary-Feminist Readings of Biblical Narratives.* Philadelphia: Fortress, 1984.

Van der Toorn, K. *From Her Cradle to Her Grave: The Role of Religion in the Life of the Israelite and the Babylonian Woman.* Sheffield: JSOT Press, 1994.

———. "The Nature of the Biblical Teraphim in the Light of the Cuneiform Evidence." *CBQ* 52 (1990), pp. 203–22.

Van Selms, A. "Judge Shamgar." *VT* 14 (1964), pp. 294–309.

Van Wolde, E. "Texts in Dialogue with Texts: Intertextuality in the Ruth and Tamar Narratives." *BibInt* 5 (1997), pp. 1–28.

Vaux, R. de. *Ancient Israel.* 2 vols. New York: McGraw-Hill, 1961.

Warner, S. M. "The Dating of the Period of the Judges." *VT* 28 (1978), pp. 455–63.

Webb, B. G. *The Book of Judges: An Integrated Reading.* JSOTSup 46. Sheffield: JSOT Press, 1987.

Weinfeld, M. "The Period of the Conquest and the Judges as seen in the Earlier and the Later Sources." *VT* 17 (1967), pp. 97–113.

Yee, G. A., ed. *Judges and Method: New Approaches in Biblical Studies.* Minneapolis: Fortress, 1995.

Zimmerli, W. *I Am Yahweh.* Ed. W. Brueggemann. Trans. D. W. Stott. Atlanta: John Knox, 1982.

Subject Index

Scripture Index

NEW TESTAMENT

EARLY JEWISH WRITINGS

EARLY CHRISTIAN WRITINGS